Social action
and self-directed groupwork

Social action and self-directed groupwork

Edited by
Jennie Fleming and Dave Ward

W&B
MMXIX

Jennie Fleming is currently a Director of Practical Participation. She started her career as a youth worker, community worker and social worker in a range of voluntary and statutory settings. Until Nov 2013 she was Director of the Centre for Social Action and Reader in Participatory Research and Social Action at De Montfort University, where she led participatory research and evaluation projects. Jennie is an experienced practitioner and researcher, committed to working in a participative and empowering way with disadvantaged and oppressed groups. From 2011- 2018 Jennie was Editor of *Groupwork* Journal and on the Board of the International Association for the Advancement of Social Work with Groups. She is Vice-Chair of the Nottingham and Nottinghamshire Refuge Forum and on the Board of Trustees for Just for Kids Law and We Belong. She is a Visiting Fellow at Nottingham Trent University.

Dave Ward is Professor of Social and Community Studies at De Montfort University, Leicester. Originally a Probation Officer, Dave has been involved in human services education, research and development work throughout his career. His particular interests lie in groupwork and in work with offenders, particularly young people in trouble, about all of which he has researched and published extensively. In particular, he has focussed on the application, through groupwork, of the values and methods of transformative education (Paulo Freire) to front-line social welfare practice, to training, to research and to teamwork and management in organisations. In recognition of his contribution to the theory and practice groupwork, Dave has been made International Honoree by the International Association for the Advancement of Social Work with Groups and Visiting Professor in Participatory Groupwork and Research to the University of Montreal, Canada.

© Whiting & Birch Ltd 2019
Published by Whiting & Birch Ltd,
Forest Hill, London SE23 3HZ

ISBN 9781861771421

Social action and self-directed groupwork

Contents

Section 3: Supporting practice, training, consultation and facilitation

Section 4: Principles into practice: Practice

Dedication
Alan Perry

We should like to dedicate this collection to our colleague and great friend Alan Perry who died before his time, aged 59, in 2008. Alan, although not specifically named in any of the papers in this collection, was a core member of the group of practitioners and academics who envisioned and developed Social Action on the ground in Nottingham in the 1980s.

Born to a working class family in Smethwick, West Midlands, Alan was a committed Christian, Oxford graduate and qualified Social Worker. His career took him from field work practice in the North-West of England, through periods spent as Social Work Student Unit Supervisor at Nottingham Council for Voluntary Service, Project Leader at the Crabtree Farm Neighbourhood Centre (a Children's Society project in Nottingham), to his final post as a senior manager at Leicester City Social Services Department.

It was in his period in Nottingham that Alan contributed his substantial intellect, his energy and warmth, and a commitment to interests of young people at risk and in trouble, to the development, conceptualisation and dissemination of Social Action. In collaboration with ourselves and other colleagues, Alan facilitated school and neighbourhood groups and spread the message of Social Action through his coaching of student social workers and participation in numerous conferences and practitioner training events.

We recall with immense pleasure the time spent working with Alan in these projects and, not least, the many hours in cars and trains and around tables in offices, pubs and our homes, debating and making sense of our experiences and planning what to do next. Indeed, it is with much gratitude that we thank Alan's partner Mary and their children Kate and Tom, as also the long suffering families of ourselves and other colleagues, for all their patience and support as we wrestled with our experiences and ideas. We hope that the fruits as revealed in this collection offer, at least, some assurance that it was worthwhile.

Introduction:
The social action and self-directed groupwork collection

Jennie Fleming and Dave Ward

Social action: Setting the scene

This collection brings together in one place articles published in two journals within the Whiting and Birch stable: *Groupwork* and Social *Action Journal*, which give attention to the theory and practice of social action and self-directed groupwork. Social action and self-directed groupwork share much in common but are not entirely interchangeable. As practised in the UK, social action is a specific philosophy and theory for social change and provides a distinct form of practice for work in the full range of human services. It has been used in many different settings in countries across the globe. It is a truly international practice that can be tried and adapted for many different settings. Self-directed groupwork, as a methodology for practice, lies at the core of Social Action. Self-directed groupwork (Mullender and Ward 1991, Mullender, Ward, Fleming 2013) is a distinctive model of groupwork practice which has been, perhaps uniquely, conceptualised in the UK but has drawn upon and, also, contributed to practice and theorising in a wide range of settings around the world. In its own right provides a fully developed empowerment-orientated social action approach to groupwork (Payne 2005).

Social action has its theoretical roots in the work of Paolo Freire (1970) The disability movement, black activism and feminism have all been strong influences on the development of the social action model (Doel and Kelly 2014). It is also strongly influenced by development theory in so far as it is based on the premise that change can happen, but only if the groups concerned own it and are involved in creating the changes they want (Whitmore et al 2011). In these ways, social action is grounded on an analysis of 'power' as a theoretical and ideological concept and, through self-directed groupwork, has integrated and adapted the theory and practice of groupwork to provide a compatible and effective methodology for practice.

Since the initial framing of social action in the 1970's and 80's, there have been other theoretical developments that have needed to be woven into the model to keep it up to date.(see Mullender, Ward, Fleming 2013). These have included postmodernism/post-structuralism, social movements and single issue campaigning, The postmodern/post-structuralist agenda, for example, has argued that earlier understandings of social issues were driven by all encompassing, 'grand', theory and were insufficiently subtle to reflect the diversity of the real world. In fact, self-directed groupwork and social action, being about bottom up, resistant, power, has always recognised diversity within groups that were nevertheless brought together by a shared sense of powerlessness and oppression and a desire to take action for change. The model continues to take on board both equality and diversity around the intersectionalities within and across, for example, gender, ethnicity, disability and sexuality, but within an updated theoretical framework (Mullaly 2010). There have been developments in groupwork and in, for example, teaching and learning, teamwork and partnership theory and practice which are applicable and have been incorporated (see Mullender, Ward, Fleming 2013)

Whilst using self directed groupwork to realise and inform the social action process, the social action approach has reflexively advanced the understanding and practice of self-directed groupwork. Through the work of the Centre for Social Action between 1989 and 2013, social action practice has extended into a range of contexts beyond its original sites in social and community groupwork. For example work has taken place in a wide range of settings in training, project development, research and education right across the human services and also in social planning and social policy development. This range can be seen within the papers in this collection . Nevertheless, as the papers in this volume also demonstrate vividly, while contexts may change, values, principles and methods remain constant.

Social action and self-directed groupwork arose initially not from theory but from practical activity through a process of analysis, understanding, action and reflection that is mirrored in their practical application. As practitioners ourselves, far back in the 1970s and 1980s, we came across individuals whose work we admired and whose values we shared. They were working to facilitate the users of social, educational and health services to confront oppression in its many forms and, in this way, were moving through such a process in their own practice (see papers in the Principles in to Practice section for examples of these early groups). We met and talked with these groupworkers and participants in the groups, read accounts in both standard and 'grey' literature and found similar practice principles to our own. Through this discourse, a distinctive model gradually emerged grounded in their's and our own work. This formed the basis of *Self-directed Groupwork: Users Take Action for Empowerment* (1991). Many many more examples and developments have emerged in the years since across the globe, a good number of which have been incorporated in a fully revised and updated edition, *Empowerment in Action: Self-directed Groupwork* (2013), and in this collection.

In the course of reviewing the practice which stimulated and underpinned both the books about self-directed groupwork, we discerned not only a shared belief in certain key values but also a number of other constant features which taken together, could be assembled into a clear model for practice. This formulation has been continually interrogated and tested through our own continuing work, including activities as researchers, consultants and trainers, through practice exchanges and the emergence of a network of like-minded practitioners and educators to a greater or lesser extent linked together at the time through the Centre for Social Action.

Many of the papers in this collection describe and discuss the social action – its principles (see particularly 'The Fundamentals' section), and practice (Principles into Practice section) however readers might find it useful to have the essence of the model described briefly here.

Social action and self-directed groupwork combine two essential and inseparable elements: six practice principles and a specific process. They are interdependent and the approach enables groups of all ages and circumstances to take action and to achieve their collective goals. It offers an easy-to-understand and open-ended process that makes it possible for people to identify and act on issues that are important to them, while working within a set of values. The six practice principles emphasise the avoidance of labels, the rights of group members, basing intervention on a power analysis, assisting people to attain collective power through coming together in groups, challenging oppression though practice, and groups being facilitated rather than led. These principles provide a clear and explicit value base.

The process involves starting with groups considering and describing what is going on in their lives collectively and identifying areas for change; they then consider why these issues exist. Next the group thinks of how participants might be able to take action to change things (a planning stage). They then undertake an agreed and planned course of action, following which the group together reflects on what has gone well, what has not, why and how things could be done differently to move further towards their goal. As this description indicates, it is an iterative and cyclical process. Social action groupworkers provide the framework for groups to consider problems, issues and concerns. Group members provide the content, using their skills, knowledge and expertise. Group members create the knowledge and understanding through active participation: describing, suggesting, analysing, deciding, experiencing and reflecting (Fleming and Ward, this volume)

'Why?' is the watchword of social action and provides the glue to cement the values into the practice. It sets social action apart from other practices, which often jump from the question 'what?' to the question 'how?' without considering the question 'why?' in between. If this is not done, explanations, responsibilities and the scope of solutions are unwittingly steered to the private world around people and within their existing knowledge and experience. These have been fashioned by their position in society and the processes which keep them there. In asking 'why?' people are encouraged to pursue an issue until the root causes have been identified and exposed.

Asking 'why?' gives people the opportunity to 'examine the internal bridles and perceived powerlessness which underpin their sense of self and guide their actions in the world.'(Young 1999: p88). It enables people to break out of what can be a demoralising and self-perpetuating narrowness of vision, introspection and self -blame created by poverty, lack of opportunity and exclusion and the neo liberal emphasis on self-responsibility. With expanded horizons of what is possible, people envisage new explanations in the wider social, political and economic context and consider how they can engage with these. Asking 'Why?' directs the spotlight onto the problems people encounter, and enables them to see opportunities to develop a wider range of options for action and change. Asking the question 'why?' is the key that unlocks the process.

This empowering practice has been pursued in a multiplicity of settings, with a range of participant groups, and by different professional disciplines and, not least, by volunteers, peers, patients, young people, carers and users of services themselves. This reflects the genesis of the model as one which bridged professional and theoretical disciplines. It was developed by social workers, community and faith group activists, volunteers, patients and users of services, students, community workers, youth workers, teachers, health visitors, paid and unpaid carers, and others, drawing the best of each and from groupwork skills and concepts. They shared a grounding in certain practice principles which provided a common value base in which social action, as an evolving and reflexive praxis, grew.

This value-base continues to allow social action to transcend conventionally defined boundaries between disciplines and settings. It has as much to offer to professionals such as educators (Cary et al this volume) and adult educators (Arches this volume), youth workers (Ballantyne this volume), community workers (Fleming and Luczynski this volume), those working in social care (Butler et al this volume) and workers in the criminal justice system (Badham et al this volume) as well as psychologists, psychiatrists and nurses, planners and architects, provided they have a 'social' or 'community' orientation to their work. Notably also, revealed in our more recent reviews, the approach has much to offer to volunteers, peers, patients, young people, carers, survivors and users of services themselves, Grounded in sharing and partnership they possess and exhibit the values and the 'imagination' (Wright Mills 1970) to envision and reach out beyond the conventionally defined boundaries of their disciplines, work settings and experiences.

The evidence shows that social action can be extremely effective in bringing about change. However, we should still heed a 'health warning': unprincipled or, even, instrumental use of such a methodology, that has been shown to have proven impact on people's behaviour, can lead to ends that serve to oppress and confine rather than empower (Anderson 1996). There are many 'fellow travellers' on the 'empowerment road' Empowerment has been adopted within neo-liberal initiatives for example by encouraging volunteer run libraries and youth work facilities, competing for resources and managing with diminished public funding (Sennett 2011). So loose has the thinking become that, unless empowerment is accompanied by a commitment to challenge and combat injustice and oppression that shows itself in actions as well as words, there will be a tendency to rewrite accounts of practice, appropriating the terminology of empowerment whilst retaining oppressive exclusionary top-down power.

Furthermore, social action achieves change, not with carefully selected groupings of people who are thought to be the most articulate and able to intervene but, potentially, with any group, whether they are users of the professional services or not. The model can be adopted by paid workers or by a group acting on its own behalf.

Having social action available, means that paid workers and natural groups have a 'ready-made' methodology of change to turn to, to help them refine their skills and techniques. An analogy we rather like is that of the learning to swim. It is certainly possible to swim without learning technique. However, with technique, it is likely that you will reach the end of the pool more quickly and more efficiently. In social action, this should mean that participants can move ahead further and faster in their achievements. Papers in the 'Supporting Practice' section set out a number of ways the development of 'technique' can be supported. Workers and activists no longer have to trust to their instincts when, dissatisfied with the failure of conventional methods for empowerment in their particular field of practice, they depart from the tried and tested ways. We are, of course, full of admiration for those who do take that leap of faith.

The fact that social action grew, and continues to grow, directly out of such people's practice is the highest testament to their achievements, and represents a valuing of the crucial contribution which thinking practitioners and activists make to the development of more acceptable forms of practice (Ward and Mullender, 1988). We would only add that, left to themselves, people often fail to find time or encouragement to write about the best new ideas and, even where these are preserved, are frequently not as rigorous in analysing them, as many who have found their way into this volume have tried to be (Beddoe and Harrington 2012 p77).

To foster the social action and self-directed groupwork approaches and to encourage the development of its intellectual expression and of critical enquiry, The Centre for Research and Training in Social Action Groupwork (subsequently honed down to, simply, the Centre for Social Action) was founded at Nottingham University, UK. Starting off, informally in the 1980s, as little more than a repository of materials accumulated in the process of formulating the Self-directed Groupwork model (Mullender and Ward 1991), the future centre quickly became a hub through which Social Action practitioners, undertaking innovatory social action work utilising the Self-directed model, from across the country could source and connect with practitioner colleagues and with like-minded academics. It accumulated information on projects and, also, practice materials which could be disseminated and shared. For those in the vicinity of Nottingham, it provided a central point for meeting together and, importantly, a 'clearing house' for support and consultation. Its structure at this time was entirely informal.

In these early days much was gained from a link between the University social and community work course, the student training unit at Nottingham Council for Voluntary Service and Nottingham Young Volunteers, a third sector youth action organisation. Besides providing placements for students in social action in a wide range of settings and opportunities for praxis and reflection on the evolving methodology, the people involved became a core activist group for networking and dissemination. The diversity of background of those involved meant that, from virtually the outset, this 'hub' carried a perspective and pursued a critical orientation. As noted previously and explained in an entry to the *Encyclopedia of Social Work with Groups* (Fleming 2009 p275-277), the work of the centre established social action as distinctive but complementary, to self-directed groupwork:

> Social Action is an approach that predominately, but not exclusively uses groupwork. It is informed by Self-directed Groupwork, ... however it is a distinct form of practice..... Whilst using Self-directed Groupwork, the Social Action approach has also advanced Self-directed Groupwork in a range of disciplines, for example training, research and education. Examples would include groupwork being used as the basis for a training methodology (Fleming 2004 [in this volume]), and as the basis for training for community workers and community activists in Peru. Social Action has been used to inform transformational change in children's services in Russia and Ukraine (Fleming 2000) and the development of more student-led learning in the US through a partnership with National Writing Project (Berdan et al 2006). Social Action has also been used to develop community cohesion and enhance the understanding within communities as to what social capital means to them (Boeck and Fleming, 2002).

The Centre for Social Action quickly found itself engaged in the development of social action on a much wider terrain. Sporadic requests to talk to interested individuals, groups and teams expanded to more formal consultancy and training contracts. International contacts put the centre on to an even wider canvas. At the same time, other organisations also adopted social action as a methodology for training and service development work. In order to manage a burgeoning portfolio the centre was accorded official standing within Nottingham University. It subsequently transferred to De Montfort University, Leicester. It was from this base that the *Social Action Journal* was launched. The Centre went from strength to strength at De Montfort University for some twenty years, surviving changes in personnel and the huge shifts that took place in Higher Education and in society more widely. Throughout this period people left to practice Social Action in other settings and environs, creating ultimately a much looser network of those committed to principles and processes of Social Action – the Social Action Net which can be accessed at http://socialactionnet.com .

Over the past 30 years, we have seen social action permeating and demonstrating relevance and results in a range of areas in education and training, in research and evaluation, in project and service development, and in management and organizational practice. The links between Social Action and education, training and learning are clearly shown by Cary et al and by Fleming and Arches (this volume). The influence of Freire's (1972) writings, on the development of the approach, have grounded it within a learning framework from the start since he was an educationalist whose work was adopted by other professions.

The two main texts setting out the self-directed groupwork approach in detail - *Self-Directed Groupwork: Users Take Action for Empowerment* (1991) and *Empowerment in Action* (2013) have been in use continually as a textbooks on professional courses, for example in social work and in youth and community work. The notion of citizen empowerment is currently core to the policies of all mainstream political parties in the UK and has become established in government policy here and beyond. Specifically it can be seen in the 'personalisation agenda' in adult social care, in 'patient choice' in the health services and in the extension of participation rights for young people in the education, children's and youth services. Thus the central tenet of social action – that service users are the experts in their own lives and can be facilitated to take action for change in directions they themselves choose – remains current.

In the course of developing and refining the social action approach in practice, we quickly realized the application of the principles and process to research and evaluation (Ward this volume). From this developed a particular approach to research, underpinned by self-directed principles and process, that has become known as 'social action research' (Fleming and Ward 1999, 2004). The six principles of social action have been reworded with the focus on research rather than practice, but their essence is unchanged (Ward 1992, Fleming and Ward 1996). Social action research is participatory in that it seeks not only to discover meaning but to explore its properties with the people who are the focus of the research.

Those who might traditionally be considered 'research subjects' become research participants and engage collaboratively with the researchers in a process of gathering, refining and interpreting data. The notion of empowerment is closely aligned with this approach (Abu Samah and Dyson and Harrison in this volume) as participants can and should be involved in all stages of the research process: deciding the parameters of the research, its framework, the questions and who should be involved; collecting and analysing the data; presenting and using the information gathered.

Social action itself often leads to the creation of new resources; training activities based on it similarly lead to action plans, research identifies things that need to change and methods for achieving this. Social action fits well with any move away from a 'one-size-fits-all' view of services and offers methods that ensure the outcomes are not 'more of the same'. Much work in regeneration and in health and social care has been criticized for not engaging communities that will be affected. Social action focuses on engagement and, because of this, on the ownership by community members and service providers of any change created. In this way the method can provide a sound and practical way forward for many organizations where they are genuinely concerned for the participation of their stakeholders (Fleming 2012).

*

The papers are divided in to 4 sections: The Fundamentals; Parallel Developments; Supporting Practice – training consultancy and facilitation; and Principles into Practice.

In the first paper, *The Legacy of Paulo Freire*, Les Price sets the scene. He examines the contribution of the Brazilian radical and transformational educationalist, asking 'What does all this mean to us, struggling in our daily work?' Price argues the case for rebuilding knowledge as a dynamic creation rather than a dead commodity, emerging 'through invention and reinvention, through restless, impatient, continuing, hopeful inquiry .... in the world, with the world and with each other' (Freire, 1985, p46). This is, says Price, a fundamental lesson for all who work within social action frameworks: our thinking, our knowledge can only be authenticated by the authenticity of thinking of the people with whom we work. While we may be shaped by our social context, in naming and understanding that context we are in a position collectively to reshape it and ourselves. Through this process we '.... come to see the world not as a static reality but as a reality in process, in transformation' (Freire, 1985, p56).

In *Values as Context*, Mark Harrison and Dave Ward outline the history and thinking underlying social action as a values-led approach to practice in which groupwork is a key element of the model. They challenge practitioners in all areas who use groupwork methods and skills to reflect critically on their work and to explore the often unspoken values which underpin their practice. Turning this challenge back to social action practitioners themselves, Jo Aubrey, in *The roots and process of social action*, critically evaluates its theoretical roots with particular reference to Freire's writings. She identifies the eclectic sources of Freirean philosophy and considers the challenges posed by other writers to aspects of his thought. The implications for the principles and process of the social action model are discussed.

Taking this critical perspective further, Maire Ni Chorcora and colleagues in *Issues of Empowerment: anti-oppressive groupwork by disabled people in Ireland*, examine the dilemmas inherent in working to empower marginalised groups, in particular, analysing the difficulties in a groupwork model which views empowerment as a political process. The authors discuss their experience, as disabled people, in the development of a group where members concern and commitment was to overcome their feelings of powerlessness. Barriers to participation and power sharing are considered and an effort is made to discover how those people who are most affected by decisions can take control, challenge their oppressors and begin to have a meaningful impact on policy making.

We have found many instances when, on describing the social action principle and process, people have immediately responded by saying 'That is a model I recognise' or 'That is just what we do'. In the next section, Parallel Developments we include three such examples where, distinctively, in unison with social action, groups incorporate a primary focus on addressing through collective action, a shared structural issue.

Jacky Drydale and Rod Purcell, in *Breaking the culture of silence: Groupwork and community development*, argue the importance of groupwork as a principle method in a community development approach to combat social exclusion and promote participation within political and democratic processes through working in partnership with communities. Through groupwork, they argue, people can be enabled to challenge oppressions by becoming vocal and active in identifying their own concerns and seeking appropriate solutions for them. In *Towards a Model of Social Groupwork with Marginalised Populations*, Margot Breton, from Canada, deploys groupwork and community organisation constructs to address problems faced by people who are in a state of 'marginalisation'. Breton describes a groupwork project addressing the needs of homeless women to illustrate aspects of the model. In another North American contribution, *Empowerment through Mutual Aid Groups: a practice grounded conceptual frame work*, Judith Lee, from the USA, proposes a conceptual framework, strongly very similar to social action in its underlying values and practice process, that unites empowerment theory to other groupwork theories, in particular the notions surrounding 'mutual aid'.

In the next section, Supporting Practice: training, consultation and facilitation, a series of papers covers in some detail various stages of the social action process. Audrey Mullender and Dave Ward write about *preparing for and initiating a group* and two papers address the core concept of *facilitation* (Mullender and Ward in 1989 and, recently, Fleming and Ward 2013). The skills involved in *the beginning stages of a social action group* are examined in some detail by Jennie Fleming and then the key roles to be played by *co-working, consultancy and training* in achieving effective social practice in papers by Izzy Terry, Eamonn Keenan and John Pinkerton, and Michael Preston-Shoot respectively. The conceptual and practical challenges and dilemmas presented by social action, as a practice committed to empowerment in a world dominated neo-liberal ideology and its assumptions about what is appropriate and possible, are given a full airing in these papers.

The next section, Principles into Practice, offers a series of articles that describe and critically evaluate social action in practice. They demonstrate its applicability in a range of settings, showing how far the approach has moved since its early days. Besides social care (Butler: *The Social Action Women's Group*), youth work (Ballantyne: *The Top End Action Group*) and community work (Fleming and Luczynski: *Fathers' Voices*), there are case examples of inter agency community based criminal justice work (Badham et al: *The Bulwell Neighbourhood Project*), prisons based work (Badham et al: *Self-directed Groupwork in a Youth Custody Centre*), work in schools (Cary et al: *Involving school students: The Youth Dreamers Group*) and in higher education (Arches: *The role of groupwork in social action projects with youth*). As we reveal in a separate volume (Mullender, Ward, Fleming 2013), these are no more than a taste of the range of what is possible and has been achieved when other sources of information about social action work are taken into account.

The concluding papers explore one such area: Social Action Research. Dave Ward, in *Social Action Research: A Methodology for Addressing 'How It Is'* sets the context for this emancipatory and participatory research approach. Mark Harrison and Simon Dyson in *Black Community Members as Researchers* and Asnaul Abu-Samah in *Empowering Research Process: Using Groups in Research to Empower People*, describe projects respectively in Black urban communities in England and within a rural village in Malaysia. Both papers address in some detail the challenges posed for researchers who are committed to revealing and tackling, in partnership with research participants, issues reflecting 'how it is' in their lives.

These papers present a range of perspectives and experiences to provide, in combination, a vivid account of social action as a values based approach committed to social justice and empowerment. In addition they contain a wealth of ideas and practices, a detailed resource which we hope will inspire and signpost without shirking the dilemmas and challenges to be considered, understood, faced and addressed.

Now, we invite you to read on ....

References (texts not included in this volume)

Anderson, J. (1996) 'Yes but IS IT empowerment? Initiation, implementation and outcomes of community action', in B. Humphries (ed.) *Critical*

Perspectives on Empowerment. Birmingham (UK): Venture Press.

Beddoe, L. and Harrington, P. (2012) 'One Step in a Thousand-Mile Journey: Can Civic Practice Be Nurtured in Practitioner Research? Reporting on an Innovative Project.' *British Journal of Social Work*, 42(1), pp74-93.

Berdan, K., Boulton, I., Eidman-Aadahl, E., Fleming, J., Gardner, L., Rogers, I. and Solomon, A. (eds.) (2006) *Writing for a Change: Boosting Literacy and Learning through Social Action*, San Francisco (CA): Jossey-Bass.

Boeck, T. and Fleming, J. (2002) *Social Capital and the Nottingham Social Action Research Project*, Nottingham (UK): Nottingham City Primary Care Trust.

Doel M and Kelly T (2014) *a-z of groups & groupwork*, Basingstoke: Palgrave Macmillan.

Fleming, J. (2000) 'Action Research for the Development of Children's Services in Ukraine', in H. Kemshall and R. Littlechild (eds.) *User Involvement and Participation in Social Care: Research informing Practice*. London: Jessica Kingsley.

Fleming, J. (2009) 'Social Action' in A. Gitterman and R. Salmon (eds) *Encyclopedia of Social Work with Groups*. London: Routledge.

Fleming, J. (2012) 'Service user involvement what it is and what it could be.' in S. Carr and P. Beresford, *Social Care, Service Users and User Involvement: Building on Research*. London: Jessica Kingsley.

Fleming, J. and Ward, D. (1996) 'The Ethics of Community Health Needs Assessment: Searching for a Participant Centred Approach' in Parker, M. (ed.) *Ethics and Community*, Preston: Centre for Professional Ethics, University of Central Lancashire, pp 284-294.

Fleming, J. and Ward, D. (1999) 'Research as Empowerment: the Social Action Approach', in W. Shera and L. Wells (eds.) *Empowerment Practice in Social Work: Developing Richer Conceptual Foundations*, Toronto: Canadian Scholars Press.

Fleming, J. and Ward, D. (2004) 'Methodology and Practical Application of the Social Action Research Model', in Maggs-Rapport, F. (ed.) *New Qualitative Research Methodologies in Health and Social Care: Putting Ideas into Practice*. London: Routledge.

Freire, P. (1972) *Pedagogy of the Oppressed*, Harmondsworth (UK): Penguin.

Freire, P. (1985) *The Politics of Education: Culture, Power and Liberation*, Westport CT: Bergin and Garvey Publishers Inc.

Mullaly, B. (2010) *Challenging Oppression and Confronting Privilege*, Don

Mills (Ont): Oxford University Press.

Mullender, A. and Ward, D. (1991) *Self-directed Groupwork: Users Take Action for Empowerment*, London: Whiting and Birch.

Mullender, A., Ward, D., Fleming, J. (2013) *Empowerment in Action: Self-directed Groupwork*, Basingstoke (UK): Palgrave Macmillan.

Payne, M (2005) *Modern Social Work Theory*, Basingstoke (UK): Palgrave Macmillan.

Sennett, R. (2011) 'A Creditable Left', *The Nation (New York)* 293, Issue 5/6, pp24-26.

Ward, D. and Mullender, A. (1988). 'The centrality of values in social work education', *Issues in Social work Education*, 8 (1) pp 46-54.

Ward, D. (1992) 'Through the Looking Glass: Practice led Research into Groupwork'. Paper presented to the *14th Annual Symposium for the Advancement of Social work with Groups*, Atlanta USA, October 1992.

Whitmore, E., Wilson, M. and Calhoun, A. (eds.) (2011) *Activism that Works*, Winnipeg, Manitoba: Fernwood Publishing.

Wright Mills, C. (1970) *The Sociological Imagination*, Harmondsworth: Penguin.

Young, K. (1999) 'The Youth Worker as Guide, Philosopher and Friend.' in S. Banks (ed.) *Ethical Issues in Youth Work*. London: Routledge.

Social action and self-directed groupwork:

Section 1
The fundamentals

The legacy of Paulo Freire

Les Price

It was with a deep sense of loss that activists and educators the world over heard of the death of the Brazilian educator Paulo Freire on May 2nd 1997. I, amongst many others, found myself mourning the parting of a man I had never met but who had influenced me a great deal over twenty years of practice as a community educator. In writing this short piece I have tried to sketch out what I consider to be Freire's legacy for those who work as formal and informal educators in social action contexts. One difficulty is adequately representing the man and his life's work.

First, a few words about the man. There is no accredited biography, authorised or not, of Freire (Taylor, 1993, p3). Indeed Freire himself always resisted the temptation to write about himself per se, although he did use the stuff of his individual experiences to inform his thinking in a truly reflective praxis. Freire the man is *in* his writing, but in a way he would regard as authentic rather than egocentric.

Freire's very early life was essentially middle class. The death of his father when Freire was in his teens precipitated the family into great poverty, a poverty which was to mark him in a most direct way. He often talked of experiencing hunger in his youth (Taylor, 1993, p14). The experience of attending university and work within literacy programmes with impoverished peasants brought together two nascent thoughts: that education could be a transforming force, but, in order to transform, it needed to be set within a philosophical framework. Such a framework would make education liberating rather than a replicator of oppressive relationships.

Time spent in North America as a visiting professor at Harvard in the late 1960s presented Freire with a perspective of poverty and oppression within a First World rather than Third World context. Freire found marginalisation, exclusion and oppression of the poor within the USA to equal that of his native Brazil. It caused him, as Sue Branford's obituary of him notes, to redefine the 'Third World' as a political place rather than a geographical one (Branford, 1997). This is a perspective many of us working inside the hinterland of the dispossessed within the so-called developed world can share. Globalisation has only sharpened this drift towards a polarised world economic order which defies the previous divisions of the compass.

It was during his time in the USA that Freire wrote his seminal *The Pedagogy of the Oppressed*. Freire had always admitted that he was more used to talking than writing: speaking is, after all, an essential component of dialogue, verbally recreating the world is a prerequisite for learning to write about it (Taylor, 1993, p3). That said, 'Pedagogy' is a dense, multi-layered and well-written work. Shaull in his foreword to the Pelican edition talks about the, 'richness, depth and complexity ....' manifest in the book (Freire, 1985). As such the book requires, indeed demands, reading and rereading, not because it is obscurantist but because it asks for a dialogical engagement with its contents. As Freire writes in his own preface to the book: 'This volume will probably arouse negative reactions in a number of readers .... the reader who assumes closed 'irrational' positions will reject the dialogue I hope the book will open.' (Freire, 1985, p11).

Freire's philosophical stall is laid out in *The Pedagogy of the Oppressed* in the most complete way. It seeks to deal with three fundamental questions that are crucial to all educators and others who seek to work with people in an anti-oppressive way. Firstly, it asks, 'What is it to be fully human?'. This allows Freire to set out his ontological position and describe the nature of being in a way that transcends the moulds oppressive relationships might place us in. Secondly, it asks, 'What is the nature of knowledge?'. Here Freire sets out an epistemological position that rehabilitates knowledge as a dynamic entity, created and recreated in dialogue, rather than a fixed commodity. A commodity is something to be 'banked' as a deposit in those people who do not yet possess it.

Finally, it asks, 'What is a liberating pedagogy?'. At this point Freire draws all the strands together of his philosophy to formulate and describe educational processes that nourish and build upon the qualities of humanness rather than destroy them, that validate knowledge creation as a joint act of living rather than a dumb act of transmitting and receiving and that turns education out on to the world as a force for life. Freire, building upon the philosophy of Hegel and Marx, attempts to wrestle the whole edifice of western philosophy to the ground in a bid for a liberating pedagogy. Little wonder then, that Freire in his own preface is certain ' .. that Christians and Marxists, though they may disagree with me in part or in whole, will continue reading to the end.' (Freire, 1985, p17). The serious intent of the book as a work of philosophy should not be doubted.

What does all this mean to us, struggling in our daily work? It may mean a very great deal, for Freire's ontology is refreshing and hopeful. It builds upon Marx's own ontological position that recognises that even though people are oppressed, are alienated, their 'species being', what Freire calls their 'ontological vocation', is always orientated towards growth and liberation. In this sense, both Freire and Marx recognise and document the capitalist trend to dehumanisation, and the ensuing brutality and inhumanity. Freire writes, 'I consider the fundamental theme of our epoch to be that of domination ...... ' (Freire, 1985, p75). He also asserts, 'Nor yet can dialogue exist without hope. Hope is rooted in .. (our). ... incompleteness..... The dehumanisation resulting from an unjust order is not a cause for despair but for hope, leading to the incessant pursuit of the humanity that is denied by injustice'. (Freire, 1985, p64). This is no blind optimism and empty rhetoric for Freire derives this position from a tightly defined philosophical base, Marx's own. As Marx himself wrote, amidst the alienation and degradation of Nineteenth Century capitalism, the human creative drive is the core of humanity,

> The whole character of a species.... is contained in the character of its life activity; and free, conscious activity is ... (our). ..... species character (Marx, 1959)

So Freire rehabilitates us as people. Though we are within contexts of oppression and dehumanisation our ontological vocation as human beings creates within us the potential for growth and change. We are within the world but we need not be its dumb recipients; we can change it and ourselves. Freire's epistemological position builds upon this. If free, conscious activity is our human entitlement then knowledge is its manifestation. However in a world of alienation real knowledge is at risk. It has been replaced by a thousand small 'competencies', a million 'transferable skills', a commodity culture in which, '...knowledge is a gift bestowed by those who consider themselves knowledgeable upon those whom they consider to know nothing.' (Freire, 1985, p46). Worse even than this, knowledge has been splintered and debased by having its organic connections with the context in which it is created ignored. The true links between the subjective and objective within knowledge have been cut. Implicit in this is the assumption of a dichotomy between human beings and the world. We are disempowered because we seem to be, '.....merely *in* the world, not *with* the world or with others.' (Freire, 1985, p66). We come to see ourselves as spectators not recreators.

Freire makes the case for us all needing to rebuild knowledge as a dynamic creation rather than a dead commodity, 'Knowledge emerges only through invention and reinvention, through the restless, impatient, continuing, hopeful inquiry..... in the world, with the world, and with each other.' (Freire, 1985, p46). Knowledge is created through dialogue. Authentic thinking, thinking that is deconstructing reality, can only take place in communication; it is a joint, collective task. This is a fundamental lesson for all of us working in social action frameworks. Our thinking, our knowledge can only be authenticated by the authenticity of the thinking of those we work with. We are all in the epistemological boat together and our professional skills and insights are about helping people to row for themselves and us, and vice versa. As practitioners we are not therefore, in a knowledge transaction, we are within a praxis, a cycle of collective action and reflection in which our role is that of problem poser and facilitator.

This hints at an answer to Freire's last big philosophical question, 'What is a liberating pedagogy?' Freire recognises that educational processes can never be neutral, that they all carry within them implicit statements about the nature of the human condition and moral judgements about what it is right and proper to 'know'. Freire understands that his ontological and epistemological perspectives inevitably lead to a pedagogy that exists to create a critical consciousness in all those it engages. As Freire writes, 'Authentic education is not carried on by A *for* B or by A *about* B, but rather A *with* B, mediated by the world, a world which impresses and challenges both parties...' (Freire, 1985, p66) (his emphasis). In dialogical action the educational process reunites ourselves with the world. Yes, we have been shaped by our social context, but in naming and understanding that context we are in a position collectively to reshape it and ourselves. Through this process we '... come to see the world not as a static reality, but as a reality in process, in transformation' (Freire, 1985, p56).

Perhaps Freire should speak the last word about his own legacy. I have already commented on his preference for producing 'talked' books rather than 'written' ones, believing as he did that knowledge is only truly created within dialogue, within reflective cycles between human beings. In a collaboration with the American educator Ira Shor in 1987 Freire talked about his own place in liberating pedagogy, 'For me, being a 'prophet' does not mean to be a crazy man with a dirty beard, or to be a crazy woman. It means to be strongly in the present, to have your feet firmly planted in the present, to have your feet firmly planted on the ground, in such a way that foreseeing the future becomes a normal thing. You know the present so well, you can imagine a possible future of transformation. Imagination at this level is side-by-side with dreams...... This is imagination. This is the possibility to go beyond tomorrow without being naively idealistic' (Freire and Shor, 1987, pp186-187)

This seems to be an apt epitaph for the man and a note of encouragement for those of us engaged in creative social action.

References

Branford, S. (1997) Obituary of Paulo Freire. *The Guardian'*, May 10th

Freire, P. (1985) *The Pedagogy of the Oppressed.* Harmondsworth: Penguin

Marx, K. (1959) *Economic and Philosophical Manuscripts.* (trans M. Milligan M.) London: Lawrence & Wishart

Freire, P. and Shor I. (1987) *A Pedagogy for Liberation: Dialogues for Transforming Education.* Basingstoke: Macmillan

Taylor, P. V. (1993) *The Texts of Paulo Freire.* Buckingham: Open University Press

This chapter was first published in 1998 in *Social Action* Vol. 3(3), pp.4-6

At the time of writing Les Price worked at the Linwood Centre, a community education unit in the south of Leicester

Issues of empowerment: Anti-oppressive groupwork by disabled people in Ireland

Maire Ni Chorcora, Eddie Jennings and Nuala Lordan
Cartoons by S. O' Shaughnessy

This chapter examines the dilemmas inherent in working to empower marginalised groups. It seeks to analyse the difficulties of a groupwork model which views empowerment as a political process. The authors discuss their experience as disabled people in the development of a group, where members concern and commitment was to overcome their feelings of powerlessness. This group sets out to learn new ways of dealing with their oppressors; and to create societal structures where people, who are most affected by decision making, can have a meaningful impact on policy making. The barriers to participation and powersharing are considered and an effort is made to understand how the power structures of society operate. The paper concludes by identifying key issues in the groupwork process which facilitated empowerment, and enabled members to take control and begin to challenge their oppressors.

The focus of this paper is on a model of groupwork intervention which seeks to challenge oppression, moving from identifying personal experience to understanding the political forces which create and maintain the status quo. The approach is closely aligned to Mullender and Ward's 'self directed approach' (1991) to groupwork. It acknowledges a clear value base, which views empowerment not merely as an enabling process, but a political position which has as its goal the changing of existing power relations. Challenging the status quo and finding ways and means to negotiate new structures, which provide for real dialogue and partnership in the decision- making organisations of our society, is central to power sharing.

The analysis of our experiences in the development of a group of disabled persons whose initial concern was the marginalisation of people with disability in Irish society highlights many of the dilemmas inherent in this model. We believe that the issues which this process has raised are not unique but relevant to all groups of marginalised people. Although every group has its own dynamic forces, the context and cultural stimuli play a major role, in determining the central issues of concern.

Anti-oppressive practice and empowerment

The concept of anti-oppressive practice has come very much to the forefront of the social work agenda. British theoreticians and practitioners have done much to highlight the key challenges facing groupworkers who work to empower marginalised groups; but the question, of whether it is possible to develop partnerships with user groups within structures which by their very nature seek to maintain the equilibrium of the power structure, still needs to be addressed. Much of our thesis has been said before, and there is already a substantial literature on power and empowering practice. Why does it need to be repeated? We believe it needs repeating because in our experience it does not often happen. It is we realise a very difficult process: our wish is to create a forum for dialogue regarding the reality of the dilemmas inherent in empowering practice.

The word empowerment slips easily off the tongue, anti-oppressive practice is a little more difficult. Both have become the 'fashionable' words for social work practice. Empowerment has 'power' as its centrepiece an attribute crucial to its understanding and use. It has to do with enhancing people's power, (Preston-Shoot, 1992), and through non-hierarchical working, empowerment sees users as subjects rather than objects in the social work process. When we talk about working toward empowerment, we are talking about developing ways of creating a transfer of power, so that people can become involved in the processes which produce plans and decisions which affect their lives.

It is worth asking the questions:

Who are the experts on knowing what it is like to live with a disability?
Who plans the services?
Why?

We are talking of moving from the personal to the political. The issue of participation, or lack of it, is forcing its way onto national and international agendas. Notably, at a time when in Europe decision making structures are getting further and further away. Some structures of our society allow people to be represented in the decision making process. However almost all of these structures do not provide genuine participation for most people affected by their decisions. Take the allocation of European funding, in the area of disability: decisions are taken in Brussels, in consultation with a national agency of non-disabled people, although there does exist in Ireland a forum of disabled people.

It is interesting to note that the language of anti-oppressive practice and empowerment is now being used by social workers. This is occurring during a time when on the political agenda and other power fronts, those with rightwing conservative policies have gained ground world wide. Mandates are being sent from Europe about the importance of user participation, and the mobilisation of self help is a key issue in the obtaining of funding. However it is clear that the interest in the corridors of power is in people becoming more self reliant, self supporting, employable. However laudable this aspiration is, it does not take into account the experience of marginalised groups; their involvement at this level has not even been considered, genuine participation is not on the agenda.

Limited information is given on the decision making process. Groups are put in competition with each other in their efforts to obtain limited funding, and it would appear that the well tried techniques of control are operant in the form of 'divide and then conquer and rule'.

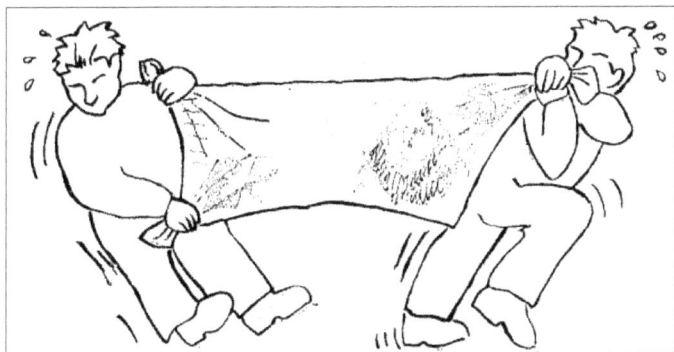

We have seen the disastrous effects of this policy on some communities in Cork, where friendships have been broken, people divided, in their scramble to obtain resources. Indeed there is now a belief among many that the continual need to compete for funding is just a strategy of those in powerful positions to keep the poor busy preparing proposals, diluting their strength and motivation to band together in opposition to the faceless controllers of resources.

There are many aspects to powerlessness. Sennett and Cobb (1972) and Conway (1979) list these as being; economic insecurity, absence of fiscal support, lack of training in critical and abstract thought, and physical and emotional stress. One thing all marginalised and oppressed groups have in common is poverty. This includes: a lack of money; a lack of rights; lack of entitlements; and a lack of access to opportunities. Speaking from their personal experience of poverty, reports from women's groups in Ireland (Daly, 1988) have stated that poverty is about feelings, how one regards oneself, and how one is regarded by others. It is about feelings of powerlessness; experiencing exclusion; rejection; being treated as inferior; lacking in status or being in some way inadequate. Members of our group report a very similar encounter, they constantly experience exclusion, being on the outside, and they are made to feel inadequate, helpless, and dependent. These feelings are central to the experience of marginalised groups.

Solomon (1976), identified three potential sources of powerlessness:

1. the negative self evaluation attitudes of oppressed people themselves;
2. negative experiences in the interaction between the victims of oppression and the outside systems which impinge on them;
3. larger environmental systems which consistently block and deny effective action taking by powerless groups.

This has indeed been the experience of all our disabled group members, who constantly encounter these levels of powerlessness. Empowerment is about gaining power and in doing so, the above mentioned areas need to be addressed. People need to develop self confidence, self esteem and control of their situation. They need to learn to be assertive regarding their rights, and to challenge the structures which oppress them. For us working in an empowering way means that group members have real power.

They control the finance.
They make the decisions.
Each member has a role to play.

– TAKING CONTROL –

Croft and Beresford (1989) talked in terms of three dimensions to empowerment: they suggested that social service agencies must be committed to the concept of empowerment; this will necessarily involve offering its users a say in the control and management of the agency, and enabling people to take up opportunities for a say in the agencies' functioning whenever possible. It is our experience that agencies do not give away their power, unless of course they want the job done on the cheap. Usually they will stay in a position of sufficient power to claim the credits. Mullender and Ward (1991) added another crucial dimension to those already mentioned. It is the importance of developing a way of working, which in its foundations, its techniques and style of operation, empowers those who experience its use. It is this aspect of empowerment we hope to address here. How can a real change of power take place in an environment which as Pernell (1989) so aptly points out:

> When the powerless stir and begin to seek some equity, the system shakes and the powerful move to restore the equilibrium, giving a little perhaps, but substantially retaining power. The social worker, then engaged in the process and goal of empowerment of the disadvantaged group or individual, may stand exposed and vulnerable to the efforts of those in power to hold the line' (p.110.).

From its origins, the function of groupwork has been seen not only as the accomplishment of (individual) personal goals, but also through group exchanges and networking as a means for achieving social change. However, in Ireland there has been a great resistance at agency level to groups that do anything other than individualise problems. Much of the groupwork which is done focuses on personal development and individual coping, and although this is very valuable, there is great difficulty moving beyond this level to becoming involved in structural change issues.

Sabotage

Efforts to establish groups to address structural issues are in fact actively sabotaged by those in positions of power, as in the following example:

A group of parents of autistic children came together due to their frustration with the lack of services. They wanted to demand better services for themselves and their children. Many of them were regarded by professionals as very disturbed families whose anger was largely a symptom of their pathology. These professionals joined them, praised them, and directed their efforts toward fund-raising, to gather money on a voluntary basis for more services. Thus the present service was not challenged, the rights of these families were not considered. The professionals maintained the equilibrium, where they continue to define the agenda.

Similarly when Combat Poverty Agency placed its first workers in Cork, to work in a particular neighbourhood, the local statutory authority (the equivalent to social services) put their workers into the same area to work in competition and make sure they would be kept informed of any developments taking place.

Yet another example is when the voluntarily run Family Centres came together (there are five in different neighbourhoods in the city) and wished to negotiate with the statutory authorities as a group, in an organised planned fashion. They were informed individually that they would do much better financially if they negotiated by themselves.

These vignettes all demonstrate quite clearly that the establishment is not supportive of group initiatives which are about to create change. After all those in the establishment do not want to lose their position in the pecking order of the power structure.

Disability in Ireland

Let us now look at the question of disability in Ireland. It is not an exaggeration to say that disabled people are one of the most marginalised groups in Irish society. They are hidden and dealt with behind closed doors. Their position in society is that of second class citizenship. This is best illustrated by the depiction of 'the collection box mentality' where people with disabilities are objects to be pitied, patronised, prayed for, and seen to be in need of nothing more than a few pounds tossed into a collection box. This money is then to be managed and spent by 'do gooders' out to save their souls in the provision of services for the disabled. These attitudes have definitely kept people with disabilities in their place. '*Grateful*'.

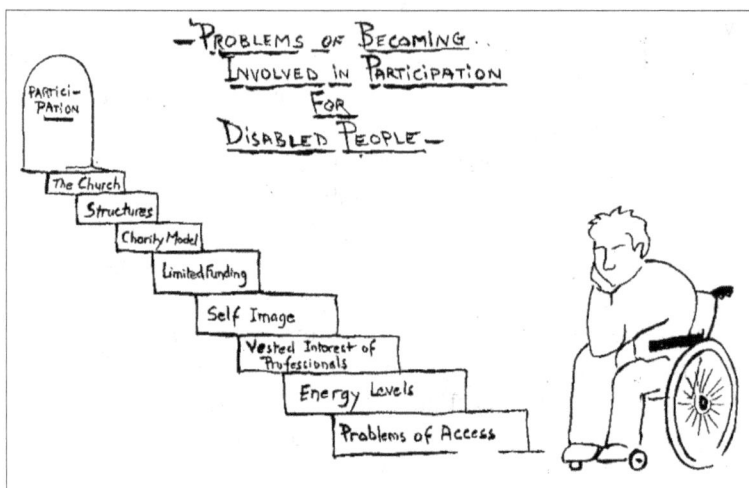

The Green Paper on Services for Disabled People (Department of Health, 1983) examined the introduction of legislation on the rights of people with disabilities. The Green paper decided against the introduction of legislation, preferring instead to rely on 'goodwill and understanding', thus leaving disabled people very much the victims of charity. There have been murmurings of consultations about how best the rights of disabled people can be promoted, but little attention has been paid to the problems of becoming involved in real participation for disabled people. Issues have been identified by members of our group as being:

Problems of access.
Energy levels.
Vested interest of professionals.
Self image.
Limited funding.
Charity model.
Structures.
The church.

The motivation to start the group.

It was the felt need of disabled people which created the group, which started when about six like minded individuals came together. Their concern was about the level of ignorance regarding the realities of disability, and the need to get the issue of Disability on the political agenda as a rights issue. They felt that it was time people with disabilities made themselves heard. But how? Many voices were necessary, group members lacked the know how, their experiences heretofore had not equipped them for this task, and indeed had left them feeling helpless and frustrated. Thus it was decided that the best place to start was with training. Some of the members were aware of the excellent training initiatives in Britain, but felt that being disabled in Ireland was a different experience. Little is written about being disabled in Ireland, the collective experience is unknown. The first task of the group was to network with other people with disabilities. Since the group had as its catchment all disabilities, members found themselves very ignorant about each others needs. Much of the groups beginnings were taken up with information exchange and learning about each others experiences. Members wrestled with understanding and developing action plans to combat the many encounters of discrimination that individuals brought to the group.

The group at this stage is made up of about 20 members, who meet on a regular basis. This group forms a steering committee where policy decisions are made. The group have received financial aid, from the European Union under the horizon programme, in partnership with the Adult Education Department of University College Cork, to launch a training program for 12 disabled persons to become disability equality trainers. Various sub-groups have been established as the need arises to get on with the work of the committee. They report on a fortnightly basis. There is a commitment to keeping everyone as informed and involved as possible. There is an action group of five members, who carry on the work of the group between meetings. This action group rotates its membership on a regular basis so that everyone gains experience at this level.

The personal experiences of two group members.

The following accounts of our experience give a factual picture of the reality of life with a disability and the ways in which we have been marginalised. It also outlines the significance of this group, and its meaning for us. Let us begin with Eddie's story:

> I was diagnosed with Multiple Sclerosis when I was 22 years old -that was nearly ten years ago. What is Multiple Sclerosis?...it's a disease of the brain and the spinal cord, central nervous system. MS interferes with the brain's ability to control such functions as seeing, walking, and talking. It's called multiple because many scattered areas of the brain and spinal cord may be affected. The symptoms can be mild or severe, and come or go unpredictably. It is called Sclerosis because the disease involves sclerosed or hardened tissue in damaged areas of the brain and the spinal cord. MS is not a mental illness, it is not contagious and is not preventable or curable yet.
>
> When I was first diagnosed I was working as a technician / buyer in an electronic plant in Shannon which is in the west of Ireland. I had recently been made a permanent member of staff, although I had not been working with this company for long. I was enjoying my time, I received a good salary, I liked the opportunity to work away from home, I had no worries, my social life was excellent.
>
> I really had no concept on diagnosis what MS was all about save what I had been told by the doctors. I hadn't met others with it so I didn't really understand what to expect. I went back to work shortly after being diagnosed as I didn't feel very physically sick. I did have double vision and I knew I dragged my foot a bit. But I felt alright, I wasn't ready to talk about it yet to any of my colleagues until I was sure of the answers. I did tell my immediate boss whom I felt would support me because he was always telling me to be sure and come to him about any problems I may have had. I did confide in him feeling it was the right thing to do. This was a mistake as I found to my peril. Not long afterwards, I was made redundant.
>
> I felt that my life had ended...Now everything was up for grabs including my future job prospects. I soon realised I would never again pass another medical examination, for I would have to disclose everything about my MS to other employers. It was a dreadful shock

for me, I felt let down. Who would have confidence in me again? When I enquired about the redundancy, I was told that it was outside local control who was to be laid off. But later I found out that I had been betrayed, information about my medical condition became known, soon after I informed my boss.

When I had worked out my notice, I felt that I had no option but to return home to Cork. I loved my independence, I loved the kind of life I had and the choices I could make because of it. I went home reluctantly without much prospects. I languished there for about a year without doing very much but getting used to my MS and getting more depressed.

I was signing on the dole but I was soon advised that I wasn't really available for work, and therefore I should go on a disability payment and be certified sick and unable for work. I was told that I should register with the National Training Agency for disabled people if I wanted a job or training of any kind. I was extremely excited about the prospect of working again. At the same time, they told me about the uncertainty of finding an employer to take me on. My opportunities were very limited.

My placement officer picked me up from my home on a Monday morning. He arrived in a beautiful tan coloured Alfa Romeo car something akin to the one I had sold the week previously as I couldn't afford it any more. We were going to visit a training centre. This was my first introduction to sheltered workshops. All the 'so called' trainees were in one room. They were people with all different kinds of disability. I felt I needed to get out of this place fast. I also felt angry that this was the only option to be presented to me. There had to be more. I never went back to see that particular placement officer. Anyway I felt he talked too much and nicely about all the great things he could do for me.

Next, I got involved in voluntary work and self-help initiatives locally and nationally. This gave me an opportunity to develop skills in community work. I eventually decided, having received professional guidance, to pursue full time education and training in Community and Youth Work at Maynooth College.

I got involved in this Disability Equality group from the very beginning, in fact I was a founding member. For a long time now we have had professionals in all kinds of areas speaking about disability, whereas we the people with disabilities are the experts. This programme is about training people with disabilities to be able to speak for themselves. It is a unique group. From the beginning people have gained loads of confidence by being part of a group which is willing to be tolerant and listen. Never before have they had such an opportunity, People just do not hear disabled people or do not give them the chance. Group members have a sense of possible power to change their own situation and circumstances. For my part, as a newly trained Youth and Community worker I have been extremely interested in disability equality training, so this project provided me with plenty of scope to develop this skill. It added a definite focus and direction to my life for which I had been looking.

Maire's experience

I am a disabled woman working in a full time post, living with my partner and two daughters. My main dilemma in life has been my struggle to be 'normal' and knowing in my heart that I had to acknowledge the fact that I am disabled.

My story began when I contracted Polio at fifteen months. It impaired my mobility in my lower spine and legs. I was immediately isolated physically and emotionally from everyone and everything that was familiar to me. I was hospitalised. For the first three months of my hospitalisation my parents were only able to view me through clear glass for fear they would catch or carry the virus outside the fever ward. So the only contact I had was with nurses and doctors and my uncle, who because he was a Roman Catholic Priest was allowed to stand beside my cot. I learned through my parents at a young age that mystique either medical or spiritual held a lot of keys. I was eventually discharged after one year, unable to walk and with my callipers on back to front.

This was the beginning for me of not quite fitting in - either outside the hospital or inside. During hospital stays I knew that I had to be a 'good girl', a 'good patient', a good polio victim, and in order to acquire the tag of 'good' I had to stifle the positive and negative emotions and do what others, the professionals expected a good girl to do.

At home my Mam and Dad desperately tried to make me normal despite the fact that I had a major mobility impairment. But they always stated the only chance I had was if I was to become as normal as possible. Being disabled for them meant that I had no future educationally, financially and sure as hell I wasn't going to be happy. So they did everything as the hopeful parents they were, in order for me not to fall into the disabled 'bracket'.

The downside for me was that even though I tried and succeeded in the normal world I was never true to myself. I am only now acknowledging that I am disabled by the social attitudes of the society we live in and the environmental barriers I hassle with everyday of my life.

Society's view is hardly one where a disabled person is economically independent - not just on a state pension but fully employed - not just a token, but a fully active sexual member of that society. Disabled people are generally disadvantaged in relation to the above assumptions and one has to ask why? I speak as a woman and I believe disabled women are even more disadvantaged. Our image of disabled women is hardly one that includes being sexually active, whatever your sexual preference. Rearing children, feeding them or caring for them is not part of the picture, and again one has to ask why not. The answer for me is that disabled people, both men and women and children, have no choices, no decision making powers. Because we are not in the position or the places where choices and decisions are made, so therefore we are forgotten, only to become more isolated and alienated than we already are.

I believe it is not until 'abilist' people in society, face the possible vulnerability of old age, or the personal fears and prospect of a disability for oneself or for a loved one, that disabled people will be welcomed as part of the human race.

For years I have swung from wanting to be seen as normal to wanting to have my disability acknowledged as part of me, But if I gave into this I would have become invisible, lonely, and genderless. These are my fears and they are real because up to now I as a disabled person have not been spoken to or listened to. My needs have not been met in the society of which I am a part.

However society does manage subtly, to deal with me at some level by putting the penny in the box, or buying the odd piece of art, or being a member of the committee that is doing such 'good work'. Charity has been as easy option for everyone. Pay lip service and forget all about us. I am learning that charity does not any longer serve to absolve society of all responsibility, charity will no longer buy our gratitude. It will serve to create a greater divide.

I am now in my 40th year and only now hearing the voices of my fellow disabled, the real story of their lives and I am learning to say I will not go away and be normal. I am learning to say I want to be part of this society and a disabled part at that.

Key issues in the group

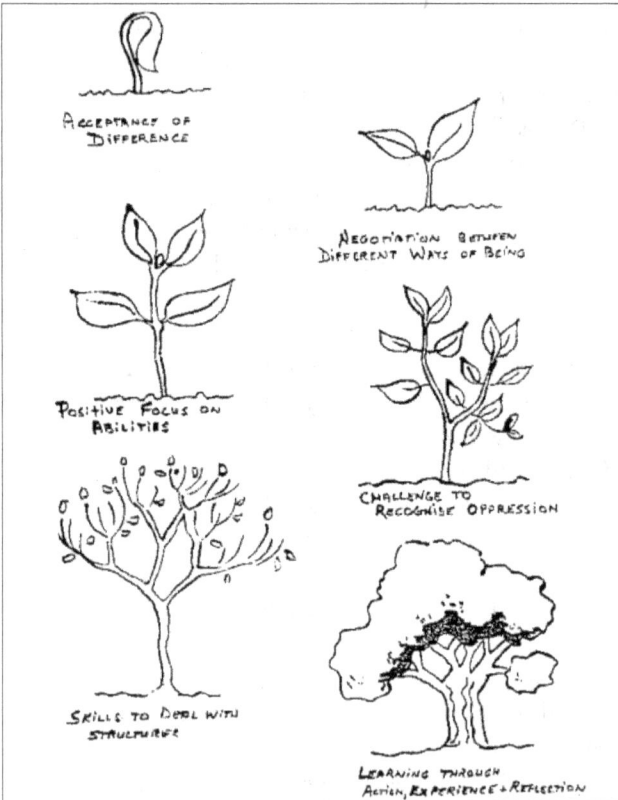

The key issues in this group which have facilitated the empowering process are:

1. Recognition and acceptance of difference,
   a. Everybody has a right to be themselves, they are OK.
   b. Everyone is different.
   c. Everyone has a way of being.
   This aspect of the group was greatly facilitated by the fact that everybody was so totally different. We all had quite different experiences of disability and thus could not presume to understand each other.
2. The group's commitment to negotiating between different ways of being. Great effort was put into meeting each others needs. Be it difficulties in communication or concentration, ways were sought to facilitate all members: for example because it is difficult for some people to concentrate for any lengthy period the group takes a break and coffee, tea and cakes are provided to recharge member's energy levels.
3. Positive focus on people's abilities. We always focus on what members can do and can contribute to the process, involving everybody as much as possible.
4. The challenging of oppression. The focus of the group has been to learn actively how to gain and to keep our own power. One of our main ground rules was the right to challenge ourselves and to recognise our oppression, as most of us were often not even aware of this oppression.

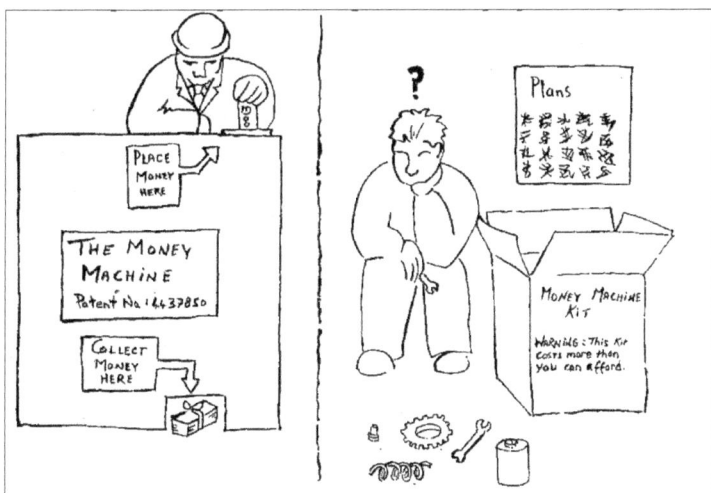

5. The development of knowledge and skills to deal with the structures of society. This is an ongoing process with each new task demanding knowledge and skills not in the repertoire of our previous experience. We opted to develop a partnership with the University, recognising that alone we would not qualify for EC funding. nor would we have a Certificate to Award. Our dealings in this partnership highlight the many issues facing groups who do not want to be taken over by the well organised and functioning elite. For example they constantly choose one member of the group to negotiate with them. This has the effect of divide and rule in the group by influencing peoples perceived status with each other. Similarly organisations want to take power for themselves so they then get to make the decisions which will eventually only suit their own needs, giving them the prestige and reinforcing the global ethos that disabled people have not the personal resources to organise their own lives.

6. Learning through action, experience and reflection. At committee level the rotation of roles has facilitated the learning of different skills and expertise, using our own creativity, acknowledging and having our needs respected. Everybody gets the opportunity to carry out tasks on behalf of the group and to experience all this involves, such as facing the panic of what to do, and the feeling of achievement in a task well done.

These aspects of the group have been positive in enabling group members to grow in confidence, knowledge and expertise. Through this experience they have recognised that they have abilities and can make things happen, they can move from dependence to taking control of their lives.

Summary and evaluation

Challenging the Status Quo –

In this paper we have endeavoured to highlight the issues and dilemmas facing any marginalised group who wish to challenge the status quo.

Change does not come easily, power is not usually given away. However as we have discovered through our experience, it is through the ongoing analysis of encounters with the establishment that the group members learn the power game. In doing so they grow in strength within themselves, as can be seen from this sample of quotes we collected from group members.

> The group is about confidence, pride in your disability and not having to hide it.
> I see it as a liberating group coming from the grass roots with individualistic experience.
> I feel equal.
> The group provides a platform to achieve specific goals and remove obstacles for all people with disabilities.
> I have developed new meaningful relationships which I feel enormously comfortable with, which I know will outlive the life of the project.

Each new action brings with it new questioning, new reflections and it takes strength and determination to succeed. The continual problem is to sustain the group in the face of such adversity. This can only be done through recognising the gains made, however small, and the acknowledgement of each others support in understanding and fighting oppression.

References

Conway, M. (1979) *Rise Gonna Rise*. New York: Anchor.

Croft, S. and Beresford, P. (1989) 'User involvement, citizenship and social policy', *Critical Social Policy*, 26.9(2)

Daly, M. (ed.) (1988) *Women Together Against Poverty*. Dublin: Combat Poverty Agency.

Department of Health (1983) *Towards a Full Life. Green Paper on Services for Disabled People*. Dublin: Stationery Office.

Mullender, A. and Ward, D. (1991) *Self Directed Groupwork: Users Take Action for Empowerment*. London: Whiting and Birch.

Pernell, R.B. (1989) 'Empowerment and social groupwork' in Parnes, M. (ed.) *Innovations in Social Groupwork: Feedback from Practice to Theory*. New York: Haworth Press.

Preston-Shoot, M. (1992) 'On empowerment, partnership and authority: a training contribution', *Groupwork*, 5(2) pp.5-30.

Sennett, R. and Cobb, J. (1972) The Hidden Injuries of Class. Garden City, NY: Vintage.

Solomon, B. (1976) *Black Empowerment: Social Work in Oppressed Communities*. New York: Columbia University Press.

This chapter was first published in 1994 in *Groupwork* Vol. 7(1), pp.63-78

At the time of writing, Maire Ni Chorcora had a longterm disability and was a founder member of DET, working in the area of disability.Eddie Jennings was a founder member of DET. He was a person with MS. Nuala Lordan was a Lecturer in Social Work at University College, Cork

Values as Context:
Groupwork and social action

Mark Harrison and Dave Ward

This chapter outlines the history and theoretical foundations of social action. Social action is a values-led approach to practice in which groupwork is a key element of the model. This relationship, however, brings into focus recent trends in groupwork practice which, it is suggested, merit critical reflection among groupwork exponents. Examples of three areas of social action activity are described: practice, training and research; and the paper concludes with a critical discussion suggesting lines for further development.

The social action approach

Social action emerged in the late 1970s and early 1980s as a distinctive approach to empowerment and was located initially in work with young people at risk and in trouble (Ward, 1979; 1981; 1982; Harrison et al, 198; Burley, 1982; Fleming et al, 1983). It was first conceptualised in detail as 'Self-Directed Groupwork' (Mullender and Ward, 1991) which Payne (1997, p.280) describes as offering 'a clear view empowerment theory focused on groupwork settings and processes.'.

Social action has been developed reflexively and in partnership by practitioners, service users and academics in the course of developing, carrying out, and evaluating interventions, training programmes and action-research. The approach has been recognised as applicable in a wide range of human service settings and to have wide currency internationally (Breton, 1994; Brown, 1996; Jakobsson, 1995; Lee, 1994; Treu et al, 1993). Besides Britain, social action work is currently taking place in projects in eastern and western Europe, North America, and Australasia. *Self-Directed Groupwork* (Mullender and Ward, 1991) has been translated in full into Ukrainian (1996) and in summary into French (1992). Many social action workers and participants link up through the Centre for social action at De Montfort University in Leicester (UK) and share experiences at the Centre's annual international summer school.

Social action has two central characteristics. Firstly, it rejects the 'deficit' and 'victim blaming' approaches which dominate social welfare, promoting instead a commitment to the capacity of all people to take action to improve the circumstances of their lives. Secondly it bases this action on a process of open participation in which people, working collectively in groups, explore the underlying social issues effecting their everyday lives as the foundation for action. Practitioners do not lead but through a non-elitist, highly skilled process, facilitate group members in making choices and taking action for themselves.

Through a continuing and reflexive process of practice and debate among workers and service users, a set of six key principles has developed which provides an adaptable framework for social action practice in a range of settings: training (eg Ward, 1989; Canton et al, 1996), research (eg Ward, 1996/7; Dyson and Harrison, 1998; Fleming et al, forthcoming) as well as practice. These are:

- Refusing to accept negative labels: all people have skills and understanding on which they can draw to tackle the problems they face. Professionals should not attach negative labels to service users.
- The right to chose and control: all people have rights, including the right to be heard, the right to define issues facing them, and the right to take action on their own behalf.
- Complex problems: individuals in difficulty are often confronted by complex issues rooted in social policy, the environment and the economy. Responses to them should reflect this understanding.
- Collective power: people acting collectively can be powerful. People who lack power and influence can gain it through working together in groups. Practice should reflect this understanding.
- Workers as facilitators: methods of working should reflect non elitist principles. Workers do not lead but facilitate members in making decisions for themselves and controlling whatever

outcome ensues. Though special skills and knowledge are employed, these do not accord privilege and are not solely the province of workers.

- Tackling all forms of oppression: social action workers will strive to challenge inequality and discrimination in relation to race, gender, sexual orientation, age, class, disability or any other form of social differentiation.

These principles have been graphically expressed in cartoon by Muldoon (1994/5) reproduced opposite; and James (1997, p.7) succinctly summarises the shift in perception they involve:

Problems	⟶	Solutions
Deficits	⟶	Assets
Clients	⟶	Citizen Decision Makers
Objects	⟶	Subjects
Problems in Individuals	⟶	Problems rooted in Systems

Theoretical and practical inspiration for social action comes from the work of Paulo Freire (1972) and the challenge has been to apply his ideas in working, initially in the UK but, subsequently, more widely afield, most notably in some of the former communist states of eastern Europe. (Mullender and Ward, 1992; 1996; Fleming and Keenan, 1998). Social action holds much in common with the theory and practice of community development. Here the challenge is to adapt the values and practice developed in collective action on structural issues from the predominantly locality based context of community work and working with 'ordinary' albeit poor people, to the more fragmented and specialist concerns of social work. Social action has been influenced strongly by the struggles of the disability movement (see for example: Oliver, 1992), black activists and writers (see for example: Cress-Welsing, 1991; hooks, 1992; Ahmed, 1990; and Gilroy, 1987) and the women's movement (see for example Hudson, 1989; Dominelli and McLoed, 1989; Langan and Day, 1992; and Evans, 1994). They indicate the complex way in which various dimensions of exclusion and oppression are distinctive but still interlink. Each overarches the others at

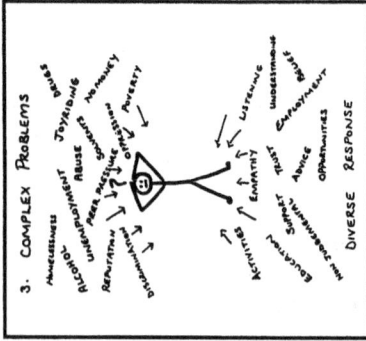

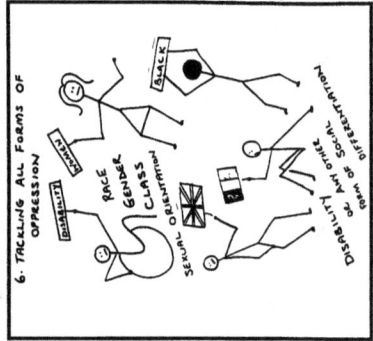

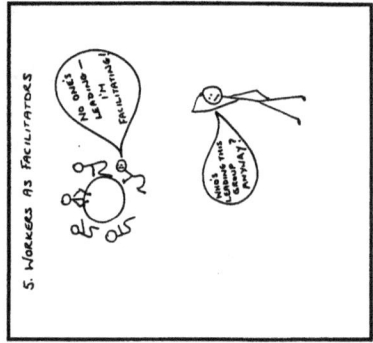

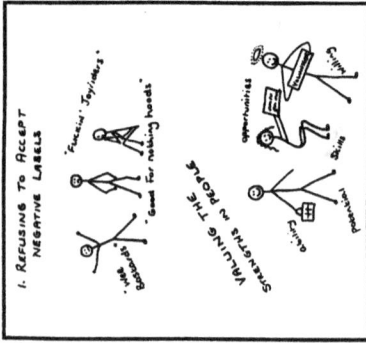

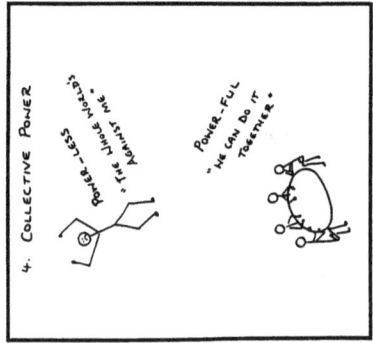

different times and in particular conditions, requiring independent action but within a coherent world-view. Methods developed in social education and in social skills training are adapted for the exploration of issues and the preparation, implementation and evaluation of action. (See Mullender and Ward, 1991, for the methodology set out in full.)

This formulation of social action differs from the normal usage of the term in North America, where generally it refers to a range of forms of

> professional effort to bring into public discourse issues which, according to the consensus between power holders and the public, should remain in the shadow of public debate. (Staub-Bernasconi, 1991, p.36)

> social action is practice and activity which are committed to social change and social justice. (Breton, 1995). While this generic definition still appertains, the focus of this paper is upon social action as an explicitly articulated practice theory and methodology which is making a prime contribution to debates about empowerment and associated working practices (Adams, 1996; Payne, 1997; Barry, 1996; Barry et al, 1998/99; and Fleming et al, 1998 in response). Groupwork is central to social action and these practices.

Why Groupwork?

Whether one takes the generic or the narrower approach to social action, groupwork is at the heart of practice. In the American context a special volume of the journal *Social Work with Groups* (Vinik and Levin, 1991) has been devoted to the inextricability of the connection:

> The group has been recognised as a social microcosm in which its members can be helped to become participants and leaders in social action through experience with the group process and through engaging in social action processes in the group's immediate social environment. (Shapiro, 1991, p.8)

American groupwork writers vary widely in how they interpret this. For many, taking a pluralistic view of social relationships, this means groups providing an arena in which competing interests might be mediated and integrated. In so far as interpersonal relationships reflect social relations within the broader social structure, groups provide a training ground for democracy and can contribute to the common good. (Shapiro, ibid). However, there are American groupworkers (for example: Breton, 1994; Lee, 1994) who, while placing the group at the centre of social action, take a more radical stance and ground their practice on principles which resonate strongly with those set out above. As Shapiro (1991, p.19) puts it: 'They recognise that not only the personal is political; practice is also political'.

Returning to our starting point in the work of Freire, groups are both the 'context' and 'instrument' of his *Pedagogy of the Oppressed*. This is because in groups personal troubles can be translated into common concerns. In groups the experience of being with other people in the same position can engender strength and new hope where there was apathy before. In groups a sense of personal responsibility internalised as self-blame can find new productive outlets. Alternative explanations and new options for change and improvement can be opened up. The demoralising isolation of private misfortune can be replaced in the course of working together with a new sense of self confidence and potency, as well as concrete gains, which individuals on their own could not contemplate. (Mullender and Ward, 1991, p.12).

But this could be read as groups and groupwork providing merely 'technical support' to some greater enterprise. We would argue that it is much more than just this. Besides achieving material changes and raising the confidence of their members, groupwork has *transformative* capacity. Mistry's (1989) description of a group for black and white women is a classic example of how groupwork, where affiliated to empowerment, can be tremendously powerful in moving people towards more humane and emancipatory relationships. So, bearing this in mind, what has distinguished groupwork, historically, from other forms of practice and connects it to social action, has been:

an emphasis on the commonalities of problems and situations _.In groupwork each issue that is raised, even when that issue at first glance seems to have no relevance to others in the group, does have applicability for all. The worker who practices *real* groupwork draws out that applicability and elicits the commonalities and asks members to examine the issues of others. (Kurland and Salmon, 1993, p.10, my emphasis)

In such groupwork groups develop lives of their own, over which the worker cannot have complete control; the agenda can be holistic and the process open and inclusive. Group members raise what is important to them, no matter what ground rules and boundaries have been set. It has been argued elsewhere (Ward, 1998) that such free-flowing characteristics are out of kilter with the current climate of social work with a resultant emphasis on structured groupwork 'programmes' with predefined purposes, audited outcomes, discipline and a focus on the individual, in fact *work-in-groups* rather than groupwork.

It is *real* groupwork that is at the heart of social action, groupwork which can align with 'concepts of equality and democracy' (Douglas, 1993, p.31) and which is 'anti-oppressive in its context, purpose, method, group relationships and behaviour'. (Brown, 1996, p.83).

Social action live

Practice

Butler (1994) writes in this journal about a social action group for women whose children were adjudged by social services as at risk of significant harm from their parents. It took place in a family centre run by a national voluntary agency, facilitated by a part-time social action groupworker. Butler, who was asked to evaluate the work of the centre, describes how social action groupwork engendered an atmosphere of equality, enabling the women 'to explore the humour, sadness and strains of family life and no longer remain silent about these.' (Butler, 1994, p.178). Central to the group agenda emerged structural dilemmas facing members: women's sexuality and their relationships with male partners, which were entangled with the processes of racism and the difficulties of bringing up mixed-parentage children. Faced with relentless hardships, the women easily identified the nature of the politics of poverty. The opportunity the group provided to unpack structural and individual issues was critical to these women's empowerment and the creation of their own solutions to the threats and dilemmas they faced. (Butler, 1994, p.163).

Training

A team of social action trainers has been undertaking training for youth social workers in Ukraine. (Fleming and Keenan, 1998). Groupwork is central to the training process. The trainers made it very clear that they had not come with solutions to Ukrainian problems. They offered the social action framework but the actual content was to be the participants'. Courses were run in three cities: Kyiv, Kharkiv, and Odessa, for workers in three districts. They were experiential, group-based and all the exercises and techniques used on the course could be used with groups of young people in the field. Each course had three parts. The first was a week long visit from two trainers and focused on the identification of problems facing young people, exploring their causes, examining different models of intervention, identifying the values base they wanted to work to and developing ideas for working in partnership with young people to address specific issues they face. The last session of this week was spent drawing up action plans. The second part encompassed the next six months during which participants attempted to put their action plans into practice and to use their learning from the course in their work, using each other for advice and support. The third and final part was a another visit from the trainers to review progress, and to reflect on and share the learning, among the whole group, from what had actually happened in the work.

Projects which the Ukrainian youth social workers have developed in partnership with young people with whom they worked included: new initiatives in 'Reform Schools', groups of disabled people enabling them to have a greater say in what happens to them, work with the police, contacting and working with 'street children', work with young men and young women on issues surrounding relationships and on violence, self-help groups for young parents.

This approach elicited a very positive response from course participants. Feedback in course evaluations included:

The atmosphere of the course - mutual support and understanding - this was very helpful in order to do creative and productive work.

The method of planning was very useful ... working out programmes ... the scheme of social action ... the methods of identifying problems young people may have.

Research

Here the example is a Health Needs Assessment commissioned by a Health Forum within a large urban regeneration agency. (Fleming, 1997). The brief was to obtain detailed information, to supplement an earlier quantitative survey, of the views of people living in the area about the quality of their lives from a health perspective and to generate ideas for actions to improve residents' health. Although not entirely group based, groupwork made an essential contribution to the research process. (See also Ward, 1996/7, for further examples.)

Adapting the social action practice model, the research team began by asking local residents and professionals, 'What are the questions we should be asking people about their health?'; 'Who should we be asking?'; 'How can we find the answers to these questions?'. It emerged that the concept of health had different meanings for different people. Local people, generally, did not see health in medical terms. They talked about 'happiness', 'satisfaction', 'energy levels', and 'being able to do all you need to do in a day'. It was agreed to use the term 'health and well-being'.

Based on these discussions, semi-structured interviews asked people individually and in groups about *what* factors they thought effected their health and well-being; *why* they thought these factors existed; and *how* they thought matters could be improved. People identified many and varied issues. Health and well-being was seen as benefiting from the support of family and friends, getting together with people like themselves and, for those that had them, jobs and financial security. Conversely, poor housing, financial worries, racism fear of crime, lack of appropriate cultural and linguistic facilities, poor environment and pollution, poor transport and mobility problems, and unemployment were said to adversely effect health.

However, the researchers were very aware of Oliver's observation (1992, p.105) that the experience of being researched can be isolating, reinforcing the dominant idea of problems being individual. Thus, meeting respondents in groups where they could bounce ideas off each other and develop ideas further was a major aspect of the project. Some of the groups were existing groups where people already knew each other and discussed things together, for example, a group of Polish elders at a social club. Others came together especially for the research, for example, a group of older Muslim men who all attended the Pakistani Centre for lunch but had not worked as a group before. Members of this group expressed common issues: difficulties in getting interpreters, poor housing, the need for adaptations for physically impaired elders. They came to realise they were not alone with their problems and identified action others could try out.

Another example of the power of group activity in this research comes from a group young Muslim women with children. Through taking part in the study they identified loneliness and isolation as very real problems which, for them, adversely effected their feelings of well being and thus their health. They decided they wanted to organise regular meetings for themselves and their children. They negotiated with Pakistani Community Centre to use the centre on the day the men were at the mosque and lobbied for recognition and funding from the local authority.

The debate continues

The potential of groupwork framed within social action principles has been highlighted by these examples. However it is important to acknowledge that social action and its roots in Freire's pedagogy has some strong critics. Points made are that social action raises unrealistic expectations about changing the world. It reifies process and leaves real problems of 'managing to survive day to day, finding a job and/or constructive activities and support networks rarely defined'. (Barry et al, 1998/99, p.68). In so doing, critics argue, it promotes action that inadvertently gives more legitimacy to, rather than questions, the existing social order (Barry, 1996, p.7). Further, it is asserted that social action, no less than any other 'method', represents an imposed worker-led agenda which in the final analysis serves the interests of the professionals at the expense of the poor and excluded. (Page, 1992; Baistow, 1994).

These are serious and challenging questions. However, they can be addressed at two levels, the practical and conceptual, and through this thinking it might be that further directions for practice can be offered. First, at the practical level, the examples presented to back up critique are invariably drawn from practice which does not follow the methodology. (see Barry, 1996, and Fleming et al, 1998, in response). In contrast, the examples above show how social action work, which has engaged people in the process of working in partnership on an open and transparent agenda, can achieve tangible material gains countering exclusion and alienation.

Second, criticism of the applicability of Freire's pedagogy leads into a debate of a different order. The point made is that Freire's work belongs to 'another time and another place':

[It is a] ... treatise on educating revolutionaries in oppressed countries about the need to similarly educate, politicise, and revolutionise the people ... In societies which are highly polarised such as Brazil, a wholly radical agenda may be the preferred route. However, in societies such as the UK, despite some stark extremes, more diverse agendas might be more appropriate. (Barry et al, 1998/99, p.67, p.69)

First, a misapprehension must be corrected. Freire wrote his major works while living in the USA, where he 'found that repression and exclusion of the poor from power were not limited to developing countries and changed his definition of 'third world' to a political rather than a geographical concept.' (Branford, 1997, p.19). Second, such thinking reflects a 'dualistic' view of the social world (Layder, 1994). It sets the 'third world' against the developed world as if what applies in one cannot do so in the other. Recent events in Europe surely show that boundaries are not so clear cut. Likewise process is set against product; big problems against little ones; changing society against joining it; worker against participant. In contrast social action, following Giddens (1984), adopts a non-dualistic position, taking the view that people are shaped by the world around them but they are also creative agents capable of effecting the shape of that world (Ward, 1982, p.4). All people, even the subordinated, are never completely powerless in situations (Foucault, 1980); they have some means in their control to influence and change things. Non-dualist practice requires 'sociological imagination' (Wright Mills, 1970), rising above either/ or explanations. This means for groupworkers a *holistic* concern for members as people and for the issues they confront in the world in which they live. The group is both context for, and instrument of, personal and social change (Douglas, 1993). The agenda could not be more demanding nor diverse.

Such 'joined-up' thinking is also at the heart of current Government policy, the search for regeneration through *The Third Way* (Giddens, 1998). It recognises that tackling structural problems is a key feature of tackling poverty and exclusion and so enabling people to mobilise their creative potential. Undoubtedly it is crucial that the right volume and quality of concrete resources are put in and are targeted to the right places. However, it is clear that this will not automatically liberate peoples capacities to find new and better solutions. What also is needed is a process that will effectively 'join up' the 'New Deal' programmes with people in need. Our experience is that many are sceptical, demotivated and, indeed, understate and devalue their potential. This is not surprising, given the social experiences and economic conditions that many have had to endure under the market-centred policies and the unrelenting 'survival of the fittest' rhetoric of the past 20 years. Social action, with groupwork at its core, addresses the necessary connections between people and policies. It does not provide a panacea but, we would argue, it does ask some of the essential questions and has demonstrated enough success, in the most unpromising of circumstances, to have the right to be taken seriously.

References

Adams, R. (1996) *Social Work and Empowerment*. London: Macmillan

Ahmed, B. (1990) *Black Perspectives in Social Work*. Birmingham: Venture Press

Baistow, K. (1994) Liberation or regulation? Some paradoxes of empowerment. *Critical Social Policy*, 42, pp.34-46

Barry, M. (1996) The empowering process: Leading from behind? *Youth and Policy*, 54, pp1-12

Barry, M., Davies, A. and Williamson, H. (1998/99) An open response to the concerns of the Centre for Social Action in Issue No.60. *Youth and Policy*, 62, pp.67-70

Branford, S. (1997) Word power to the poor. *The Guardian*, May 10th, p.19

Breton, M. (1994) On the meaning of empowerment and empowerment-oriented social work practice. *Social Work with Groups*, 17, 3, pp.23-37

Breton, M. (1995) The potential for social action in groups. *Social Work with Groups*, 18, 2/3, pp.5-13

Brown, A. (1996) Groupwork into the future: Some personal reflections. *Groupwork*, 9, 1, pp.80-96

Burley, D. (1982) *Starting Blocks*. Leicester: National Youth Bureau

Butler, S. (1994) 'All I've got in my purse is mothballs.' The social action women's group. *Groupwork*, 7(2), pp163-179

Canton, R., Clarke, A., Knight, C. and Ward, D. (1996) *Training for Work with Mentally Disordered Offenders: Setting the context*. (Report to the Home Office), Leicester: Dept. of Social and Community Studies, De Montfort University

Cress-Welsing, F. (1991) *ISIS Papers*. Chicago: Third World Press

Dominelli, L. and McLoed, E. (1989) *Feminist Social Work*. London: Macmillan

Douglas, T. (1993) *A Theory of Groupwork Practice*. London: Macmillan

Dyson, S. and Harrison, M. (1998) Black community members as researchers: Two projects compared. in M. Levalette, L. Penketh and C. Jones (eds) *Anti-Racism and Social Welfare*. Aldershot: Ashgate

Evans, M. (ed) (1994) *The Woman Question*. London: Sage

Fleming, J. (1997) Research in the Context of Human Services in Crises. in R. Adams (ed) *Crisis in the Human Services: National and international issues*. Kingston upon Hull: University of Lincolnshire and Humberside

Fleming, J., Harrison, M., Perry, A., Purdey, D. and Ward, D. (1983) Action speaks louder than words. *Youth and Policy*, 10(3), pp.16-19

Fleming, J., Harrison, M. and Ward, D. (1998) Social Action can be an Empowering Process. *Youth and Policy*, 60, pp.46-62

Fleming, J., Harrison, M. and Ward, D. (forthcoming) *Research as Empowerment: The social action approach*. Aldershot: Ashgate

Fleming, J. and Keenan, E. (1998) *Youth on the Margins in Northern Ireland, England and Ukraine*. Leicester: Centre for Social Action: De Montfort University

Foucault, M. (1980) *Power, Knowledge: Selected Interviews and Other Writings*. New York: Pantheon

Freire, P (1972) *Pedagogy of the Oppressed*. Harmondsworth: Penguin

Giddens, A (1984) *The Constitution of Society*. Cambridge: Polity Press

Giddens, A. (1998) *The Third Way*. Cambridge: Polity Press

Gilroy, P. (1987) *There Ain't No Black in the Union Jack*. London: Hutchinson

Harrison, M., Perry, A. and Ward, D. (1981) Letting the young set the agenda. Community Care, 3rd December, pp.20-21

hooks, bel. (1992) *Ain't I a Woman*. London: Pluto Press

Hudson, A. (1989) Changing perspectives: Feminism, gender and social work. in M. Langan and P. Lee *Radical Social Work Today*. London: Unwin Hyman

Jakobsson, G. (ed) (1995) *Social Work in an International Perspective*. Helsinki: Helsinki University Press

James, T. (1997) Empowerment through social change. *Bridges*, Summer, pp.6-7

Kurland, R. and Salmon, R. (1993) Groupwork versus Casework in a Group. *Groupwork*, 6, 1, pp.5-16

Langan, M. and Day, L. (eds) (1992) *Women, Oppression and Social Work*. London: Routledge

Layder, D. (1994) *Understanding Social Theory*. London: Sage

Lee, J. (1994) *The Empowerment Approach to Social Work Practice*. New York: Columbia University Press

Mistry, T. (1989) Establishing a feminist model of groupwork in the probation service. *Groupwork*, 2, 2, pp.145-158

Mullender, A. and Ward, D. (1991) *Self-Directed Groupwork: Users take action for empowerment*. London: Whiting and Birch

Mullender, A. and Ward, D. (1992) En groupe l'union fait la force. in J. Lindsay (ed) *Textes de Base sur le Modèle de Groupe Autogéré*. Quebec: École de Service Social, Université Laval.

Mullender, A. and Ward, D. (1996) *Self-Directed Groupwork: Users take action for empowerment*. (translated into Ukrainian), Amsterdam and Kyiv: TACIS/ Geneva Initiative

Muldoon, R. (1994/5) The demystification of social action groupwork principles. *Social Action*, 2, 3, pp.9-10

Oliver, M. (1992) Changing the social relations of research production. *Disability, Handicap and Society,* 7, 2, pp.101-114

Page, R. (1992) 'Empowerment, oppression and beyond: A coherent strategy? A reply to Mullender and Ward (CSP Issue 32). *Critical Social Policy,* 35, pp.89-92

Payne, M. (1997) *Modern Social Work Theory.* (2nd Ed) London: Macmillan

Shapiro, B. (1991) Social action, the group and society. *Social Work with Groups,* 14, 3/4, pp.7-22

Staub-Bernasconi, S. (1991) Social action, empowerment and social work: An integrative theoretical framework for social work and social work with groups. *Social Work with Groups,* 14, 3/4, pp.35-51

Treu, H-E., Salustowicz, P., Oldenburg, E., Offe, H. and Neuser, H. (eds.) *Theorie und Praxis der Bekämpfung der Langzeitarbeitslosigkeit in der EG.* Weinheim, Germany: Deutscher Studien Verlag

Vinik, A. and Levin, M. (eds) (1991) *Social Action in Groupwork. (Social Work with Groups,* special issue,14, 3/4). Binghampton, NY: Haworth Press

Ward. D, (1979) Working with young people: The way forward. *Probation Journal,* 26, 1, pp.2-9

Ward, D. (1981) The Chaplefield intermediate treatment project. in R. Adams, S. Allard, J. Baldwin and J/ Thomas (eds) *A Measure of Diversion.* Leicester: National Youth Bureau

Ward, D. (ed) (1982) *Give 'em a Break: Social action by young people at risk and in trouble.* Leicester: National Youth Bureau

Ward, D. (ed) (1989) *Social Action Training Pack.* Nottingham: Centre for Social Action, University of Nottingham

Ward, D. (ed) (1996/7) *Groupwork and Research (Groupwork,* special issue, 9, 2)., London: Whiting and Birch

Ward, D. (1998) Groupwork. in R. Adams, L. Dominelli and M. Payne *Social Work: Themes, issues and critical debates,* London: Macmillan

Wright Mills, C. (1970) *The Sociological Imagination.* Harmondsworth: Penguin

This chapter was first published in 1999 in *Groupwork* Vol. 11(3), pp.88-103

At the time of writing, Mark Harrison was Director, Centre for Social Action, De Montfort University, Leicester, and Dave Ward was Head, Dept of Social and Community Studies, De Montfort University

The roots and process of social action

Jo Aubrey

This chapter discusses the theoretical roots of social action in the work of Brazilian adult educator Paulo Freire, who proposes an alternative to conventional educational methods, based on the concept of problem posing education, which entails mutual learning and dialogue between students and teachers. For Freire, the notion of dialogue is based upon the principles of equality and critical thinking, which enables oppressed people to challenge their existing circumstances. The eclectic sources of Freirean philosophy and the challenges of other writers to aspects of his thought are examined. The paper describes how members of the Centre for Social Action have translated the theories of Freire and other writers into a set of principles and the social action process, which have been used as the basis of work in the community with a wide range of disempowered groups.

Paulo Freire

To unravel some of the concepts surrounding social action as both a model and a process, it is first necessary to examine some of the theories and philosophies that have influenced it. The most fundamental of these lies within the work of Paulo Freire.

Freire was an adult educator in South America. In 1964 he was exiled from his native Brazil during a military coup as a result of his work with the rural poor. He continued his work in Chile and went on to teach at Harvard University before returning to Brazil to become the Minister of Education in Sao Paulo. (Institute of Paulo Freire) The core of his philosophy was a critique of traditional educational methods that denied the experiences of students and which at its heart is a consensual form of control. Ellul (1964) suggests that traditional methods of education have a number of different features, which aim to adapt learners to consensual controls. These are: career choices (specialization); authority (dependency); and the good life (consumerism). He goes on to argue that school also encourages competition (the rule of the fittest), whilst at the same time maintaining order (social conformism).

Freire (1972) was critical of this form of what he termed 'banking education' which he believed negates the experiences of students and as such holds no relevance for them. He goes on to describe the role of the teacher in the traditional educational setting:

> His task is to 'fill' the student with the contents of his narration – contents which are detached from reality, disconnected from the totality that engendered them and could give them their significance. Words are emptied of their concreteness and become a hollow, alienated and alienating verbosity. (p.52)

What Freire is arguing is that the curriculum presented to students within a traditional educational setting, is out of context for them and meaningless in terms of their own lives. Freirian philosophy also maintains that many of the experiences of students are rooted in oppressive structures. As Heaney (1995) says:

> Curriculum which ignores racism, sexism, the exploitation of workers and other forms of oppression at the same time supports the status quo. It inhibits the expansion of consciousness and blocks creative and liberating social action for change. (p.1)

Freire's pedagogy, seeks to change the social order and to bring this about through unity and common experience. The 'curriculum' is transformed into an open forum which places teacher and student on the same level and which on the one hand aims to produce a critical consciousness in people, whilst at the same time they learn the skills that they need to transform their own lives.

Taylor (1993) suggests that Freire was influenced by many different schools of thought, ranging from Aristotle to traditional Catholic theology and international Marxism, as well as many diverse philosophies and theories of education. He further maintains that Freire often 'poaches' ideas and blends them into his own ideas, using them to support his own arguments and observes that, the text that Freire offers is actually a complex tissue of his own work and the threads of other pedagogies and philosophies which he has woven all together across the loom of his experience and his genius. (p.34)

Pedagogy of the Oppressed

The main tenet of Freire's pedagogy can be seen within a letter he wrote to literacy teachers in Chile in 1971, where he stated that,

> To be a good liberating educator, you need above all to have faith in human beings. You need to love. You must be convinced that the fundamental effort of education is to help with the liberation of people, never their domestication. (in Maclaren and Leonard, 1995, p.25)

In *Pedagogy of the Oppressed* (1972) he expands upon this theory of banking education and goes on to suggest that it mirrors many elements of an oppressive society. It regards humans as manageable beings who are easily manipulated and who are expected to adapt. The more they adapt, the easier they are to oppress. Finding it hard to keep themselves and their families, they are far less likely to come together to fight against the system that oppresses them.

Freire (1972, p.61) proposes an alternative which he terms problem-posing education, which is based on dialogue. He continues: 'Through dialogue, the teacher of the students and the students of the teacher cease to exist and a new term emerges: teacher-student with student-teacher.' This relationship is based upon mutual learning where the teacher recognizes that he learns from the students just as much as they learn from him, both growing as part of this process.

The objective of this problem posing education is that it enables people to become critically aware and allows them to unveil reality. Once they have an understanding of the world and of themselves as subjects within the world, they develop the power to transform it. In other words, they come to a critical understanding of the means through which they are oppressed and as a group they take action to change it. Most importantly people begin to ask the question 'why?' Freire maintains that this is the question the oppressors do not want the oppressed to ask, for if they do, it will mean a challenge to their power.

For Freire, the entire notion of dialogue is based upon equality, for one is not able to enter into a dialogue if one sees oneself as superior, or the group that has the monopoly on knowledge and truth, or if one is afraid of being displaced. As stated at the beginning of this section, Freire maintains that to enter into dialogue one has to have faith in humankind and one must also be a critical thinker, ready to unwrap the structures that hold the oppressed down, and with them challenge and transform that which keeps them in their place. If one is a naive thinker, one sees oneself as an object in the world that has to adapt; a truly critical thinker believes that the important thing is to change that reality. Critical thinking perceives the universe as, 'a domain that takes shape as I act upon it.' (Furter, 1966, p.26 in Freire, 1972, p.73).

Without critical thinking, Freire maintained that the oppressed remain within a culture of silence. The dominant members of society control the oppressed and alienated and, 'prescribe the words to be spoken by the oppressed through the control of the schools and other institutions, thereby effectively silencing the people.' (Heaney, 1995, p.9). Freire explores this culture of silence in global terms and argues that in so-called under-developed colonized countries it can be seen in its stark reality.

For Freire, the means through which people can break out of this culture of silence is the process of see-judge-act. It is through action and reflection and the dialogue that is part of that, that people can make sense of their situation and be enabled to take steps to transform it. However there are flaws in the approach which are both practical and ideological. Blackburn (2000) suggests that fundamentally Freire makes several assumptions concerning the 'oppressed'. Firstly he argues that Freirean pedagogy assumes that the oppressed are powerless, when in fact it is difficult to measure the extent to which people do not have power. The most oppressed groups in society could be said to have certain power in that they have the ability to sabotage and they have the option of non-cooperation. Blackburn (2000) uses the oppression of the Guatemalan Indians to explore this point. He maintains that whilst they were suffering extreme and often violent forms of discrimination, they developed a 'culture of resistance' based upon their own experiences. As Blackburn (2000) argues and as has been argued above, Freire used the theories of many writers and philosophers to develop his pedagogy and these were based largely upon leftist European schools of thought and traditions. Blackburn, (2000, p.11) concludes by arguing that within this perspective, 'Freirean and other participatory activists have tended to dis-value traditional and vernacular forms of power.'

There are also certain issues surrounding the extent to which Freire neatly categorizes people as either oppressed or oppressors and it would seem that in a complex world it is not as easy to split people into such distinct groupings (Blackburn, 2000). For example, in some contexts a man may be able to oppress a woman, but within a different setting, such as within the work context, the woman may possess more power than the man because of her status. Similarly a black man and a white man may both have oppressor characteristics, but a white man will be less oppressed because he lives within a society that is fundamentally racist. In this way it is feasible to suggest that people can be oppressors and oppressed at the same time but in different situations.

On a more practical level there are further problems within Freire's pedagogy and these issues concern the role of the facilitator or 'teacher-student'. Wuyts et al (1992) suggest that Freire is never actually clear who the facilitators will be. He speaks of a revolutionary leadership but does not specify of whom it will comprise and the extent to which they will develop their own critical consciousness. Freire also speaks of the facilitators as having very special qualities, in that they need to be able to allow the group to act based upon their own needs and interests and should not impose their own agenda upon the group. Blackburn (2000) argues that this presents a problem on different levels. In the first instance he maintains that the leader will have his own perceptions of power and oppression so that when he goes to facilitate a group he goes in with an agenda based upon his or her understanding. Secondly, the group that he goes to work with may perceive their situation very differently, they may not label themselves as powerless or oppressed and may not want to use the empowerment model of the facilitator.

Also, in terms of the educators, there are further difficulties relating to the recognition of their own position of power. It is possible that facilitators may fail or be unable to, 'strangle the oppressor within them, and may consequently misuse their position to manipulate those over which they (potentially) have so much power.' (Rahnema, 1992, p.124) Freire places many expectations upon the educator, who is at the end of the day human and, as such, entirely capable of manipulating or abusing power whether they are conscious of it or not.

Groups and organisations, particularly within the development context have used Paulo Friere's methods to work with oppressed people. Based upon their own professional and personal backgrounds, they will work with people in different ways and will develop the system to suit their own contexts. The Centre for Social Action is an example of this. Whilst they have been heavily influenced by the work of Paulo Freire, the CSA has its own style of working.

As well as Frierean thought, the Centre has been influenced by the disability movement, (Oliver, 1990; 1992), black activism (Cress Welsing, 1991; Hooks, 1992) and feminist movements (Dominelli and McLeod, 1989; Hudson, 1989). Based on all of these influences the CSA:

> Opposes models based on individual pathology that have dominated social welfare. Rather social action concentrates on the circumstances in which people find themselves. Individual pathologies are no substitute for serious consideration of the social condition of service users. (Fleming and Ward 2004 forthcoming)

Over the years the CSA has developed its own individual principles which guide its work. It is therefore necessary at this point to define social action as it is used by the CSA and to place it within its historical context. Finally the process of social action itself will be presented and explored.

Social action

Within its British context self-directed groupwork, or social action, is based first and foremost upon anti-oppressive principles and the notion that people can gain collective strength through working in groups. Mullender and Ward (1993) maintained that as a result of consecutive Conservative governments, an approach was needed within a social and community work setting, that took account of the problems that people experienced as a result of oppressive social policies. They saw this approach as being openly collective with a value base that embraced all the principles of anti-oppressive working. Mullender and Ward (1991) also recognize the work that has been undertaken with feminist and anti-racist approaches and that rather than seeing these as separate struggles,

> Male as well as female workers must find a practice which supports the women's movement and white practitioners, as much as black, have a responsibility to work in a way which supports the activists' struggles. (p.10)

In this way practitioners are asked to 'combine their efforts with those of oppressed groups without colonising them.' (p.11)

Social action as it is used by the CSA, began its development during the 1970s. Youth work during this decade was based upon models of social education. Arches (2001, p.1) argues that problems facing young people tend to be attributed to, 'individual pathology or the breakdown of social norms.' During the latter half of the decade there were moves to encourage young people to design and implement their own services and the term social action came about as practitioners saw themselves moving away from the social education origins of youth work into action centred community work. (Mullender and Ward, 1993).

Ward and Boeck (2000, p.45) assert that there are three main characteristics of social action. Firstly, 'it was designed to distance itself from the 'deficit' and 'blaming the victim' approach.' Secondly social action advocates that only through careful questioning and understanding of the reason 'why', can the question of 'how' be tackled. In other words to return to Freire, social action aims to engender in people a critical consciousness in order that they are able to identify the underlying causes that keep them in the situation that they are in. Ward and Boeck (2000) continue that through asking the question why:

> people have the opportunity to widen their horizons of what is

possible, to break out of the self-perpetuating narrowness of vision, introspection and 'victim blaming' induced through poverty, lack of opportunity and exclusion. (p.46)

Finally social action is process rather than outcome oriented. People are guided through a process which does not work towards a final result, activity or action but which is a 'way forward of discovery, of liberation, of dialogue, of conscientization.' (Ward and Boeck, 2000, p.46). Once groups are clear about the situation and the underlying causes, they are then able to take action based upon the conclusions they have reached during the 'why' stage of the process. Once the action has been taken, the group reflects upon what they have achieved and the process begins again.

The principles of social action

The Centre for Social Action (2001) is committed to working in an anti-oppressive way and as such, has created six principles which guide its work. These principles,

> encapsulate a set of beliefs about the unrecognized skills and capacities of people who may be marginalised by the wider community and assert their rights to determine their own future, the inherent power of collective working and the ethical principles that should inform professionals working with groups such as these. (p.2)

They are as follows:

1. *Social Action workers are committed to social justice. We strive to challenge inequality and oppression in relation to race, gender, sexuality, age, religion, class, culture, disability or any other form of social differentiation.*
   Within this principle the Centre for Social Action recognises that all forms of oppression are inter-linked and one cannot simply be committed to one cause at the expense of all the others. There is also a sense that social action workers should carefully consider the groups with whom they are working and ensure that they are clear about how oppressive comments or

actions are addressed. (Mullender and Ward, 1993). Also the responsibility for challenging oppressive remarks should not lie with members of the oppressed group.

2. *We believe all people have skills, experience and understanding that they can draw on to tackle the problems they face. Social action workers understand that people are experts in their own lives and we can use this as a starting point for our work.*
    This principle challenges the problem focussed nature of mainstream social and community work practice. It challenges the notion that people's problems can be solved by professionals who know better; it recognises the fact that people are fully aware of their needs and an understanding of the roots of those needs will come to the surface through the process.

3. *All people have rights including the right to be heard, the right to define the issues facing them, and the right to take action on their own behalf. People also have the right to define themselves and not have negative labels imposed upon them.*
    Once again this principle highlights the fact that within social and community services, the user rarely has choice in terms of the assistance that they are given. Mullender and Ward (1993, p.34) maintain that, 'It is no longer tenable for workers to deprive clients of key information on the assumption that they know best.' Mullender and Ward (1993, p.34) go on to suggest that service-users should not be given assistance based upon the assumptions of the professional, rather they should be, 'empowered to opt in or out of groups and campaigns, to define their own issues and to set their own agenda for change.'

4. *Injustice and oppression are complex issues rooted in social policy, the environment and the economy. Social Action workers understand people experience problems as individuals but these difficulties can be translated into common concerns.*
    This principle emphasizes the most important aspect of the social action process: asking the question 'why?' To encourage people to describe their situations and ask them what can be done to change them merely scratches the surface and does

not allow people to explore *why* their circumstances are such. Without this question, 'there can be no awakening awareness either of wider scale oppression or of the possibility of moving beyond fatalism and self-pity into raised consciousness and the pursuit of rights.' (Mullender and Ward, 1993, p.36)

5. *We understand that people working collectively can be powerful. People who lack power and influence to challenge injustice and oppression as individuals can gain it through working with other people in a similar position.*
   The process of social action is ostensibly about groupwork. Groups that have used social action vary, but mainly they consist of people who come together to address an issue which affects them collectively. Arches (2001) examines the work undertaken by a group of young people living on an estate in Nottingham. They had been involved in burglaries and the courts requested a social enquiry of the circumstances of some of the young men in the area. The report found that the young people on the estate were bored and frustrated, with limited leisure facilities for them to use. The probation officer began using social action with the young people and over a five year period the young people raised funds, went on trips, held meetings with police and councillors, and enlisted support from adults on the estate. Although the youth club that they eventually created was destroyed by fire shortly after it was opened, Arches' (2001) research over 20 years later reflects the impact that social action had upon the young people involved in the project, particularly communication and interpersonal skills.

6. *Social action workers are not the leaders, but facilitators. Our job is to enable people to make decisions for themselves and take ownership of whatever outcome ensues. Everybody's contribution to this process is equally valid and it is vital that our job is not accorded privilege.*
   Facilitation of a social action group is non-directional, workers are committed to ensuring that the group keeps control of both the agenda and the content and that the group itself decides upon direction and action, based upon the work that they

have undertaken together. However, Arches (2001) maintains that this can be difficult and there are problems with the fact that once the involvement of the CSA is over, the group must not be left floundering. Many of her respondents spoke very favourably of social action facilitators and the fact that they did not try to lead or direct the projects. However from her research it is also clear that continuing consultation and training from the facilitator would have been of benefit, as would activities and discussion concerning potential threats and difficulties that the group may encounter after the departure of the facilitator.

The principles are an important feature of social action and they provide a firm basis that guides social action workers. However, it could be argued that, as in the case of some of the criticisms of Freire discussed above, social action demands much of its workers who are expected not to influence the group, merely to facilitate the process. However there must always be the risk that facilitators will subconsciously attempt to move the group in ways that it may not necessarily want to go. Workers will have prejudices of their own, they will also have professional values and beliefs and it may be difficult to keep these buried during the course of their work. The next section will examine some of the other criticisms of social action including an exploration of some of the issues concerning the facilitators.

Critiques of social action

Social Action professes not to impose an agenda upon the groups and communities with whom it engages. However, Barry et al (1999, pp.68-69) would challenge this and maintain that social action itself is indeed an imposed agenda and that it is, 'a method of working devised *by* professionals *for* groups of participants. It has not evolved through the efforts of those it purports to empower.'

It could be argued that any method which aims to work with oppressed or minority communities has an agenda. Mullender and Ward (1993) clearly state that the agenda of social action is to empower people through working collectively together to improve their situations or circumstances. Most importantly it asks people to examine the root causes of the problems they are facing in terms of economics, environment and structural inequalities. This is the aspect of the process that attracts most criticism from Barry (1996) and Barry et al (1999).

They argue that in their experience young people do not want to examine the structural and political inequalities that impact upon their lives. Barry et al (1999) maintain that,

> For many disadvantaged young people, the problem is managing to survive day to day, finding a job and/or having constructive activities and support networks. (p.68)

By this last quote, Barry et al (1999) seem to be arguing that as well as having to cope with the day to day stresses of their own lives, they also need other activities and support structures that give them concrete day to day solutions to the everyday problems they are experiencing. They argue that social action, which asks young people to uncover the roots of their disadvantage, is simply not giving the practical support and assistance that is needed.

In terms of their perceptions of the needs of young people, Barry et al (1999) have four main criticisms of social action with young people. The first is that in their experience young people generally do not want to address national or political issues – they want to focus upon themselves and their own realities rather than the wider structural picture. Secondly they prefer a more directive approach and rather than facilitation, they prefer emotional support from those who work with them. Thirdly, Barry et al (1999) suggest that social action can be accused of raising expectations of young people in the long term. They go on to argue that goals should be short term and achievable rather than tackling issues that may not offer immediate results. Finally they argue that the self directed nature of social action may be too difficult and demanding for some young people, who after all, have been used predominantly to directive models of youth work practice.

One of the other criticisms that Barry (1996; 1999) makes is also the fact that self-directed groupwork can potentially overlook positive input from the facilitator. She argues that the facilitator role within social action is simply about guaranteeing anti-oppressive practice and the facilitation of self-direction. Rather Barry et al (1999) feel that,

> Those working with young people should also consider the possibility of injecting their own ideas into the debate with young people ... it could be about sharing with (them) innovative and pro-active ways of improving their situation. (p.69)

Barry (1996) argues that there is also the issue of young people acting in isolation. As the self-directed groupworker attempts not to impose content, the young people act alone and this, she maintains, can be demoralizing and that it is only through partnership working that young people can really make a difference within their own lives:

> Without the goodwill, cooperation, openness and collaboration of others who can give them that trust and recognition as partners, then regrettably the powerful voice of young people may well remain unheard. (p.11)

Essentially, within her criticisms of social action, Barry et al (1999) are asserting that sometimes young people simply do not want to ask the question 'why', and that to take them through a process which makes them examine the political, social and economic roots of their problems is simply a way of imposing an overtly political agenda upon those who do not really want it. Rather they want a more directive approach that will support and encourage them to change their individual lives.

In a counter argument to Barry (1996;1999) Fleming et al (1999) maintain that the 'why' stage of the process is in fact the most important and that simply looking at the 'what' and the 'how' is a traditional model of youth work that enables people to act, but does not empower them in any way. They maintain that traditional models of youth work use the 'what' and the 'how' and that simply to ask these questions is to,

> collude with the process in which explanations and responsibilities and the scope of the solutions are sought in the private world around young people and within their existing knowledge and experience.' (p.49)

By not asking the question 'why', Fleming et al (1999) argue that young people are kept in their place. The question 'why' offers young people a route out of this blame, for only by seeing the structures that oppress them are they able to, 'see opportunities to develop a much wider range of options for action and change.' (Mullender and Ward, 1993, in Fleming et al, 1999, p.49)

Ward (2000) goes on to argue about some of the actual dangers of not asking the 'why' question. A preoccupation with the 'what' and the 'how' in the United States has led to what Murray (1999) terms a custodial democracy – a situation where mainstream society walls off the excluded, either by sending them to prison or maintaining the deteriorating inner cities. The privileged mainstream remain comfortable and those excluded are told that they cannot function as full citizens. Asking the question 'why' offers options that the 'what' and the 'how' do not present. These latter approaches keep people in what Freire termed a state of naïve consciousness, preventing them from exploring the inequalities that stand in their way forward, and keeping problems and issues within the realm of the personal and the local rather than, 'enabling (people) to envision a much wider range of options for action and change.' (Ward, 2000, p.5)

Within social action literature, there are many examples of how communities and groups of young people have gained through working within this method. Whilst some of these examples are been given by people who are committed to social action, Arches (2001) provides a less predisposed evaluation of three projects and examines their impact over time. She interviewed people who had been involved with a social action project twenty years ago and asked them to talk about how the project and the social action work undertaken had changed their lives. It seems that from the interviews conducted, the project participants had experienced changes within their relationships and behaviour that was having an impact upon their own families over two decades later. One of the participants in the evaluation spoke thus:

> I've got a 12 year old son now – and I know from what I went through to get this and that, I'm trying to show him values. If you work hard and try something you can achieve your aims ... I was part of something – I was part of making something work by sticking together and persevering – you can change people's lives. I'm proud of that. (Arches, 2001, p.14)

More specifically people in the evaluation group spoke about the fact that had it not been for the group they would probably have become involved in criminal activity. Whilst there are many youth work projects that could boast about similar results, the social action evaluation reveals something more about the *way* that they were worked with and the values which emanated from it. One participant in Arches' research spoke of the facilitator in terms of the respect that he had had for the group. He also spoke of values and the fact that the group had remained in control: 'We were in charge, we set the guidelines, we wanted to get on it.' (Arches, 2001, p.16) A further quote demonstrates this yet more clearly: 'What's the difference between ATAG (Ainsley Teenage Action Group) and a youth club … well we wanted it! We wanted it, we loved it.' (Arches, 2001, p.5)

Barry et al (1999) argue that the social action approach was created within a South American development context and therefore has little relevance for young people in Western 'developed' countries. However, as has been discussed above, the central tenets of Friere's pedagogy are pulled from European philosophies and theories of education. Yet, aside from this academic debate, Arches' research has shown that people who have used social action within a British context have not only gone on to use the process again, but also say themselves that their interpersonal skills have improved and that their family lives and relationships are better as a result of the group with which they were involved twenty years ago.

Within his broad criticisms of social action Blackburn (2000) uses a similar critique to that of Barry (1996) and Barry et al (1999) in that he maintains that people who are used to a banking type of education do not have sufficient skills to be able to cross over into self directed work. This criticism would seem once again to be rather patronising in that it does not recognise that people are automatically labelled as having limited skills, just because they do not have formal educational qualifications, or are deemed 'socially excluded'. However it could be suggested that professionals who are used to individualizing problems and pathologising, find it yet more difficult to allow service-users to determine what their problems are, why they exist and how they can be remedied. The problem it seems lies not with the jump from banking to self-directed education, but with the professionals being faced with a challenge from those who they have perceived for so long as inadequate and in need of help. When people begin to determine their own destinies through a process that exposes and challenges the mainstream, the role of the professional and the power which accompanies it, becomes uncomfortably threatened.

Process is the key to social action, and the examples given in the articles that follow demonstrate that participants in social action groupwork understood this. They began by questioning the way in which social action begins with the very basics, but soon recognized that through creating a firm knowledge basis, they were far more able to ask 'why' their problems existed, and to develop change based upon a critical awareness of their situation and its complexities.

References

Arches, J. (2001) *Using Social Action to Achieve Social Change: The impact of social action on individuals taking part.* Unpublished research paper. Summary, Research Notes September 2002, available on www.dmu.ac.uk/dmucsa under Research and Reports

Barry, M. (1996) The empowering process: Leading from behind. *Youth and Policy,* 54, 1-12

Barry, M., Davies, A., Williamson, H. (1999) Debate. An open response to the concerns of the Centre for Social Action in issue no. 60. *Youth and Policy,* 62, 67-69

Blackburn, J. (2000) Understanding Paulo Freire: reflections on the origins, concepts and possible pitfalls of his educational approach. *Community Development Journal,* 35, 1, 3-15

Centre for Social Action (2001) Social action principles updated and renewed. *Centre for Social Action Newsletter,* 3, 2-3

Cress-Wellsing, F. (1991) *Isis Paper.* Chicago: Third World Press

Dominelli, L. and Macleod, E. (1989) *Feminist Social Work.* London: Macmillan

Ellul, J. (1964) *The Technological Society.* New York: Alfred Knox

Fleming, J., Harrison, M., Ward, D. (1998) Social action can be an empowering process. A response to the scepticism of Monica Barry. *Youth and Policy,* 60. 42-62

Fleming, J. and Ward, D. (forthcoming) Methodology and practical application of the social action research model. in F. Maggs-Rapport (Ed.) *New Qualitative Research Methodologies in Health and Social Care: Putting ideas into practice.* London: Routledge

Freire, P. (1972) *The Pedagogy of the Oppressed.* Harmondsworth: Penguin

Heaney, T. (1995) *Issues in Freirean Pedagogy.* http://nlu.nl.edu/Resources/Documents/FreireIssues.html

hooks, b. (1992) *Ain't I a woman: Black women and feminism.* London: Pluto Press

Maclaren, P. and Leonard, P. (Eds.) (1995) *Paulo Freire. A Critical encounter.* London: Routledge

Mullender, A. and Ward, D. (1991) *Self Directed Groupwork: Users take action for empowerment.* London: Whiting and Birch

Mullender, A. and Ward, D. (1993) The role of the consultant in self-directed groupwork. *Social Work with Groups,* 16, 4, 57-80

Murray (1999) All locked up in the American Dream. *The Sunday Times,* 7th February, p.7

Oliver, M. (1992) Changing the social relations of research production. *Disability, Handicap and Society,* 7, 2, 101-114

Rahnema, M. (1992) Participation. in W. Sachs (Ed.) *The Development Dictionary. A guide to knowledge as power.* London: Zed Books

Taylor, P. (1993) *The Texts of Paulo Freire.* Buckingham: Open University

Ward, D. and Boeck, T. (2000) Addressing social exclusion. The social action research contribution to local development. in A-L. Matthies, M. Javela and D. Ward, (Eds.) *From Social Exclusion to Participation. Exploration across three European cities.* Jyvaskyla, Finland: University of Jyvaskyla

Ward, D. (2000) Twenty years of social action. Lessons for participation in the 21st century. Paper presented at the launch of the *Centre for Social Action Review,* 15th March 2000.

Wuyts, M., Mackintosh, M. and Hewitt, T. (Eds.) (1992) *Development Policy and Public Action.* Oxford: Oxford University Press in association with the Open University

This chapter was first published in 2004 in *Groupwork* Vol. 14(2), pp.6-23

At the time of writing Jo Aubrey was Project Manager at the Global Youthwork Project, National Youth Agency, Leicester

Social action and self-directed groupwork:

Section 2
Parallel developments

Empowerment through mutual aid groups: A practice grounded conceptual framework

Judith A.B. Lee

Social work practice with oppressed groups requires theory that connects the personal and political levels of empowerment. This paper proposes a conceptual framework grounded in practice with groups of homeless women that unites empowerment theory and other social work theories to address this need. A content analysis of 40 'empowerment group' meetings will be presented and discussed.

Social work practice with people who experience oppression requires theory that connects the personal and the political. Empowerment theory grounded in practice is challenging social workers internationally to rethink practice formulations. Though the words used may be different, for example the concepts of 'self-directed groupwork' or 'social action groupwork' in England and France and "base communities' in South America, the notion of developing practice concepts to aid people in seeking personal and political power and self-determination is of immediate and global interest (Breton, 1988; Friere, 1990; Brown, 1990; Keenan and Pinkerton, 1988; and Mullender and Ward, 1989).

The word 'empowerment' has slipped into popular and social work vernacular. Like most jargonised words, it is in danger of losing clear meaning. 'Empowerment' is now used to describe just about everything we do in social work, but everything we do is not empowering. According to semanticists: '...unexamined key words..., the illusion of meaning where no clear cut meaning exists, can hinder and misdirect our thoughts' (Hayakawa, 1962). We must take responsibility for using language precisely so that important concepts can retain original meaning and direct our thinking and practising. It is also important to develop conceptual frameworks for practice from actually doing the practice (Davis, 1985; Mullender and Ward, 1989). This grounding can be a prerequisite for the empirical testing of practice notions (Glaser and Straus, 1967).

A content analysis of 40 'empowerment group' meetings with homeless women who are predominantly black and Puerto Rican and residing in shelters will be presented and a conceptual framework for empowerment through social work will be suggested. The practice which grounds this effort is based on the author's consultation and direct practice with homeless women in shelters from 1982 through to the current time (NASW News, 1983; Lee, 1986; 1987; 1989). In the content analysis, the author reviews the process recordings of 16 workers who attended her "Empowerment Through Groups" workshops in 1988 and 1989. The groupwork practice analysed takes place in shelters in the Greater Hartford area of the State of Connecticut. The particular shelters cited here are relatively small and comfortable urban shelters for women who are alone or with their children. Connecticut is the richest state per capita in the USA but ironically Hartford is one of the ten poorest cities in the country (1980 Census). Housing is very expensive and minority unemployment is high. In better times', when State rental subsidies were plentiful, women stayed in the shelter up to three weeks. But in had times' (currently) women may extend their stays up to three months to save enough money to secure housing. Most groups, therefore, tend to have an ongoing nucleus of women with open-ended transitional membership as well. Women without children may be part of these groups while most homeless men reside in men's shelters. Some reside with their families in the area's one 'family shelter'. Men's shelters tend to be larger and have less program and staff to focus on services including working with groups.

The author also worked with the administrators of the shelters to enlist their support in the empowerment group effort. Most saw the groupwork as positive, though some worried about the 'extra work' it might cause. In one shelter the executive director actually joined her workers in offering the empowerment group service and she was more of a political activist than her workers were initially. Managers and staff in these non-traditional Hartford agencies tend to have political awareness and commitments to social justice unlike most of their counterparts in the bureaucratic city shelters in New York City and other large cities (Lee, 1986). Workers and managers in the Hartford area women's shelters agreed that oppression was a force to be reckoned with. They saw the women as experiencing oppression on at least three interrelated levels: they are poor, they are women, and they suffer the effects of racism (Gutierrez, 1988). They are often young and have small children (Mills and Ota, 1989; Johnson and Kreiger, 1989). Developing efficacy in personal, interpersonal and political power is, therefore, relevant.

This paper will locate empowerment theory within the context of broader social work practice theory. After defining terms, it will suggest a conceptual framework including professional purpose, a value base, theoretical foundations and methods and skills. The concepts for this framework, informed by the literature, were derived from actual practice and qualitative study including the content analysis presented here.

A foundation to build on

Empowerment concepts supply a next step in the evolving thinking on the professional purpose of social work and in developing its action principles. They flesh out and strengthen the broader base of an ecological perspective and a life model approach to practice (Germain and Gitterman, 1980; Germain, 1990). They add direction and action principles consistent with serving oppressed groups.

> In an ecological view, practice is directed toward improving the transactions between people and environments in order to enhance adaptive capacities *and* improve environments... Both knowledge and values support the professional objectives of 1) releasing, developing, and strengtheningpeople's innate capacity for growth and creative adaptation; 2) removing environmental blocks and obstacles to growth and adaptation; and 3) positively increasing the nutritive properties

of the environment (Germain, 1979).

Recent critics of this approach have ignored the definitions of adaptation which Germain poses above (Gould, 1987). Clearly to 'remove environmental blocks and obstacles' and "to increase the nutritive properties of the environment' involves actively changing the noxious environment. It does not negate the possibility of a conflict stance toward intractable oppressive systems. It does emphasise principles of mutuality and reciprocity between worker and client as a way of promoting identity, autonomy, competence and relatedness for people and for systems. This perspective also details *How* personal growth is achieved in the processes of stress, adaptation and coping. It supplies a basis for the personal and the political sides of the equation of empowerment (Germain, 1979; 1990). Further, it challenges workers to 'restructure situations' and to 'create resources where they are absent'. It discusses political skills and organisational change processes (Germain, 1979,1990). Germain notes that next steps would include further development of practice principles which deal with how to change structurally oppressive environments (Germain, 1990, pp.148-149). Practice principles that mandate workers to move back and forth with clients from the individual to the group, to the structural change level as is needed in the situation, are also key foundation concepts (Woods and Middleman, 1989). A close look at actual practice with oppressed groups and a synthesising of concepts from empowerment theory may well provide the next steps in conceptualisation.

Empowerment theory

Blaming the Victim (Ryan, 1972) and *Black Empowerment* (Solomon, 1976) are landmark pieces in focusing the profession on personal and political power and their interrelatedness. Solomon develops action principles and identifies 'direct and indirect power blocks'. Indirect power blocks represent internalised negative valuations (of the oppressor) which are 'incorporated into the developmental experiences of the individual as mediated by significant others'. Direct power blocks 'are applied directly by some agent of society's major social institutions'. Solomon's concepts are specifically directed to the powerlessness of African-American people, but she notes that other groups that traditionally have been negatively valued - the handicapped, women, and gay men and lesbian women have also begun to 'push for reduction of their powerlesness' (1976, p.21). Solomon is specific regarding the concept of empowerment: 'It deals with a particular kind of block to problem-solving: that imposed by the external society by virtue of a stigmatised collective identity' (p.21). Bearing this in mind, the word 'empower' is not intended to describe psychologically, interpersonally, or existentially oriented interventions with dominant group clients.

The definition of empowerment used in this paper is Solomon's (1982, p.19):

> A process whereby the social worker engages in a set of activities with the client... that aim to reduce the powerlessness that has been created by negative valuations based on membership in a stigmatised group. It involves identification of the power blocks that contribute to the problem as well as the development and implementation of specific strategies aimed at either the reduction of the effects from indirect power blocks or the reduction of the operations of direct power blocks.

Solomon directs the practitioner's attention to both types of power blocks to the adaptive capacities affected by internalised negative valuations and to direct environment blocks. She (1982, pp.26-27) suggests that empowerment activities can have one agent or more of the following goals: that the client perceive herself as causal agent and the worker as a knowledgeable collaborator or partner in the problem solving effort; and to help the client to perceive the power structure as multipolar and... therefore open to influence. The practice stance is one of 'combining forces' rather than giving aid (pp.26-27). Further, all social work roles must be examined for inherent paternalism. We need to be careful to advocate or act as social broker with and not 'for', to examine any concepts of treatment and care', to examine the possible 'one-up' position in the traditional concept of teacher. Simon's (1990, p.32) discussion of the paradox of empowerment is relevant here:

> The one function that social workers or, for that matter, anyone

else cannot perform for another person is that of empowerment. Empowerment is a reflexive activity, a process capable of being initiated and sustained only by the agents or subject who seeks power or self-determination. Others can only aid and abet in this empowerment process.

Empowering roles may include: resource consultant, particularly using the group modality; the sensitiser role in which the client can use the practitioner to work on self knowledge critical for the solution of problems which stem from social and psychological power deficits; and the teacher/trainer role in which the worker assists people and systems in the acquisition of information, knowledge, or skills. Another principle is to help recipients of help become dispensers of help, as is compatible in the mutual aid group or social network situation (Solomon, 1982, pp.345-353; Germain 1979; 1990).

The 'radical pedagogy' of Paulo Friere (1973) is easily related to empowerment in social work (Lee, 1988; Gutierrez, 1988; Breton, 1988; Parsons, 1988; Friere, 1990). His notion (1973, pp. 11-13) of the dialogic process is particularly relevant:

> Every human being is capable of looking critically at his world in a dialogical encounter with others... In this process, the old paternalistic teacher-student relationship is overcome. A peasant can facilitate this process for his neighbour more effectively than a 'teacher' brought in from the outside. Each man wins back his own right to say his own word, to name the world.

Friere's methods are directed to the collectivity, they are group and community oriented methods of dialogue. Liberation theology, particularly from South America, with its notions of base communities as units of social and political change and use of consciousness raising, are also pertinent to social work thinking (Breton, 1988; Germain, 1990). Friere(1973,p.20)defines conscientisation as learning to perceive social, political and economic contradictions and to take action against the oppressive elements of reality'.

Gutierrez cites consciousness raising as goal, process, and

outcome in empowerment work (1990; 1989a; 1989b). Speaking of the personal and institutional levels of empowerment thinking, she says (1989a):

It is not sufficient to focus only on developing a sense of personal power or developing skills or working toward social change. These three elements combined are the goal of empowerment in social work practice.

Gutierrez (1989a) sees developing critical consciousness, reducing self blame, assuming personal responsibility for change, and enhancing self efficacy, as critical to empowerment. She (1989a, p.9) also cites the following empowering interventions: basing the helping relationship on collaboration, trust and shared power; utilising small groups; accepting the client's definition of the problem; identifying and building upon the client's strengths; raising the client's consciousness of issues of class and power; actively involving the client in the change process; teaching specific strategies utilising mutual aid, self help, or support groups; experiencing a sense of power within the helping process; mobilising resources or advocating for clients. Noteworthy are her comments on the importance of groupwork to empowerment practice and her research on the effective use of groups with Latino college students (Gutierrez, 1989b).

Parsons (1988; 1989) also emphasises the importance of the group. She (1989, p.10) defines empowerment as an outcome and a process which comes initially through validation of peers and a perception of commonality.

The idea of building collectivity is central to the helping process. Collectivity involves the process of merging energy of individuals into a whole... It goes beyond treatment in a group. It contains Schwartz's notion of the provision of a mediating or third force function for people who need to attain resolution to their situations from those systems, and who in turn must shape those systems and assist in their functioning. The collective provides an opportunity for support, mutual aid, and collective action on behalf of the whole.

Parsons identifies at least three kinds of) empowerment: a developmental process which begins with individual growth, and possibly culminates in larger social change; a psychological state marked by heightened feelings of self esteem, efficacy, and control; and liberation, resulting from a social movement which begins with education and politicisation of powerless people, and later involves a collective attempt on the part of the powerless to gain power, and change those structures which remain oppressive, (Parsons, 1989). The use of the mutual aid/empowerment group' seems to unite the ends of this continuum as parts of a whole process. This is clearly seen when empowerment theory is united with a mutual aid group approach in practice with a range of oppressed people (Lee, 1989).

Mutual aid groups: The interactionist approach

The mutual aid group concept was defined and advanced in social work by William Schwartz in the 1960s, a time when social work was compelled to consider collective unrest and collective action.

> The group is an enterprise in mutual aid. A collection of people who need each other to work on certain common tasks to which the agency is hospitable (Schwartz, 1974a).

This definition emphasises people helping each other with issues they have in common. It assumes mutuality and reciprocity between members and between members and the worker. It delineates five tasks of the worker: to make a simple unjargonised contract offer and to reach for client's stake and feedback in a mutual contracting process; to point out the common ground between members; to detect and challenge obstacles to the work; to give information; and to help the group complete its work (Schwartz, 1974a). "Mutual aid groups', as used in this paper, are groups that conform to these definitions of purpose and task. The stance of the worker and the tasks defined are compatible with empowerment theory. The 'giving of information' and 'pointing out the common ground' includes the consciousness raising process in areas of the group members' oppression, or for example, fostering pride as

---

A conceptual framework:
Empowerment through mutual aids groups

Professional purpose: dual simultaneous concern for people and environments; to enhance adaptive potentials of people and to change environmental and structural arrangements that are oppressive.

Value base: preference for social work activites which give priority to work with oppressed groups; individual adaptative potentials *and* environmental/structural change through collective action.

Theoretical foundations: practice theory that encompasses the knowledge of individual adaptive potentials, mutual aid group processes and dynamics, and larger scale and structural change, with special attention to concepts of empowerment on the personal, interpersonal and socio-economic political levels.

Method and skills: the use of mutual aid groups to identify and work on direct and indirect power blocks toward the ends of personal, interpersonal and political efficacy. A collaborative relationship that encompasses mutuality, reciprocity, shared power and shared human struggle. Collective activity which reflects a raised consciousness regarding oppression. Specfic skills in addressing indirect and direct power blocks on all three levels of living.

---

members of a minority group, be it ethnic pride or gay pride and so on. The 'obstacles to work' may include the indirect or direct power blocks noted by Solomon (1976). The larger theoretical context of this mutual aid group approach is one in which the worker acts to mediate the process by which group members and systems reach out to each other even when the tie between the two may be almost severed by structural or systems inequity (Schwartz, 1974; Lee, 1986). This assumes that such inequities cannot be tolerated and change must occur.

The chart opposite pulls together the conceptual framework which flows out of the preceding theoretical foundations and the grounded theory approach which will now be described.

The practice

The author did a content analysis of 40 group records (N=40) produced by 16 workers (including herself) learning empowerment groupwork in a consultation group with the author while working in shelters for homeless people during 1988-1989. The records described practice primarily with younger (age 18-35) black (African-American and some Carribbean) and Puerto Rican homeless women. This is consistent with the national profile of homeless women (Johnson and Krieger, 1989).

With beginning workers, the contracting process happened in stages. They grasped the mutual aid group concepts first and got the group going. After three to four sessions and repeated consultation they were better able to build in an empowerment focus. The content of the work expanded to the wider socio-economic and political level only after the empowerment focus was clear to worker and group members. This necessitated consciousness raising amongst the workers in the workshop. The following analysis was done in two stages: first as workers were able to develop a mutual aid group, and then again after the empowerment focus was clear to the workers and group members.

Pre-empowerment stage

The following categories of group members' concerns were derived from reviewing the records in the pre-empowerment stage. They are in order of frequency (frequency meaning the number of meetings (of 40) in which the behaviours were observed).

Deep sadness (F=37)

Crying in the group, or statements like 'I am so depressed', 'I am feeling lower than a snake's belly'. 'It's hard to stay up'. Rose said, 'If I start to talk I cry all night'. Bettina responded, I cried today in my room... I have 3 kids and nowhere to go: how could I do this to them?'. Rose said, It makes you feel worthless'; several responded 'yeah'.

Sharing survival skills/coping skills (F=36)

Group members often acted as resource experts. Pam said, "I have an eviction notice, I am out by the 20th. I tried legal aid. I had a trial and my witness didn't show. I felt so bad, it was all over for me'. After several suggested other legal routes, Pam said they had been tried. Mary said, 'I guess you just got to go to X agency, speak to Mrs. Y and ask for a subsidised housing application'. Ana said, That Z agency is better for that and you can get the worker to call for you or go with you...'.

In later stage group meetings, vulnerabilities were also shared, and developing skills to work on a problem was also a strong theme in the mutual aid. Gloria said, 'I have to admit it. I am scared of talking to landlords. On the phone I am scared of the answering machine, in person I don't know what to say'. Tasha asked what was scary to Gloria? Gloria said she stammers when she is anxious and can't think. Spontaneously Ruth said, 'Let's make believe I am the answering machine, you can say...'. Connie said, Its good to write it down and memorise it just before you go there...'. Ruth said, Wait she's still not saying it, we are. Gloria, now how would you say it after you heard us?'. Gloria picked a simple 'speech', and said it in different ways, making it her own. The members applauded it. Gloria wrote her version down and read it to the group...

Aloneness (F=32)

Mary said, I feel like everyone abandoned me and I am left here all alone. No one cares'. Pam responded, You have to make it alone - no one does care'. That is not true', said Tasha, we care, you are not alone'.

Self-blame (and lowering of self-esteem) (F=28)

'I am worth shit, my family says I'm no good, I guess I am'. 'I hate myself for bringing this on my children'. 'My children deserve a better mother'. 'I was so stupid...'

Frustration with systems (F-28)

'They give us a constant runaround. They lost my application *three* times'. I got lost in the shuffle'. 'They don't even answer the phone'. The landlord told me to put down roach traps. I got rid of the roaches and the mice came, I got a cat but a rat came bigger than the cat'.

The use of humour (F=24)

A style of 'playing the dozens' or topping another's experience over who suffers most with the grim realities of living in poverty: 'I finally got them to fix the leak in the roof and the floor broke in'. The laughter produced by this round of stories would enable the worst to be told without immobilising depression and it would also be a way to state survival abilities with some bravado and some pride.

Anger and rage (F=18)

This was also thinly hidden in these accounts, but it was only expressed directly on rare occasions. 'When that rat bit my baby I had to threaten to kill the landlord. I had to act bad, nice didn't get it. You can't let nobody walk on you; you walk on them first'. More often the anger was expressed with sad affect as in this excerpt: Pat said, 'I got mad at the housing people...' 'What did you do?' asked Kim. 'I just cried...' Pat replied. Stories of fighting for their rights argumentatively and sometimes physically, also contained their anger and fear.

Interpersonal struggles (F=15)

The groups were also used to solve problems of living together in the cramped quarters of shelters. Ada said, 'I can't stand Molly, she's always making eyes and flashing herself at my husband when he comes to meet me...'. After a silence Matilda said she wanted to apologise for the way she acted the other day. She didn't mean to say anything 'racial' but she was angry when Pat's daughter hit her two- year old son. Pat said she thought Maria (now gone) had been trying to start a 'war' of Puerto Ricans vs. Blacks and that Matilda wasn't really that way, things are better now that Maria is gone... Everyone agreed and the focus went to Maria...

An analysis of the pre-empowerment phase categories

These categories: deep sadness; sharing survival and coping skills; self-blame and the lowering of self-esteem; frustration with systems; the use of humour; anger and rage; and interpersonal struggles represent important areas of work and coping strategies for disempowered women (Adams-Sullivan et al, 1987; Berlin, 1988; Bricker-Jenkins and Hooyman, 1987; Gutierrez, 1988).

The generalised contracting process that produced this work (despite the specific empowerment focus in the workshops) looked like: We're here to discuss any concerns you have and also to see how we can support one another. You all have valuable knowledge and I'd like to use this as a time for you to share. Does anyone want to begin? Carla said, "I do...". The level of work this produced is important but short sighted in an empowerment focus. What has to be built in, to the worker and to the group members, is an understanding of the dynamics of oppression and of indirect and direct power blocks. This takes time, dialogue, self-examination, reading of literature and teaching. When this is absent or in the early stages the inspection of the data shows that the work, however helpful, was also arrested at the personal and interpersonal levels of empowerment, for example, in the last example (under 'interpersonal struggles') the worker should have begun to raise consciousness about the oppression that both Puerto Ricans and African-Americans face, to point out the common ground and the need for unity as a next step.

At pre-empowerment skill levels, workers could indeed help people move from aloneness to connection and mutual aid, from depression, self-blame and indirectly expressed anger to direct expression of feelings, finding strengths, coping, and negotiating systems better. Before her direct practice with homeless women this author would have thought that was enough, and maybe even called it empowering. Certainly the women felt accompanied in their struggles, that others were there and could help, that others care. They felt more competent. It could stand as good groupwork - but not yet as good empowerment work.

The empowerment stage

After several meetings of workers with their groups and several workshops on the empowerment focus, the workers were able to offer a clearer understanding of the empowerment group purpose as part of the contracting process. Here is an example:

We finished talking about Gloria's eviction. The worker then suggested that dealing with severe housing issues was bigger than any one person or groups' problem. It had to do with things that were wrong in our society, with the way poor people and black or Puerto Rican people were treated and where the money went and where the power was. They each needed the strengths and skills we named with Gloria's situation to deal with systems and with life' but they also needed to know that being there is not their fault and getting out or making it better is not an individual task alone. Sandy immediately said, 'Let me tell you about Knight Village and what I'm doing'. She spoke eloquently of a tenant run complex, a residents' advisory council and of speaking at city council and legislative hearings.

With this specificity contract and clarity, the categories of work then expanded in these groups to include the following consciousness raising and organising activities:

Frank work on racism (N-18)

Both as experienced in the shelters and in society: Maria said, 'I know I didn't get the job because I am Puerto Rican...'. The story is told and critically examined. Donna said, The landlord didn't want no young black woman with three kids, she shut that door'. 'Was it the black or the young?', asked Chris. The black', answered some group members. 'The young and kids', said Pam, who is older and also black. The woman part', said Mary. "Let's look at it', said the worker... And, 'Why are we all black and Spanish and *here*', asked Pat. 'Why do you think?', asked the worker.

Frank work on power and class (N=8)

The following excerpt from a meeting shows this clearly: Sandy said she had testified at the state legislature about where tax money was going and that it wasn't going to affordable housing. After many questions on what the 'legislature' was, which Sandy and the worker answered very specifically (including how many legislators were women, black or Puerto Rican persons, thus making the power structure multipolar), the worker asked if group members understood about these social, political and economic issues? Sandy and Vera said yes, but the others said no. The worker filled in about the Federal Budget - 52 cents on the dollar was for defence and less than two cents for housing. They angrily added their knowledge of where tax money was going. The worker talked about the nationwide 'Housing Now' march and the symbolic demand of 'four cents on the dollar' instead of two cents. Paula said astutely, 'They think we aren't even worth the two cents', and everyone agreed. The worker said, 'Yes, and let's get clear on who "they" are. Who has the money and power?' Sandy answered, 'The rich men'. The worker responded, 'What rich men?' Kim laughed and said, "Rich white men, the millionaires and big companies. They have most of the money in this country and we have none!' All agreed - that is who controls the country, the economy and public policy. The worker said we need to talk about how we can make our voices heard. They said, we can vote and we can tell it like it is. Energy was high as each one added a piece to the equation. Pam said, 'We are not useless people, junkies or criminals. They think we'll go away but we won't, cause the poor are gonna rise up'. Paula said, Yes, like Tracy Chapman's song, "Revolution", if we're gonna be someone we can't take this treatment for ever'. The worker said the Housing Now' march was one way not to take it and they eagerly agreed to go, planning baby sitting and how to take part'.

Organising for and taking collective action (N=12)

The example given above also shows moving into a collective action strategy. Of the 16 workers' groups, six moved into this level of work on varying issues. Others were slowly moving in that direction, and some workers could not get there themselves or with their groups. A collective action strategy in one shelter involved writing a letter to the mayor of their city who is an African-American woman. They appealed to her as a 'woman like them' and invited her to the Shelter. They described very specific issues in the letter. They received a personal letter in response and were asked to call to negotiate the date. This gave them a sense of access to a multipolar power structure, which was responsive in this case. This group and others have testified at legislative hearings. Other groups are planning to organise a local march to make the homeless visible. Some have talked about civil disobedience as a possibility.

Reflecting on the new categories

Taken together the earlier categories and these reflect empowerment groupwork that takes place on the personal, interpersonal and political/institutional levels of dealing with indirect and direct power blocks. These categories are full of energy and hope. Work in these areas seems to lift depression and self blame and also finds direction for anger and develops new coping skills. Yet work in the newer empowerment categories is accomplished less frequently and often with self consciousness on the workers' part since it is a newer level of practice, and perhaps because workers' own consciousness is not fully raised in these areas. On the other hand, some workers were comfortable only with action oriented tasks and had difficulty hearing and responding to personal pain.

Pulls experienced in the work

Workers (myself included) sometimes felt tom in terms of the direction to move with the work. Any given piece of work in the group can be handled on any of the three levels. Finding the common ground between the levels was an advanced skill to be learned. Workers needed to learn where group members were and move accordingly while moving with and from the personal pain, including taking personal responsibility for change, to the political (and collective action) and back again. The personal and interpersonal levels seemed more comfortable for most workers. Workers tended to dichotomise either the personal or the political initially and only the more advanced learned to put the two levels together so that the personal and political were one.

Next steps

Further exploration of a qualitative and quantitative nature is needed to test whether reaching for both levels of work (the personal, including interpersonal, and the political) produces strengths in both areas in members' lives, perceptions, *and* social change activities, and to explore further the benefits of using this conceptual approach in practice. For homeless/oppressed women personal pain and the need for change and political action are often spontaneously expressed in the same breath. That is where the 'clients' are. It was the inexperience of workers that tended to respond to one level of work at the expense of the other. Further study of 'empowerment groups', where both levels are attended to, will further refine the conceptual framework suggested here.

Acknowledgement

The author is deeply grateful to Mary McAtee of the Connecticut Coalition for the Homeless; to the inspiring members of The Successful Women's Group' of My Sisters Place; and to the workshop participants for preparing and sharing their work. Special thanks go to Judith Beaumont, Executive Director of My Sisters Place, Gail Bourdon and Jean Konan, social workers at My Sisters Place, and Mary Beth Cullina of Marshall House, a Salvation Army facility. It has been a joy to learn and grow with them.

References

Adams-Sawyer, Z., Adams-Sullivan, M, Brown-Manning, R, DeLaCruz, AC and Gamer, C. (1986) 'Women of color and feminist practice' in Bricker- Jenldns, M. and Hooyman, N. (eds.) *Not For Women Only: Social Work Practice For A Feminist Future.* Silver Spring, Md: NASW.

Berlin, S. (1987) 'Women and mental health; anger, anxiety, dependency, control' in Burden, D.S. and Gottleib, N. (eds.) *The Women Client:Providing Human Services In A Changing World.* New York; Tavistock, pp.146-161.

Breton, M. (1988) 'The need for mutual aid groups in a drop-in for homeless women: the sistering case' in Lee, JAB. (ed.) *Group Work With The Poor and Oppressed.* New York: Haworth Press, pp.47-62.

Bricker-Jenkins, M. and Hooyman N. (1986) *Not For Women Only: Social Work Practice For a Feminist Future.* Silver Spring, MD: NASW.

Brown, A. (1990) 'Recharging groupwork batteries', *Groupwork,* 3(1), pp.3-7.

Davis, L.V. (1985) 'Female and male voices in social work', *Social Work,* 30, pp. 100-113.

Friere, P. (1973) *Pedagogy of the Oppressed.* Seabury Press: New York.

Friere, P. (1990) 'A critical understandingof social work,' *Journal of Progressive Human Services,* 1(1), pp.3-10.

Germain, C.B. (ed)(1979)Social Work Practice: People and Environments-An Ecological Perspective. New York: Columbia University Press.

Germain, C.B. and Gitterman, A (1980) *The Life Model of Social Work Practice.* New York: Columbia University Press.

Germain, C.B. (1990) 'Life forces and the anatomy of practice', *Smith College Studies for Social Work,* 60(2), pp.138-152.

Glaser, B.G. and Strauss, A (1967) *The Discovery of Grounded Theory.* Ill: Aldine Publishing Co.

Gould, K (1987) 'Life model vs conflict model: a feminist perspective', *Social Work,* 32, pp.346-351.

Gutierrez, L.M. (1990) 'Working with women of color an empowerment perspective', *Social Work,* 35(2), pp. 149-155.

Gutierrez, LM. *(1989a)Empowerment in Social WorkPractice: Considerations for Practice and Education.* Paper presented at the Annual Meeting of the Council on Social Work Education. Chicago, Illinois.

Gutierrez, LM. (1989b) *Using Group Work To Empower Latinos: APreliminary*

Analysis. Paper presented at the Annual Symposium of the Association for Advancement of Social Work with Groups. Montreal, Canada.

Hayakawa, S. (ed.) (1962) *The Use and Misuse of Language*. Greenwich, CT: Fawcett.

Johnson, AK and Kreuger, L.W. (1989) Toward a better understanding of homeless women', *Social Work*, 34(6), pp.532-540.

Keenan, E. and Pinkerton, J. (1988) 'Social action groupwork as negotiation: contradictions in the process of empowerment?, *Groupwork*, 1(3), pp.229-238.

Lee, JAB. (1983) "Who's looking out for the homeless?1, *NASW News*, Silver Spring, MD, pp.4-5.

Lee, JAB. (1986) "No place to go: homeless women' in Gitterman, A and Shulman, L. (eds.) *Mutual Aid Groups and The life Cycle*. Illinois: The Peacock Press, pp.245-263.

Lee, JAB. (1987) "Social work with oppressed populations: Jane Addams won't you please come home?* in Lassner, J. Powell, K and Finnegan, E. (eds.) *Social Group Work: Competence and Value in Practice*. New York; Haworth Press, pp.1-16.

Lee, JAB. (ed.) (1989) *Group Work With the Poor and Oppressed* New York: Haworth Press.

Lee, JAB. and Swenson, C.R (1986) 'The concept of mutual aid' in Gitterman, A and Schulman, L (eds.) *Mutual Aid Groups and The Life Cycle*. Illinois: The Peacock Press, pp.361-380.

Mullender, A andWard, D. (1989) 'Challenging familiar assumptions: preparing for and initiating a self-directed group', *Groupwork*, 2(1), pp.5-26.

Mills, C. and Ota, H. (1989) 'Homeless women with minor children in the Detroit metropolitan area', *Social Work*, 34(6), pp.485-490.

Parsons, RJ. (1988) 'Empowerment for role alternative for low income minority girls: a group work approach' in Lee, JAB. (ed.) *Group Work With the Poor and Oppressed*. New York: Haworth, 27-46.

Parsons, RJ. (in press) 'Empowerment as purpose and practice principle in social work', *Social Work with Groups*.

Pinderhughes, E. (1982) 'Afro-American families and the victim system', in McGoldrick, M., Pearce, J. and Giordano, J. (eds.) *Ethnicity and Family Therapy*. New York: The Guilford Press, pp.108-122.

Ryan, W. (1972) *Blaming The Victim*. New York: Vintage.

Schwartz, W. (1974a) 'The social worker in the group' in Klenk, R and

Ryan, R (eds.) *The Practice of Social Work.* Second Edition. Calif: Wadsworth, pp.208-228.

Schwartz, W. (1974b) 'Private troubles and public issues: one social work job or two?' in Klenk, R and Ryan, R (eds.) *The Practice of Social Work.* Second Edition. Calif: Wadsworth, pp.82-99.

Schwartz, W. (1986) 'The group work tradition and social work practice' in Gitterman, A and Schulman, L. (eds.) *The Legacy of William Schwartz: Group Practice As Shared Interaction.* New York: Haworth Press, pp.7-28.

Simon, B.L. (1990) 'Rethinking empowerment?', The *Journal of Progressive Human Services,* 1(1), pp.27-39.

Social Work (1977) Special issue on conceptual frameworks, 22(5).

Solomon, B.B. (1976) *Black Empowerment: Social Work In Oppressed Communities.* New York: Columbia.

Solomon, B.B. (1982) 'Social work values and skills to empower women' in Weick, A and Vandiver, S.T. (eds.) *Women, Power and Change.* Washington, D.C: NASW, pp.206-214.

Solomon B.B., (1986) 'Social work With Afro-Americans' in Morales, A and Sheafer, B. *(eds.) Social Work:A Profession of Many Faces.* New York; Allyn and Bacon.

Woods, G.G. and Middleman, R *(1989) The Structural Approach to Social Work Practice.* Second Editioa New York: Columbia Press.

This chapter was first published in 1991 in *Groupwork* Vol. 4(1), pp.5-21

At the time of writing Judith A.B. Lee was Professor of Social Work at the University of Connecticut School of Social Work, and President of the Association for the Advancement of Social Work with Groups

Toward a model of social groupwork practice with marginalised populations

Margot Breton

Marginalised populations are often served in non-traditional settings staffed by volunteers or para-professionals. Social workers who want to reach these populations need to develop a model of practice which takes into account the realities of both these populations and these settings. This paper offers a step in this direction. It uses groupwork and community organisation constructs to address issues related to the group form appropriate to this type of practice, to the tensions generated by professional practice in non-professional settings, and to the particular problems produced by the state of marginalisation. A groupwork experience with homeless women in a para-professionally staffed program (the *Sistering* drop-in) illustrates some aspects of the model.

The setting

Sistering is a Toronto city drop-in which was established in 1981 to serve socially isolated, homeless and/or transient women. Many of these women (more than 50%) are chronic or ex-psychiatric patients. Some of the older women lost their homes through widowhood, separation or hospitalisation of a spouse, the younger are unemployed. Many are victims of violence (physical abuse, incest) (Breton, 1984). The program is funded 70 per cent by the Ontario Ministry of Health, 20 per cent by the United Way, six per cent by the Municipality of Toronto, and the balance by membership and donations.

The drop-in, housed in a community centre, strives to be a competence-promoting environment offering both nurture and optimal challenges. Nurture and challenges, support and opportunities, these concepts underlie the *Sistering* philosophy.

Thus the goals of the drop-in are:

1. to provide a daytime 'refuge' where isolated, transient or homeless women can rest and recuperate;
2. to promote learning and consciousness-raising experiences through which the women may gain or regain some degree of control over their lives.

It is because of the belief in the inherent abilities of the women to make the most of the support and the challenges offered that *Sistering* is located in a community centre. People use community centres for a multitude of purposes, mainly recreational and educational. Youngsters and adults alike use the swimming pool and the other sports or athletic resources; and all age groups may join friendship clubs, or enrol in language classes and various skills courses. The point is that community centres serve the needs of the community - and locating the *Sistering* program in a community centre says that the women who attend belong to and are part of the community.

This does not imply that the women who attend *Sistering* do not have special needs; but then so do the troubled teenagers who meet with a worker to sort out their problems, or the isolated seniors who join a regular card-playing group to relieve their loneliness. However, like the teenagers and the seniors, the women also share common human needs for understanding, for help in problem-solving, and for relationships. For the chronic mental health patients, the location in a community centre is part of a strategy of normalisation. For all the users, it is a strategy to reintegrate them into their community.

The variation in the *Sistering* population means that the program must allow for diversity. It is a tribute to the maturity of the Sistering program that the women are increasingly challenged to participate in the running of the drop-in and to decide what activities best meet their needs. This is a crucial issue, for without this active participation the nurturing aspects of the program will inevitably feed into the helplessness training' which has characterised the socialisation of the majority of women the world over.

Sistering recognises that some of the women who are struggling to deal with chronic mental anguish and disabilities may always remain more dependent, more inactive and in greater need of support than the rest of the women - in other words some will rely more heavily on the nurturing components of the program. However, they as much as anyone need the opportunity to test their strengths and to evaluate for themselves what they can and cannot do.

As for the women who are victims of the feminisation of poverty, who are hit by unemployment and the continuing crisis in affordable housing, or have escaped from violent relationships with mates or parents, Sistering can provide opportunities for them to gain a clearer perspective of the nature of their problems, and to realise the extent to which structural socio-economic and political forces (versus personal inadequacies) have landed them in the hostel system.

It is difficult to come to this kind of realisation in isolation: alone, most of us tend to blame ourselves for the problems we face. Sistering helps by encouraging the women who want to do so to share relevant information concerning the events which have led to their plight. Some individual women gain support from talking with a staff member; however, when the women share information with each other - in a 'sistering' fashion - they gain not only support, but an awareness of 'being in the same boat'. This can become a powerful dynamic of mutual aid, because it helps to hear that others face the same problems, and also because listening to one another's stories is a simple but real act of helping (Gitterman and Shulman, 1986); and the women soon realise that they are helping each other by sharing their stories. When this process of mutual aid occurs not by chance but is systematically developed in a small group context, and skilfully guided over a period of time, it is truly the beginning of empowerment for the women, as their sense of competence is awakened (or reawakened) and affirmed by their demonstrated capacity to help others, and as they realise that commonly experienced socio-economic factors play a primary role in the situations in which they find themselves.

However, to maintain a sense of competence and to be empowered, it is necessary to move from consciousness-raising to action and to testing oneself in the world. *Sistering* challenges the women to test themselves when it helps them to pursue their health care, housing, welfare, and other rights. The right to have fun must be mentioned here; when *Sistering* provides opportunities for the women to engage in recreational activities, and to use the resources of the community centre, it is challenging the women to activate their rights to a full life - it is not giving the women 'something to do' to while away a super abundance of time.

The Wednesday Discussion Group

A few years ago, amid considerable staff apprehension about the introduction of a social work component into the program, a small, open-ended, time-limited group, the Wednesday Discussion Group, was initiated. At that time, the organisational structure of *Sistering* included an elected volunteer board of directors, a paid executive director/ administrator, three paid para-professional direct service staff, but no professional social workers. "The mandate of the group was to provide structured opportunities for the enhancement of social functioning in a discussion group format' (Stewart, 1986). In the planning stage, the social worker employed exclusively to lead the proposed group met with members of SUGI (Sistering Users Group Incorporated, made up of long-time users of the drop-in) and together they identified health-related issues as a major concern, and as an appropriate focus for the Wednesday Group's discussions. These issues included:

1. 'Assembly line' treatment in hospital out-patient services: as most women used emergency services and the high turnover of interns/residents exacerbated consistent treatment follow-up, access to community-based medical and dental care was seen as a pressing need.
2. OHIP (Ontario Health Insurance Plan) coverage: women had difficulties accessing appropriate coverage and were not aware of their rights to this coverage.
3. Access to drug and dental cards.

A number of other issues were identified, such as access

to emergency welfare funds, housing (tenant/landlord rights, lease protection, group homes, hostels, boarding homes related problems), problems with the bureaucracies of traditional social service institutions, nutrition problems while on limited funds, and stress generated by all the above-mentioned problems.

It was agreed that staff and SUGI members would inform the drop-in users that a discussion group was to start on the Wednesday of the next week, that anyone who wished to attend could do so, and that a commitment to attend regularly was not required.

During the first meeting of the Wednesday Discussion Group, the proposed health focus was discussed and approved by the women. A tentative structure, as well as short and long-term goals for the group were agreed upon: the meetings would begin with physical relaxation exercises (perceived by the staff and the group worker as a positive and concrete health-oriented feature), then information on community resources would be shared and systematically collected for compilation into a *Sistering Resource Handbook* to be produced by the group before its termination. Other possible activities would include inviting resource people to provide information about medical care and other matters, writing letters to housing authorities about the discrepancies in the services provided to male versus female hostel users, and viewing films to help in the identification and discussion of various issues and problems.

The structure was changed at the second meeting to allow for a 'check-in' procedure which provided an opportunity for the women to discuss immediate and pressing issues or problems and to share strategies they had employed successfully or unsuccessfully in similar situations. At the fourth meeting, the women decided the physical exercises would come at the end of the meetings, as by then, having had a chance to get acquainted, they would be less uncomfortable and self-conscious about doing these exercises (Stewart, 1986). The group met for 16 weeks, with a three week break halfway. The meetings lasted two hours. Attendance varied: when the weather was beautiful (the group started in mid-April and ended mid-August), the turnout was small (5-7 women); when the weather was not great, the turnout was large (12-15 women).

Over these 16 weeks, the women contributed to the *Handbook*, viewed and discussed five films (all on gender-related issues, e.g.

the feminisation of poverty, images of women in North American society), invited three speakers and prepared intensely for these sessions, videotaped themselves on three occasions role-playing problematic situations, then reviewed and discussed the tapes (much support from the executive director of the drop-in was initially necessary to alleviate the women's apprehensions), and wrote one letter in response to a newspaper column which they felt was insensitive to the vulnerability of women to abuse from husbands or mates.

Group practice with marginalised populations: theoretical constructs

To model a group practice aimed at effectively engaging marginalised populations, assumptions are made firstly about aspects of group form most appropriate for, or most likely to characterise, this type of practice: these aspects relate to open and time-limited systems. Secondly, assumptions are made about the tensions generated by the divisions of labour and of power between professionals and nonprofessionals. Lastly, assumptions are made about marginalised population and their motivation to participate in a community, and about the socio-economic and chronic features of their problems.

Group form

Open groups

Group openness can refer to the internal openness within a 'closed' group (Lang, 1980), to the openness of a group to new members in an 'open-ended' group (Schopler and Galinsky, 1984), or to the openness of a group to its environment (e.g. Lewis, 1983; Moore, 1983). Given the nature of a drop-in, the Wednesday Discussion Group had to be conceptualised as an 'open-ended' group, and indeed the membership of the group changed at every meeting, although as often happens in open-ended groups, it had a small core of members who attended with some regularity.

The basic assumption made in this paper regarding group

openness is that a group is part of a community, and that when working with socially and economically marginalised populations it is essential to recognise the permeability of a group's boundaries to the community of which it is a part. In this perspective, an open group constantly interacts with that community as it promotes the right of its members "to participate and share in the life of the community' (Boff, 1985, p.25). An open group is in a permanent state of potentiality. Its optimal functioning is not at the point of 'maturity' when internally the group functions fully and effectively (Lang, 1972). An open group functions optimally when it is influenced by and influences the community in such a way that the greatest possible benefits ensue to the group, its members and the community.

In a group such as the Wednesday Discussion Group, the immediate environment, in this case the drop-in itself and later on the host agency or community centre, can be seen as the 'community' with which the group members first interact. Thus learning to interact effectively with the wider social environment, or learning to become socially competent, is made easier as the learning tasks are tailored and paced in relation to the abilities of the group members. In the case of marginalised populations not to promote exchanges with the community only consolidates their state of marginalisation. To promote these exchanges, the present model addresses issues of group membership, group participation and group space, i.e. issues of symbolic and physical group boundaries.

Membership and participation in open groups

Membership involves belonging to a group, whether one is active or not; participation involves actively sharing in pursuit of the group goal(s). The group open to the community will be one that maximises the participation of all individuals who share in the pursuit of the group goal(s).

While much has been written on the member role (see Falk, 1988), the role of participant per se has received relatively little attention. It is in the analysis of community work that the participant role is addressed most explicitly. For example, Lewis

(1983, P-12) points out that in adult community groups, members do not have the requirement of 'adhering to group norms for behaviour'. In pursuing the group goal, they act, in and out of the group, as the situations demand and their particular creative powers allow. This implies a radical acceptance of the notion that participation can vary qualitatively and quantitatively, and that the essential factor in participation is commitment to and pursuit of the goal(s) of the group.

In the Wednesday Discussion Group, some members were more ready than others to participate and showed more initiative and ability in relating their own particular problems to the general issues raised in discussions. For example, after viewing the film The Stress Mess' which focuses on how people contribute to raising their own levels of negative stress because (among other reasons) they have difficulty saying 'no', one of the participating members raised a problem she regularly encounters with other women 'bumming smokes' from her. This struck a cord with several women, particularly those who identified with difficulties saying 'no' to friends. Discussion centred on why they might be feeling those problems so acutely and the women identified a fear of losing those friends if they didn't share their tobacco. The women were able to support one another ... and shared strategies to deal with the problem (Stewart, 22 May 1985).

Furthermore, in a group open to the community, distinctions between 'insider' and 'outsider' would be less important in identifying participants than commitment to the group goal(s). Thus a willing-to-help community member, by virtue of his/her commitment to the group goal(s), would be thought of not only as a 'resource', purely external to the group, but also as a participant - a valued, though temporary, part of the group. The mediating function of the social worker could then be extended to other relevant (and skilled) community members. Especially in working with marginalised populations, incorporating, as it were, the community into the group may be the first step in incorporating the group in the community. In typical groupwork fashion, the speakers invited to the Wednesday Discussion Group were perceived as 'resources'. It may be that social work practice as a whole needs to look at participation in change endeavours in terms of partnerships and partners, concepts which could bridge the differences between 'insider' and 'outsider' and would allow for the range of functions and roles necessary to effectively address the personal and the structural components of the complex problems faced by marginalised populations.

Group space

Conceptualising the group as open to the community creates a challenge in terms of group identity. The formulation must allow for cohesion as well as for permeable boundaries, i.e. the focus has to be a dual one, keeping a balance between looking inward and looking outward. One aspect of this challenge concerns the physical arrangements for group meetings. Just as there is a need for new perceptions of socio-emotional boundaries (i.e. new concepts of insider/outsider roles), there is a need for new perceptions of physical boundaries (i.e. new ideas about group space). Practitioners who work with marginalised groups in non-professional settings, and who conceive these groups as open to the community, need to continue the social groupwork tradition of being creative in respect to the use of space. For example, the Wednesday Discussion Group had to accommodate to holding its meetings within the *Sistering* drop-in room, which, though large and organised to accommodate a number of simultaneous activities as well as different degrees of closeness between people, nevertheless did not allow for a completely private space. However, what looked like an obstacle to group cohesion and identity turned out to be an opportunity to establish identity and do 'boundary work' (two necessary conditions for developing effective relationships with a larger system such as a community) by impressing upon everyone in the room the distinction between the unstructured or loosely structured nature of the drop-in as a whole and the group as a special, structured feature of the drop-in.

The openness of the spatial arrangement led not only to learning about boundaries and differences between systems, but to learning about different ways of participating in different systems. Indeed, the women who were not ready to engage in the group, but were attracted to it, could participate from a distance. The participation was uneven, with some merely observing and drawing it all in silently and impassively, others joining non-verbally but expressively (following with their eyes, smiling, frowning, shaking their heads), while a few occasionally put in a sentence and then retreated to the safety of their outlying posts. Scaled down demands in terms of group participation may be necessary for people marginalised and 'on the outside' to learn to trust others as well as to trust their own capacities to participate. An open spatial arrangement, by giving individuals the opportunity to join and participate in a group at their own pace and in their own way, and by providing them with grounds for informed decisions about joining and participating, can prepare individuals to join (or rejoin) a community and to exercise their right to participate in that community.

Time-limited groups

Though group practice with marginalised populations need not involve pre-set time-limits and perhaps should not, it often does. Pressures created by time constraints can have a debilitating effect on a group or can be harnessed to 'mobilize strengths', as Shoemaker suggests (Alissi and Casper, 1985). In all work with marginalised populations, mobilising strengths is of the essence; in group practice, this involves in particular respecting the conditions for adult learning and engaging in meaningful group activities.

The conditions for adult learning

In the model of practice under discussion here, goals are conceptualised as adult learning goals; thus the importance of identifying the conditions which facilitate adult learning.

Knowles (1975) has suggested that adults learn best when they are in control of what and how they learn (of content and process). He bases his theory on the assumptions that an adult's self-concept involves self-directedness; that adults understand in terms of their experience; that an adult's need to perform various social roles produces the readiness to learn; and that most adults have a problem-centred orientation to learning, i.e. they are concerned with action and with applying what they learn. If these assumptions are correct, it would appear that adults are motivated to 'mobilise strengths in using present experiences in the group to become more productive in their lives' (Alissi and Casper, 1985, p.5). Therefore, a model of practice with marginalised populations will be concerned not so much about 'helping' or 'motivating' people to mobilise strengths, as about giving them the opportunity to do so - which implies adopting an adult learning paradigm.

This paradigm has implications in terms of self-determination and of empowerment, issues central to practice with marginalised populations if we assume that this practice is geared not so much to 'assisting' marginalised individuals with their needs, as to providing them with opportunities to mobilise their strengths and exercise their right to participate in the life of the community (Breton, 1989). Community organisation research on 'constituency self-determination' has identified various controlling mechanisms whereby organisations and their staffs constrain 'constituents' from participating in decisions which affect their lives (Brager and Specht, 1973). For example, the research indicates that staff use the argument that constituents are not 'ready' as a means of control, and the argument that constituents are not 'representative' of their milieu as a means of limiting their decision-making. This second argument was used by the staff in the early stages of the *Sistering* drop-in. A *Welcome Book* had been set up so that (among other purposes) the women could express anonymously what they thought of the drop-in and what changes they would like to see. It was a rudimentary tool which took into account the fact that many of the users would not communicate their criticisms or requests verbally to the staff. This instrument was perceived correctly by the staff as engaging the women in decisions concerning the operation of the drop-in, and it was soon discarded on the grounds that the commentators were not representative of the drop-in population.

The existence of controlling tendencies (of both professionals and para-professionals), as well as the realisation that lower socio-economic groups in general make relatively little use of voluntary associations (Rothman, 1974), suggest that group practice with marginalised populations requires educational approaches and techniques which encourage and facilitate participation. Such educational approaches have been developed in *Sistering* over the past ten years, as the program has learned to provide an effective blend of nurture and optimal challenges. Three years ago, one of the users, a woman who was then 74 years old and the president of SUGI, effectively lobbied City Hall to keep *Sistering* open on weekends. Backed up by her function as president of the user group, she had a petition drawn up and signed by about 60 women users, presented it to the Board of Directors at the Annual Meeting, and the next day gave a (short) speech to the Mayor and the Metro Social Services and Housing Committee. This woman had come to *Sistering* two years previously, 'not caring whether I was dead or alive' as she admits, but the drop-in and its program had restored her self-esteem and her sense of competence, and taught her to participate in and influence her community: she had become empowered (Milne, *Sistering Newsletter,* 1988).

The use of activities

However, participation can serve to obscure the failure to achieve social change (Brager and Specht, 1973). This warning from community organisers echoes social group workers' concerns about the misunderstanding and misuse of groups and group activities (Levinson, 1973). When activities are developed primarily as means to keep people busy or happy, they have the anaesthetic effect of deterring individuals from taking the kind of action that produces significant change in their lives. However, given the opportunity to engage in meaningful activities, the opposite is true: the Wednesday Discussion Group, for example, produced a *Resource Handbook* which not only provided specific information on easy-to-access community services, but allowed the homeless women in the group to regain some degree of control over their lives as they actively participated in solving resource-access problems that had plagued them constantly.

With marginalised populations, meaningful group activities are those through which the participants learn collectively to take social actions, as well as individually to take personal actions, which will impact their situation and/or problems. Practitioners (both professionals and para- professionals) are often tempted to dismiss time-limited groups, especially if participants come from disadvantaged populations, as incapable of taking action on important issues. The present model rejects this view, and assumes that marginalised individuals can and will participate in purposeful, learning-related and change-inducing group activities.

However, it does recognise that consciousness-raising, mobilisation and organisation, the three essential steps in social action, take time. Practitioners, while not giving up on time-limited groups, should not automatically opt for them either.

Professional practice in non-professional settings

The model also assumes that practice with marginalised populations must reach and engage the populations on their own turf (Breton, 1985). This means that professional practice can be expected to take place in host-settings such as soup kitchens and drop-ins run by volunteers or para-professionals - which indeed is often the case (see Lee, 1988). The model further assumes that mutual respect and effective communication are essential conditions for productive coexistence between professionals and paraprofessionals, just as they are for effective co-leadership of groups, and that these conditions rest on appropriate divisions of labour and of power.

The division of labour

The pioneers in community organisation assumed that one of their most important functions was to create links between systems (Newsletter, 1947). They recognised that effective communication between groups of people demands that problems of inter-organisational relationships be addressed. This recognition is essential to the establishment of a successful professional practice within a para- professional setting: first, everyone must understand that two systems are involved and secondly, a linkage function must be assigned and a plan for its effective performance must be worked out. This rational approach will prepare professionals and para-professionals to deal effectively with the conflicts that normally surface between systems. The social worker who led the Wednesday Discussion Group noted the absence of formal channels of communication and decision-making between herself and the

Sistering staff; nor were there formal channels between the group itself and the staff. From an organisational point of view, the group did not exist. Little wonder that problems involving the division of labour between the professional worker and the para-professional staff developed early and were never surmounted.

The second condition for effective coexistence between professionals and paraprofessionals is mutual respect. It is too often assumed, in practice, that mutual respect can survive the vicissitudes of intergroup life without active nurturance. This is a costly assumption, perhaps held because little guidance is available on how to sustain mutual respect - save for appeals to everyone's good will, which is ineffectual. A more realistic approach may be to investigate the concept of domain as it is understood in community organisation: 'A domain is an area of space, time or function which everyone "agrees" belongs to a certain organisation' (Tropman, 1974, p.149) - we could substitute the words "to a certain part of the total system'. Tropman goes on to note that: 'Competition occurs when two or more organisations are involved in the same domain'. For professionals and paraprofessionals to operate successfully within the same setting or service, they must specify as clearly as possible their respective 'domains'. Furthermore, they should expect a certain degree of competition, as they are all involved in the pursuit of the general objective of assuring the welfare of the users of that particular service or setting. When competing Visions' of that welfare surface, as they most assuredly will from time to time, the fact that all parties are prepared for the occurrence of competition will assist them to cope directly with the issues and problems raised, instead of either pretending they don't exist or resorting to destructive bickering and/or sabotage. It must be emphasised that when competing visions of the welfare of service users are accepted in a spirit of mutual respect, they act as a powerful mechanism to further the interests of the users. This is not to say that a discussion of competing visions will automatically lead to an optimal solution. For example, the *Sistering* paraprofessional staff distrusted social work services offered within the program, perceiving them as threats to the drop-in concept and to the nurturing aspects of the program. Board members and the program consultant, on the other hand, saw these services as adding to and complementing the program. These competing visions of the users' welfare were recognised and discussed informally", however, the staffs reservations did not change, and this was not confronted. Consequently, the professionally-led social work group never received the support it needed to have the utmost impact.

A related critical variable for efficient intersystem functioning is awareness of interdependency. Community organisers have warned that there should be a clear understanding of the aspect of interdependence between various parts of a system (Tropman, 1974). Whether this interdependence refers to goals or to means, it must be acknowledged openly, and all concerned must be prepared to deal with the problems and irritants that inevitably result from interdependence.

The division of power

The issues raised above apply equally to a discussion of the division of power. Suffice it here to emphasise that for professionals to work effectively in paraprofessional settings, discussions about respective areas of influence and power must take place in a formal context before a particular program is introduced, as well as after it is in operation. In approaching these discussions, it may be wise for practitioners to incorporate elements of negotiating and/or of bargaining models into their frame of reference. Practitioners often pay dearly for their relative unsophistication in these areas, and for their reluctance to admit that their practice involves an exercise of power.

A sophisticated approach to the division of power includes a sophisticated approach to the distribution of scarce resources. Service providers know that resources of staff, money and equipment are scarce, and that: 'Often there are intra-agency fights over the allocation of these resources' (Tropman and Erlich, 1974, p.166). Sensitivity to scarcity of resources is a sine qua non for professionals who practice in a paraprofessional setting. Discussing the scarcity, coming to terms on a fair allocation, accepting that some 'fights' might occur and being prepared for this eventuality increase the chances of productive coexistence between professionals and paraprofessionals. Reluctance to deal openly with scarcity of resources, on the other hand, leads to unproductive power plays.

For example, because of limited resources, the *Sistering* group met in the same room as all the other drop-in users. Dining an evaluation meeting following the termination of the group, the staff commented that they had had to spend a lot of time 'helping' the social groupworker by keeping other drop-in users from making too much noise. The social worker could not recall when they had had to spend time helping her out. Obviously, power struggles had taken and were still taking place. I believe the staff had interpreted the group's demands for concentrated attention (i.e. demands for work) as meaning that the group would have more power to influence the members than they had. That is why they resented having to spend some moments now and then asking other drop-in users not to disturb the group. This would also explain why the worker's records show that, occasionally, the staff would interrupt an intense group discussion to make a trivial announcement. Had issues of influence and power been discussed openly, there would have been less of such dysfunctional and disruptive power plays.

The state of marginalisation

A model which recognises the right of the marginalised to participate in the life of the community must also recognise their right to decide if the cost of participating in a given community is too high. Such a model assumes that marginalised people are decision-makers motivated at least in part to avoid failure, to avert risk and to maintain control over their lives (Breton, 1985). Thus it can be expected that they will hesitate to participate in a community when they sense that this community, via its institutions and power structures, contributes to their state of marginalisation and presumably would reject them again. Social workers are perceived, correctly, as part of the health and social welfare institutions of a community and as part of its power structures; if they want to effectively reach and engage marginalised populations, they must also be seen as having the will and the ability to work with these populations toward changes in those institutions and structures.

Socio-economic and political features of problems

The problems of marginalised populations are, in great measure, socio-economic in origin. Insufficient low-income housing, unemployment, inadequate community-based mental health services for the deinstitutionalised, to name but a few - these are not problems the marginalised have created for themselves. Moreover, these problems are political in that their resolution is dependent on policy decisions involving various power centres and structures in the society. To incorporate this reality into their practice, social workers need not neglect the personal aspects of problems, but must highlight their 'macro' or socioeconomic and political dimensions through a combination of consciousness-raising and of establishing dialogues and relationships between the marginalised and community representatives which can lead to social action and concrete changes (Lee, 1986). In the present model, it is assumed that consciousness-raising on the nature and resolution of problems needs to take place not only within marginalised populations but also within the community, which includes volunteer or para- professional host-settings and their staffs as well as professional social work institutions and social workers. As for establishing dialogues and relationships, again it is assumed that social workers will model competence, i.e. effective interaction with the environment, and take on an active teacher role both within marginalised populations and within the community.

The chronic nature of situations

Morales (1981) noted that the teacher/trainer role can lead to client empowerment. The issue of empowerment is crucial in work with marginalised and disadvantaged populations. However, it is a particularly difficult issue because chronic problem situations produce a tendency towards hopelessness and apathy in the people caught up in them (Solomon, 1976). At the same time, chronic situations produce in would-be helpers a tendency to give up challenging people in favour of supporting them - and support without challenge does not lead to learning and does not lead to empowerment. It is especially important for professionals who practice in paraprofessional settings to make systematic and sustained efforts to share with paraprofessionals the ability "to understand the artificial dichotomy between support and demand' (Gitterman and Shulman, 1986).

Moreover, one of the forms support often takes is that of protecting individuals from the harsh social, economic and institutional environments which have been instrumental in creating their problems. This nurturing approach has its value and its place in services to the disadvantaged. However, if this protective/nurturing stance results in the closure of boundaries between individuals or groups and their environment, if it isolates and insulates individuals or groups from their community, then the approach becomes part of the problem.

Conclusion

To further develop a model of social groupwork practice with marginalised populations, research is needed on how the dynamics of mutual aid impact the transactions between the group, the paraprofessional setting and the community. Given that groups cannot meet all the mutual support, affiliation, and social needs of the participants or, to paraphrase Janchill (1979), given that 'groups cannot go it alone', this research must address the following issues: Should social workers be more aware of the mutual support functions of communities? On the other hand, recognising that all communities are not supportive, should they think of both marginalised groups and the communities from which they are marginalised, as 'under-developed communities', as this concept is understood in community-organisation and development theory? If so, should practitioners think of group work with marginalised populations as necessarily involving some form of community development work?

At this point, one cannot but recall Margaret Hartford's warning that an ecological perspective (such as in the model discussed in this paper) throws an enormous amount of information in the lap of workers, and that it takes discipline not to forget about acting and reacting 'with caring and compassion, and concern for the benefit of each individual participant and the group collective whole' (Hartford, 1985, p.97). However, the times are such that social workers cannot afford the luxury of looking only at what goes on inside groups. Perhaps even working at the interface of groups and communities is not quite enough. As the situations of marginalised populations become more desperate, the task of influencing social policy urgently beckons all social workers.

References

Alissi, AS. and Casper, M. (1985) Time as a factor in social group work, *Social Work With Groups*, 8(2), pp.3-15.

Boff, L. (1985) *Church: Charisma and Power.* New York: Crossroads.

Brager, G. and Specht, H. (1973) *Community Organizing.* New York: Columbia University Press.

Breton, M. (1984) 'A drop-in program for transient women: promoting competence through the environment', *Social Work,* 29(6), pp.542-545.

Breton, M. (1985) 'Reaching and engaging people: issues and practice principles', *Social Work With Groups,* 8(3), pp.7-21.

Breton, M. (1989) 'Liberation theology, group work, and the right of the poor and oppressed to participate in the life of the community', *Social Work With Groups,* 12(3), pp.5-18.

Falk, H.S. (1988) *Social Work: The Membership Perspective.* New York: Springer Publishing Company.

Gitterman, A and Shulman, L. (1986) *Mutual Aid Groups and the Life Cycle.* Itasca, Ill: Peacock Publishing.

Hartford, M. (1985) 'Book review', *Social Work with Groups;* 8(1), pp.95-98.

Janchill, Sister M.P. (1979) 'People cannot go it alone' in C.B. Germain (ed.) *Social Work Practice: People and Environments.* New York: Columbia University Press.

Knowles, M. (1975) *Self-Directed Learning.* New York: Association Press.

Lang, N. (1972) 'A broad-range model of practice in the social work group', *Social Service Review,* XLVI, pp.76-89.

Lang, N. (1979) 'Some defining characteristics of the social work group: unique social form', *Social Work With Groups: Proceedings, 1979 Symposium.*

Lee, JAB. (1986) 'No place to go: homeless women' in Gitterman, A and

L. Shulman (eds.) *Mutual Aid Groups and the Life Cycle.* Itasca, Ill: Peacock Publishing.

Lee, JAB. (ed.) (1988) *Group Work with the Poor and Oppressed,* New York: The Haworth Press.

Levinson, KM. (1973) 'Use and misuse of groups', *Social Work,* 18(1), pp.66-73.

Lewis, E. (1983) 'Social group work in community life: group characteristics and worker role', *Social Work With Groups,* 6(2), pp.3-18.

Milne, C. (1988) 'How Evelyn saved the weekend drop-in program', *Sistering Newsletter.*

Moore, E.E. (1983) 'The group-in-situation as the unit of attention in social work with groups', *Social Work With Groups,* 6(2), pp.19-31.

Newstetter, W.I. (1948) 'The social intergroup work process' in *Proceedings of the National Conference of Social Work.* New York: Columbia University Press, pp.205-217.

Rothman, J. (1974) *Planning and Organizing for Social Change.* New York: Columbia University Press.

Schopler, J.H. and Galinsky, M J. (1984) 'Meeting practice needs: conceptualizing the open-ended group', *Social Work With Groups,* 7(2), pp.3-21.

Solomon, B.B. (1976) *Black Empowerment: Social Work in Oppressed Communities.* New York: Columbia University Press.

Stewart, S. (1986) *Records of the Wednesday Discussion Group.*

Tropman, J.E. (1974) 'Conceptual approaches in interorganizational analysis', in Cox, FJM. et al. (eds.) *Strategies of Community Organization.* Itasca, ID: Peacock Publishing.

Tropman, J.E. and Erlich, J.L. (1974)'Strategy, introduction' in Cox, FM. et al. (eds.) *Strategies of Community Organization,* Itasca, Ill: Peacock Publishing.

This chapter was first published in 1991 in *Groupwork* Vol. 4(1), pp.31-47

At the time of writing Margot Breton taught social work at the University of Toronto

Breaking the culture of silence: Groupwork and community development

Jacky Drysdale and Rod Purcell

This article intends to introduce the reader to the principles and actions of community development, through one of the principal methods; groupwork. It does this by offering one case example of the groupwork aspects of a community development group. This example is set in the context of the growing importance of a community development approach to meeting current political imperatives; such as combating social exclusion, working in partnership with communities (either of interest or geography), and promoting participation within the political and democratic processes. Some reflections are offered on the history of community development and its value base. Community development seeks to challenge oppressions and encourage people to be vocal and active in identifying their own concerns and seeking appropriate solutions for them.

The here and now

Since the mid 1990s community development has been undergoing a rediscovery in the United Kingdom. The turning point was marked by a speech given by Virginia Bottomley, then Secretary of State for Heritage in September 1996. That speech recognised the significance of the social exclusion of citizens, and the need to reverse this trend through partnerships with communities.

From May 1997 many UK Government speeches (see for example, Blair, 1997) and policies have placed social inclusion at their heart. They acknowledge the need to support communities in relating with government and agencies (HMSO, 1999a), to encourage proactive self-help, and recognise the importance of personal growth and learning throughout the life cycle for all citizens (Cmd.4048). This is clear in the health sector from the document 'Our Healthier Nation' (Cmd.3854 and Cmd.4269) and the development of Healthy Living Centres and Health Actions Zones.

In the social and economic spheres the community development process requires local involvement in rural and urban regeneration bids (Social Inclusion Partnerships and Single Regeneration Budget programmes). The process contributes to environmental sustainability through, for example, the implementation of local Agenda 21 initiatives; These initiatives support sustainable development as a result of Chapter 28 of Agenda 21, the United Nation's sustainable development action plan for the 21st century, which was agreed at the Earth Summit in Rio de Janeiro in 1992. The process is also part of community safety initiatives, the development of housing associations and housing co-operatives, of issues relating to community planning and the decentralisation of government, and of planning for real and community care (HMSO, 1998.). Overall, community development is concerned with the promotion of active citizenship.

In the late 1990s then, community development is practiced in diverse settings under a wide variety of names across the community, voluntary and local authority sectors (CoSLA 1990; Purcell 1998; Barr, Drysdale and Henderson 1997). Community development is no longer the province of a group of community workers. It has become a method of working for social welfare organisations, housing agencies, health service workers, health promotion workers, educators, economic development workers, town and country planners and ecologists who seek to promote change in partnership with communities. This expansion necessitates a clear understanding of the approach and clear links to other skills located within the training and experience of these professions. Groupwork may be one of these generic skills.

One example of a community development group

Tuckman (1965) produced a model that explores the development process of a group, through the stages of 'Forming', 'Storming', 'Norming' and 'Performing'. The model was later elaborated to include a 'Mourning' stage. As with all groups (Whitaker, 1985), community development groups start by encouraging individuals to interact with each other, by learning skills and increasing knowledge about themselves and each other, by establishing moods and atmospheres. In community development these stages encourage the development of personal empowerment and ensuring that action is taken to challenge oppressive practices.

The processes involved can be illustrated by examining the establishment of a drugs forum through a community council and a community health project in a Scottish town (see Barr, Drysdale and Henderson, 1997). A group of local residents on a housing estate expressed concerns about the increase of drug use after a young person had died. The community council and the community health project joined forces to acknowledge the visibility of drug use in the area. They discussed with agencies and politicians what local people could do to reduce drug misuse. Some of the people were already experienced community activists, and they managed to recruit a variety of other local people who were parents or who had an interest in the issue. This was the 'forming' phase of the group. Forming is when the group members are preoccupied with getting involved and being included.

In general people will become engaged with community development groups for a number of reasons (Henderson and Thomas, 1992) which may alter with time:

- to protect their personal and/or family interests;
- for social and cultural activities and support;
- to improve the quality of life within their community;
- to preserve or create community assets;
- to examine opportunities or repel threats whether real or perceived.

For this community group there were aspects of protecting family interests, improving the quality of life in the area and repelling a threat. Through the action of meeting together as a group, and with the support of a community worker, people began to recognise a common interest and to reach a contract for group action. When people began to critically evaluate themselves and their social situation, they gave credence to the possibility of change, which enabled them to build confidence and assertiveness over time.

However, to reach this point the people involved had to deal with the stage of storming. During this process people tested out themselves and other people in the group. Roles were sought or rejected, and power was a significant dynamic. The initial view expressed by the group was that the identification and expulsion of drug dealers, who lived locally, would solve the problem. This view exposed many differences of understanding, of values and of attitudes within the group. As is often the case during this stage, people also made some irrelevant contributions, as group norms were not yet established. Yet the debate generated some frank discussions and highlighted the need to try to establish what would be a fair and just response.

On further investigation, and as a result of researching the experiences of other neighbourhoods, the initiative was rejected as ineffective. Clearly through that difficult stage of seeking cohesion, shared concerns were strong enough to enable networking and discussions with other interest groups. The role of the worker in supporting and facilitating the group through these difficult times was crucial. This role reflects the experiences of groupwork writers such as Schwartz (1961), Shulman (1984), Douglas (1976) and Doel and Sawdon (1999). During that phase the group had to respond to prejudices relating to young people, drug users, rival territories and attitudes towards agencies and services. Members needed to disclose their views and have their ideas and prejudices challenged. The group needed to increase their awareness, knowledge and skills about the real issues.

Then came the 'norming' phase of the group's development. During 'norming' a culture of trust and belonging developed. A belief system emerged that, though not entirely consensual, could be sanctioned by everyone. The group established and enforced policies of equal opportunities, and later, when they received funding to employ staff, made stringent efforts to ensure that local people had equal opportunities to be appointed to the jobs. Through the storming and norming stages issues of dealing with oppression were made central to the work of the group.

The phase of the group where thoughts and ideas were translated into tangible actions (performing) came when the group improved its networks within the community. The tasks were focused and the group began to function effectively. The group started to expand its membership by including a wider range of people. They established a community organisation and publicised it in the area. They visited local schools and youth organisations. They exchanged information and ideas with local agencies and with other people concerned with drug misuse in the area. From this phase clear outputs and outcomes emerged. The members also wanted to work with young people in extending their access to, and knowledge of, a drug free lifestyle. To this end a workshop that involved local people and agencies in mutual learning, and managed to develop a partnership that could have some impact on the problem they had defined.

The workshop was a great success and the 'performing' stage was in full flow. The group also instigated a local drug forum. They worked in partnership with local voluntary and statutory agencies to identify gaps in the services, including a needle exchange point to reduce the numbers of needles found in the street. They worked with families, neighbours and friends around the apprehension of having this exchange clinic situated on the estate, by highlighting the benefits, and monitoring the difficulties. They received a small grant to develop an 'Alternative to Drugs Programme' for drug users in the area. One night each week users who were drug free got involved in other activities and in peer support. These activities involved appointing, training and managing staff, and accountability for budgets.

We would like to emphasise that the group process was not a linear experience: indeed workers changed, members left and were replaced and so various aspects of 'mourning' were experienced. The fact that a bid to become a partner in the development of a local drug team failed was a particular low point. Yet after each set back the common objectives could be revisited. A struggle similar to storming followed, but a consensus for joint work was re-established.

In community development terms such stages of group development are needed to create strong community organisations, and enable the participation of local people in political and democratic power relationships.

For the drug forum, the ability to influence policy and practice followed soon after the conference. The drug forum became influential, and was invited to work closely with health staff, social work staff and the voluntary agencies to develop policy and practice in the locality. This could have been the final phase of the community development process when people begin to understand how to use their own power to influence policy and practice. However, in community development the process continues so that achievements are sustainable. Therefore, while there are often transitions and changes, endings are less frequently encountered than in other forms of groupwork.

What is community development?

Community development is the underpinning theory of community work practice and has a long history in the UK. Its nature and purpose has changed over time (for fuller discussion, see the community development writer Popple; 1995).

> It is an approach which strengthens local democracy and the capacity and voice of communities to participate actively in determining the process and outcomes of social and economic change. A range of professionals and agencies can adopt this approach. (Scottish Community Work Forum, 1994)

The beginnings of community development can be traced back to two discrete foundations, 'benevolent altruism' (such as that associated with Victorians like John Ruskin) and grass roots community action. The first influence came through the working men's educational institutions of the 19th century, the early University settlements and various self help schemes developed amongst the poor of the Victorian era (Jacobs and Popple, 1994; Craig and Mayo, 1995).

From the 1920s onward community associations were developed around social and cultural activities, particularly on the inter-war housing estates. Much of the focus of this work was centred on social, educational and leisure activities. However, it was in the post war era that community development as we recognise it today began to fully take shape. The transfer to independence of the former British colonies throughout the 1950s and 1960s led to the return to the UK of community development workers who had been instrumental in building local administrations for independence. Alongside this in the 1960s was the growth of a more grass roots based radical practice in working class communities, for example the squatters movement and campaigns around housing (O'Malley, 1977; Radford, 1970).

The Community Development Projects from the late 1960s and 1970s, were funded by the Home Office, and attempted to tackle pockets of urban poverty. These projects developed a political, economic and structural critique of poverty (see: CDP inter-project editorial team, 1977). Many people have argued that they failed to develop a linked model of practice (Loney, 1983; Waddington, 1983). Yet throughout the 1970s and early 1980s practice became increasingly incorporated into local government activity through urban programme funding, the growth of the Youth and Community Service in England, the Community Education Service in Scotland and the movement in some authorities towards community social work practice (Cockburn, 1977; Barclay Report, 1982).

From the mid 1980s onwards community development was affected by a number of other influences. Firstly, feminist theory (Hanmer and Rose, 1980; Rowbotham, 1992) and practice were adopted by community development workers. This led to consideration of gender, process and personal politics. Secondly, the ethnic minority communities highlighted issues of race and culture alongside the traditional class analysis of community development (Sivanandan, 1990). Simultaneously community development became a victim of local authority funding cuts and of the Thatcher dictum that rejected the whole notion of society. The Major and now the Blair administrations have begun to reverse this decline.

Various contemporary definitions of community development have been put forward by various bodies such as the Association of Metropolitan Authorities, Voluntary Activities Unit of the Home Office, Combat Poverty Agency in Ireland, Federation of Community Work Training (see Barr, Hashegan & Purcell, 1996). They all have the following principles in common. Community development:

- involves promoting change;
- seeks to challenge social exclusion and promote full citizenship;
- is anti discriminatory in its outlook, and practice;
- encourages empowerment of individuals and groups through increased participation in decision making;
- has an educative function in relation to the community and the organisations which work with those communities;
- seeks to collectivise and develop new forms of association and organisation.

If the values and principles above tell you what community development aims to do, the next question is how it achieves this. In October 1996, the Scottish Community Development Centre completed research commissioned by the DHSS in Northern Ireland. That project produced a report that provided a functional analysis of the dimensions and elements that were necessary for a community development process to be claimed (Barr, Hashegan & Purcell, 1996). The process involved four core dimensions:

1. Personal empowerment;
2. Positive action;
3. Community Organisation;
4. Power relationships and participation.

These dimensions are interrelated and should be viewed as a 'checklist' to decide to what extent community development is taking place. It is however important to have some idea about the practical manifestations of these rather abstract terms.

These elements reflect the values and purposes of community development highlighted above. In addition the model requires the outputs and outcomes of community development to be identified and measured in both quantitative and qualitative terms. These outputs and outcomes relate largely to the degree of *empowerment* at individual, family, group and community levels and the changes in the *quality of people's lives*.

1. Personal empowerment	2. Positive action
• the development of informal skills and knowledge (through the community development activity) by local people • formal or non formal training and education about the purpose of the activity, or the process of working • a conscious belief in the possibility of change • development of leadership	• understanding of needs in relation to discrimination • existence of equal opportunity policies • evidence of equal opportunities practice • affirmation and assertion of cultural heritage and identity

3. Development of community organisations	4. Power relationships and participation
• investigation and monitoring of community needs • nature of the recorded activities run by community organisations • levels of activity in community organisations • support networks between people/community organisations in the community	• openness and accountability of community organisations • understanding of policy frameworks and political systems • effective influence by community organisations on public policy or practice

Community development and groupwork

Promoting change that combats social exclusion and discriminatory attitudes and practice cannot solely be an individual activity. Oppressive conditions and discrimination originate within institutional and cultural levels of society. Changing these requires individual personal growth, but its success lies in the ability to generate effective organisations that can challenge institutions, agencies and governments, and create movement in terms of understanding, policy and practice. This is the logical conclusion of ideas developed by groupworkers such as the 'mutual aid system' proposed by Scwhartz (1961, p.7-34) or Lee's 'empowerment group approach' (1994, p.208-261).

Mutual aid and empowerment necessitate mutual learning experiences by citizens in terms of the rights and responsibilities of their citizenship and by governments in terms of recognising and responding to people's experiences and aspirations. As Lee (1999) wrote:

> The very existence of the group provides potential for personal and political empowerment and for strengthening and restoring human connection. (Lee, 1999, p.8)

Community development is a change activity. It seeks to galvanise people who are disadvantaged or excluded to examine their experiences and commonalties and to determine and prioritise their needs. Through this process people are enabled to organise around their common needs. This animation of people can be in a geographical location or around issues or experiences that motivate people to take action.

In community development, perhaps more sharply than in some forms of groupwork, there should be clear outputs (products of the action; e.g. establishing drug advice services) and outcomes (effects of the action; e.g. change in drug use patterns). The process that facilitates this also receives significant attention. There are both individual and group components, but community development is founded on the principle that the medium of collective action is essential:

> ... that every human being, ... is capable of looking critically at his world in a dialogical encounter with others. Provided with the proper tools for this encounter, he can gradually perceive his personal and social reality as well as the contradictions in it, become conscious of his own perception of that reality and deal critically with it. (Schull, 1972 in Freire, 1972, p 8)

For community development to take place it is not enough just to be aware of the group dynamics and the stages 'forming – storming – norming –performing -mourning'. Workers need also to understand the personal development experienced by group

Group process:
Forming
Storming
Norming
Performing

Developing individual
consciousness—
Moving boundaries—
Breaking silence

Group tasks
for promoting change

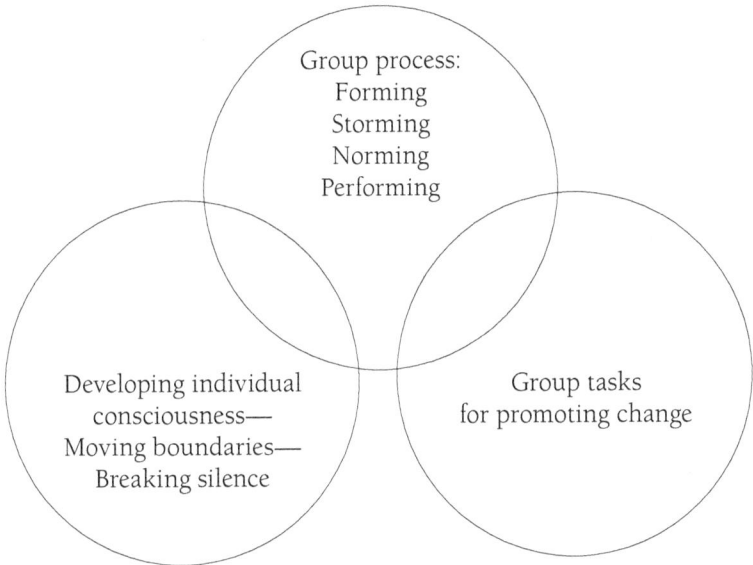

members and assist the group to focus on the essential tasks that need to be pursued if change is to be achieved. Community development happens almost exclusively in groups. However, this does not mean that groupwork theories are acknowledged or practised effectively. When groupwork is used as the principal method of promoting community development, there is a clear awareness of the personal level, and of group dynamics; there is a clear plan and process for change, and mutual learning is identified and acknowledged. The authors have called this 'community development groupwork'.

The personal and task-oriented aspects of community development groupwork can be explained through the work of Freire (1972 and 1974) and Henderson and Thomas (1992). The above diagram illustrates the overlap of these activities.

Paulo Freire (1972; 1974) has explored how groupwork techniques can help people develop their critical understanding of themselves and their life. Freire's approach is used widely in the developing world and his approach also works well in the UK. It can be applied to any group setting.

Freire argues that the role of the worker in the group setting is to act as a facilitator. The worker in a community development context should not be leading the group to a predetermined end, but enable group members to gain a greater understanding of their personal, family and community situation. For this to happen group members have to develop a more critical level of consciousness. Lee (1994) uses many quotes and ideas from Freire and his three main levels of consciousness to explore both individual and groupwork practice. These are explained below.

Firstly, there is 'Magical Consciousness' when people accept the oppressions of external powerful forces; they do not fully comprehend the socio-economic or other social contradictions that exist in our world. They do not believe in the possibility of change because they are caught in the 'Culture of Silence'. Such silence can operate at a community level, for example in a community living in substandard housing, where there are few job opportunities and where schooling and health services are inadequate. Magical consciousness also operates at the personal level, for example among women subject to domestic violence who feel trapped and where their suffering is unheard and unacknowledged.

Freire defines the next level as 'Naïve Consciousness'. This is where people can reflect on their situation and begin to make connections with social, economic and political issues. However, the worldview at this level is very much one of individualised experience. For example, the non-availability of good housing may be blamed on single parents or the shortage of jobs on immigrants. At this level issues are subject to simplistic analysis and emotional responses often with other social groups being classified as deserving or undeserving.

The major step of viewing life through 'Critical Consciousness' does not come until people engage with the context of the outside world on an analytical basis. The impact of structural and cultural discrimination is understood, and problems move from being private troubles to becoming public issues (C. Wright Mills, 1959). It is essential to the community development process that the object of the work and activities are generated by the group themselves as a result of this process of consciousness development.

Related to these levels of consciousness is Freire's concept of 'Boundary Situations'. He contends that we all repress ourselves through imposing a boundary on our own actions as a result of internalising the cultural norms of oppressive institutions and belief systems. Through using a problem posing technique, the groupworker should facilitate the group to question these assumptions, to develop a more critical view of themselves and their community and shift their self defined boundaries. If this expansion of boundaries is achieved, belief in the possibility of change becomes conceivable. The group is then able to move from the Reflective phase to developing a Vision of a better personal and collective future, and go forward to Plan and undertake Action to these ends.

Henderson and Thomas (1992) developed a model that outlines the various tasks each community development group has to accomplish to effectively promote change. These tasks can be identified as:

- Making contacts and people coming together;
- Forming and building an organisation;
- Clarify goals and priorities;
- Keeping the organisation going;
- Dealing with friends and enemies;
- Leavings and endings.

The processes that lead to accomplishing these tasks are not necessarily linear. Community development groups often work over a long period of time. After all, promoting change is never easy. The group may loose and recruit members constantly throughout its life. The group may also have a number of successes as well as failures. The ability to sustain group activity through the highs and lows requires particular skills and awareness on the part of the groupworker.

Conclusion

Success in community development groupwork involves working on multiple processes simultaneously. The process involved in the stages of forming, storming, norming and performing are common to many groups. In addition the development of group members' critical understanding of themselves and the wider group tasks is necessary. As these processes unfold, changes in the aims, purposes and activities of the group can be expected (Mullender & Ward, 1991; Lee 1994; 1999). The challenge for the groupworker is to understand these multiple processes and to facilitate their progression. The reward is the empowerment of individuals with collective strength and cohesion to contribute to positive change in their communities; to break the 'culture of silence' and promote a more active exchange between policy makers and citizens. Achieving this shift may convert the rhetoric of current policies into the reality of an improved quality of life for ordinary people.

Three major sources

We include for further reference, three diverse approaches to undertaking groupwork in community development settings:

- Lee, J.A.B. (1994) *The Empowerment Approach to Social Work Practice.* New York. Columbia University Press.
  This is an excellent example of using a community development approach to working with individuals and groups of people. While Lee does not overtly use the term community development, her work follows closely the value base of community development by trying to find ways to deal with oppression and 'seek liberation' for people in poverty or those experiencing social welfare difficulties

- Hope, A and Timmel, S. (1995) *Training for Transformation.* (3 volumes) Zimbabwe: Mambo Press
  This is a practical book that provides many accessible exercises for the application of Freire's work to groups. Book 1 focuses on the basic method and the reflection and vision stages. Book 2 is concerned with group dynamics, developing leadership and participation, decision

making, planning and evaluation. Book 3 looks at linking global issues to the local context and how to develop local trainers and workshops.

- Henderson, P. and Thomas, D, (1992) *Skills in Neighbourhood Work.* London: Routledge
  The book takes an implicit pluralist approach with the focus very much on working within a neighbourhood. It is valuable as a 'how to do it' guide. Each of the chapters provides a thoughtful range of issues to be considered by the groupworker. For those who are new to working with community groups this book will prove to be indispensable

References

Agazarian,Y. and Peters, R. (1981) *The Visible and Invisible Group: Two perspectives on group psychotherapy and group process.* London: Routledge & Kegan Paul

Barclay, P. (1982) *Social workers: their role and tasks: The report of a working party ; set up in October 1980 at the request of the Secretary of State for Social Services by the National Institute for Social Work; under the chairmanship of Peter M. Barclay.* London: National Institute for Social Work

Barr, A, Hashegan, S. and Purcell, (1996) *Monitoring and Evaluation of Community Development in Northern Ireland.* Belfast: Voluntary Activity Unit. DHSS

Barr, A., Drysdale, J. and Henderson, P. (1997) *Towards Caring Communities.* Brighton: Pavilion

Benjamin J., Bessant, J. and Watts, R. (1997) *Making Groups Work. Rethinking practice.* St. Leonards, Australia: Allen and Unwin.

CDP Inter-Project Editorial Team (1977) *Guilding the Ghetto. The state and poverty experiments.* (Cmd 3854) London: HMSO

Cockburn, C. (1977) *The Local State.* London: Pluto Press.

CoSLA (1990) *Recommendations for the Way Forward in the Identification of Standards Linked to Vocational Qualifications: Community work feasibility study.* London: Care Sector Consortium, Voluntary Organisations Group

Craig, G. and Mayo, M. (1995) Community Empowerment: A reader in participation and development. Atlantic Highlands, NJ: Zed Books

Doel, M. and Sawdon, C. (1999) *Teaching and Learning Creative Groupwork.* London. Jessica Kingsley

Douglas, T. (1976) *Groupwork Practice.* London. Tavistock.

Douglas, T. (1983) *Groups: Understanding people gathered together.* London. Routledge

Freire, P. (1972) *Education: The Practice of freedom.* London, Writers and Readers Publishing Co-operative

Freire, P. (1974) *Pedagogy of the Oppressed.* Harmondsworth: Penguin

Hanmer, J. and Rose, H. (1980) Making sense of theory. in P. Henderson, D. Jones and D.N. Thomas (eds) *The Boundaries of Change in Community Work.* London: Allen and Unwin

Henderson, P. and Thomas, D. (1992) *Skills in Neighbourhood Work.* (2nd ed). London: Routledge.

HMSO (1998) *Working Together for Healthier Scotland: A consultation document.* 1998. (Cmd 4048). Edinburgh: HMSO

HMSO (1998) *Opportunity Scotland: A paper on life long learning.* Edinburgh: HMSO

HMSO (1998) *Modernising Community Care: An Action Plan.* London: HMSO

HMSO (1999a) *Bringing Britain Together: A national strategy for neighbourhood renewal.* London: HMSO

HMSO (1999b) *Towards a Healthier Scotland.* Edinburgh: HMSO

Hope, A, and Timmel, S. (1995) *Training for Transformation.* (3 volumes) Zimbabwe: Mambo Press.

Jacobs, S. and Popple, K. (1994) (eds.) *Community Work in the 1990s.* Nottingham: Spokesman

Lee, J.A.B. (1994) *The Empowerment Approach to Social Work Practice.* New York: Columbia University Press.

Lee, J.A.B. (1999) Crossing bridges: Groupwork in Guyana. *Groupwork,* 11,1, pp.6-23

Loney, M. (1983) . *Community against Government: The British Community Development Project 1968-78.* London: Heinemann Educational

Mills, C.W. (1959) *The Sociological Imagination.* Harmondsworth: Pelican

Mullender, A, and Ward, D. (1992) *Self-Directed Groupwork: Users take action for empowerment.* London: Whiting and Birch

O'Malley, J. (1977) *The Politics of Community Action.* Nottingham: Bertrand Russell Peace Foundation

Popple, K. (1995) *Analysing Community Work: Its theory and practice.* Buckingham: Open University Press.

Purcell, R. (1998) *Mapping of the Community Work Occupational Domain to Research Potential Numbers for the N/SVQ.* Sheffield: Community Work Forum

Radford, J. (1970) From King Hill to the Squatting Association. in A. Lapping (ed) *Community Action*. (Fabian Tract 400) London: Fabian Society

Rowbotham, S. (1992) *Women and Movement: Feminism and social action*. London: Routledge

Schull, R (1972). Forward to *Pedagogy of the Oppressed* by Paulo Freire. Penguin: Harmondsworth

Schwartz, W. (1961) The social worker in the group. in *New Perspectives on Services to Groups: Theory, organisation, practice*. New York: National Association of Social Workers.

Scottish Community Work Forum (1994). Edinburgh: Scottish Community Education Council

Shulman, L. (1984) *The Skills of Helping Individuals and Groups*. (2nd ed) New York: Columbia University Press

Sivanandan, A. (1990) *Communities of Resistance: Writings on black struggles for socialism*. London: Verso

Touraine, A. (1981) *The Voice and the Eye. An analysis of social movements*. Cambridge: Cambridge University Press

Tuckman, B.W. (1965) Developmental sequence in small groups. *Psychological Bulletin*, 63, pp.384-99

Waddington, P. (1983) Looking Ahead- Community work in the 1980s in D.N. Thomas (ed) *Community Work in the Eighties*. London: NISW

Whitaker, D. (1985) *Using Groups to Help People*. London: Routledge

This chapter was first published in 1999 in *Groupwork* Vol. 11(3), pp.70-87

At the time of writing Jacky Drysdale was Lecturer in Social Work, and Rod Purcell was Lecturer in Community Development and Adult Education, both at Glasgow University

Social action
and self-directed
groupwork:

Section 3
Supporting practice:
Training, consultation
and facilitation

Social action groupwork as negotiation: Contradictions in the process of empowerment

Eamonn Keenan and John Pinkerton

This paper is about the process and outcomes to date of a series of discussions between a social action worker and a social work lecturer in Belfast. The central theme of the paper is contradiction within practice committed to empowerment. It is an attempt to take our discussion and theorising further by bringing it to a wider audience. Our aim is to contribute to defining the nature of social action groupwork and to identify appropriate forms of support.

You must assume responsibility for your own professional growth and evolution. No one can develop your practice for you. You must do the work yourself. But at times it can be a painful and difficult experience and you will need support, guidance and encouragement. So assuming responsibility for your professional growth involves setting up a support system which will contain you while you question and examine your practice. (Jarlath Benson, 1987, p. 244)

This article is a statement by and about two actors in just such a support system: one a member of Save the Children Fund's (SCF) Belfast based Youth Unit and an experienced social action groupworker, the other a social work lecturer, with a special interest in practice strategies which resource members of families to work on needs they identify as their own.

The 'times' that prompted Eamonn to set up his support system, and include John in it, are times of change. In Northern Ireland, as elsewhere, SCF is in the process of realigning its work - a realignment neatly summed up in the title of the division's youth work strategy paper 'Challenges to Powerlessness'. Change is disconcerting. Even for a Worker like Eamonn, with a social action perspective, the newly explicit commitment by SCF to empowerment threw up its challenges. Finding a way of articulating the experience of this challenge was the business of a series of monthly meetings we have been having. This paper is about the process and outcome of those meetings to date and thereby, we hope, a contribution to defining the nature of social action groupwork and to identifying forms of support appropriate for those engaged in it.

Getting started

As the starting point for our meetings, we had Eamonn's concern to make sense of and define his role in relation to the opportunity and demands SCF was making on him by re-designating him the primary social action worker for the Belfast Youth Unit. We judge 'concern' to be the appropriate term here because what we are referring to is Eamonn's lived, felt, sense of challenge about the possibilities and pitfalls of his situation; the felt need that had led him, with encouragement from his agency, to set up a support system that included outsiders such as John.

To Eamonn's concern we added what we identified as John's motivation for agreeing to join the support network; his concern about how to develop and check out ideas about practice now that he only experienced it in a very occasional and limited fashion. Through describing and discussing our concerns with each other we generated a set of issues that we could share. We reckoned that we could do limited, focused work on these issues. In addition we expected spin-offs for each of us in other work we wanted to do on the concerns that we had identified. We recognised that work as being our own separate, more personally immediate business.

In this way, we negotiated a shared task, from which we hoped to gain both shared and separate things. We regard terms such as supervision, consultancy or support as too loose and tending to suggest a one up status for the supervisor, consultant or support person.

We agreed on four issues to work on together over a six month period. Each of them we saw as an area of particular challenge and fraught with tensions. The areas were:

1. personal practice ideology;
2. the relationships between service workers and users;
3. operationalising agency objectives as tasks;
4. the role of the voluntary sector

As so often with agenda setting we were overly ambitious. We have only managed to do work of any significance in relation to the first two areas. This is reflected in what follows.

Practice grounding

As we were both concerned, albeit in different ways, with practice, our next step was to explore the relationship between the issues we had identified and Eamonn's practice. We had the issues, so what we needed next was the practice to relate them to. We opted to do this retrospectively by identifying an incident which had involved one of the groups Eamonn was working with.

The group consisted of six young women, aged between 17 and 18. They are a natural peer group all from the same area; a large modern housing estate on the outskirts of Catholic West Belfast, where socio-economic deprivation and the 'troubles' are part of everyday life. Eamonn's stated commitment from the outset of his work with this group was to use a social action approach. In addition to this being his preferred style of work, he perceived it as appropriate to the young women's situation. His intention was to facilitate the group in addressing issues that they had identified as important to them. Reflecting this, his approach was to address issues within the group which were clearly located within their own life experience. Their issues were about their feelings of containment, abuse and control. These were experienced within relationships in the home, the neighbourhood and at work.

Coincidental with the beginning stage of the group, Eamonn received notification of a residential weekend being organised for young women to discuss their needs. The information indicated that only two women would be accepted from any one project. Eamonn brought the material he had received to the group for discussion. Two of the group had prior commitments for the weekend in question but the other four were all keen to attend. They asked Eamonn to telephone the organisers and try for the two extra places they wanted. This he agreed to do and was successful in getting the additional places. As transport posed a major difficulty for the young women, he also agreed to drive them to and from the residential venue.

Many youth workers will identify with this fairly typical chain of events. What made Eamonn choose it for our discussion was that it had left him, a social action worker, attempting to empower the group with a nagging feeling that he had failed to match his practice to his theory. The information about the residential weekend came to him, the adult, male worker; he gave the information to the group; he telephoned and negotiated the four places; he supplied the transport. The dependency of the group members on the worker was clearly reasserted at each step. But even worse in his view was the way that he had lost a string of opportunities to engage the young women in understanding what was happening.

Of course, Eamonn knew he could justify what happened on the basis of the reality constraints he was working with. The information came to him as part of a routine mailing to organisations working with young people. The group was only in its infancy and its members had not yet established themselves in taking responsibility for this sort of situation. Telephones and transport were not readily available to group members. The limits of time demanded an immediate response or the places might have been taken. Certainly, opportunities had been lost for group members to gain skills such as negotiating over the telephone, but really that was secondary to the chance being offered by the weekend for learning at a more in-depth and intensive level.

But identifying these 'realities' did not help. Eamonn continued to be nagged by what he saw as the 'facts' that the group was dependent on him for information, it had handed over responsibility for its own activities so easily, and that by acting as he had, he had maintained an unequal relationship that had removed from the group opportunities for developing its autonomy. In Eamonn's view, what he aspired to as a social action groupworker, and what he actually had done, were in conflict. Yet he still could not see what other options there were for him which could have resolved the conflict. Refusing to have done these things for the group, and thereby losing the opportunity provided by the weekend, would have been just as clear a statement of dependency; but a repressive rather than a benign dependency.

Towards an analysis

Having identified this practice incident and Eamonn's views and feelings about it our next step was to relate it to our list of issues. Personal practice ideology was top of our list.

By personal practice ideology, we mean the set of ideas that all workers carry around inside their heads with which they think their everyday work experience. This set of ideas form a framework of reference points by which workers can describe and evaluate and thereby engage with the situations they find themselves facing. It is these conceptual frameworks that allow workers to make sense of a practice situation; as it is, as it ideally might be, and as realistically it might be made to become.

By way of this conceptual framework, or practice ideology as we prefer to call it, options are identified and choices made inside the head of the worker. Practice ideology provides and furnishes the conceptual space in which a worker manoeuvres prior to opting for any particular course of action. The outcome of the action that results from this thinking work, conceptual manoeuvring, may be perceived as success or failure, but either way it creates a new experience for the worker's ideology to make sense of. The new experience will either reinforce or challenge the practice ideology that prompted the choice of the particular course of action that resulted in the experience. It seemed to us that Eamonn's practice experience with his group was an example of a challenge to a worker's practice ideology. So as our next step we turned to trying to spell out Eamonn's implicit practice ideology so that we could be clear about what it was that was being challenged.

Personal practice ideology

Eamonn felt it relevant to begin by identifying some of the broad underpinnings of his personal ideology. First was a sense of class identity. Like the young women in the group he came from a background of socio-economic deprivation, lack of educational achievement at school and the experience of interventions by statutory agencies that were generally ineffective. Linked to this class identity was a rejection of the inequality and restricted life chances it represented. This rejection had led him to study as a mature student and from there into youth and community work. On the way he incorporated Freire's notion of 'conscientisation' into his personal ideology. From the ideological reference points he already had he could engage with Freire's ideas:

> ... discovering myself oppressed I know that I will be liberated only if I try to transform the oppressing situation in which I find myself (Adult Learning Project).

> Those who work for liberation must not take advantage of the emotional dependence of the oppressed. ... Using their dependence to create still greater dependence is an oppressor tactic (Freire, 1980, p. 42).

As for ideas specifically about youth and community work he found that what Smith (1981) and Davies (1981) were arguing for synchronised with his basic ideology. They defined an agenda for work with young people in a way that Eamonn was ideologically disposed to value. Davies' assertion that state social policy towards young people is aimed at gaining:

> ... young people's containment, and if possible their uncomplaining adjustment to the often personally demeaning demands of a reconstructed economy and political order under growing stress (p. 14)

was a description that is in line with Eamonn's idea of class oppression. When Smith suggested that there were strategies and professional skills that could help young people:

> ... gain for themselves the necessary knowledge, understanding and develop the feelings, attitudes and values to be able to think and act

in ways that will increase their control over their own lives and their ability to speak for themselves,

he legitimised both Eamonn's continued identification with his class background and his educational and occupational movement away from it. Within this ideological framework he could understand his becoming a qualified youth and community worker as a way of gaining something to offer others like himself in their struggle against oppression.

For illustration of what this approach meant in practice, Eamonn looked to the Nottingham Young Volunteers. The practice principles by which that project worked combined descriptive and prescriptive aspects in line with the practice ideology he had developed. As part of its prescription for empowering young people it emphasised the power of groupwork. As Ward put it quite clearly:

> The key task is to create opportunities for choice which mean something to the young people themselves.... The achievement of the task will entail such young people achieving and exercising power in order to bring about changes. This is best achieved collectively (Ward, 1982, p. 6)

Spotting the contradiction

Having set out Eamonn's practice ideology in this way, we were then in a position to try and tease out what it was within his experience of the incident involving the group that had challenged his ideology and set up his nagging sense of dissatisfaction. We aimed to make explicit the way in which his practice experience had provided a critique of his personal practice ideology. In this way we hoped to develop that same ideology. He had not been prepared to compromise and change his personal practice ideology in order to accommodate the incident. At the same time he also had not been prepared to dismiss the self-criticism his personal ideology was insisting on in relation to the incident. The result of this was his feeling of failure to match practice to theory noted earlier.

It seemed to us that at the very heart of Eamonn's practice

ideology was the idea of a dichotomy; to be powerless/to be empowered.

The young women in his group were either dependent on him or they were independent of him. He received the notification of the residential weekend or they received it. Yet in direct contradiction to that idea of dichotomy, to be powerless/to be disempowered, stood his own biography and experience of work with young working class men and women. Both of these demonstrated that the experience of deprivation and inequality, whether socio-economic, cultural or emotional, is never passive. People respond. They may adapt, challenge, or collapse, but whichever, they make some form of response to their situation. How that response is seen, active or passive, acceptable or unacceptable is a matter of judgement. It was Eamonn, by way of his practice ideology with its core dichotomy, who had judged his provision of services to the group unacceptably active and the group's actions unacceptably passive.

Thus, it appeared to us that Eamonn's practice ideology, despite its central concern with power, failed in any useful way to actually register the power differential that generated the group incident. As the older, male worker, any exhibition of Eamonn's power that asserted the inequality between him and the young women in the group was oppressive and, therefore, was not ideologically acceptable. As for the young, female group members, any use, and thereby acknowledgement, they made of the power differential was dependency. It was, therefore, an unacceptable source of frustration to Eamonn.

Thus we spotted at the centre of Eamonn's practice ideology the contradiction between his idea of powerlessness as passivity and what he knew about the capacity of deprived and oppressed individuals and groups to respond to their situation. It was this contradiction that was giving him his problem with that hoary old groupwork process issue leadership. Leadership, the exercise of differential power, was experienced as particularly acute within Eamonn's social action practice ideology as it was precisely the exercise of power inequality which was its target for change. We concluded that any useful development of Eamonn's practice ideology would have to find a way of incorporating such inequality as a means of change in addition to being a target for change.

Towards social action as negotiation

Through our discussions it had become clear to us that, just as we had entered into a- relationship with different concerns, so too the relationship between social action groupworker and group members had to be based on differences. This was a direct challenge to a basic element in Eamonn's ideology which emphasised identification, lack of difference between himself and those he worked with. We had come together seeing our difference as holding out the opportunity of gaining from each other, and thereby contributing to each other. The difference, as we now see it, between Eamonn as worker and the young women group members was one of access to resources; notification of certain events, experience in telephone negotiation, transport. Therefore, far from being a block to the process of empowerment, negotiation around access to resources as expressed in the incident was inevitably the basis for a social action intervention.

Negotiation has been identified by Payne (1986) as one of the practice skills required for community social work.

> Negotiation is appropriate, then, where there is disagreement between two or more parties about something that is relevant to them, and there is discretion among the parties about the action they can take, and potential power to achieve a result satisfactory to both sides (p. 51)

By replacing 'disagreement' in the first line of the quote with 'difference', negotiation as defined by Payne gives the addition we required to Ward's practice principles. By using it, it is possible to extend Eamonn's practice ideology to bring into its frame of reference the differences between worker and group members and how these can be collectively addressed. What exactly the implications of this would have been for the group incident we focused on, is open to speculation and further work by us. However, some general ground rules are clear if once again we return to the process of our meetings. We had started with different agendas, reflecting our independent concerns, and then negotiated an agreed agenda of issues which have focused our discussions. So too for the social action worker and group members, the starting point must be to identify the different concerns that have brought them together and relate these in a way that allows for an agreed agenda. In this way differences are not resolved but can be more effectively addressed.

This may be a painful process for the worker as it involves disentangling personal practice ideology in a way that confronts closely held assumptions.

Empowerment, the key element in social action as a practice ideology for group workers, is no longer seen as something that only happens to group members. The worker too gets his/her 'piece of the action' - is empowered. It becomes possible to acknowledge that the social action worker is looking for a gain in terms of personal satisfaction, professional recognition, meeting agency aims or whatever. Thus the worker can explicitly bring his/her own agenda to the negotiation that we now see as central to the business of empowerment.

Conclusion

In summary, what we think we have learnt about social action group- work, and the support which workers involved in it require, is this.

Firstly, workers need to include in their support network at least one contact which gets them out of the quagmire of personal introspection, group process, and agency pressure, so as to work on clarifying and modifying their sense of direction; their personal practice ideology. This work should consciously be based on the same model of social action as workers are bringing to their groupwork. This includes recognition of the differences in personal/practice ideologies between the contact person and the worker. These exist prior to their work together, and are also generated during the course of their creative dialogue.

Secondly, we think that any model of social action must start with a recognition of differences, particularly inequalities in power, and regard group process as the most potent way of working the creative tension within these differences. Social action groupworkers need to accept that they cannot know where the working of this creative tension will lead. Perhaps then the most they can aim for is clarity about their own power base and their own agendas and how these are changing as part of negotiations with group members.

Our advocacy of extra support for social groupworkers to enable recognition of the manner in which their groups are beyond their control may be disconcerting for some; particularly in these days of limited resources and 'output measurement'. But that is what we advocate and we see it as no more than the application and realisation of what Bill Schwartz once said: that as groupworkers we must be *'secure in our own ignorance'*.

References

Adult Learning Protect, *Definitions of Key Concepts of Freire, Some Notes.* Edinburgh

Benson, J.F. (1987)' *Working More Creatively with Groups,* Tavistock: London

Davies, B. (1981) *Restructuring Youth Policies in Britain. The State We're In.* Occasional Paper No. 21 Leicester: Leicester National Youth Bureau

Freire, P. (1980) *Pedagogy of the Oppressed.* Harmondsworth: Penguin

Payne, M. (1986) *Social Care in the Community.* Basingstoke: BASW/ Macmillan

Smith, M. (1981) *Creators Not Consumers.* Leicester: National Association of Youth Clubs

Ward, D. (ed.) (1982) *Give 'Em a Break* Leicester: National Youth Bureau

This chapter was first published in 1988 in *Groupwork* Vol. 1(3), pp.229-238

At the time of writing Eamonn Keenan had been employed by Save the Children since 1981, working largely with adolescents in West Belfast. John Pinkerton had been a social worker in Belfast's Northern suburbs before teaching groupwork at Ulster Polytechnic and, from 1984, Queen's University, Belfast.

Challenging familiar assumptions: Preparing for and initiating a self-directed group

Audrey Mullender and Dave Ward

The self-directed groupwork approach aims to empower group members to set their own goals for external change. The membership of self-directed groups is often, voluntary and non-selected. In this paper, the preliminary stages of the approach are examined in detail and are contrasted with more conventional groupwork methods. A key feature of self-directed groupwork is that workers must begin by thrashing out an agreed and explicit value position from which their practice will flow. They then embark upon a process of 'open planning' in which, rather than making all the initial decisions for the group, they hand over as much responsibility as possible to the members. Neither the length of the group nor the frequency of meetings is predetermined; members themselves decide on the timing and location of meetings. The conduct of the group is also negotiated by workers and members together. The message to be conveyed is that the group belongs to its members right from the start.

In an earlier paper (Mullender and Ward, 1985), we outlined a model which we called 'self-directed groupwork' and which has subsequently been incorporated into a number of groupwork typologies (Brown, 1986, p. 20; Preston-Shoot, 1987, p. 17). The essential features of self- directed groups include a dominant focus on empowering members to achieve external change, and open, voluntary and non-selected membership.

The self-directed groupwork model is part of a total approach which encompasses an underpinning system of values; it is not an abstract method of intervention which might have arisen in a vacuum. One definition of an 'approach' is that it is *'the total embodiment and expression of a philosophy which rests upon identifiable theory and assumptions'* (The Nottingham Andragogy Group, 1983, p. 37). What makes our model unusual is that its philosophy and assumptions are not only made explicit, but are firmly embedded in the groupwork practice itself (see Table 1). No model is, in fact, value free but many are presented as if they involved only a set of *'organised procedures ...or processes'* (ibid., p. 37), thus requiring the reader to elicit their value bases by implication or interpretation. In other cases, the published accounts of a particular model may lay claim to a philosophy whilst leaving scope for practitioners to use the model without being consciously aware of the values which its use implies. This would not be possible with self-directed groupwork because, central to the model, is an explicit commitment to a set of values *from which the practice itself must flow*.

This first stage of the model involves the groupworkers in thrashing out their agreed value position before they move on to the normal beginning stages of preparing to run the proposed group. It is, of course, easy enough for us to state that the groupworkers must reach a clear value position – far harder for them to achieve it. The process of establishing that they do, in fact, agree precisely on the values which underpin the self-directed approach, and that these values represent their starting point for intervention, will, almost inevitably, involve a series of meetings at which each person's views can be expressed and a collective stance reached. Only preliminary agreement of this kind about the sources from which ideology, understanding – and resultant action – will flow can assure the success of the group. If anyone feels at this stage that they are not able to agree with the others and decides to opt out of involvement, then we would regard this as a success rather than a failure since it demonstrates that the preliminary planning stage is being carefully and conscientiously carried out.

Important assistance in this phase of preparation for a group can be provided by a consultant to the worker team who is able to stand outside the workers' own deliberations (Ward, 1982, pp. 23-24). The person who plays this role needs to have had direct experience of self- directed groupwork practice, not only so as to have a greater awareness of what is being planned, but also because his or her interventions can set an appropriate tone for the

Table 1

First stage of the self-directed groupwork model The groupworkers must begin by arriving at an agreed value position and selecting a methodology of practice accordingly. If this methodology is to be that of self-directed groupwork, their value position will look like this:

i.   The worker team reaches the view that the people who use their existing services are not 'sick' or 'deviant', but that they are basically normal people facing difficult circumstances which stem largely from structural factors. Another way of expressing this is to say that people themselves are not the problem; they are caught in a wider web of problems, often including a lack of essential facilities, unemployment, adverse attitudes and prejudice against them.

ii. The workers accept empowerment as valid aim which can be pursued through addressing structural issues, in day-to-day practice, by means of groupwork.

iii. The workers consider that potential group members are not empty vessels; they have strengths, skills, understanding, the ability to do things for themselves, and something to offer one another.

iv. The workers believe that potential group members have rights, including the right to more control over their own lives.

v.   In all their work, the workers determine to challenge oppressions – whether by reason of race, creed, gender, class, age, disability or sexual orientation. They recognise that this implies continual efforts to confront the prejudice and discrimination which permeate their own attitudes and practice.

Footnotes
1.   The self-directed model can be adopted by one or more groupworkers or by a group acting on its own behalf. The latter possibility should be borne in mind at all points where, for ease of expression, we refer to the input or views of groupworkers.
2.   For the remaining stages of the model, see Mullender and Ward, 1985, p. 165, commencing at step (e) and allowing for renumbering.

group that is to follow. In so far as the consultant uses classic self-directed techniques like brainstorming, and provides a framework for discussions rather than pre-set content, he or she models the groupworker role in a self-directed group. Overall, by listening, questioning and testing impressions, the groupwork consultant can help focus on issues and draw conflict out into the open so that workers themselves can resolve it – just as they will assist the members to do in the group.

An actual group example can be used to illustrate what happens when a worker team leaves conflict unexpressed and hence fails to reach an agreed value position in advance of establishing a group. In this example, which relates to the Rowland Dale group, a group for parents who had physically abused their children, two out of three group- workers strongly believed that structural inequalities lay at the root of the members' abuse of their children, whilst the third was of the opinion that more money or better housing would not help because the families concerned would simply get themselves into a mess all over again. These fundamentally opposing views were not discussed or resolved before the group commenced and no consultant was involved. The third, isolated, worker left the group after only a few meetings. No lasting harm was done, but the differences of viewpoint had for a time hampered the group's ability to discuss matters from members' own perspectives (which concurred with the view that social structural factors were central in the problems they faced, and also drew attention to the fact that child abuse 'procedures' had involved a secretive and heavy handed use of authority) because meetings had continually degenerated into discussions between the workers. It would certainly have been preferable if the third worker had departed before the group started, rather than after.

Realising that this emphasis on agreeing values in advance is an unconventional starting point for running a group, we want to go on and consider in what other ways the planning and preparation stages of self-directed groups differ from more traditional groupwork models.

Open planning

Once the groupworkers have reached a common position in relation to their values, there are a number of other matters which remain to be considered before a group is actually instituted. We regard these as amounting to establishing a climate or an environment in which self- directed groupwork can take place. In most forms of traditional group- work, this initial planning stage consists of making a series of decisions about the goals of the group, its membership, leadership, and the circumstances in which it will be run, each of which decisions closes off other options by choosing one amongst them. Self-directed group- workers, in contrast, need to start off by opening up horizons as far as possible so that the group members will be enabled to take as many decisions as possible for themselves. We call this a process of 'open' as opposed to 'closed' planning. The skill is in knowing what *not* to plan in advance because it is better left to be discussed with the potential group members.

All writers on groupwork give considerable attention to planning, on the assumption that it *will* be appropriate to decide a whole range of things in advance. Douglas (1976, pp. 41-42), for example, offers a *check-list for starting a group* designed to give the worker *a reasonable certainty about what he* [sic] *intends to do* since that will make it easier to convince a sceptical client of the value of the group. He makes no mention of the alternative means of winning a potential member over to the idea of a group: by involving them fully in its planning and making it truly 'their' group. This would be the approach favoured by self- directed groupworkers and it would include giving the individual concerned the choice whether to attend the group or not.

Although less is decided in advance, preparation is no less important in self-directed groupwork than in any other model. Indeed, we would echo Brown's view (1986, p. 27) that:

> The preparation stages may lack the demands, enjoyment and involvement of actual group meetings and activities, but they require just as much creative energy, clear thinking and skill in communication. Some groups are stillborn or die later because social

workers underestimate the time and care which good preparation requires.

It would now be appropriate to look in greater detail at each facet of groupwork planning, to examine the effect of keeping this process as 'open' as possible.

Unfettered goal setting

The key feature which the worker team must not pre-empt in its own preparations is goal setting. Indeed, it is a central characteristic of self-directed groupwork that group members set their own goals (and any group able to do so can use the approach). In fact, of course, the groupworkers do start out with an overarching purpose in mind for the group, based on their initial forging of agreement about their underpinning values. This broad purpose, however, should be set at no greater level of specificity than the general concept of empowering members to confront and move on from their shared experience. The latter may be of an entirely personal nature at first, for example a common experience of having a child with learning difficulties, but it is crucial to the model that the option to progress to broader social considerations is not shut down by the groupworkers. In the example just given, for instance, it would commonly be the case that, if not self-directed, a group would be run on therapeutic lines intended to help members to 'come to terms' with their experiences. Whilst discussion of feelings and the opportunity for mutual support remain very important in any group of this kind, it is equally likely that common themes of anger about under resourcing of obstetric and neo-natal care, or unsatisfactory service provision, may emerge over time if discussion is allowed to flow without being checked by workers' assumptions about what is appropriate or what the group is 'for' (see fuller example in Mullender and Ward, 1985, p. 157.) Equally, a self-directed group for people who have suffered bereavement might progress into issues concerning industrial diseases, or inequalities in health care, or changes in widows' benefits, and might decide to campaign around issues such as these.

It is by no means contradictory for the groupworkers to be clear about their overall purposes and explicit about group process, and yet to leave group members free to determine the detailed goals for the group. Indeed, helping them to do so is an essential part of empowerment. Only the group members have had the life experiences which legitimate their establishment of these kinds of priorities. In order to establish and pursue their priorities, however – at least initially – many groups will require skilled facilitation.

Non-selected membership

'Open planning' involves moving away from the selection of members on the basis of referrals sought in response to predefined criteria. Many groupworkers seek referrals almost by default, as if this were the only possible way of conducting the initial stages of a group. In self-directed groups, on the other hand, the only criteria for inviting people along to an initial group meeting are that they must freely choose to attend and that they are either a natural group or, alternatively, that they have enough in common to offer the potential for developing a group identity; there is no selection stage of any kind. 'Having enough in common' may include being all women, or all black. It would normally also include some additional shared experiences of oppression, as with the members of a self-directed group of Asian students at a further education college who all felt they had been treated unfairly by the college authorities. They successfully campaigned for their meetings to be included in the normal weekly timetable and, with the help of two Asian groupworkers, went on to negotiate on a range of matters concerning the way they felt their particular needs had previously been ignored within the college.

Although the members of self-directed groups may have heard about the group initially through their social workers or health visitors, or through any other professionals who have a significant involvement in their lives, they cannot be 'referred' as such; the group is merely suggested to them for their own consideration as a potentially useful or interesting idea. Although it is not associated with any process of selection, many self-directed groupworkers, except when working with a natural group, do nevertheless employ the same procedure of meeting potential members individually before the group starts as will be familiar from more traditional methods of groupwork (Manor, 1988).

Perhaps we might see Stock Whitaker's idea of a *two-way process* (Stock Whitaker, 1975, p. 431) as becoming more one way in self-directed groupwork; the groupworker will not be making a decision during this meeting whether or not to invite the individual to the group because enough will already be known about them to make this an automatic process. The potential member, however, will still need all the information the worker is able to give about the group. As Stock Whitaker continues (and allowing for 'therapist/group leader/client' terminology and gender specific language which the present authors would not find acceptable):

> The therapist tells the client that a group is being organized; the client naturally wants to know what sort of group and what will happen in it ... the therapist explains as best he can; the client reacts with enthusiasm (rare) or certain reservations; the reservations are explored and client and group leader together decide whether or not the client will give the group a try. . . . The client's intuition is often very reliable. I do not of course mean that the client's first 'I think I'd rather not' should be accepted as it stands. That should be the starting point for a mutual exploration, not the end of the conversation.

What the workers will be explaining to potential members of a self-directed group is that it will be *their* group at which they will meet others – or be with others they already know – who are facing similar problems to their own, and that the workers will only be there to help them discuss what form the problems take, which of them are experienced as the most severe, why these problems exist and what, as a group, they might choose to do about it.

Almost by definition, the people who are most likely to make excellent use of self-directed groups are also, and rightly, very cagey of professionals who come offering them new kinds of help; they have usually had many negative experiences of authority and of well-meaning intervention in the past. They may also see themselves as struggling on alone against the world and may find it hard to see what relevance a group could have or – since they will generally have had many personally devaluing experiences in the past – what anyone could think they might offer to it. Most of all, they are likely to be feeling pretty hopeless about the prospect of any remedy for their present troubles, and may take some convincing that this proposed group has any more chance of success than all the other failed solutions in the past, or that it is anything other than a new way of the powers that be pointing the finger at them as authors of their own misfortunes (Ryan, 1971). All these matters can be explored in pre-group meetings with potential members. All that is required from them is agreement to give the group a try and willingness to continue these discussions in the group itself; they do not have to be convinced in advance that it will succeed.

Open membership

In addition to being non-selected, the membership of self-directed groups is truly open; there is no requirement that any member should stay throughout the group's life, so that anyone may opt in or out at any intermediate stage, and, of course, this means that the overall group membership fluctuates over time.

Whilst apparently alert to factors such as the increased range of 'learning opportunities' in open membership groups (Preston-Shoot, 1987, p. 31), writers on groupwork invariably exhibit a bias in favour of closed groups: '*A closed group does seem to promote cohesion and trust and may provide security for members who initially are apprehensive or lacking in confidence*' (*ibid.*, p. 31). There is an apparent fear, shared by many theorists, of working with open groups:

> Some groups seem to operate with a revolving door, with members constantly dropping out and being replaced. In such a group continuity is lost, and the members are likely to be preoccupied much of the time with mourning lost members, working out fantasies about what the survivors did to drive the members away, or dealing with new people coming in (Stock Whitaker, 1975, p. 435).

We would not suggest that those remaining in the group either can or should completely ignore the coming and going of other members, but nor would we accept an interpretation that sees this as always problematic. Since those attending a self-directed group know from the start that membership is entirely open and that people only come of their own volition, it may be nothing out of the ordinary for a particular individual to stop attending when they lose interest or move on to deal with other, more pressing things in their life. As the group has often not been brought together by the worker, members and ex-members may continue to bump into each other outside of group sessions and, even where they did meet initially through the group, they may forge friendships or informal neighbourhood contacts which take on a life of their own. Similarly, members may bring friends along to group meetings and be flexible enough to welcome new members as useful additions to the group's combined strength and efficacy.

At other times, self-directed groups do hit patches where established members become reluctant to accept new faces and develop into something of a 'clique'. These may well be times when the workers have to help them examine and reflect on the process that is going on in the group and whether it is helping or hindering the group in the pursuit of its goals. They may need to encourage existing members to recall how they felt before they joined the group; to think how many more people 'out there', who are facing the same kinds of oppression and inequality as themselves, could potentially benefit from group membership to raise their confidence and awareness. These others may also have a major contribution to make to the group's ideas and activities so that their loss, if they are not recruited to the group, would also be the group's loss.

As far as any threat to continuity is concerned, it is possible to preserve a feeling of continuity in a self-directed group, in the pursuit of goals which the group itself has set, by means of a kind of 'group memory' that is also owned by the whole group. This can take the form of written records of group meetings, photographs, press cuttings, sometimes even a video film or televised item about the group, and anything else which the group finds it appropriate to keep. Sometimes such materials are stored and only occasionally referred back to, to boost group morale or keep the members to the goals and tasks they have set themselves. Other groups may routinely use records of the direction they have set and their achievements to date in the same way that some professionals use written contracts with their clients. Flip-charts, for example, on which issues and plans of action have been brainstormed and analysed, can usefully be retained and regularly displayed at future meetings to form the basis of subsequent work. The Nottingham 'Who Cares' group, with which one of the authors was involved as a coworker, operated in a similar way by gathering together all its memorabilia into a box which came to every meeting and took on a certain significance as the embodiment of where the group had been and what it had done.

Group size

The notion that the ideal number for a small group ranges from three, and preferably from six, to 12 members is a further example of received wisdom which is not applicable in self-directed groupwork. The entire literature of groupwork is essentially one of work with *small* groups. Douglas (1976) and Heap (1977), both give serious and balanced consideration to the question of group size but come down firmly on the side of the small group, whilst Stock Whitaker (1975, p. 434) asserts:

> A group of 12 or 15 or more is too large for many purposes. If one's intention is to plan, or to hold open discussions (even when the topic 1 is well structured), groups of this size almost always devolve into a small core of active participants and a fringe of onlookers.

She does go on to add that large groups may be desirable in certain residential or hospital ward settings, simply so that everyone can be included. Whilst self-directed groupwork has been successfully practised under similar circumstances, we would have no qualms about extending our view of the acceptability of such large groups to a wide range of other contexts.

In self-directed groups, since not even an upper limit is set, it is not uncommon to find attendances in excess of 20, and 40 is not unheard of. The Asian students' group and the Nottingham

'Who Cares' group which were mentioned earlier, certainly both exceeded 20 members at times. With the exception of Kreeger (1975), the theoretical literature on groups of this dimension tends to have an orientation which is out of harmony with our own (see, for example, Jones, 1968, on therapeutic communities; Bozarth, 1981, on Rogerian residential workshops, which reached 50 to 150 people). Interestingly, Bozarth (*ibid.*, p. 118) comments that ' *The role of the facilitators in the large group is no different than in small group therapy or encounter groups using the well-known client-centred model',* showing that he, at least, is not overawed by the prospect of working with such large numbers.

As a consequence of the membership fluctuating over time in self-directed groups, clearly the size does also. The workers need the necessary skills to work with three members at one meeting and over 20 at another, as happened, for example, in the Nottingham 'Who Cares' group. Large attendances called for the use of techniques to raise issues, such as brainstorming, exercises to prioritise those issues and to set tasks arising from them, and games designed to help the group to look at its own process. (Examples of all these may be found in ACW, 1981; Hope and Timmel, 1984; Jelfs, 1982.) At other times, when only a few members are present, it is important not to retreat into the feeling that they represent a more 'authentic' small group and to treat them, therefore, as if they *are* the whole group by letting them take fresh decisions that contravene all the work which has been done in the group up to that point. One way of holding on to what the large group has set as its priorities is to display its work to date (in the form of flip-charts, for example) at every meeting and to keep that in the forefront as representing the direction in which the group is aiming to move, however many of its members are actually able to attend at any given time.

Self-directed groupworkers may, then, require greater flexibility but, given this, they do not find that large numbers of group members need remain on the side lines or that the issue of trust within the group cannot be satisfactorily handled, despite Preston-Shoot's fear (1987, p. 32) that, in large groups, both intimacy and freedom of expression are threatened.

Although Brown (1986, pp. 40-41) and Preston-Shoot (1987, pp.

32-33) reflect the tendency in more recent literature to think about size less rigidly, and in relation primarily to the broad purpose of the group, they still remain wedded to upper limits on numbers: in the region of 12, or six to eight, respectively. Brown (1986, p. 40) passes the sensible observation that, at the upper end of his own recommended range of group size: 'Problem-solving takes longer, but may produce better solutions'. Similarly: 'For problem-solving, activity and "open" groups, larger groups provide more resources and can work well '. Nevertheless, he still does not appear to feel comfortable with the notion of the larger grouping, in that he states that the observed 'tendency to sub-grouping', rather than being minimised by the worker, 'can be used constructively by sub-dividing the group for various tasks and activities' (ibid., p. 41). It is as if practitioners and theoreticians are anxious to return to the more familiar territory of the small group as quickly as possible. A further axiomatic principle appears to be that large groups lead to loss of control: 'Larger groups usually require more management and structure'. Although we would agree that the size of the worker team may usefully increase with the size of the group itself, this is not to ensure that the groupworkers keep a grip on the group but, rather, to facilitate their ability to pick up the wealth of ideas and energies which will flow from the members. An additional role which can usefully be played by one of the groupworkers, for example, over and above the more standard ones, is that of 'spotter'. This involves the worker concerned in sitting amongst group members and listening out for those who clearly have ideas to contribute but who are perhaps more inclined to whisper these to a neighbour than to share them with the whole group. The 'spotter' can encourage them to have the confidence to address their views to the group.

Like community groups, self-directed groups may go through periods of feeling that numbers have shrunk too far and decide to publicise the group to attract more members. This may be done through word of mouth when, for example in young people's groups, members will bring their friends along to the next meeting. Alternatively, a group may consider putting posters up in its usual meeting place, or may even advertise in the press, as the Rowland Dale group considered doing when it needed more members to help it run independently of worker support.

Open ended length

Just as the number attending a self-directed group is not fixed in advance, so the workers need to learn not to pre-set the duration of time during which the group will meet. It is not easy to move away from the kind of 'gut level' feeling in many professional settings which has come to associate small groups with a duration of six, eight or 12 weeks. It is not untypically acknowledged that therapeutic groups may last for several years but, in general, timespans are calculated according to the length of commitment workers feel they can make, rather than the exigencies of the group itself. This is compounded by the unfortunate tendency to regard any form of 'self-help' activity as able to become member-led after a very short period of time (Wilson, 1987) so that, again, workers' own involvement in the group may last only a matter of weeks. In self-directed groupwork, group members themselves decide for how long they find the group to be serving a useful purpose, which frequently extends over a period of years until long term goals for external change are achieved – for example, the successful campaign by a young people's group for a youth club on their estate, or by a local women's group for a women's centre (in both cases with the group firmly in control of the management committee).

Groupworkers may hand the responsibility for facilitating the group in its work over to colleagues after a time (subject to the group's agreement), or eventually over to members themselves, but workers should not expect to be associated with the group for less than a good few months – and years would be better. Such a long term commitment makes a team of at least three workers especially desirable, so that sickness and leave can be covered. These workers need not all be from the same agency – for example, the facilitators with the Rowland Dale group were a social worker and a health visitor – but their necessarily long term commitment does have resource implications. The proven effectiveness of the approach in a wide range of settings would probably need to be its own justification.

Frequency of meetings

Once again, the frequency of meetings constitutes a feature which is not fixed in advance of self-directed groupwork. There is a tendency, in adult-led long term groups, to assume that meetings will take place once a month whilst short term groups may well meet weekly. In self-directed groups there is a far greater element of the members determining what feels right for them and what will best enable them to meet the group goals they have set.

In the Nottingham 'Who Cares' group, for example, the group-workers – who were new to the self-directed approach – had made the assumption in advance, following the model of most adult meetings, that the group would meet monthly. After the group had actually started, the members – all teenagers in the care of the local authority – stated that they would prefer to meet weekly. It seems likely that they were more accustomed to weekly groups, on the model of Scouts or Guides for example. They also found it easier and more realistic to plan their lives a week rather than a month ahead. The reasons for this included the routines established within the children's homes where most of them lived, their schools' weekly schedules of homework and of out-of-school commitments such as team sports, their own sense of time which revolved around a somewhat shorter timescale than that of adults, and their vague awareness that control over their use of time, and even over where they might be a few months hence, was not in their own hands – which made it important to achieve as much as possible as quickly as possible. The lack of fit between the group leaders' expectations of monthly meetings and the members' wish for weekly meetings led to a compromise that the group would meet fortnightly. This suited no-one particularly well, did not harmonise with anyone's other commitments so that it became difficult to remember the meeting dates, and caused problems in fitting meetings around holidays and half- terms. The workers learned from this that they should not have predetermined or made assumptions about the frequency of meetings, but should have left this for negotiation with the group members. They could then have negotiated their own commitment to the group on whatever basis resulted; if necessary, for example, by recruiting additional assistance in running the group so that a sufficient number of groupworkers could be present on each occasion without making unrealistic demands on anyone.

Timing of meetings

Similar principles relate to the timing of meetings. Brown (1986, p. 41) rightly regards discussing meeting times with members as desirable 'within many approaches to groupwork; we would not claim this as specific to self-directed groupwork, but it is of particular importance there. A groupworker team who made advance plans for a women's group, for example, might assume that it would be easier for women with family commitments to attend an evening group because they could then share child care with their partners; in fact, were they to consult the women themselves, they might find that they were single parents who could only manage a daytime group with a crèche for the youngest children. Only by discussing the matter with the potential members concerned would this necessity emerge. Of course, the same would be true for any kind of group but with the additional factor that a self-directed group needs to bear its own goals in mind when deciding what would be most suitable. It may, for example, be needing to reach the widest possible potential membership, or one specific group of people for whom timing is of crucial importance – as was the case with the young people in care who joined the Nottingham 'Who Cares' group because they needed to seek permission to be allowed out in the evening.

Location of meetings

In seeking to involve members in determining the most appropriate location for group meetings, one factor to bear in mind may be the places where they would tend to congregate naturally. With young people, for example, the most natural setting in which to find them initially could be a street comer or a public open space of some kind. This does not mean that all subsequent meetings have to be held out of doors, but it is a reminder that most groupwork takes place under quite artificial conditions and that much effort is typically expended on bringing individuals together into groups instead of working with the untapped potential of natural groups. It is important for self-directed groupwork to tap into the natural dynamics of group interaction as far as possible because this is what the workers are there to facilitate; they are often not attempting to create a new group identity from scratch but to enhance what already exists, in embryo at least.

A wonderful example of a detached youth worker who was very skilled in self-directed groupwork techniques doing precisely this occurred when he came across a natural group of young people 'hanging around' on .a housing estate. Wanting to encourage them to voice their own experiences of living on the estate, but knowing that the process of engaging them in joining together into an officially recognised group and moving to an indoor location would lose the young people's natural spontaneity, the groupworker proceeded to pull a piece of chalk out of his jacket pocket and to hold a 'brainstorming' session with them there and then, by writing on the paving stones. This led to the group negotiating for somewhere to meet and setting goals around issues which members decided to tackle. Natural group dynamics may also be harnessed in a residential or day care setting where members already know each other and where the group can meet in its normal, everyday context. The use of self-directed groupwork in penal settings should remind us, however, that a group's everyday setting is not necessarily one in which it feels perfectly at ease: there still remains the need to engage the group in the work and to go through all the stages of 'open planning'.

Where individual members are being brought together for the express purpose of starting a self-directed group and there is, therefore, a completely open choice of venue, the initial one or two meetings should normally be held on 'neutral' territory away from the professionals' normal workplaces, such as a community centre, and the preferred location of future meetings should be discussed with those members who come along at this initial stage. Once again, we are emphasising that no aspect of planning should unnecessarily be taken out of group members' hands. It is not normally appropriate for workers to provide transport to a self-directed group unless for some special reason, for example, if members have disabilities and some require help. In residential, day care and penal settings, members are already together in one place. Outside of this, group meetings will normally take place in the members' own neighbourhood, within easy reach of their homes so transportation should not be needed. Also, it is sometimes questionable as to how far attendance remains truly voluntary when transport arrives without fail every week; it is easier to attend by default than to contemplate the choice of whether to go or not.

Reaching agreement on the conduct of the group

Self-directed groupwork is grounded in the notion of a working agreement between workers and members. As has been outlined, many of the elements of the group's functioning – such as where and when the group will meet – are negotiated between the parties. The group members also decide for themselves whether they want to attend, and they are responsible, as a group, for setting the group's goals.

There remain a number of other matters, however, on which it is necessary to reach agreement in the very earliest stage of the group's life (Brown, 1986, pp. 45-46): these include any rules for the conduct of the group; the related issue of confidentiality – both between workers and members, and between the group and the outside world; the relationship between membership of the group and any individual help which members may be receiving from one or more of the agencies involved, including any with a statutory component; and what members and workers can properly expect from one another – in particular, what role the workers will play.

Group rules

Rules for the conduct of self-directed groups are established by the group members themselves. In the Nottingham 'Who Cares' group (for young people in the care of the local authority), for example, after one or two rather boisterous and noisy meetings the young people decided on the rule that only one person should speak at once and that the others should listen. It would, of course, have been perfectly possible for the workers to predict that such a rule would be needed ánd to have delivered it to members as an expectation at the first meeting. This, however, would have flown in the face of the whole philosophy and practice of self-directed groups and would have been entirely counterproductive. It would have established a 'them and us' feeling between workers and members and would have placed the former firmly in a leadership role, with the members left to choose between subservience and rebellion. Furthermore, if the groupworkers had later gone on to suggest to members 'This is your group and it is up to you to decide how you want to use it and what you want to achieve', the members would have had no reason to believe that this was actually how the workers intended to operate.

Confidentiality outside the group

The same 'Who Cares' group also had to tackle the issue of confidentiality between the group and the outside world. The residential staff who were caring for most of the young people felt somewhat threatened by the existence of the group and would sometimes 'pump' them for information as to what went on there. The group considered this situation and reached the opinion that they had a right to discuss matters which concerned them in privacy but that, at the same time, there was no point in fostering suspicion of the group's activities unnecessarily. As a result, the members decided to hold occasional 'open evenings' for their field and residential social workers at which the group's progress and plans could be reported on, in a way which the whole group had had a chance to plan, and support would be enlisted for the group's continued existence since it could be seen to be an important factor in its members' lives. In between these open meetings, members could feel free to keep the content of group sessions confidential without feeling that they were betraying individual social workers or carers. Such freedom was absolutely essential if they were to have the necessary space to share their adverse experiences of the care system and to reach decisions on how to tackle these. The groupworkers regarded themselves as bound by exactly the same expectations.

Confidentiality in the group

A different aspect of confidentiality, that between workers and members, was faced by the Ainsley Teenage Action group, a group for young people on a council estate who had been harassed by the police and who had nowhere to congregate without getting into further trouble. The worker team with this group was meeting regularly with a consultant to help them keep in view their overall philosophy of empowerment of the young people in the group, and to develop the kinds of skills and techniques which would make this a reality. When the existence of these consultancy sessions first came up in conversation between the workers and the young people, the latter were angry that there were discussions going on about *their* group from which they felt excluded, in just the same way as the residential workers had felt shut out from the 'Who Cares' group. In this case, however, the fact that it was the members of the group themselves who were experiencing this feeling of exclusion raised a very real dilemma for the worker team. Workers and members together discussed the situation, with the group- workers strongly holding the opinion that they had a right to their own professional development and, indeed, that they could not offer an adequate service to the group without it. On the other hand, they did not want to create any 'no go' areas in their work, nor to leave the members feeling that they were being talked about behind their backs. On reflection, it became clear that the workers did have a right to, and a need for, time and space for their own reflection but that this should not be kept confidential from group members. Indeed, as the group developed its own levels of skill and awareness, the members became increasingly able to offer valuable feedback to the workers about how helpful they were experienced as being and how they might have responded differently at particular points in the group sessions. It was agreed, therefore, that any members who wished to do so would be free to attend the consultancy sessions, provided that the focus of these remained on the performance of the workers and they did not develop into mini-group sessions outside of the meetings proper. In addition, the records of the consultancy sessions would be open to the group members to read, just as the records of self-directed group sessions themselves are normally open to members – and, indeed, are quite often written by them.

Group membership and individual work

Part of the process of negotiating a working agreement with the members of a self-directed group consists of clarifying which matters it is proper to bring to the group and which should be dealt with outside of it. Brown and Caddick (1986, p. 101) have questioned how the self- directed approach '*incorporates the agency's goals in relation to individual behaviour*', with particular reference to social control functions, and also '*whether there is a place within it for individual members to work at their own... personal matters, perhaps of health, role-change or relationship*'. Unequivocally, we would answer that a groupworker using the self-directed model would not put any of these matters on the agenda *in the group*. Individual members themselves are, of course, always free to mention in a group meeting that they have had a bad week, or any other current preoccupation, but this would be because it arose in the course of conversation and not in the expectation that the group would 'down tools' to focus on the matter, as might happen in a group which had a therapeutic purpose. When an individual problem arises spontaneously, it may well be discussed but is often a prelude for either workers or other members to refocus on the goals or tasks in hand. For example, in a group held in a penal setting, a number of people wanted to know about parole or visiting arrangements; answers to specific factual questions on these matters, as well as strong expressions of discontent by particular individuals, led into broader discussions of how to 'play the system' for an early release and of the unfairness of the 'system' overall. What is not appropriate at such a time is for the workers to move into an individualised perspective which would be at odds with the overall goals of the group.

This is not to say, however, that individual needs are ignored. On occasion, the same or a different worker does retain a continuing one- to-one casework relationship, sometimes on a statutory basis (discussed in more detail below), with a group member outside of the group. Where this is the case, the worker is able to make it clear to all group members that he or she (or the rest of the team) remains available to offer individual support at times of difficulty. The probation officer who worked with the Ainsley Teenage Action group left open the offer of individual contact for occasions like this, although he did not impose it as a regular requirement alongside group membership. Some members did indeed ask to see him individually when they felt they needed to do so. As a group develops over time, however, members increasingly offer each other this support both inside and outside the group and, where they feel something to be beyond their scope, will often help the person concerned to seek appropriate sources of help outside the group.

We would not deny that very many group members feel that their personal problems have eased, or that they have become more able or more motivated to tackle them, as a result of their membership of a self-directed group. These benefits we have elsewhere referred to as 'secondary advantages' of membership of self-directed groups (Mullender and Ward, 1985, p. 156). Also, it is true to say that workers and individual members get to know each other better because of the group, and may discuss the group's progress, and how membership of it is helping this particular member, as part of any individual work outside of the group; this process would not, however, work the other way round and does not mean that the groupwork is subservient to, or less important than, individual work.

Statutory requirements

The viability of self-directed practice where statutory orders are in force may be seen as open to question (Brown, 1986, p. 20). In our view, however, membership of a self-directed group is not precluded for those on such orders, or those who are subject to statutory monitoring or investigation, provided that there is no actual or implied requirement that they will join the group. This is of crucial importance in self-directed groupwork since voluntary membership has already been shown to be a basic feature of the approach (see above p. 10).

A helpful consideration here is the differentiation made by Bottoms and McWilliams (1979, p. 177) between constraint and coercion. Coercion, they argue, is unacceptable, whereas constraints exist in all situations in which people interact. They merely provide a framework within which real choice remains possible. This notion of choice can be developed further by considering the idea of primary and secondary contracts (Bryant *et al*, 1978; Raynor, 1985; see also Mullender, 1979). The primary contract, the court order, provides a framework of constraints – officially termed 'conditions' – such as the requirement in a probation or supervision order to report regularly. Beyond this framework, the person who is subject to the order remains free to choose whether to enter into one or more secondary contracts, which may include receiving individual help through casework or joining a group. In the Ainsley Teenage Action group, for example, the probation officer who set up the group gave members the option of fulfilling the reporting requirement of their orders by attending the group. He made it absolutely clear that, should they withdraw from the group, their primary contract – the statutory order – would not be broken, provided that they worked out an alternative arrangement for contact. Since subsequent withdrawal from a secondary contract would not prejudice the conditions of the court order (which remains in force), the existence of the order itself does not prevent potential group members from exercising a real choice.

Mutual expectations

In sum, it is essential that a potential group member's preliminary expectations on first joining a self-directed group are explored and clarified, as would be the case with any method. The role that the workers can be expected to play, for example, requires careful elucidation. It needs to be clear from the start that they will not be telling members what to do but will be placing full responsibility on them to decide. This firm placing of responsibility back with group members may have to continue, intermittently, throughout a group's life. For example, one women's action group has been in existence for several years and now employs its own worker, but she still finds that the group occasionally attempts to pass decision making to her; she then needs to remind members of how much they have achieved already and to stress that new tasks and responsibilities are not beyond their capabilities.

Conclusion

Many of the features of planning and preparing to run a self-directed group involve the groupworkers in unlearning previous assumptions about the classic features of groupwork. The first stage of the group-workers' activities, as outlined in this paper, has covered all the preparations and planning for the group as well as getting the members together on the basis of a preliminary working agreement as to how the group will run. In short, the process we have described has been that of the groupworkers moving out of a leadership role into that of facilitators. The group members, too, may need time to become accustomed to the workers playing this less familiar role and may need gently reminding at various points during the life of the group that they cannot look to the workers to have all the answers. Since members are keenest to seek the safety of depending on the workers and conforming to their wishes at the very beginning of a group (Brown, 1986, p. 74), it is particularly important that workers in self-directed groups should convey the message that these groups are member-centred right from the start – that is, from the point when initial preparations for the group begin to be made. As they 'get the message' that the workers are not going to give them an easy way out by telling them what to do, members begin to look more to each other to make decisions. The workers, meanwhile, attempt always to help the group members determine where they want the group to go, rather than imposing their own goals or direction onto the members.

This brings us back full circle to the question of values. We consider that there are problematic issues surrounding both 'leadership' and 'control' in groups. We would always wish to ask to what ends such control is directed, and over which areas of members' experience it is exercised. It is not sufficient to treat control, or the power on which it depends, as value-free or value-neutral as, for example, does Douglas (1976, pp. 71-73) when he discusses both the degree and the sources of the groupworker's power as questions primarily of what makes the worker most effective. Power-ful leadership roles are presented by Douglas as alternatives to be adopted or discarded by the professionally skilled worker in order to achieve his or her own ends for the group. We would personally be unhappy with any analysis of power which was not *value-laden* (Lukes, 1974, p. 57), or which omitted to note that the significance of control *to the recipient* is related as much to the ends to which it is exercised as the means by which this happens. Leadership, by definition, cannot be simply a technical exercise in management; it must always involve explicit or implicit intentions and purposes which, if left to default, will reinforce rather than question dominant social values. The self-directed approach is deeply grounded in value-based considerations of who determines what those intentions and purposes shall be; its underpinning rationale is one of handing back the power over decision-making to service users.

'Empowerment', a term which can be used to encapsulate these values, has become fashionable in recent months. In this paper we have attempted to show that its achievement through the medium of a self-directed group demands a high level of awareness and skill, so that careful planning of the group remains consonant with the groupwork-ers' overall values.

References

Association of Community Workers (1981) *Community Workers' Skills Manual* London: ACW.

Bottoms, A.E. and McWilliams, W. (1979) 'A non treatment paradigm for probation practice', *British Journal of Social Work-,* 9(2), pp. 159-202.

Bozarth, J.D. (1981) 'The person-centred approach in the large community group' in Gazda, G.M. (ed.) *Innovations to Group Psychotherapy.* Springfield, Illinois: Charles C. Thomas. Second edition.

Brown, A. (1986) *Groupwork.* Aldershot, Hants: Gower. Second edition.

Brown, A. and Caddick, B. (1986) 'Models of social groupwork in Britain: a further note', *British Journal of Social Work,* 16(1), pp. 99-103.

Bryant, M., Coker, J., Estlea, B., Himmel, S. and Knapp, E. (1978) 'Sentenced to social work?' *Probation Journal* 25(4), pp. 110-114.

Douglas, T. (1976) *Groupwork Practice*. London: Tavistock.

Heap, K. (1977) *Group Theory for Social Workers*. Oxford: Pergamon.

Hope, A. and Timmel, S. (1984) *Training for Transformation*. Gweru, Zimbabwe: Mambo Press.

Jelfs, M. (1982) *Manual for Action*. London: Action Resources Group.

Jones, M. (1968) *Beyond the Therapeutic Community: Social Learning and Social Psychiatry*. New Haven: Yale University Press.

Kreeger, L. (ed.) (1975) *The Large Group*. London: Constable.

Lukes, S. (1974) *Power: A Radical View*. Basingstoke, Hants: Macmillan.

Manor, O. (1988) 'Preparing the client for social groupwork: an illustrated framework', *Groupwork*, 1(2), pp. 100-114.

Mullender, A. (1979) 'Drawing up a more democratic contract', *Social Work Today*, 11(11), 13th November, pp. 17-18.

Mullender, A. and Ward, D. (1985) 'Towards an alternative model of social groupwork', *British Journal of Social Work*, 15, pp. 155-172.

Mullender, A. and Ward, D. (1988) 'What is practice-led research into group-work?' in Wedge, P. (ed.) *Social Work – A Third Look at Research into Practice: Proceedings of the Third Annual JUC/BASW Conference*, London, September, 1987. Birmingham: BASW

Nottingham Andragogy Group (1983) *Towards a Developmental Theory of Andragogy*. Nottingham: University of Nottingham, Department of Adult Education.

Preston-Shoot, M. (1987) *Effective Groupwork*. Basingstoke, Hants: Macmillan.

Raynor, P. (1985) *Social Work, Justice and Control* Oxford: Blackwell.

Stock Whitaker, D. (1975) 'Some conditions for effective work with groups', *British Journal of Social Work*, 5(4), *pp*. 423-439.

Ward, D. (ed.) (1982) *Give 'Em a Break: Social Action by Young People at Risk and in Trouble*. Leicester: National Youth Bureau.

Wilson, J. (1987) 'Helping groups to grow', *Community Care*, 667, 2 July, pp. 20-21.

This chapter was first published in 1989 in *Groupwork* Vol. 2(1), pp.5-26

At the time of writing Audrey Mullender and Dave Ward were Lecturers in Social Work at Nottingham University.

Facilitation in self-directed groupwork

Dave Ward and Audrey Mullender

This paper continues the exploration and explication of self-directed groupwork as a distinctive approach within the practice of groupwork. Here, the major role of the groupworker is proposed as that of 'facilitator' rather than 'leader' of the group. The crucial skills and parameters of facilitation are discussed, and set in the context of the more usual conceptual framework of maintenance and task functions. It is argued that facilitation involves a different emphasis, which is no less rewarding or demanding of identifiable skills.

The value-base of self-directed groupwork (Mullender and Ward, 1991) is grounded in the work of a range of practitioners. By opening themselves up to hearing what service users are saying, they have shown that it is possible to empower group members to set their own goals and take action collectively to achieve them. This implies drawing out the strengths in group members and helping them to determine where they want the group to go, rather than imposing one's own aims or direction onto them. In so doing, groupworkers need to define their overall role not as leaders but as *facilitators*.

The facilitator's role allows scope for working with the pre existing leadership structure in a natural group without undermin ing it (Brown, 1986, pp.52-53) or challenging it in a damaging way. The main issue in such a case will be the negotiation of a role for the group facilitators and setting boundaries around the group as such. The Ainsley Teenage Action Group, for example - which consisted of a number of young people who were getting into trouble regularly because they had nothing to do on their estate but 'hang around' and attract inevitable police attention - had to establish when it was 'in session', as opposed to being simply a gang of friends 'hanging around' together, before it could undertake any group planning or activities. It also had to consider whether to accept what the groupworkers were saying they could offer to the group - in terms of helping them look at the issues which concerned them and decide for themselves if anything could be done - despite previous bad experiences of professionals. Once the users are engaged in a piece of work, the workers can then begin to find ways of encouraging them to speak out about their lives and the problems which confront them as a means of moving towards the setting of goals and taking action by the group.

An initially frustrating and unfamiliar role

All this can feel very time-consuming and frustrating. Developments would often be quicker and more predictable if the workers went ahead and took decisions. The refusal to be directive can be difficult both for workers and for members, but the process is nonetheless necessary if users are going to take responsibility for decisions and events. It is especially difficult for workers with a background in statutory social work, who may be more used to taking decisions for themselves and others, to sit back and consciously stop themselves from directing the decisions of a group, allowing the group to move at its own pace and learn from its own mistakes.

Often, people who are unfamiliar with the role fall into the trap of going too far the other way and becoming totally non-interventive. This is not what is implied by facilitation. It means playing an active role but being sensitive to the differences between this and a dominant one. It means resisting the sense of passive acceptance which members can bring to a group, especially at the beginning. It does not mean falling over backwards to keep one's self and one's own views invisible and unheard.

A clear example of this is that there are some things workers will be prepared to be involved in, and others not. Since involvement is constructed as a partnership of workers and users, it would be dishonest for workers not to share the things they feel strongly *about. It can also mean that they collude with the group in being* oppressive of others. Workers' expectations and assumptions are easily taken for granted, as being in agreement with the group, if left unspoken. In the Ainsley Group, for example, sexism, and to a lesser extent racism, were confronted because they were issues about which the workers had developed their own fundamental practice principles. They were not introduced out of context as separate topics but were discussed and challenged as and when they oc curred. It is essential to be honest with members about your 'bottom line', about what you can and cannot accept.

As well as needing to think carefully about their facilitative role for the sake of their own clarity in practice, workers need to work hard at explaining and maintaining this role in the group. Member will be more used to professionals as figures of authority, and as providers or with-holders of resources. Consequently, they will expect the workers to tell them what to do and how to do it, and to procure everything the group needs to make it function. It takes frequent direct explanation and practical demonstrations for group members to recognise that they can look to the workers for help but not for instruction. Workers have initially to be directive about being non-directive. They must hold strongly to their view about what means would best facilitate the group to achieve its aims but not attempt to influence what those aims should be.

Facilitation in context

Group maintenance

Perhaps 'facilitation' is largely another term for what Douglas (1976, p.71) refers to as 'maintenance functions' and Brown (1986, p.54) as 'maintenance-leadership functions'. However, as conceptu alised in the standard literature of groupwork, these are only par tially appropriate in self-directed groups and workers have to adapt them to the value framework of empowerment. Some are frankly inapt: 'setting standards' (mentioned by both the above authors) and evaluating group functioning against them (Douglas, 1976, p.71), would not normally be a function of the workers adopting a self directed approach because group members should be helped to set and maintain their own standards. They also carry out their own evaluation.

On the other hand, there is no difficulty in absorbing into the approach the skills which Douglas refers to as 'encouraging' and 'gate-keeping' (that is, 'attempting to keep communication channels open'). Those in Brown's list which are relatively unproblematic similarly include 'en couraging participation', 'helping communication', 'observing proc esses', 'listening actively' and 'building trust'. These are basic tools for the job, without which none of the other functions can be performed. 'Energising' is also a fundamental skill, provided it is channelled towards the goals which the group has set for itself and not in a direction of the workers' own choosing. Indeed, these functions all need to be exercised in a style which is compatible with the overall principles of empowerment. Hence, in the normal course of group meetings, the workers would share with group members the task of ensuring that sufficient space is created in discussion for individuals to have their say. The Nottingham 'Who Cares' Group perceived this immediately as its own responsibility and wrote its rules accordingly to include: 'Only one person to speak at once'.

Continuing to consider what is and is not facilitative, we see that 'compromising' should always refer to the worker's own 'idea or status', as Douglas intended, and not that of the group. In place of the concept of compromising, indeed, we might prefer that of flexibility. The workers in self-directed groups need always to be actively on the look-out for the impetus, arising collectively from group members, to influence or modify group objectives. They should not experience this as opposed to their own ideas, because their own ideas should not have been predominating in the first place. In the face of fresh initiatives from the group, it can also be unhelpful and de-skilling for the members at times if the workers attempt to hold to previously agreed decisions. This requires careful reflection. With consul tancy support, the workers may need to make themselves aware of the intrusion of their own preferences into such judgements.

'Expressing group feelings' (Douglas, 1976, p.71) or 'evaluating the emotional climate' (Brown, 1986, p.54), in order to be empower ing and facilitating, require that the worker should merely state what he or she is experiencing, not attempt to interpret it. Where a worker does try to pick up and voice the prevailing mood or feelings in the group (which can assist participants' voices to be heard), members must at all times feel perfectly free to disagree with what the worker has sensed to be the case - there should be no hierarchy of control over this, just as there is not over any other aspect of the group's functioning.

The skill of 'harmonising' or, as Douglas (1976, p.71) goes on to define it, 'attempting to reconcile disagreements, reducing tension by pouring oil on troubled waters, getting people to explore their differences' also clearly remains a useful one but should not be used presumptuously by workers simply to cool people out. Anger is often justified and it is, in fact, crucial that members should come to trust and even to value their own anger if they are to arrive at a real comprehension of the oppression they have personally experienced.

We would urge that the group itself needs to learn the skills of 'resolving interpersonal conflict' (Brown, 1986, p.54), for example by giving both sides' views an adequate airing or by recognising that a particular person is facing personal difficulties and is distraught and temporarily unreasonable. It should do so, however, in the growing understanding that such expressions of hostility often represent a misdirecting towards one another of anger which could more fruitfully be focused on the actual source of their oppression, and hence channelled into motivation to achieve external change. At other times, an individual may direct anger inward into self-blame.

Here again, both workers and other members can ease the way for them to realise the inappropriateness of this. Page (1983, pp.9-10), who is a community worker, highlights some of these latter functions as being under-emphasised in the literature. The reality of groupwork is that the skills workers often need to use most effectively are those of dealing with people who have little or no experience of working collectively and who may need a good deal of individual support within the group early on, mediating conflict, and attempting to mend relationships where trust has broken down. As a feminist, Page argues that these personal, or process, aspects of work must be recognised and attended to: dealing with mistrust, post- or pre-meeting flak, the things which remain unsaid to those for whom they are intended, people's discomfort with each other or the situation in which they find themselves. In con trast, she argues, the rhetoric is often constructed around a macho discourse on strategies, tactics and action. In other words, the military metaphors should not be dismissed as accidental They represent the prevalence of powerful, male imagery in much of our thinking about effective intervention. If we are serious about anti oppressive working, we have to rethink the meta-language which we use to talk about practice as much as the practice itself because the two are heavily intertwined. In this way, we will draw nearer to a truly facilitative style.

A reducing role in group maintenance

Overall, the involvement of workers in group maintenance will reduce over time as groups become able to take on more and more of the responsibility for these matters. As the group becomes more confident and able to take over responsibility for process analysis as well as for its own task activities, so workers can recede more into the background - acting as a reference point, perhaps, rather than as a catalyst for change. Members then gradually begin to treat them as consultants or co-activists, rather than as professionals. There may still be times when the workers move to the fore again temporarily. For example, a group may hit the doldrums for a period, or it may become static simply because members are enjoying the performance of tasks for their own sake rather than as a means to an end, or because the social pay-offs of group membership have caused them to lose sight of their longer term aims. Generally, though, in a mature self-directed group, such episodes should be short-lived A brief return to the more active facilitation of earlier stages in prompting the group to set and carry out clearly defined goals, will normally get matters back on course.

Task functions

The values of empowerment, translated into groupwork practice, will mean that group members move increasingly to the fore in carrying out task functions on behalf of the group. Over time, they will become able to share or to take over an increasing number of what Douglas (1976, pp.70-71) lists under this name and Brown (1986, pp.53-54) as 'task-leadership functions'. The workers willneed to act less as information bearers, for example, as the group first learns how to follow suggestions on where and how to find the data it needs for decision-making and taking action, and later develops the skills to know itself where to look and whom to consult. Similarly, initially it may tend to be the workers who set out all the alternative courses of action and their likely consequences for consideration and decision by the group or who notice that the group is nearing a decision. As time goes by, however, the members will become increasingly able to facilitate their own decision-making in this way. In particular, although in the early days of a group the workers may accede to the group's request that they should undertake a minimum of tasks which are outside the access or current skills of group members, the need for this should progressively disappear during the life of the group.

An example of a task-function which should quickly be handed to group members is that of judging when group members are ready to act as advocates or negotiators on behalf of the group. Here, it is crucial that the group should trust itself as soon as possible to make the approaches to seek official support, funding and the like, since this will greatly influence the degree to which the group is taken seriously and will also give members control over their own group. No one else should negotiate anything away on their behalf or decide what compromises are acceptable. A negotiator is only ever a 'go between' from users to outside bodies; he or she is not empowered to make delegated decisions on their behalf. It is true, however, that some individuals - and sometimes whole groups - will not be suffi ciently confident to act as the voice of the group until membership has engendered in them considerably more confidence, so the work ers may need to go with them initially. The words used to frame the group's demands should, as far as possible, however, be those of group members and the workers should check out, in discussion with their consultant, that they are not seizing on perceived lack of confidence to cover their collusion with outside bodies who find their professional aura more acceptable in negotiation than the nega tively labelled service users who constitute the group membership.

A midway point may be reached at which members can 'do the talking' in meetings with outside authorities, prospective funders, and the like, but where it is useful for a groupworker still to be present at the meeting in order to see fair play. We see this role as that of a 'line judge' because, unlike a referee, this individual does not take overall control of the meeting, or play an active part in it at all times. He or she will merely ensure that the representatives of the group are not 'out-played' from the start by the domination of those with whom they are negotiating, and s/he will signal if the latter overstep the mark. It is all too easy for skilled negotiators to play to their own rules and not to allow less experienced people a fair say. The groupworker as 'line judge' keeps communication smooth and open, along previously mutually agreed lines, but without intervening to alter its direction.

As with group maintenance, there are some task functions listed by other authors which are inapplicable in empowerment work because of the value-base of the work. Taking those functionsoutlined by Douglas (1976, pp.70-71), we would suggest that workers taking a self-directed approach should largely refrain from 'information or opinion-giving' and, equally importantly, from Brown's additional notions (1986, 53-54) of 'giving directions' and 'diagnosing'. These are all too directive and hence discourage participants from raising their own issues and setting their own goals. The workers should be aiming to share with the group all the other task functions, and increasingly to hand these over as the group matures and members become able to ask each other for information or to decide when a consensus has been reached.

We would add to the lists compiled by other authors that the workers should share in the encouragement of appropriate risk-taking by group members in considering new approaches to tasks and trying themselves out in new situations - often preceded by 'rehearsal' within the safety of the group. There is a careful balance to be drawn between, on the one hand, preparing the ground adequately for group members to take on new tasks and responsibilities and, on the other, allowing members to learn through their own mistakes. Sometimes, it may be necessary to ask the group to judge whether members going too far, too fast, could inflict irretrievable damage on future chances of success.

Workers should be aware that, as professionals, their own style of approaching tasks may not be the one the group will adopt. In negotiating with external bodies, for instance, workers have a tendency to set out and consider the strengths and weaknesses of the other party's point of view before deciding how best to oppose or circumvent it. To the group, this may initially look like selling out and taking sides against them. Service users may take a far simpler stance than the workers, based on their experience or anticipation of hostile interaction. This purity of vision can often be immensely invigorating both for members and workers and to attempt to temper it is to risk diluting the user perspective. On occasions, however, the adoption of too rigid a position may be counterproduc tive. In the last analysis, the workers can only advise the group in these terms; the eventual decision as to how to proceed must lie with the group.

The parameters of the facilitator's role

Despite the last statement above, in considering the facilitator's role overall, we would strongly emphasise that there is no less skill involved in this kind of work than in groupwork which is led from the centre. Although control of the direction the group takes lies with members, the groupworker is far from non-interventive. In fact, he or she will say and do a great deal, and exercise considerable expertise, but with a strong tendency to focus on group process and only indirectly on group content. Groups may require assistance, for example, to come together most effectively to exchange views, to form opinions, or to generate the knowledge or the skills needed to meet the task in hand.

In the Ainsley Teenage Action Group the workers assisted the teenagers a great deal in formulating and meeting their aims. They were helped not only to form themselves into a group and to set their own objectives (to obtain their own youth club and persuade the police to be less provocative), but to learn the skills involved in meeting high-ranking police officers and councillors, raising funds, assessing the views of other young people and of adults on the estate, organising and chairing a public meeting, serving on a committee and eventually, several years later, deciding on the uses to which the new youth club would be put.

As was mentioned earlier, there may be a false idea that, because workers adopting a self-directed approach do not impose agendas on the members, they therefore must express no views at all of their own. In fact, however, it may be perfectly appropriate, for example, for the groupworker to retain a veto on his or her own continued involvement with the group - to be used, perhaps, if the members decide after full consideration to pursue an objective which is racist and with which the worker does not feel able to be identified.

On the other hand, it is not acceptable within the model for the practitioner to be working to a 'double agenda'. Reid and Epstein (1972, p.49) use this term for a situation where:

> The client may indeed acknowledge a problem that he[sic] wants help with, but the caseworker or agency see him as having other problems, usually of a graver sort, that are more deserving of attention.

The implication is that this difference of view is not brought into the open. We would extend the concept to groupwork when, for example, the groupworker has made a professional assessment that what is really needed is to employ the group merely as a locus within which individual change can occur, but allows the members to think that the group is a vehicle for external change. If the goals of a group are some form of external change determined collectively by its members, any radical departure from them - for example by a groupworker who assesses the members individually as somehow deficient and needing to change - would be unethical and contrary to the values of self-directed practice.

An example of facilitation in practice

It is perhaps easiest to convey more of the 'feel' of facilitation by looking at an example in greater detail. The Ainsley Teenage Action Group will again be used for this purpose (see Mullender and Ward, 1991, for a fuller account.) The groupworkers began by establishing themselves as a trustworthy and reliable presence in the lives of the young people, working consistently to the practice principles of self directed groupwork. This meant that, for example, they refused to accept members' negative labels but sought from them their own definitions of the problems they faced They were also committed to the possibility of the young people taking action on these issues through the group. The workers continually affirmed, acknowledged and respected what the young people brought to the group, encouraging them to find their own strengths and take their own decisions; in short, treating the young people as adults not as children.

For a group to become self-determining, it is necessary for the workers to create a relaxed informal setting in which the members feel comfortable and confident. As the Ainsley Group gained mo mentum, ways had to be found to promote a meeting where there was a relaxed informal attitude on the one hand, and as much participation as possible on the other, without exercising undue control. Being used to being told what to do, members found it hard to discipline themselves and to control their own sessions. In the early days, some lacked the confidence to participate at all, while others dominated aggressively and gathered cliques of supporters. The workers might have been tempted to use individuals as allies to try to achieve more control, but they did not consider this acceptable, ethical or, in the long run, likely to be effective.

The use of structured exercises, such as brainstorming, suggested by the workers and taken on by the group, helped to some extent but was by no means the whole answer. Eventually, a system for managing these problems emerged naturally and was positively encouraged by the groupworkers. The members came to allow themselves a wilder 'relax' session at the beginning of each meeting, followed by getting down to 'Business'. This gradually became an accepted part of the meeting routine.

Sometimes the 'relax', or general discussion time, took up the whole session and no formal 'work' appeared to get done. What the workers discovered, however - by careful observation followed by analysis in consultancy sessions - was that in these informal ses sions a lot of 'business' was sorted out among the young people themselves, often pulling together discussions that had taken place outside club meetings, on the street or at school. After this, the business sessions, when they took place, were productive, sharp and decisive, and exercises could be used discriminatingly, to meet group purposes rather than workers' concerns about control.

What the workers had to recognise and accept was that, on

occasions, the members were taking decisions independently and without their awareness. They needed to tune into the wavelength of this informal but powerful decision-making process, whereby members might reach their own separate conclusions and not feel the need to communicate with them. This really tested the workers in their determination to facilitate the group in owning its own decisions and goals.

Conclusion

The term 'self-directed groupwork' encapsulates a style of working in which groupworkers do not 'lead' the group but facilitate people in making decisions for themselves and in controlling whatever out come ensues. Though identifiable skills and knowledge are em ployed, these do not accord special privilege or power and are not solely the province of the workers; they pass increasingly to the members as the group matures.

Facilitation in Self-Directed Groupwork

To adopt this style effectively, groupworkers must want to work with people and not to direct intervention to or at them. The groupworker must consequently value his or her most effective contribution as being facilitation rather than leadership in the traditional sense and not seek opportunities to jump into the driving seat. Workers may assist with finding means to achieve the group's desired ends, but they do not dictate what those ends should be. They will probably continue to make suggestions and offer alterna tive scenarios for consideration by group members, but their chief involvement will be in easing and highlighting group process, never in setting the aims of the work undertaken by the group. When these skills are successfully employed, the rewards of working in this way can be considerable because the group can be helped to set, and to achieve, complex and ambitious goals which make a real difference to their day-to-day life.

Acknowledgement

The authors wish to acknowledge the major contribution which has been made to their thinking by discussions with the innovative practitioners who have shared with them the development of the self-directed groupwork model, in particular the members of Social Action Training.

References

Brown, A (1986) *Groupwork*. Second Edition. Aldershot, Hants: Gower

Douglas, T. (1976) *Groupwork Practice*. London: Tavistock.

Mullender, A and Ward, D. (1991) *Self Directed Groupwork: Users Take Action for Empowerment*. London: Whiting and Birch.

Page, M. (1983) 'Language and community politics - or exorcising the old ideal!', *Talking Points*, 42. London: Association of Community Workers.

Reid, W. and Epstein, L. (1972) *Task Centered Casework*. New York: Columbia University Press.

This chapter was first published in 1991 in *Groupwork* Vol. 4(2), pp.141-151

At the time of writing Dave Ward was Senior Lecturer in Social Work at Nottingham University and Audrey Mullender was Director of the Centre for Applied Social Studies, University of Durham.

Facilitation and groupwork tasks in self-directed groupwork

Jennie Fleming and Dave Ward

In this paper we will briefly set out the principles and process of the self-directed groupwork model but our main focus will be on how people are putting the model into practice and changes we have observed in relation to groupwork tasks and facilitation within its application over the past 3 decades. Whilst we have found that self-directed groupwork continues to be practised by a range of professionals it is equally used by self-run groups with no input from a professional worker.

Introduction

Self-directed groupwork was formally constructed by Mullender and Ward in 1991, in *Self-directed Groupwork: Users take action for empowerment*. At the start of their book they wrote that the model had 'grown directly out of the efforts of many groupworkers and group members to find a way of working together that is rooted in anti-oppressive principles'. They recognised the centrality of the work of practitioners in pushing out the boundaries of groupwork and contributing to the development of the self-directed groupwork model. This is no less true for *Empowerment in Action: Self-directed groupwork* (Mullender, Ward, & Fleming, 2013) where the self-directed groupwork model is revisited and refined for current and future groupwork practice, in which we continued to draw heavily on the generosity of groupworkers and group members to tell us their stories and share their wisdom about groupwork.

The development of self-directed groupwork has always drawn strongly on people who have shared with us their knowledge of self-directed groupwork; they have given deep and rich insights into the reality of groupwork and most importantly have enriched our thinking and knowledge about self-directed groupwork and how it is being put into practice. In the same manner as Whitmore et al (2011) express, we have attempted to connect and relate 'individual ideas, thoughts and groups coming together to create a story reflecting the richness and complexity' of what groupworkers and, in many instances, group members told us (Whitmore et al, 2011, p.19). This paper draws on a body of information specially collected by the authors about people's understanding and use of self-directed groupwork.

Self-directed groupwork

Self-directed groupwork and, alongside it, Social Action, (which is a specific theory and practice for social change that uses self-directed groupwork as a strong element (Fleming, 2009) are continually developing as a way of working. These changes take place within the framework of values, principles and processes that evolve over time and change in detail but are non-negotiable in terms of an over-arching view of the world.

A notable feature of the self-directed approach is its clear and explicit value-base which is outlined in the form of six practice principles emphasising: the avoidance of labels, the rights of group members, basing intervention on a power analysis, assisting people to attain collective power through coming together in groups, challenging oppression though practice, and groups being facilitated rather than led. The most current version of these principles is set out below:

1. We are committed to social justice. We strive to challenge inequality and oppression in relation to race, gender, sexuality, age, religion, class, disability or any other form of social differentiation.
2. We believe all people have skills, experience and understanding that they can draw on to tackle the problems they face. We understand that people are experts in their own lives and we use this as a starting point for our work.
3. All people have rights, including the right to be heard, the

right to define the issues facing them and the right to take action on their own behalf. People also have the right to define themselves and not have negative labels imposed upon them.

4. Injustice and oppression are complex issues rooted in social policy, the environment and the economy. We understand people may experience problems as individuals but these difficulties can be translated into common concerns.

5. We understand that people working collectively can be powerful. People who lack the power and influence to challenge injustice and oppression as individuals can gain it through working with other people in a similar position.

6. We are not leaders, but facilitators. Our job is to enable people to make decisions for themselves and take ownership of whatever outcome ensues. Everybody's contribution to this process is equally valued and it is vital that our job is not accorded privilege.

(Mullender, Ward, Fleming, 2013, p. 49).

Self-directed groupwork combines two essential and inseparable elements: these six practice principles and a specific process. They are interdependent; the principles elevate the process beyond a set of techniques that, otherwise, would be barely distinguishable from other practices. Conversely, the principles without the process are unlikely to foster action or change. The approach enables groups of all ages and circumstances to take action and to achieve their collective goals. It offers an easy-to-understand and open-ended process that makes it possible for people to identify and act on issues that are important to them, while working within a set of values. The process involves starting with groups considering and describing what is going on in their lives collectively and identifying areas for change; they then consider why these issues exist. Next the group thinks of how participants might be able to take action to change things (a planning stage). They then undertake an agreed and planned course of action, following which the group together reflects on what has gone well, what has not, why and how things could be done differently to move further towards their goal. As this description indicates, it is an iterative and cyclical process. Self-directed groupworkers provide the framework for groups to consider problems, issues and concerns. Group members provide the content, using their skills, knowledge and expertise. Group members create the knowledge and understanding through active participation: describing, suggesting, analysing, deciding, experiencing and reflecting (Fleming and Ward, 1999).

Inherent in the six principles is an assumption of a social structural analysis of the issues facing marginalised groups. Self-directed groups do not have therapeutic purposes. All the groups that have helped develop our understanding of self-directed groupwork are groups that are not primarily about meeting individual needs of the participants - though this may of course happen and beneficial intrapersonal and interpersonal outcomes may come about as a result of participation in self-directed groups. Rather the focus is on addressing a shared 'external' issue (Munford and Walsh-Taipati, 2001, p.70).

Having said that, self-directed groupwork is grounded in a great many generic skills, as identified, for example, in the *Standards for Social Work with Groups* (Abels and Garvin, 2010) and shared in application with critical and structural approaches to social work (e.g. Mullaly, 2010). Indeed, Cohen and Mullender (2000) have pointed out that members of self-directed groups may actually achieve a greater degree of individual change than members of deliberately therapeutic groups, simply because of the benefits of getting involved and of coming to believe in themselves through what they are doing. Certainly, given that self-directed groupwork is grounded in generic groupwork skills, it is perhaps not surprising, therefore, to see progress on several fronts in well-run groups. Mullender and Ward (1985, 1991) have always seen the individual change achieved in self-directed groups as a 'secondary advantage' and it remains the fact that it is the external change goals that predominate. Self-directed groupwork starts with the external and focuses there, celebrating the 'secondary advantage' of individual growth and change.

Over the years there have been a number of articles in *Groupwork* exploring the theory and practice of self-directed groupwork and Social Action, for example Ward and Mullender (1991); Harrison and Ward (1999); Fleming and Luczynski (1999); Aubrey (2004); Cary et al (2004) and most recently Arches (2012).

The groups

We recently undertook some research to find out how relevant people thought self-directed groupwork was to them, what self-directed groupwork was taking place currently and whether people were working in ways that related to the model. We found ourselves having conversations with people in the UK, Ireland, France, USA, Canada and New Zealand. We found a wealth of groupwork happening, both based in and arising directly from self-directed groupwork or Social Action approaches. We drew also from many people who, when we described the process and principles of the model, immediately responded with 'that is just what we do' or said that they could easily recognise the model in what they were doing.

In the course of our research we found self-directed groups in a wide range of settings, for example in schools and in a variety of independent movements outside the predominating contexts of health and social care. Thus, we found groups in the UK, for example, developing community support for older and disabled people and self-advocacy groups of people with dementia; groups of mental health service users in France and Canada; a range of groups supported by professional workers for family support in the UK, New Zealand and Canada. We came across projects of refugees and immigrants and a university lecturer in the US using self-directed groupwork as both method and subject in a Service Learning programme, with the students then taking self-directed groupwork to groups of young people in the community (Arches, 2012). There are young people in Baltimore, USA, who have worked hard over many years, facilitated by a high school teacher, to achieve their own community-based youth-run centre (Berdan et al, 2006; Carey et al, 2004) and, in the UK, young people using a self-directed groupwork approach to organise campaigns against 'mosquito' devices set up to keep them out of public spaces (BBC, 2011). We met young people who had formed *Asian Pride* a self-directed group for lesbian, gay, bisexual and transgender Asian and Pacific Islanders in the US (http://www.asianprideproject. org/). We even found that some groups such as Advocacy in Action and Turning Point, who had contributed to Mullender and Ward (1991), were still active.

Self-directed groupwork has elements in common with participatory research groups and action research (McIntyre, 2008). Indeed self-directed groupwork has informed the development of Social Action research, where researchers drawing on the principles and process set in motion a process of engagement working with interested parties to shape research agendas, make decisions about research focus, ensuring their voice is heard in ways they consider appropriate and controlling outcomes with a commitment to research leading to change (Mullender, Ward, Fleming, 2013, p.165, 166).

What we did find in England at least was that the involvement of social workers and probation officers in groupwork has almost evaporated over the past 20 years. In the 1990s groupwork was a core element of social work training; now very few universities in England teach it (although this is not the case around the world). As the focus of state social work has narrowed to the oversight and management of individuals and families, groupwork seems to be seen as less relevant. Another significant change was that in 1991 the role of facilitator in a group was predominantly considered the province of a professional worker (Ward and Mullender, 1991); however in 2012 we found much self-directed groupwork in the voluntary sector and many groups with no 'professional' involvement at all. There are many self-run, service user led and egalitarian groups facilitated by group members. In these groups roles are often fluid, with groupwork tasks being recognised and shared amongst members.

Groupwork roles

What has become readily apparent is that the distinction between facilitators and group members was blurred in many groups. The descriptions of facilitation in Mullender and Ward (1991) and Ward and Mullender (1991) were based on the assumption that the group leader/facilitator would be an outsider, and they would control the *process* that the group went through. What was distinctive at that time was that the focus and the content of the groupwork were decided by the members. However, in reality, within self-directed groupwork the groupwork tasks and facilitation functions have never been the sole province of the groupworkers, whether they are peers or outside workers, paid or voluntary. In the model, group maintenance, for example, is shared as far as possible with all group members, and increasingly so over time. Where a facilitator does exercise such functions, this is done, not through any special privilege or superior understanding, but on behalf of the group.

It is often the case that a facilitator will require the skills to work with people who have had little or no experience of working collectively and who may need a good deal of individual support within the group early on, mediating conflict and attempting to mend relationships where trust has broken down. From a feminist perspective, Page (1983) argued that such personal, or process, aspects of work must be recognised and attended to as carefully as the rather macho-sounding issues of strategies, campaigns, tactics and action. This is encompassed in the self-directed groupwork/ Social Action principle that states:

> methods of working must reflect non-elitist principles: the facilitator's role is to enable people to make decisions for themselves and take ownership of whatever outcome ensues.

Everybody's contribution to this process is equally valued and we should rethink the meta-language used when talking about 'taking action' as much as the action itself, since the two are heavily intertwined.

The 'outside' facilitator

Facilitators in self-directed groups, when they are health and social care professionals from outside the group, need to base their style of intervention firmly on recognising that all members already have skills, understanding and ability. They should employ a non-patronising approach based on the belief that people already know and understand many of the issues surrounding the reality of their lives (Longres and McLeod, 1980, p.269). They also need techniques for encouraging group members to ask themselves the broader questions about the political, economic and social factors that contribute to the actual difficulties they face in their lives. Provided they can do this, health and social care professionals have a significant contribution to make:

> Workers do have a certain knowledge and expertise that derives from their own experience - from training and from their involvement in practice. This expertise will be largely demonstrated in their ability to develop discussion and to be used as a source of information. It is not an expertise that requires deference from the group, but it is the special contribution made by the .... worker. (Longres and McLeod, 1980, p. 270)

That such an approach is valued by group members is illustrated by the comments made years later, by a group member of the Ainsley Teenage Action Group (one of the self-directed groups run in Nottingham in the 1980s and described in *Self-Directed Groupwork*), facilitated at the time by a Probation Officer, a youth worker and a university social work lecturer:

> Why did we show up for two hours every week? We were in control, we were in charge. We set the guidelines. When we first started off, we thought we would do it and just not get into trouble — then it carried on, and people started to listen to us..... You were just on the sidelines. We did what we wanted to do without people being in charge. You let us get on with it basically.
> (group member)
> Arches and Fleming (2007, pp. 40, 42)

Changing roles: Handing over to the group

The self-directed groupwork model always allowed for group members taking more control as time went on. As groups progress through the stages of the model, members frequently take on more and more responsibility for the group. They increasingly share both groupwork and practical tasks with the original facilitators who may be paid workers or fellow, perhaps founding, group members. As Ward and Mullender wrote, *the involvement of workers in group maintenance will reduce over time as groups become able to take on more and more of the responsibility'* (1991, p.145)

Together, everyone engages in what Longres and McLeod (1980, p.271) refer to as *'the process of discovery, development and change'*, whilst the facilitator encourages group members to recognise the capabilities they obviously possess. In this way, the groupworker task changes from an emphasis on structuring the decision-making process to creating space and opportunities for group members to work autonomously. Different group members come to the fore and use new found skills and confidence; there can be less reliance on key individuals who perhaps had a role in establishing the group initially, as ownership becomes more widely held and a larger number of people take responsibility for both tasks and group maintenance.

An example of this change of roles took place within a neighbourhood-based group of young people in Nottingham. On the first occasion, when the group members ran a summer holiday activity scheme, the facilitators had to assist members in detail on all aspects of the planning and running of the scheme. The next time round, the groupworkers stayed in the background and played a more advisory role. In direct terms, they only needed to provide, or to point members towards, for example, information on sources of funding, regulations relating to play schemes and on the practicalities of running their scheme. This left members free to consolidate and extend the skills and awareness they had developed previously. This process is also visible in the Youth Dreamers, who have written in *Groupwork* in the past (Carey et al, 2004). Youth Dreamers is a long standing group of young people working with a teacher in Baltimore to develop a youth-run centre (http://www.youthdreamers.org/). As young people have become more knowledgeable about writing applications for funding, contacting potential supporters, contributing to meetings with adults and confident to facilitate after-school sessions for other young people, the role of the supporting teacher has retreated more into the background to become seen as a resource to the group (Berdan et al, 2006, p.35).

To be sensitive to these changes and to adapt their practice accordingly, facilitators need to be on their toes - using evaluation processes to stay alert to the way the group is evolving. The same questions form the framework of evaluation as those which lie at the heart of the practice itself:

- What are the issues and problems members face?
- Why do these problems exist?
- How can we as facilitators enable members to achieve change?

Of course, at any stage of the process, in order to keep the work progressing non-oppressively, these questions must be guided by and asked within the framework of the six principles which underpin all self-directed groupwork. These principles can be viewed dually, both as underpinning values but also practically, as directions for undertaking practice.

As groups develop and mature, they become able to spot and handle challenges and tasks by themselves. They become increasingly secure in the authority of their own knowledge base (Munn-Giddings and McVicar, 2007). For example, the Youth Dreamers acknowledge the different levels of support and contribution members can offer and point out it is possible for young people to be involved at a range of levels: from being members of the Board, facilitating sessions on a regular basis, taking part in one-off events and, of course, simply using the centre. Participants can move between these levels of involvement and responsibility as they gain experience and confidence.

Some of the 'seasoned' Youth Dreamers in considering a series of questions posed to them by the authors, have reflected on how the Social Action/self-directed groupwork principles can be seen in their work and how they influence the roles that Youth Dreamers take. For example, one of their responses, in their own words, says:

People have choice about how they share their skills, understanding and ability:
Newer youth don't have the same ownership as the original crew so the buy-in is a bit more challenging. They come into the beautiful house and have no idea how hard we worked to create it. We always include a component of

peer teaching where the 'seasoned' Youth Dreamers 'teach' the 'fresh' Youth Dreamers about how we got to this point. This includes scavenger hunts through the house and our photo timeline, peer lessons in grant writing, fundraising, designing after school programs, etc.

We value people's strengths in a number of ways that include:

o   *We realize that not everyone has the same strengths, so we respect people's strengths and ideas.*

o   *Volunteers help by choice, running and creating programming that utilizes their individual strengths, to teach and mentor students.*

o   *We use creativity and groupwork to encourage and aid our children in learning and perfecting new skills.*

o   *People have rights; rights to decision to take part, on the issues, and action; to choose; to be heard; to control the agenda.*

o   *Since the Youth Dreamers began, decision making has been a group process where everyone has a part and opinion in decision making.*

o   *Youth Dreamers has a board of directors, composed of eight youth and eight adults who work together to form committees to run our programming and make important financial, social, and other such decisions. This shows youth and adults working together to achieve a common goal.*

o   *All adults work hard to facilitate the voice of youth, allowing them to take the lead with icebreakers, peer teaching, grant writing and more.*

One of the Youth Dreamers who was part of the initial group of young people, writes again in response to questions from the authors, about how their Dream House is run now:

We are the pioneers of what happens in our organization. We have a team of Youth Dreamers (the Dream Team) who meet once a month to evaluate programs and seek ways to improve. Our Dream Team reflect, analyze, and evaluate each of our programs, and decide what types of fundraisers and events we want to take on. They essentially manage the nonprofit and run the center. Everyone has a voice and is encouraged to use it, even our Board of Directors in which both youth and adults serve on. We use their expertise, experience, and guidance to ensure that we are making ethical and safe choices that align with our mission, vision, and goals.

Withdrawing

The open-ended nature of self-directed groups, means that eventually the facilitators, especially if they are professionals or from outside the group, may need to judge when it is appropriate to withdraw completely from the group. Even if they were the initiators, they do not necessarily need to continue forever. However:

> Letting go of almost anything you have been instrumental in starting is not easy. When a carers' group moves from being social worker led to member run, everyone - both members and professionals involved - needs to think through the issues ....

> Professionals ... often have unreal expectations about this sort of change. They underestimate the complexity of it and the time it will take. (Wilson, 1988, p.34)

When a group is contemplating becoming self-sustaining, action and direction, like participation, may require formal and explicit structures based on democratic principles (Freeman, 1970, pp.7-8). These include delegating responsibility and distributing authority to those best able to handle it, rather than to the most popular or most dominant individuals. Various groups have chosen to rotate or share tasks amongst all members. The group itself, according to Freeman, needs to determine who will exercise power and authority and who will have access to information and, to ensure that this transition does not entail becoming oppressive in the process, to share both as widely as possible.

There is no single clear process of how power can be transferred in professionally-initiated groups to the members (Seebohm et al, 2010). It is a two-way process. As the members gain more autonomy, the groupworker too must be preparing to release control and move out of the 'central person' role (Preston-Shoot, 2007, pp.146-150). This needs to be done in a skilled and measured way, giving attention to both practical and relationship aspects of the group's functioning. Rather than a uniformly paced withdrawal, as would be the case in structured conventional groupwork, letting go involves the skill of gauging when the group has become sufficiently self-motivating and self-resourcing for the facilitators' contribution to its functioning, at both task and emotional levels, no longer to be essential. Unless the group has become resourced from elsewhere or has achieved its purpose and is drawing to a natural end, it is crucial for the facilitators to make a realistic assessment, in discussion with group members, of the group's strengths and functioning at the time, not arising from a pre-determined idea of what is appropriate in general terms.

This stage in a group's life needs to be viewed flexibly and there are a variety of ways that members can be supported to achieve more shared and distributed power. Strategies can include coming initially to alternate meetings, then, in consultation with members, every third meeting and so on; or at the end of each meeting, when plans are being made for 'what next', part of the discussion could be whether the facilitator needs to attend or not. In the work done at the Service Learning project in the USA, (Arches, 2012), college students develop their own skills in self-directed groupwork before going out to work with school students. The college students rotate the role of facilitator amongst themselves in university class – so developing with their peers both the skills and confidence to take on facilitation roles.

Some groups claim to be self-directed, but follow a scheduled number of weeks of facilitation. They often do not long outlive the workers leaving, thereby providing an example of two common errors made about how facilitators can reduce their role in groups. First, withdrawal is built into the planning of a group in advance and, second, that it is a 'once and for all' activity. This is often the case where groupworkers have been attracted by the efficacy of the WHAT, WHY, HOW process in beginning a group and engaging the motivation of members, but have not fully understood and adopted the statement of principles of Self-directed Groupwork out of which flow an open-ended timescale and withdrawal only by negotiation and in agreement with members. CIFAN is a group of North American public organisation workers who were unhappy about the directive and authoritarian management approaches which are being introduced into their workplace. A trade union officer found out about the self-directed groupwork process and, after a brief introduction to the approach, decided to apply it to a series of three meetings she was convening. An agenda for action was formulated at the end of the third meeting and roles and responsibilities were delegated to a small number of volunteers. Follow-up meetings were called but were poorly attended and the campaign did not gain momentum. The facilitator had viewed the self-directed approach as a strictly time-limited intervention, very possibly on assumptions arising from other areas of her work. Members had had an initial experience at the three meetings, which, according to all accounts, they experienced as positive and empowering but the premature termination of self-directed facilitation had cast them adrift, and unable to build on the foundations hastily created in just 3 meetings.

Nevertheless, many groups have moved to a position in which 'professional' facilitation is minimal. One vital feature of the Youth Dreamers has been how the 'seasoned' Youth Dreamers support the integration of 'fresh' Youth Dreamers and how they work together to both keep the vision alive over a very long period of time, and also allow new ideas and developments to be incorporated. Over time the young people have come to take more and more control and responsibility for the actions of the group.

Self facilitated groups

Other groups have never sought – or have, indeed, positively rejected - involvement from 'outsiders' to support them. We came across a number of examples of such groups in our recent investigations.

One self-run group that recognised the self-directed process in what they did was a local young people's group that campaigned against 'mosquito' devices (instruments which emit high pitched noise aimed at deterring young people from gathering in certain public areas) on city council properties in their city. There was a core group of about 6 or 7 young people who did most of the action and met face to face. There was also a wider group of young people with more virtual involvement, for example through email, Facebook and Twitter (about 30 of them). The core group members used facebook groups to attract interest and gauge the opinions of a very wide group of young people about the devices – all wanted a ban.

As part of their campaign they linked with national children's rights organisations and spoke with local and national politicians. When they were successful with their local campaign they developed an action plan based on detailing the work they had undertaken and made it available to other groups of young people to use if they wanted. The campaigns gained support of the Children's Commissioners in England and Scotland (BBC, 2011) and this specific group was used as a case study in *Positive for Youth* a document produced by the Parliamentary Under Secretary of State for Children and Families in the UK Department for Education (Department for Education, 2011, p.68). One of the core group members, who was familiar with Social Action principles and process, says that their group could be called a Social Action group and he could recognise both the principles and process in how they worked together and what they did, although they had not overtly set out to *be* a Social Action group.

Advocacy in Action is a group that positively chooses not to have professional involvement. There are no workers in Advocacy in Action but there are 'facilitators'; these can be any member and people can take different facilitating roles within the group. For example, a woman with learning difficulties facilitates a group of women who have experienced sexual abuse. They do recognise that there are tasks that need to be done to maintain a group but do not see these as the province of any particular person as everybody contributes to this. They recognise the skills of all group members and value equally the qualities people bring to the groups - for example the importance of a smile or holding a hand when people do not feel included. In their experience people are keen and ready to take on responsibility for group process and to work together in such a way that all are able to do this.

Members of Advocacy in Action feel it is important that people watch and learn from others within the group and have the opportunity to model ways of being in a group. No one has been on a course about groupwork or how to run groups - they develop the skills themselves in practice and these are then shared among group members. In like manner, they recognise that people have the right to define their own experience and within Advocacy in Action make room for people to make decisions for themselves, creating what they describe as 'growing spaces'.

Family Advocacy Network is a service user led network. Groupwork is their primary means of working. Like Advocacy in Action, it has been a conscious decision not to have a professional facilitating a group - they prefer to do it themselves. Members seek to create a safe environment which they say that they find easier to do without professional involvement. A consequence of this safe environment is that people do feel able to show their emotions – they get angry or cry because of their frustrations or grief. Given setbacks and disappointments that members experience in their lives, this is not surprising and it is seen as vital that people feel able to express emotions in the group, considering this to be an important feature of service user led groups.

In Family Advocacy Network roles are informal and often members just see a need and fulfil the role. They have found that supportive peer-to-peer relationships are often less predominant in professionally facilitated groups than in service user led ones. They acknowledge it is possible that facilitation might be smoother and more practiced with professional involvement but there are issues of power and control that cannot always be resolved – they say that different needs and different agendas are highlighted if professionals are involved. With professionals present they have found that some group members become very quiet and can be intimidated – they quickly stop asking questions. After all, professionals as gatekeepers are often the problem in people's lives and are not seen as potential allies:

> We need to organise ourselves and offer own support, we can invite professionals in if we think it would be useful. (interview with group member)

Commonality of experience is very important for members of Family Advocacy Network. For example, one member had cared for his parents with dementia and had found he was fighting lots of 'mini-battles' to get past 'all the people who say 'No!''. He could see others struggling with precisely the same things and the group began informally with people sharing knowledge and experience, for example, of having been to a tribunal, of helping others prepare themselves or of going with them to a meeting. At the group sessions a member presents their problem or issue or particular challenge they are facing; then the other group members speak about it, drawing on their own experience to advise and offer insights. As well as achieving practical successes, recognising solidarity with others who have similar experiences can be uplifting. The discussions in the group have helped members understand that others face the same kinds of problems and obstacles as they did; they recognise the social oppression of people such as themselves but also their own potential power and ability to have greater control over their lives. Furthermore, participants have built friendship and support networks through the group which, as well as relieving isolation, have fostered awareness, self-confidence and self-esteem.

Conclusion

The term 'self-directed groupwork' has always encapsulated a style of working in which facilitators do not lead the group, but facilitate people in making decisions for themselves and in controlling whatever outcome ensues. The model has always been grounded upon the recognition that the skills and knowledge of facilitation do not accord privilege or power to the facilitator, and has never considered that this role and ensuing tasks were the province only of the facilitator. Rather, they pass increasingly to group members as groups develop. What has been exciting to observe is how, since the model was first formally conceptualised in 1991, this key element has evolved further. In many groups participants have really 'taken over' and in some, indeed, they have decided, from the outset, not to designate the tasks of facilitator to any specific individual, least of all to a professional, but rather to share them amongst all group members.

Acknowledgements

The authors wish to acknowledge the major contribution that has been made to their thinking by discussions with innovative group facilitators who have shared their knowledge and experiences with us and so have contributed to the application and development of the Social Action/self-directed groupwork model. People who specifically contributed material to this paper are: Miriam Harris, Dominique Davis, Keyani Kenny, Aniya Hodges and Chris Lawton of Youth Dreamers; Julie Gosling of Advacacy in Action; Larry Gardiner of Family Advocacy Network and Joan Arches UMASS; Harrison Carter of the Campaign against Mosquito Devices

References

Abels, P. and Garvin, C. (2010) *Standards for Social Work Practice With Groups* (2nd edition). Alexandria(VA): Association for the Advancement of Social Work with Groups

Arches, J. (2012) The role of groupwork in social action projects with youth. *Groupwork*, 22, 1, 59-77

Arches, J. and Fleming, J. (2007) Building our own monument: A social action group revisited. *Practice*, 19, 1, 33-47

Aubrey, J. (2004) The roots of social action. *Groupwork*, 14, 2, 6-23

BBC (2011) Teenagers should challenge use of mosquito devices. *BBC News website*. [Accessed 20 December 2011 at http://www.bbc.co.uk/news/uk-politics-16273076]

Berdan, K., Boulton, I., Eidman-Aadahl, E., Fleming, J., Gardner, L., Rogers, I. and Solomon, A. (Eds.) (2006) *Writing for a Change: Boosting literacy and learning through social action*. San Francisco: Jossey-Bass

Berdan, K. (2006) Reflections on the Youth Dreamers. in K. Berdan, I. Boulton, E. Eidman-Aadahl, J. Fleming, L. Gardner, I. Rogers, and A. Solomon (Eds.) (2006) *Writing for a Change: Boosting literacy and learning through social action*. San Francisco (CA): Jossey-Bass (pp. 31-41)

Cary, C., Ried, C. and Berdan, K. (2004) Involving school students in social action in America: The Youth Dreamers Group. *Groupwork*, 14, 2, 64-79

Cohen, M. B. and Mullender, A. (2000) The personal in the political: Exploring the group work continuum from individual to social change goals. *Social Work with Groups*, 22, 1, pp.13-31 (Reproduced in 2005, *Social Work with Groups*, 28, 3/4 and simultaneously in Malekoff, A. and

Kurland R. (Eds.) *A Quarter Century of Classics (1978-2004): Capturing the Theory, Practice and Spirit of Social Work with Groups* (pp.187-204)

Department for Education (2011) *Positive for Youth: A new approach to cross-government policy for young people aged 13 to 19.* London: Department for Education. Available at http://media.education.gov.uk/assets/files/pdf/p/positive%20for%20youth.pdf]

Fleming, J. (2009) Social Action. in A. Gitterman and R. Salmon (Eds.) *Encyclopedia of Social Work with Groups.* New York and London: Routledge (pp.275-277)

Fleming, J. and Luczynski, Z. (1999) Men United: Fathers' voices. *Groupwork,* 11, 2, 21-38

Fleming, J. and Ward, D. (1999) Research as empowerment: The social action approach. in W. Shera and L. Wells (Eds) *Empowerment Practice: Developing richer conceptual foundations.* Toronto: Canadian Scholars' Press (pp370-389)

Freeman, J. (1970) *The Tyranny of Structurelessness.* [Accessed at 27 October 2011 at www.jofreeman.com/joreen/tyranny.htm]

Harrison, M. and Ward, D. (1999) Values in context: Groupwork and social action. *Groupwork,* 11, 3, 80-103

Longres, J. and McLeod, E. (1980) Consciousness raising and social work practice. *Social Casework,* May, 267-276

McIntyre, A. (2008) *Participatory Action Research.* Thousand Oaks, CA: Sage

Mullaly, B. (2010) *Challenging Oppression and Confronting Privilege.* Don Mills, Ont: Oxford University Press

Mullender, A., Ward, D. and Fleming, J. (2013) *Empowerment in Action: Self-directed groupwork.* Basingstoke: Palgrave Macmillan

Mullender, A. and Ward, D. (1991) *Self-Directed Groupwork: Users take action for empowerment.* London: Whiting and Birch

Mullender, A. and Ward, D. (1985) Towards an alternative model of social groupwork. *British Journal of Social Work,* 15, 155-172

Munford, R. and Walsh-Tapiata, W. (2001) *Strategies for Change : Community development in Aotearoa/New Zealand.* Palmerston North, NZ: School of Social Policy and Social Work

Munn-Giddings, C. and McVicar, A. (2007) Self-help groups as mutual support: what do carers value? *Health and Social Care in the Community,* 15, 1, 26-34

Page, M. (1983) Language and community politics - or exorcising the old ideal! *Talking Points,* 42. London: Association of Community Workers

Preston-Shoot, M. (2007) *Effective Groupwork*. Basingstoke: Palgrave Macmillan

Seebohm, P., Munn-Giddings, C. and Brewer, P. (2010) What's in a name? A discussion paper on the labels and location of self-organising community groups, with particular reference to mental health and Black groups. *Mental Health and Social Exclusion,* 14, 3, 23-29

Ward, D. and Mullender, A. (1991) Facilitation in self-directed groupwork. *Groupwork,* 4, 2, 141-151

Whitmore, E., Wilson, M. and Calhoun, A. (2011) *Activism that Works*. Black Point, Nova Scotia: Fernwood Publishing

Wilson, J. (1988) When to let go. *Community Care,* 26th May, pp.34-35

This chapter was first published in 2013 in *Groupwork* Vol. 23(2), pp.48-66

At the time of writing Jennie Fleming was Reader in Participatory Research and Social Action, and Director, Centre for Social Action, De Montfort University. Dave Ward was Professor of Social and Community Studies, De Montfort University

On empowerment, partnership, and authority in groupwork practice: A training contribution

Michael Preston-Shoot

A key question confronts teachers of groupwork: how can empowerment, partnership and anti-oppressive practice be implemented in agency contexts where statutory duties predominate? This question directs practitioners and teachers to the dilemmas inherent in social work and probation practice, and to apparent contradictory expectations of qualifying training. These in turn are reflected in two influential models of groupwork practice. This paper presents one approach to groupwork training which is designed to enable practitioners to adopt and retain an approach to their practice which is centred upon the principles and goals of anti-oppression, empowerment and partnership.

Key challenges confront groupworkers. The first is defining empowerment and working in partnership in an agency context of statutory authority and legal mandates. Working in partnership is generally presented as an uncontroversial 'good thing', involving a transfer of power from agencies and workers to users. The core elements of negotiation, contracting, information and skill sharing, and involvement in decision-making aim to provide users with greater control over their lives. Empowerment similarly aims to enhance people's power. Through non-hierarchical working empowerment sees users as subjects rather than objects in the social work process. It aims to identify their stories, concerns and experiences, concentrating particularly on the sources and effects of oppression. It aims to enable users to engage, individually and collectively, as change agents with powerful organisations, by tackling internalised negative self-valuations, developing support networks and a collective identity, building on strengths, and taking planned action.

However, both partnership and empowerment have a complex aetiology. The legislative framework provides encouragement, indeed in some instances duties, but also contradictions and constraints. This confusion is compounded by uncertainty concerning with whom workers are in partnership. Professional defensiveness arising from role ambiguity and insecurity, coupled with the bureaucratic top-down nature of welfare organisations and the structural position of powerlessness experienced by service users further complicate the principle (Braye and Preston-Shoot, 1992a).

A second challenge is enabling practitioners to negotiate familiar practice dilemmas and the questions they raise:

1. care vs control - what values and principles should we operate?
2. welfare vs justice - what criteria should determine the intervention?
3. needs vs resources - are services needs-led or provider-led?
4. humanitarianism vs economics - are considerations of cost or effectiveness to predominate?
5. agency vs professionalism - to whom are practitioners accountable (Braye and Preston-Shoot, 1990)?

A closely related third challenge is to identify the key skills and competencies of anti-oppressive groupwork practice. Groupwork theory has been relatively silent until recently on how groupworkers can take action on racism, sexism, disablism, heterosexism and other inequalities in relation to issues of group content, process and leadership/facilitation (Mistry and Brown, 1991; Mullender and Ward, 1991). The requirements for qualifying practitioners (CCETSW, 1989) contain little mention of groupwork and nothing which clarifies the essential components of an anti-oppressive approach to groupwork practice. Practitioners must pursue instead contradictory requirements for practice competence. They must counteract discrimination and oppression, mobilise users' legal rights and promote choice. Yet they must act within organisational and legal structures, and understand the social (controlling) functions of the law, even though these may contribute to the oppressions experienced by users. Qualifying practitioners must be able to work as advocates and in partnership. However, where necessaiy, they must use authority and make decisions on behalf of users, working within organisational decision-making processes which may exclude users or limit their participation. They must promote antidiscriminatory and anti-oppressive policies and practices, but also understand accountability and contain the dilemmas between professional judgement and agency policy (CCETSW, 1989).

These practice dilemmas and contradictory expectations are encapsulated in legislation. Some is enabling, designed to challenge discrimination (Sex Discrimination Act, 1975; Race Relations Act, 1976), to foster partnership (Children Act, 1989) or to promote participation in assessment, service design and delivery (Disabled Persons Act, 1986; NHS and Community Care Act, 1990). Other legislation is frankly repressive: immigration controls, enactments on sexual orientation, and social security provisions being examples (Braye and Preston-Shoot, 1992b).

How, then, should practitioners proceed? How should they challenge, and enable users to challenge isolation, oppression, disadvantage and discrimination from an agency base where statutory duties predominate, where these organisations are not noted for radical aspirations, and where services frequently individualise users' problems rather than challenge the social attitudes and structural inequalities in which oppression and discrimination are rooted (Evans, 1978; Kingston, 1982; Dominelli, 1988; Hanmer and Statham, 1988)?

Groupwork has not escaped these dilemmas. The distinctive features of one model include the conjunction of care and control, of individual-centred aims arising from user need with agency function and its statutory context (Brown et al., 1982). Such groups are leader-centred, particularly in relation to aims, membership, and structure. However, a user-centred paradigm now challenges many basic assumptions about groupwork planning and practice (Mullender and Ward, 1991). It emphasises user control of group design, focus and aims, and social change goals involving the confrontation of oppression and entrenched mechanisms of power.

These challenges require a creative response from groupwork teachers. This must help practitioners critique current groupwork practice and theory, and work towards forms of groupwork which respond to the real needs of disadvantaged groups (Senior, 1991). It must recognise the dangers of a divide between theory and practice subcultures (Sheldon, 1978), and seek to develop practical working concepts from a base of sound theory and critical appraisal of the context in which practice takes place. This paper presents one such response, developed in workshops for qualifying and post-qualifying practitioners.

Defining the questions

The question 'are authority, empowerment and partnership compatible?' must be reframed. Recent legislation affecting both adult services and child care requires enabling and protective powers and duties to be implemented, where possible, in partnership or with the involvement and participation of users and their families or carers. Moreover, there is ample evidence of ineffective or unethical practice. The clash in perspective (Mayer and Timms, 1970) between users and workers about targets for change and/or the means to achieve them is familiar. These disagreements can be based on workers' assumptions about needs, class, poverty, gender and problem-solving. Also familiar are the depressing outcomes and potential side-effects of much professional intervention: passivity, disempowerment and dependence, mystification and loss of control to tackle problems effectively (Illich, 1975 ; Smale, 1983). Intervention appears to undermine individuals and their existing networks, and imposes on individuals values of an oppressive and discriminatory society, especially in relation to gender and family. Alongside this is evidence of the manipulative and coercive use of techniques normally associated with partnership and empowerment, such as written agreements (Nelken, 1989); of the reflection by institutions in their policies and procedures of structural inequalities and oppressive stereotypes; and of the use of power and authority in patronising, colonising, non-participative and unaccountable ways (Barclay, 1982; Croft and Beresford, 1989).

In contrast stands the development of anti-oppressive practice, particularly by women, disabled people and black people. This has highlighted power imbalances, injustices, and assumptions contained in how dominant groups define roles and explain 'problems'. Notions of individual pathology and inadequacy, racism, disablism and sexism have been challenged. Existing service provision has been exposed as inadequate and discriminatory. Anti-oppressive work demonstrates how connecting personal experiences with social, political and economic factors, identifying people's skills and resources, and providing information and resources is empowering. People are enabled to initiate change at individual, group and agency levels (see for instance, Soloman, 1976; Ernst and Goodison, 1981; Eichenbaum and Orbach, 1985; Donnelly, 1986; Women in Mind, 1986; Rooney, 1987; Mullender, 1988; Rhule, 1988; Dominelli and McLeod, 1989; Mistry, 1989; Ahmad, 1990; Oliver, 1991). The work moves from remedying 'individual problems' or symptoms to sharing understanding of experiences and taking action on the structures which restrict opportunity. Thus, the rephrased question must be 'in what ways can empowerment and partnership be applied in groupwork in a statutory agency context and enhance anti-oppressive practice? How might practitioners be enabled to practise it?'

In giving prominence to inequalities of race, gender, disability, age, sexual preference, poverty and class, groupwork training must distinguish, in a way which CCETSW does not in its requirements for qualifying practitioners, between anti-oppressive and antidiscriminatory practice. These are often used interchangeably. However, a clear distinction may be made (Phillipson, 1992). Antidiscriminatory practice is reformist. It seeks to challenge and change unfairness or inequity in the way services are delivered. In respect of some issues relating to racism and sexism, this practice is supported by a legal framework. However, this framework is not unproblematic. It does little to challenge the structures that maintain inequality (Braye and Preston-Shoot, 1992b) or to protect people from (continued) discrimination. Anti-oppressive practice is more far-reaching and is not supported by a legal framework. Indeed, it seeks to achieve a fundamental realignment of power, values and relationships, beginning with an acknowledgement of structural inequalities and exploitative legal, social, and economic relationships, and their impact on individuals and groups.

Empowerment and partnership within an anti-oppressive practice framework become approaches for tackling structures of oppression; for identifying how power is defined, exercised and experienced; and for enabling people to acquire the confidence to take effective action to address their exclusion, isolation and powerlessness. These definitions relate not only to what groupwork may aim to accomplish in relation to social change, that is to goals outside the group, but also to how groupwork itself is affected by the impact of structural inequalities. Put another way, groupwork training and practice must consider how group process and content are affected, for instance, by race and gender (Mistry and Brown, 1991; Phillipson, 1992), and how concepts of partnership and empowerment can address the personal and interpersonal impact, as revealed in groups, of structural inequalities and social constructions. Otherwise, groupwork's potential to overcome the privatisation and individualisation of 'personal ills', and to reduce powerlessness, isolation and stigma will not be realised.

Defining focus

On what then should groupwork training focus to enable practitioners to meet the challenges of anti-oppressive groupwork practice outlined above? The framework developed here follows CCETSWs tri-partite division of values, knowledge and skills, subdividing each into practitioner-self; practitioner-agency; and practitioner-group members.

Values

Practitioner-Self:
- an ability to confront personal values and assumptions, and the impact of these on personal and professional development;
- an ability to examine personal strengths and gaps, especially in relation to anti-oppressive practice;
- an ability to take and use feedback;
- a commitment to anti-oppressive behaviour.

Practitioner-Agency:

- an ability to appraise critically agency roles, tasks and functions, and the relationship between these and wider sociopolitical values;
- a willingness to identify and challenge oppressive and discriminatory practices and policies.

Practitioner-Group members:

- a commitment to principles of user autonomy and participation; to developing the strengths and resources of group members; to protecting and empowering those at risk of or experiencing abuse and exploitation; to the value and dignity of individuals (MUSWTP, 1991);
- identifying and challenging oppressive behaviour;
- promoting practice which actively challenges racism, sexism, disablism, ageism, heterosexism, and issues related to class and poverty.

Knowledge

Practitioner-Self:

- a critical understanding of power and authority, of sources of inequality and oppression, and of social constructions of childhood, gender, ethnicity, age, sexuality and disability;
- ability to use supervision and learning for personal and professional development;
- understanding competing theoretical perspectives on group development, leadership and process;
- understanding competing theoretical models of inequality and its impact (consensus and conflict models of authority and social relationships; medical and social models of disability and health).

Practitioner-Agency:

- a critical understanding of the impact on agencies of political, social, legal, economic and racial factors; of the reproduction through agencies of structural inequalities (MUSWTP, 1991);

- knowledge of agency decision-making and policy-making structures, and how to gain entry to these;
- knowledge of agency policy and practice in relation to inequalities, equal opportunities, and groupwork.

Practitioner-Group members:

- a critical understanding and application of models of group leadership/facilitation, process and development;
- understanding the impact on individuals and groups of social and cultural constructions, of inequality and oppression, of social policies and legislation (powerlessness, identification with the aggressor, submission to dominant values, struggle);
- knowledge of how power is exercised through images of gender, race, competence and status.

Skills

Practitioner-Self:

- addressing the manifestation in groups of structural inequalities; the use of power and authority in groupwork planning and practice;
- connecting the personal and political, groupwork practice and its context;
- using awareness of the impact of self on others;
- understanding and managing the complexities and tensions inherent in anti-oppressive practice;
- applying the values of user empowerment and partnership, and managing the resulting practice dilemmas;
- managing accountability to the group and the agency.

Practitioner-Agency:

- using power and authority creatively to address imbalances of power between users and agency;
- managing the dilemmas between different roles and sources of authority, and between personal and agency values;
- representing the tasks, roles and functions of the agency to users, and enabling users' views to be heard within the agency;

- avoiding authoritarian or defensive practice;
- assessing agency effectiveness in promoting anti-oppressive practice. Challenging attitudes appropriately. Challenging assumptions within how problems are defined and solutions framed;
- sustaining work relationships with colleagues;
- promoting groupwork, partnership and empowerment in the agency. Involving managers in groupwork planning.

Practitioner-Group members:
- identifying power issues in group process and how these are influenced by race and gender;
- addressing conflict and difficult issues;
- engaging with expressed feelings;
- facilitating the group's work in respect of coming together, building trust, discovering resources and experiences, sustaining commitment, defining problems and taking action;
- integrating theory and knowledge of anti-oppressive practice, empowerment and partnership into planning and the group's work;
- connecting personal experiences of powerlessness with wider themes. Identifying issues of inequality;
- promoting non-exploitative relationships through information exchange, mutual education, working in partnership, support, addressing oppressive behaviour, moving between the group's centre and edge depending on the process and task stage of the group;
- evaluating with members the outcome of the group.

The exercises which follow represent one means of providing learning opportunities to connect with these components of competency. However, since facilitated discovery is more effective than lecturing or information giving (Gillespie-Sells and Campbell, 1991), and since the focus is on partnership and empowerment, the traditional didactic training model is replaced by one which provides for partnership in planning and process. The possibility exists, where the entire content and process is trainer-led, that participants' questions will not be addressed and/or that the process will reinforce passivity and powerlessness and be experienced as disempowering and deskilling.

The model adopted here mirrors aspects of self-directed groupwork. The first task is to identify participants' groupwork concerns and issues, their reasons for attendance if choice was possible, and the resources (knowledge, attitudes, skills and experiences) available to them. The trainer also identifies their resources, including the exercises and their relevance to questions of personal development and anti-oppressive groupwork practice. From this starting point a programme is negotiated which utilises these resources. The emphasis is not just on individual change, reflected in the acquisition of knowledge and skills, but also on achieving change in the organisational context in which participants practise. The trainer does not direct or instruct the group but works with it in addressing members' concerns and the values, knowledge and skills for creative practice. The trainer is a facilitator rather than leader (Mullender and Ward, 1991), active but not dominant, and clear about non-negotiable values or content. This must include the requirement that issues of inequality and oppression permeate the work, and the experience that anti-oppressive practice requires training which addresses the core values, knowledge and skills outlined previously.

This approach to teaching has a clear rationale which should be explicit: namely that open planning models partnership and empowerment, ensuring the relevance to the learning needs of the programme negotiated; and that moving away from the expert, didactic model towards one of mutual education enables participants to use their resources and to exercise their ability to take responsibility for defining the issues which concern them and identifying appropriate action. Practitioners cannot be expected to empower those with whom they work if they themselves are not empowered in their training and practice experiences.

Negotiation involving a mutual sharing of concerns, resources and ideas occurs prior to the actual training event It concludes with an agreed statement of group objectives and learning outcomes - values, knowledge and skills which participants should be able to demonstrate afterwards. A contract is agreed which covers the outline programme to be followed and such process issues as the creation of a safe space for learning. This contract is confirmed at the beginning of the training event. The exercises are used for personal reflection followed by discussion in small and larger groups. In plenary sessions themes rather than personal material are identified. These form the basis for subsequent skill development and action plans where workers take forward their training into practice. Experience demonstrates that participants value highly the opportunity for reflection provided by the exercises. Each exercise takes approximately 45 minutes.

Preparing for practice: Values

Values are one foundation for effective practice, providing the context for groupwork skills centred on empowerment and partnership. This is because values filter what is seen and the sense made of this. They shape purpose, beliefs and, therefore, practice. They inform how issues of power and control are perceived and addressed. Moreover, constructing services based on partnership and anti-oppressive principles involves the creation of a new culture (Jones and Jowell, 1987) which re-values service users, addresses their marginalisation by society and service providers, and offers cogent responses (Mullender and Ward, 1991) to the struggle against material and social disadvantage. Consequently, appraisal is required of how personal values affect groupwork practice, determine the range of options perceived, and influence planning and intervention. Otherwise socially constructed and internalised personal values will permeate practice. Not having examined their own cultural inheritance and personal vulnerabilities, practitioners will be unable to identify and challenge the assumptions around which others have structured their lives or the constructions those with power place on such matters as family life, gender, caring, mental distress, and race (Preston-Shoot and Agass, 1990).

The following exercises address this personal value base in relation to individuals and groups, authority and power, discrimination and oppression, and professional roles - key themes in groupwork practice.

Individuals and groups

How practitioners respond to the challenges of antidiscriminatory practice will be influenced by their personal history and cultural inheritance. That this can re-emerge in practice in the form of attitudes, values, scripts, anxieties, prejudices and blocks has long been known to psychotherapists and family therapists whose training requires focus on personal material (Francis, 1988) using, for instance, geneograms and eco-maps (Stratton et al., 1990).

Exercise One: think of things you have learned in (a) your family and (b) other groups that are important to you now. Think of things you learned but have since rejected. How do these affect your work?

Exercise Two : identify key experiences for you as a child, young person, adult. In what ways have these experiences influenced your self-image, current personal relationships, and professional work?

Exercise Three: what have you learned, and from whom, about work and unemployment, poverty and disadvantage, parents and children, health and illness, authority and power? Which of these beliefs have you accepted and which rejected? How does this affect your work?

Authority and power

For empowerment, partnership and anti-oppressive practice to be sustained in groupwork, there must be an analysis of power and control, with an emphasis on altering the imbalance of power between workers and users, and on identifying and valuing the sources of power held by users.

French and Raven (1959) provide a classification of power which may usefully be juxtaposed with a threefold division of authority (Payne and Scott, 1982). The power to reward (with resources or approval), to coerce or punish, and to legitimate equates particularly with positional authority which derives from location in groups and organisations, and from status which, itself, may be linked with gender, statutory power and race. Power deriving from knowledge and expertise connects with sapiential authority which originates in training, experience, information and resources. Referrent power, deriving from charisma and willingness by others to refer to individuals, relates to authority of relevance whereby authority is assigned by virtue of knowledge possessed and seen as relevant to a user's situation.

A further distinction may be drawn between one, two and three dimensional power relationships (Rees, 1991). In practice which is one-dimensional the agenda is controlled by the worker. Compliance is demanded within assumed agreement on dominant values by which society is organised. The professional and the political are separated. Two-dimensional practice is reformist but the questions which workers ask are within officially sanctioned rules and procedures. Ideologies and social structures are not questioned. Three-dimensional practice explores the political context explicitly. Focus is given to how power has been used to define people's interests. The emphasis is on empowerment: mutual education; the suspension of assumptions about services; the creative exercise of power to maximise people's control over choices.

The next exercises (Braye and Preston-Shoot, 1992b) begin to direct practitioners to how they define and work through issues of power and authority.

Exercise Four: identify situations when you have accepted or rejected another person's authority? What influenced your decision? What helped or interfered with you acting on that decision?

Exercise Five: when in your work do you feel powerful? Where does this power come from? When in your work do you feel powerless, and why? What does it feel like to be powerful or powerless?

Exercise Six: how does your power affect users? How does your exercise of power and authority empower or disempower them? What power and authority do users have? How easily may they exercise it in relation to you and your agency?

Exercise Seven: identify situations in which you are or anticipate working. What power and authority do you need to work effectively there? What power might you transfer to users? How might you enable users to identify and use their power and authority? What do you feel about giving up power and control? What effect would this have on the work?

Clearly, different participants will have access to different types of power and authority. Nor will all the parties involved have equal power. A prerequisite for empowerment and partnership is, therefore, acknowledgement of power imbalance arising from material and social disadvantage, professional language and mystique, and discrimination. From this it follows that practice must seek to use and enhance the power and authority held by users, whilst recognising that professional power and authority remain, legally mandated, and may have to be exercised on occasion without user consent or co-operation. However, since this involves the transfer of power from workers to users, some focus on feelings about control is essential. These feelings may be anxiety about relinquishing control or the destructive potential of groups, fears about the worst that could happen if power was shared, lack of confidence or low self-esteem, or concerns that group members will perceive the worker as incompetent or become hostile (Preston-Shoot, 1987a; Heap, 1988). Otherwise the worker's response may be to emphasise control and professional expertise, to adopt a directive approach. This tends to close down expression of opinions and feelings, and to deny individuals and groups opportunities to extend their skills.

Oppression and discrimination

The impact of racism, sexism and other forms of oppression on personal values and the professional task has been exposed clearly but remains an urgent challenge at individual and societal levels since power continues to be used oppressively (Dominelli, 1988; Hanmer and Statham, 1988). If groupworkers are to enable service users to challenge the way power is exercised, practitioners themselves must examine their relationship to the state and their use of power (Rees, 1991).

Exercise Eight: 'racism and me'.
- How would I describe my racial identity?
- How, if at all, is that different from how I have described it before?
- When was I first aware of my racial identity?
- When was I first aware of people whose racial identity was different from mine?

- What messages did I receive about my racial identity and other people's racial identity?
- What effect has this had on my personal relationships and outlook, and on my work?
- When have I discriminated against people of a racial identity different from mine? What do I think makes me do this?

Exercise Nine: ask yourself similar questions about class, gender, family and disability. Critically appraise your practice: in what ways do you reinforce existing power structures, stereotypes and assumptions in your work?

Exercise Ten: when you work with someone whose gender, racial origin, class or sexual preference is different from your own, what is the effect of this on your relationship? What is the impact of who you are and of your behaviour on them? What is the impact for you of who they are (Braye and Preston-Shoot, 1992b)?

Professional role

The practice dilemmas inherent in social work, the changing nature of the roles required of practitioners, and the organisational cultures in which practitioners are located can make it difficult for groupworkers to identify their resources and to practise on the basis of clearly articulated values. For practitioners to work in partnership and to be experienced as empowering, they must themselves feel empowered.

Exercise Eleven: what would colleagues and users say are encouraging and discouraging patterns in the way you work? What would you say are your resources - values, knowledge, skills and experience? What have you learned from training which helps you to negotiate the practice dilemmas and to work in partnership? What have you learned that obstructs this?

These exercises can be informed by principles for empowering practice identified elsewhere (for instance, Jones and Jowell, 1987; Preston-Shoot, 1987b; Mullender and Ward, 1991). However, for values to be a springboard for action, to be visible in practice, they must be connected with knowledge of and skills for empowerment and working in partnership.

Preparing for practice: Defining partnership

Exercise Twelve: what do you understand by partnership? How far and in what ways has your groupwork practice reflected working in partnership? How would group members know you are working, or are wanting to work in partnership with them?

Essential to effective practice is a clear understanding of how partnership can be defined and is being applied in particular situations. Partnership may be seen as a continuum (Amstein, 1969; Pugh and De'Ath, 1989) from involvement and consultation in decision-making processes within pre-determined limits controlled by service providers, to collaboration in defining issues and options, and beyond to user control of these processes. Partnership does not necessarily mean that participants have equal power. It does imply recognition and open discussion, however, of how power is distributed and used. It means clarity regarding the extent to which group members are involved in, or control decisions regarding duration, focus, size, membership.

From this understanding, the skills for partnership can be defined. Whilst a feature of the entire groupwork process, they will be especially prominent in the early stages of the group and will involve:

1. Group workers presenting their own values and encouraging a collective exploration of values (Benson, 1987) and resources as one means of defining possibilities open to the group. This will involve groupworkers clarifying which value principles are non-negotiable, such as taking up oppressive behaviour, even though this might conflict with other principles, such as user self-determination (Mullender and Ward, 1991).
2. Groupworkers clarifying their own role, particularly what is and is not negotiable. It is impossible, however tempting, to

keep authority 'secret'. Indeed, to hope that the need to exercise statutory authority will not arise may ultimately prove more disruptive to group process than to acknowledge the possibility at the outset, to recognise users' anxieties about it, and to establish principles about its use. Role clarity must include the nature of accountability owed to employer, group, self, society and social work.

3. Redistributing power by maximising users' choices. Groupworkers may be invited to assume levels of responsibility and control which are disempowering. They may be invited to be an expert (tell us what to do; is this normal?) or to be a nurturing figure. They may be compared, by implication unfavourably, with previous workers, or be invited to comment on an interesting, inviting problem. Such 'trips' reinforce passivity and dependence, hierarchy and status. The skill is to be curious about what is happening. This involves self-questioning about what power and control users have, or perceive themselves to have. From here workers may address any pressures users feel to comply with their suggestions, or to remain silent in the face of unfairness. Throughout the emphasis is on negotiating roles.

4. Being open to feedback, to user perceptions. This involves encouraging group members to 'speak bittemess' (FRG, 1991; Mullender and Ward, 1991), and acknowledging the oppression, humiliation and fear that may have been central to their experience. A companion activity is to place oneself in the user's position. This may enable preconceived ideas to be challenged. For example, one practitioner, when focusing on 'racism and me', described outbreaks of violent protest by black people as 'self-destructive' and 'unhelpful'. When asked to imagine herself as a black British person, experiencing disadvantage and discrimination, and the limited opportunities to challenge these features of life, she gained a different perspective.

5. Prioritising the group's aims as defined by group members, acting on their problem definition and analysis. The groupworker's task is to share information and knowledge but not to impose definitions or skills. It involves helping the

group to identify what it might achieve rather than pressing for particular change.

6. Negotiating and reviewing written agreements in order that they reflect the current level of expressed expectations, knowledge, resource use, trust, and understanding about the purpose of the work (Corden and Preston-Shoot, 1987).

This working together, based on openness and a shared sense of purpose and responsibility may, of itself, be empowering. However, partnership does not guarantee empowerment.

Preparing for practice: Defining empowerment

Exercise Thirteen : what might users experience as empowering or disempowering about your groupwork planning and practice?
Some empowering interventions are common to all groupwork. These include:

1. scene setting and creating a safe space for the group's work;
2. normalising members' experiences, such as when joining a group;
3. listening and demonstrating a concern to understand;
4. providing information and counteracting professional mystique;
5. identifying and developing members' skills and strengths;
6. exploring what may be blocking the group's work (unrealistic goals, conflictual relationships, other systems, inadequate resources);
7. becoming less central as the group develops (Heap, 1966).

Mullender and Ward (1989) refer to helping groups discuss the nature of problems and possible solutions, and reflect on the process of the group and its work. These interventions can counter powerlessness and promote personal and inter-personal change.

However, the concept of empowerment is limited if seen only as a form of enabling by professionals (Adams, 1990). This is because such interventions may maintain users' dependency, whether benign or repressive (Keenan and Pinkerton, 1988). They may maintain the invisibility of oppression in members' lives (Dominelli, 1988) and fail to address the distribution of power - male/female, black/white, rich/ poor, able-bodied/disabled. Moreover, a limited concept of empowerment may reinforce the cult of the expert rather than promote autonomy. In so doing it may obscure the limits on statutory agency employees empowering users and the consequent importance of advocacy structures (Mullender, 1991) when users' needs and rights lead them to question the services of which the workers are a part.

The concept of empowerment will equally be limited if groupworkers fail to consider the impact on users of disadvantage and oppression. Barber (1991) explores the psychological legacy of powerlessness: accepting the unacceptable, renouncing responsibility for oneself, and belief in the futility of action. He also explores attributional theory to account for individual differences of response to marginalisation and powerlessness. Self-esteem and action are more likely to follow when a person's attributional style, their explanation of their circumstances, is governed by universality (anyone in my position would feel...), specificity (my response is just to this situation), and transience (my response may change, so may the situation). It is less likely to follow from a position of personality (it is my fault), globality (wide generalisation to other situations) and stability (a fixed belief system).

From this understanding the pre-requisite skills can be identified for empowerment and anti-oppressive groupwork practice which tackle the structural underpinnings and psychological legacy of powerlessness (Barber, 1991):

1. Identifying how group members interpret their situation. This involves clarifying the contextual and cultural features which influence the meanings they attach to their experiences. If the attributional style of members in the group predispose them to "helplessness', a first task will be to address this pessimism and personal blame and an on-going role will be to help members resist a return to powerlessness (Rees, 1991). The skills which follow are central to this.
2. Creating opportunities for members to acquire knowledge, understanding and skills to act in ways which will increase their power, control and choice. This involves enabling people to make connections between the personal and political, and to

reflect on the consequences of the distribution of power (Rees, 1991). These opportunities involve access to independent advice and advocates, the provision of information, and support in using unfamiliar or daunting structures so that users are not intimidated or frightened out of their rights (BASW, 1980).

3. Challenging labels, stereotypes and behaviour applied oppressively or inappropriately and/or which reduce the authority of the user's voice. This involves challenging, and enabling groups to challenge the way group members, and services 'for' them have been perceived. For these barriers to be confronted requires an analysis of the power blocks - those internalised as negative self-evaluations (Lee, 1991) and those existing within agencies.

4. Negotiating the groupworker's role and responsibilities on the basis of the different concerns and agendas which have brought the group together (Keenan and Pinkerton, 1988). The role may include developing group cohesion, education, resource development, and supporting the group devise and implement strategies of intervention which will give it entry into political processes (Barber, 1991; Lee, 1991). Put another way, the role entails balancing support and help to group members with work which will enable the group to perform its agreed tasks and address political and structural arrangements (Adams, 1990).

5. Enabling discussion of power in the group - who has it and how it is being used. This may involve challenging oppressive behaviour, such as men dominating discussion in a mixed gender group, or inviting the group to reflect on how gender, for instance, has influenced group task allocation or process. Given the potential for group members to feel 'pressurised' into conformity, a continuing task is to review how safe the 'space' is to express differences or to highlight unfairness. At times groupworkers may have to be central in suggesting discussion of group processes and in tackling imbalances of power. Open advocacy may be appropriate, such as supporting a woman whose statements about the effects on her of working with sexually abused children had been treated dismissively

by a man in the group. Open challenge to individuals may be necessary, using techniques such as circular questioning and interventions (Stratton et al., 1990).

The training sessions aim to facilitate workers develop these skills by either detailed review of recent or current practice, and/ or critical appraisal of groupwork planning undertaken in the workshop. Workers are asked to reflect particularly on partnership, the use of power, and empowerment during discussions, simulations and goal setting. In appraising their groupwork practice, particular emphasis is given to how partnership and empowerment is practised. Thus, in their planning have they pre-determined the group's framework and/or content? Have they made assumptions about how the problem is defined? For example, workers planning a group for women whose children had been abused by male adult family members, had devised objectives which failed to take into account the power imbalances between the adults involved. Planning also must consider venue, time, and the language in which services are offered if the group is to be perceived as potentially empowering. When the group first meets, how is the content negotiated and early processes managed? Have workers assumed responsibilities without prior negotiation with the group? For instance, in beginning groups with warm-up exercises, groupworkers may be imposing assumptions about personal space, trust and touch. In negotiations which conclude with a group contract, has everyone been enabled to voice their views and anxieties, have people's strengths and resources been identified and have the groupworkers, where necessary, tackled power relationships within the group? Looking at the objectives agreed, what opportunities will the group promote for members to gain a greater degree of control over their lives, challenge forces which are experienced as oppressive (Mullender and Ward, 1991) and change assumptions? Given that agencies are not infrequently part of the problem rather than part of the solution, how are the workers engaging with the agency to promote change, and how might they facilitate the group's entry into the organisation?

Choosing models

Exercise Fourteen: in the group you have planned or are running, what influenced you towards a particular model? What factors did you consider?

The competencies required of qualified practitioners require social workers to understand and intervene in the structural patterns which perpetuate the problems they encounter in their practice (CCETSW, 1989). This corresponds with service users increasingly challenging models of service provision which are oriented towards individual pathology rather than structural inequalities and social role expectations, and towards defining for users their needs and appropriate provision to meet them (Oliver, 1983; Llewelyn, 1987; Chamberlin, 1988). These requirements and challenges, together with the principles of empowerment and partnership, must call into question the traditional worker-led model of groupwork practice.

Barber (1991) argues that it will only be through casework with individuals that practitioners will discern patterns and themes which indicate the need for change at broader system levels through groupwork and community organisation, with users and workers becoming social activists. Again, however, the competencies and challenges addressed above indicate that training can and must provide the knowledge which will equip practitioners to engage with service users in discussion about the impact of these wider systems.

Training must explore available theoretical perspectives for informing a group's aims, objectives and activities. One group for women offenders combined concepts from feminist, offending and welfare perspectives (Jones et al., 1991). Such perspectives should be underpinned by a two-fold analysis of power relationships. First, how have structural inequalities, such as racism and sexism, which might be imported into group planning and work been addressed (Mistry and Brown, 1991)? One means of clarifying these issues, besides appraising groupwork plans presented by participants, is to analyse filmed group sequences for the workings of power and powerlessness; stereotypes and oppressive behaviour, group stages and the influence on these of ethnicity, disablism, gender, and models of practice; and leadership styles. Two which are particularly informative are Twelve Angry Men' and the group meetings portrayed in 'One Flew Over The Cuckoo's Nest.'

Secondly, how have groupworkers managed their involvement in planning and working with the group? Through reviewing how groupworkers have undertaken their work, or engaging in planning groupwork, participants will unravel how the agenda, group's duration, membership, and activities were determined. The extent to which the group was invited to accept uncritically worker and/ or agency views will become clear, as will whether negotiation was based on a three-dimensional view of power relationships (Rees, 1991).

Even if the self-directed groupwork model is not used exclusively, it may be adapted. Agency goals concerning individual behaviour, task-focused problem solving, and mutual support underpinned by statutory authority, may be included alongside degrees of open planning, social and political action rather than individual goals, non-hierarchical leadership, and activities which aim to restore to participants greater control over their own and the agency's resources and a sense of self outside their stereotypes (Bodinham and Weinstein, 1991; Jones et al., 1991). The role of training and supervision is to invite consideration of possibilities, to explore the potential of partnership and empowerment.

Negotiating dilemmas

Exercise Fifteen', in your group, what practice dilemmas did you anticipate you might encounter? How did or could you approach them in negotiations with group members?

Practice dilemmas will be central to many groups located within statutory agencies. For example, an agency may perceive its role in relation to adults with learning difficulties as the provision of services. A group may be more interested in changing the attitudes exhibited by agency employees through service provision towards people with learning difficulties. Agencies, sponsoring groupwork for parents and children where there are concerns about child abuse, may be prioritising their child protection responsibilities. The parents may be concerned with poverty, housing and other issues which impact upon them and their children. Probation officers must negotiate the welfare versus justice practice dilemma, the demands of the criminal justice system alongside the personal and social needs of offenders.

Since such practice dilemmas are not peculiar to groupwork, workers can focus on the skills they use in other settings. How have they practised partnership with service users, particularly when using, or considering the use of statutory authority? How have they used their authority creatively? How have they empowered users in discussions about risk factors, the concerns of their employing agency, problem definition, and decisions about where change efforts should be focused? From this practice base skills which are transferable into groupwork content and process may be identified. For instance, there are skills in contributing explanations of problems which take group members beyond self-blame and in offering ideas for intervention which provide them with information about their usefulness and a choice to reject them. There are empowering and disempowering ways of challenging oppressive behaviour in a group. One strategy here is for groupworkers to simulate a group experience which concerns them, to practise empowering and disempowering ways of managing particular events. An example is how workers negotiate the extent to which they can enter into partnership with group members and their goals, and the extent to which they must adhere to agency interpretations of their functions. This example takes groupwork training and practice into clarifying agency attitudes.

Preparing for practice: Managing the agency experience

For practitioners to feel empowered and supported in this work, practice must be underpinned by a clear organisational value base. However, the hierarchical power structure of many welfare organisations, and the conflicting imperatives to which they are subject, can result in organisational values being unclear or distant, and/or policies being experienced as constraints and the antithesis of professional social work. Accordingly, groupwork training must provide strategies for practitioners to develop groupwork practice in overstretched, demoralised, 'hostile' settings.

Exercise Sixteen : what organisational procedures and practices reflect a commitment to empowerment and partnership? Which do not? How may the agency manage its powers and responsibilities in a manner which empowers users and workers? How may it develop partnership in determining and challenging the nature of service provision and delivery? How might you build on the positives? What tasks might be indicated here, with whom and when?

In some teams or organisations a debate may be possible on how the tensions between authority and empowerment may be negotiated, leading to the development of policies on such issues as rights versus risks and the involvement of users in reviewing services. In other settings, however, the groupworker is own agency may be part of the problem. The agency may endorse the principles and objectives of groupwork, empowerment and partnership, but not a strategy for implementing them; or it may not have or endorse the principles.

One exercise here is for groups to list the opposing forces - the constraints and opportunities existing in the agency. Who in the organisation has power and authority to promote groupwork and anti-oppressive practice? Who are the key people to engage? What gaps in provision does the agency identify? Does the agency focus on equal opportunities, and interpret this as being about sameness rather than fairness (Senior, 1991), or does the agency promote anti- oppressive practice by acknowledging structural inequalities, their manifestation in organisational procedures, and the need to promote practices which address these imbalances of power. This analysis may enable groupworkers to:

1. identify the nature of the problems and the audience to be targeted;
2. anticipate possible objections to groupwork and to practice

based on principles of empowerment, partnership and antioppression, and to address these views before they are voiced in opposition;

3. identify the agency's functions, acknowledge its constraints, and promote interventions in a way which enables the agency to perceive that its service objectives are being met;

4. advance alternative ways of understanding and tackling issues or problems, especially clarifying the room for manoeuvre which the agency might have;

5. present proposals which have a clearly articulated theoretical and practice rationale;

6. identify and use informal and formal channels of communication and negotiation in the agency.

A second exercise is the development of a secure base for groupworkers, a support and consultation network to underpin practice. This may usefully be done by means of an action plan (Preston-Shoot and Braye, 1991). The action plan begins with the issues practitioners confront: from where and whom might they obtain the support necessary to develop anti-oppressive groupwork practice, and to promote partnership and empowerment as an agency issue? How might they clarify the mandate which their agency is prepared to give groupworkers in relation to their work? How might they build a support system to establish and maintain groupwork in their agency? How might they find out what issues and themes are emerging in their colleagues' work? What issues and themes might users have in common? Having identified the key issues, the action plan moves on to identifying strategies for working on them: research to establish user and colleague definitions of issues; staff group discussions to identify interest in groupwork; making links with key managers. These strategies can then be reframed into objectives and tasks. Whether the final action plan is produced by individuals or by a group of practitioners, the final component is to set a date when the outcome of the plan will be reviewed and a new plan agreed.

Conclusion

This paper began with key challenges facing groupworkers. A model has been presented which provides practitioners with learning opportunities to develop and consolidate the values, knowledge and skills for anti-oppressive groupwork practice. The exercises, simulations and discussion have proved thought-provoking and, sometimes, been experienced as emotionally demanding requiring time for the experience to be worked through. Nonetheless, the centrality of oppression, partnership and empowerment, alongside the more traditional groupwork training focus on such building blocks as size, duration, preparation and focus, has been welcomed as challenging and informative for practice. Indeed, because the approach outlined here addresses major contemporary priorities in social work and the concerns of the participants themselves, in evaluation feedback workers have described feeling empowered and engaged. They have welcomed the opportunity to re-examine basic groupwork theories and methods, to consider recent developments, and to share experiences. Equally, for practice to develop, opportunities should be provided in follow-up training days and consultation or supervision for review of learning and work. Where action planning has focused in part on establishing support groups, this has enabled the enthusiasm generated by the workshop to be translated into on-going practice initiatives.

The challenge of empowerment and partnership, of anti-oppressive practice, is to enable people to speak 'truth to power' (Stanton, 1989): group members to groupworker and agencies; groupworkers to agencies. The model presented in this paper provides one means for developing and sustaining the secure base from which this may happen.

References

Adams, R (1990) *Self-Help, Social Work and Empowerment*. London: Macmillan.

Ahmad, A. (1990) *Practice With Care*. London: Race Equality Unit

Amstein, S. (1969) A ladder of citizen participation, *Journal of the American*

Institute of Planners, 35, July, pp.215-24.

Barber, J. (1991) *Beyond Casework*. London: Macmillan.

Barclay,P. (ed.)(1982) *Social Workers, Their Role and Tasks*. London: Bedford Square Press.

Benson, J. (1987) *Working More Creatively with Groups*. London: Tavistock

Bodinham, H. and Weinstein, J. (1991) Making authority accountable: the experience of a statutory based women's group, *Groupwork*, 4(1), pp.22-30.

Braye, S. and Preston-Shoot, M. (1990) On teaching and applying the law in social work: It is not that simple, *British Journal of Social Work*, 20(4), pp.333-53.

Braye, S. and Preston-Shoot, M. (1992a) Honourable intentions: partnership and written agreements in welfare legislation, *Journal of Social Welfare and Family Law*, November.

Braye, S. and Preston-Shoot, M,, (1992b) *Practising Social Work Law*. London: Macmillan.

British Association of Social Workers (1980) *Clients Are Fellow Citizens*. Birmingham: BASW.

Brown, A., Caddick B., Gardiner, M. and Sleeman, S. (1982) Towards a British model of groupwork, British Journal of Social Work, 12(6), pp.587-603.

Central Council for Education and Training in Social Work (1989) *Requirements and Regulations for the Diploma in Social Work*. Paper 30. London: CCETSW.

Chamberlin, J. (1988) *On Our Own: Patient Controlled Alternatives to the Mental Health System*. London: Mind.

Corden, J. and Preston-Shoot, M (1987) *Contracts in Social Work.*. Aldershot: Gower.

Croft, S. and Beresford, P. (1989) User involvement, citizenship and social policy, *Critical Social Polity*, 26.9(2), pp.5-18.

Dominelli, L. (1988) *Anti-Racist Social Work*. London: Macmillan

Dominelli, L. and McLeod, E.(1989) *Feminist Social Work*. London: Macmillan

Donnelly, A. (1986) *Feminist Social Work in a Women's Group*. University of East Anglia Social Work Monograph. Norwich: UEA.

Eichenbaum, L. and Orbach, S. (1985) *Understanding Women*. Harmondsworth: Penguin.

Ernst, S. and Goodison, L. (1981) *In Our Own Hands. A Book of Self-Help*

Therapy. London: The Women's Press.

Evans, R. (1978) Unitary models of practice and the social work team in Olsen, M.R (ed.) *The Unitary Model.* Birmingham: British Association of Social Workers.

Family Rights Group (1991) *The Children Act 1989 -An FRG Briefing Pack.* London: FRG.

Francis, M. (1988) The skeleton in the cupboard: experiential geneogram work for family therapy trainees, *Journal of Family Therapy,* 10(2), pp.135-52.

French, J. and Raven, B. (1959) The bases of social power in Cartwright, D. (ed.) *Studies in Social Power.* Ann Arbour. ML

Gillespie-Sells, K. and Campbell, J. (1991) *Disability Equality Training: Trainers Guide.* London: CCETSW.

Hanmer, J. and Statham, D. (1988) *Women and Social Work.* London: Macmillan.

Heap, K (1966) The groupworker as central person, *Case Conference,* 12(7), pp.20-29.

Heap, K (1988) The worker and the group process: a dilemma revisited', *Groupwork,* 1(1), pp. 17-29.

Illich, I. (1975) *Medical Nemesis - The Expropriation of Health.* London: Calder and Boyars.

Jones, A. and Jowell, T. (1987) May the force be with you, *Social Services Insight,* 10 July, pp.19-21.

Jones, M., Mordecai, M., Rutter, F. and Thomas, L. (1991) The Miskin model of groupwork with women offenders', *Groupwork,* 4(3), pp.215-30.

Keenan, E. and Pinkerton, J. (1988) Social action groupwork as negotiation: contradictions in the process of empowerment, *Groupwork,* 1(3), pp.229-38.

Kingston, P. (1982) Power and influence in the environment of family therapy, *Journal of Family Therapy,* 4(3), pp.211-27.

Lee, J. (1991) Empowerment through mutual aid groups: a practice grounded conceptual framework, *Groupwork,* 4(1), pp.5-21.

Llewelyn, S. (1987) Ethical issues in psychotherapy for women in Fairbairn, S. and Fairbairn, G. (eds.) *Psychology, Ethics and Change.* London: RKP.

Manchester University Social Work Training Partnership (1991) *Approved Proposal for the Diploma in Social Work.* MUSWTP.

Mayer, J. and Timms, N. (1970) *The Client Speaks.* London: RKP.

Mistry, T. (1989) Establishing a feminist model of groupwork in the probation service, *Groupwork*, 2(2), pp.145-58.

Mistry,T. and Brown, A (1991) Black and White co-working in Groups, *Groupwork*, 4(2), pp.101-18.

Mullender, A (1988) Groupwork as the method of choice with black children in white foster homes, *Groupwork*, 1(2), pp. 158-72.

Mullender, A. (1991) Nottingham Advocacy Group: Giving a voice to the users of mental health services, *Practice*, 5(1), pp.5-12.

Mullender, A. and Ward, D. (1989) Challenging familiar assumptions: preparing for and initiating a self-directed group, *Groupwork*, 2(1), pp.5-26.

Mullender, A. and Ward, D. (1991) *Self-Directed Groupwork: Users Take Action for Empowerment*. London: Whiting and Birch.

Nelken, D. (1989) Discipline and punish: Some notes on the margin, *The Howard Journal*, 28(4), pp.245-54.

Oliver, M. (1983) *Social Work with Disabled People*. London: Macmillan.

Oliver, M. (ed.) (1991) *Social Work, Disabled People and Disabling Environments*. London: Jessica Kingsley.

Payne, C. and Scott, T. (1982) *Developing Supervision of Teams in Field and Residential Social Work*. Paper 12. London: NISW.

Phillipson, J. (1992) *Practising Equality. Women, Men and Social Work*. London: CCETSW.

Preston-Shoot, M. (1987a) Groupwork presents its challenges and its rewards to those with the right initiative, *Social Work Today*, 18(27), pp. 12-13.

Preston-Shoot, M. (1987b) *Effective Groupwork*. London: Macmillan.

Preston-Shoot, M. and Agass, D. (1990) *Making Sense of Social Work: Psychodynamics, Systems and Practice*. London: Macmillan.

Preston-Shoot, M. and Braye, S. (1991) Managing the personal experience of work, *Practice*, 5(1), pp. 13-33.

Pugh, G. and De'Ath, E. (1989) *Working Towards Partnership in the Early Years*. London: National Children's Bureau.

Rees, S. (1991) *Achieving Power. Practice and Policy in Social Welfare*. North Sydney: Allen and Unwin.

Rhule, C. (1988) A group for white women with black children, *Groupwork*, 1(1), pp.41-47.

Rooney, B. (1987) *Racism and Resistance to Change*. Liverpool: Merseyside Area Profile Group.

Senior, P. (1991) Groupwork in the Probation Service: Care or control in the 1990s, *Groupwork*, 4(3), pp.284-95.

Sheldon, B. (1978) Theory and practice in social work: a re-examination of a tenuous relationship, *British Journal of Social Work*, 8(1), pp.1-22.

Smale, G. (1983) Can we afford not to develop social work practice?, *British Journal of Social Work*, 13(3), pp.251-64.

Soloman, B. (1976) *Black Empowerment: Social Work in Oppressed Communities*. New York: Columbia University Press.

Stanton, A. (1989) *Invitation to Self-Management*. Ruislip: Dab Hand Press.

Stratton, P., Preston-Shoot, M. and Hanks, H. (1990) *Family Therapy Training and Practice*. Birmingham: Venture Press.

Women in Mind (1986) *Finding Our Own Solutions. Women's Experience of Mental Health Care*. London: Mind.

This chapter was first published in 1992 in *Groupwork* Vol. 5(2), pp.5-30

At the time of writing Michael Preston-Shoot was Senior Lecturer in Social Work and Head of the Social Work School, University of Manchester

Brierley youth action project
The role of consultancy in its development and progression

Izzy Terry

Introduction

The purpose of this report is to outline and illustrate the part consultancy has played in the successful development and progress of Brierley Youth Action Project, one of the three Bradford GEST (Dept of Education Grants for Educational Support) detached youth projects. This innovative project was set up in 1993 as a preventative response to crime prevention amongst young people between the ages 13 and 17. Consultancy has always been built into the Social Action approach; its importance acknowledged for the development of good practice and as support for workers (Ward, 1982; Mullender and Ward, 1991).

This report will primarily focus on consultancy I carried out for over a year from February 1994 to May 1995. I was funded as a freelance consultant initially from BYAP funds and then by grants from Bradford City Challenge and Francis C Scott Charitable Trust for consultancy, training and research under the umbrella of the Centre for Social Action. New funding is now needed for this essential work to continue.

Brierley Youth Action Project (BYAP) is based in Brierley which is a predominately white working class estate three miles south of the centre of Bradford. It has been neglected and under-resourced for many years, with high unemployment, poverty and crime rates. It forms part of the City Challenge area which is now undergoing a regeneration programme and housing improvements. The project has a full time project leader, Nola O'Neill, a part time worker, Simon Baker, and some volunteers and students. It is based at the Bob Cryer Centre; a small portacabin behind the Community Centre that it shares with some other projects. More details concerning this project and the Social Action approach can be found in the GEST Project review reports (Harris and Harrison, 1994; Harris, Pryke, and Harrison, 1995).

I am an experienced youth worker, groupworker, and trainer who has been committed to the Social Action approach since working at Nottingham Youth Action in 1983. I also bring experience of helping groups to acknowledge and work with conflict constructively and I'm exploring the use of movement in groups as an alternative means of communication. In terms of my composition and related life experience I am a white, able-bodied, heterosexual woman of middle class origin.

Consultancy and setting up the project

It was through the co-working and supervision relationship built up while working in Leeds between myself and Nola that I became involved in consultancy work with BYAP. When she was in the initial setting up stage of the project we discussed the principles and values of Social Action and I informed her of the Centre for Social Action. These discussions then helped in redefining the aims and objectives of the project in consultations with her line manager in Bradford Youth Service.

The full-time project workers for the other GEST projects (in Keighley and Allerton) were also keen to develop innovative ways of working with young people. So in November 1993 they all invited Mark Harrison from the Centre for Social Action (funded by Bradford Youth Service) to run a two day training course in Social Action for full and part time workers from all three GEST projects.

After this a firm commitment to the Social Action approach was adopted by all the projects. However they recognised that they would need ongoing support and advice from experienced practitioners of the approach, in order that it be developed successfully in practice with the young people. Consultancy sessions evolved with Mark Harrison on a bi-monthly basis with all the projects. I later took over a more regular consultancy with two of the projects' teams, starting with BYAP; meeting them on average once every two weeks.

Nature of consultancies

Although at times at BYAP we had stops and starts we soon acknowledged how vital it was to have consultancies regularly. If not, the work easily drifted, issues built up and got missed, becoming increasingly difficult to deal with. Consultancy needed to be as much about celebrating, acknowledging and building on good practice as dealing with difficult and problematic practice, so this was firmly built into each session.

The team consultancy sessions soon became overloaded with practice issues, so regular consultancies for individual groups were also developed. In BYAP they have often involved workers from other agencies who can bring different skills and knowledge. Consultancy ideally needs to begin before the group starts so that principles and aims and objectives can be argued; failure to do this often means that disagreement and confusion about these emerge between workers later in the life of the group.

Some of the issues raised in the consultancies clearly needed more time and consideration. These included issues such as challenging oppression, creating positive identity in young people and dealing with conflict constructively. So we arranged specific training days – some led by myself, to consider some of these issues. The one on conflict also involved young people, and other GEST projects were invited.

The role of the consultant within the Social Action approach

It is important for a consultant to be a guide and facilitator who is independent from the direct face to face work of the project or piece of work, doesn't have managerial responsibilities for the workers, and has a firm commitment to and understanding of the principles and practice of the Social Action model.

It is important to acknowledge that although some of the functions of a consultant may overlap with those of a manager (depending on their style), a consultant doesn't have overall responsibility for the work. Indeed the consultant needs to be clear about which issues raised in consultancies are management ones that need to be dealt with by the project leader and/or their line manager. This can sometimes become confusing and difficult for full time workers who are both team managers and group workers within the projects and consultancies.

I will outline here the various functions as a consultant I developed over time; some are also highlighted in *Self Directed Groupwork* by A. Mullender and D. Ward (1991), a comprehensive guide to the Social Action approach.

- to encourage the workers to explore, formulate and be clear about their values/principles underpinning the work and the Social Action model.
- to demonstrate the use of the Social Action model through leadership of the sessions and to help workers to understand the nature of each stage (What? Why? How? Act, Reflect).
- to encourage, support and reassure the workers when they are sticking to the principles and remind them of the principles if work seems to be deviating or drifting away from them under the pressures of day to day reality.
- to support workers by reflecting back on previous sessions, drawing out the key issues and planning for the next.
- to enable workers to reflect on specific examples of 'good' and 'difficult' practice, so maximising their learning and understanding of the Social Action approach and the interventions and dilemmas it creates for workers.
- to encourage and help workers try out new skills, interventions, and techniques in a safe environment before using them with young people.
- to assist the workers in discharging, acknowledging and dealing with some of the disturbance and anxiety that arises for them from the work.
- to enable the workers to reflect on the overall progress and development of the work/group over time, helping them to see a long term perspective rather than just, for example, focusing on last week's 'incident'.
- to enable workers to be clear about their differing roles and responsibilities, and within partnerships and small teams provide opportunity for the full time worker to relinquish their facilitative and leadership role during the consultancy session.

- to help create an environment that encourages open and honest communication (including validation and constructive criticism), develops trust, values differences, enables workers to DEAL creatively with conflicts between themselves and others.
- to help workers (individually and collectively) anticipate, manage and respond constructively to rumours, suspicion, criticism and overt opposition to the practice from those outside the worker team, all of which are inevitable to a certain extent when new or unfamiliar ways of working are introduced.
- to help the worker team develop understanding, models and strategies for effective work with other agencies, enabling the workers to build on their common concerns and to manage their conflicts or dilemmas.
- to encourage workers to consider the structural, political, and external issues that affect young people's lives and how young people could respond to these.
- to be aware of the resources available to the project and their duration, helping the workers develop their practice within the often limited resources available (prioritise) and encouraging them to identify whose responsibility it is to raise more funds for the work.
- to enable workers to highlight and identify specific training needs, and to draw out areas where more time is needed to look at specific issues – eg challenging oppression.

How were these functions carried out within sessions?

I used various common groupwork strategies such as listening, questioning, challenging, reflecting back, sharing my own experiences, validating, encouraging, and clarifying. Consultants also bring their own style, energy, life experiences and personality to the sessions; some of the particular perspectives I brought to the consultancies with BYAP included:

- my experience, analysis and involvement gained from collective political organising and campaigning especially around anti-racist and feminist issues
- the acknowledgement that people have feelings as well as

thoughts which can be powerful sources of motivation, inspiration and conflict within their work

- the commitment to exploring the concept of the 'personal is political' and vice versa in groups and relationships
- the use of movement and drama as our bodies and moving selves are important vehicles of communication and expression
- searching for and drawing out the conflicts as these situations can provide opportunities for positive change if acknowledged and dealt with constructively
- the use of humour and play, as learning and fun and enjoyment can be connected together.

As well as increasingly realising that I had a lot to offer the team it was also important to recognise and be clear about what I wasn't able to offer them, being honest about my limitations and lack of direct experience of particular issues, situations and perspectives in certain areas.

Examples of some of the issues and dilemmas considered in consultancy sessions with BYAP

Although these issues and dilemmas came out of the work of BYAP many of them are common, in my experience and knowledge, to many other Social Action projects with young people.

- How do we guide groups through the Social Action model? How can we get a clear picture of WHAT THE young people's concerns and issues really are? They were not always what they expressed initially, so we needed sometimes to wait to get the full picture. We need strategies for helping them prioritising these issues.
- How can we enable them to understand the causes of their concerns and issues (Why?) so that they believe the need for external and political change, however small, rather than focusing just on individual change. The other stages of the model were also given consideration.
- The Social Action approach can be quite demanding and hard work for the young people and workers. We realised that in

order to keep up motivation for all concerned there needed to be a balance between work and play within the groupwork sessions and in the progression of the group overall. We also explored ways of integrating work and play more within the Social Action approach.

- If and when major difficulties arose within groups (which wasn't often) eg theft, violence, damage to buildings, workers sometimes felt a desire to take over and sort things out; indeed young people often expected them to do so. This created anxiety and pressure for workers and they needed clear strategies and support for helping the young people take responsibility and control of their actions so that they could effectively learn from their mistakes and move on as a group.

- At times the pace at which groups seemed to be sorting things out seemed too slow for the workers; they needed support in managing their feelings of impatience, frustration, and anxiety. They also needed to sort out ways of helping the group to look at the pace at which they were going and/or help them cope and deal with external factors eg waiting for or receiving negative replies and action from other agencies that may slow down group progress or meeting external deadlines requesting that the group pace speeds up.

- Given that there is inherent conflict between adults and young people, group members especially in the early stages of the group may 'test out' the workers' respect for them and their personal boundaries. In some groups at BYAP they asked the workers challenging questions about their lives or tried to see how much they would tolerate in terms of 'disruptive behaviour'. Workers needed to develop strategies for responding to these situations, such as assertively sticking up for themselves and what they believe (the values and principles of the approach), remaining respectful towards the young people despite their 'challenging' behaviour, and reflecting back the challenge or question on to the young people.

- Sometimes arguments and disputes both within and outside the group affected the attendance at group meetings, or group membership. This hindered the decision making of the group and the achievement of their task. This created dilemmas for workers; should they intervene, and if so how? They sometimes needed support in developing mediation skills.

- We spent time ensuring that group dynamics and process got adequate attention from the young people and workers within group meetings, so that young people got positive experiences of being in a group and collective decision making and action. We needed to be aware of not allowing this way of working to become too task orientated at the expense of the group process.

- Some other adults eg parents, local residents, and councillors at times expected the workers to have a controlling rather than enabling role with the young people's groups. We explored ways of receiving and dealing with criticism and explaining clearly our role.

- Young people needed to have their say and be heard in meetings they had arranged with adults from organisations that affected their lives, estate and/or group task. Workers explored ways of preparing groups and themselves to enable this to happen as effectively as possible.

- Although the emphasis of the work is with groups, individual young people from or attached to those groups sometimes requested help and support from workers. Occasionally this became very time consuming and often stressful, putting a lot of pressure on a small worker team. There was a need to balance the time commitments of this work with the group work and explore ways of making connections between the two.

- Word gets round! We considered how to respond to young people's requests for groups or individual work on an estate with very little alternative youth provision or services for them to choose from. Due to its limited worker resources the project had to be very careful not to become overwhelmed with too much groupwork.

- When the project acquired its office premises there was much discussion about the advantages and disadvantages of this. Given that it was to be shared by workers and young people, conflicts and dilemmas arose about its ownership, usage, responsibility for keys, opening times for young people, and its connection with other centre users. Decisions had to be made about all these issues and tested out.

Conclusion

Hopefully this report has adequately outlined and illustrated how essential consultancy is and can be to projects such as BYAP (and the other GEST projects) who are committed to innovative youth work practice with young people, alongside adequately supporting themselves as workers in what can be very demanding and stressful work.

I will leave the last words to the BYAP workers (N O'Neill and S Baker) when I asked: 'So what do you reckon to consultancies then?'

They're a real confidence booster; they've helped me realise that I can do the job. It's really important that you're independent and an outsider.

They've helped us to lay the fabric of a supportive culture for ourselves as a team.

In consultancies I can get out of my management and leadership role and contribute as a team member. They help me get some distance from the project. It's been essential that you're rooted in the Social Action philosophy and practice and that you're an experienced practitioner.

You give us ideas that we can use directly with young people; it's like you know what works.

I've liked your provocative and challenging style; you acknowledge our feelings and motivation as well as our skills. I also appreciate your humour and wouldn't have missed the movement.

I don't miss 'em till I do 'em; I sometimes think I can do without 'em yet when we have one I definitely feel the difference! They need to continue.

References

Harris, V., and Harrison, M. (1994) *Review of Social Action Projects in Bradford*. Leicester: Centre for Social Action, de Montfort University.

Harris, V., Pryke, J., and Harrison, M. (1995) *Review of Social Action Projects* in *Bradford BYAP*. Leicester: Centre for Social Action, de Montfort University.

Mullender, A., and Ward, D. (1991) *Self Directed Groupwork; Users Take Action for Empowerment.* London: Whiting and Birch.

Ward, D. (ed.) (1982) *Give 'em a break; Social Action by young people at risk and in trouble.* National Youth Bureau now National Youth Agency.

This chapter was first published in 1996 in *Social Action Journal* Vol. 3(1), pp.15-18

At the time of writing Izzy Terry had been involved in social action work with young people for 14 years. She did social action training and consultancy work in West Yorkshire and also works in Leeds with a young women's group

The beginning stages of a social action training event

Jennie Fleming

This article describes in detail how social action trainers approach the beginning stages of the groupwork process, which is recognised as a crucial stage in the formation of any group. Examples of how group members are facilitated to get to know each other, agree the purposes of the group, their expectations and the ground rules which should operate are presented under the headings of 'introductions and warmups', 'identity', 'purpose' and 'methods', drawing particularly on the experience of social action groupwork with Russian social workers and American teachers. Certain exercises have been found to be particularly helpful in achieving group cohesion and purpose and these are described. The role of the facilitator and the advantages of co-working in these circumstances are discussed briefly.

Social action training

Groupwork is at the core of social action training. We rely heavily on the building of groups to enable peer education to take place and for learning to be sustained beyond the training event, through groups continuing to support, sustain and challenge each other.

We carry out social action training with a wide variety of people: community members in Southwark in London, young people in Nottingham, teachers across the United States, social workers in Russia and in Kyiv Ukraine, Youth Offending Teams in Birmingham, or health workers in Leicester. The training sessions can take place over one or two days or a series of training inputs over a period of years, with the opportunity to develop practice in-between times. The topics range from an introduction to social action as an approach and way of working, to specific aspects of professional development.

Much has been written about social action as a way of

working with groups (see for example Harrison and Ward, 1999; Fleming and Luczynski, 1999; Fleming, 1999; Mullender and Ward, 1989 and 1991; Badham et al, 1989). The Centre's website www.dmu.ac.uk/dmucsa has information about the work and approach of social action. To summarise briefly, social action is a value-based approach to practice. It incorporates a set of principles and a problem solving approach, where social action workers provide the framework for the consideration of problems, issues or concerns and raise questions to encourage analysis and understanding, and consideration of appropriate actions. Participants provide the content, using their skills, knowledge and expertise. Group members create the knowledge and understanding, through active participation: describing, suggesting, analysing, deciding, experiencing and reflecting.

In this paper I am going to address a very specific aspect of social action groupwork: the beginning stages with a training group. The role of groupwork in learning and in the early stages of groups have been the topic of recent articles in Groupwork (Silverlock, 2000; Lizzio and Wilson, 2001). Groupwork is at the core of social action training. We find it possible to transfer much of what we know about groupwork generally to training with groups. Social action is not about doing things for people, so social action training is not usually about pre-prepared handouts and lectures. It is about the group taking responsibility for their own learning and creating their own materials. A training event is far more likely to have handouts sent out after the training, when flipcharts created by the participants have been typed up, than created before a training event. Social action training is about encouraging people to reflect on what is, why it is like this and how it can be changed. Training is an on-going process of reflection, deep consideration and action planning. However short a training event may be, there is always consideration of action and some time for planning: social action is about change.

The experience of training teachers in America and social workers in Russia will be drawn on for examples. All participants on these particular training sessions would fit into Lizzio and Wilson's category of 'informed consent – I know what this is about and I choose to be here' (Lizzio and Wilson, 2001, p.16), although we are well used to working with other motivations or, indeed, the lack of them.

An inevitable consequence of focusing in this paper on the beginning stages of the groupwork process is that other things will be left out. For example, we will not consider the planning and preparation that happened, nor give attention to how people were selected to be in the groups concerned. It will not cover the process and progress of a group beyond the beginning. However see Peterson et al, (2000) for more details of the Centre's work with teachers in America and for discussion of Social Action as an educative process (Fleming, 2003). Douglas (2000, p.13) points out that 'few people when discussing groups start at the beginning' so this article hopes to go some way towards redressing this balance.

Beginnings of groups

Many writers about groupwork highlight the importance of the beginnings of a group. Preston Shoot (1987, p .98) says that the right beginnings for a group are vital. The classic formulation of the stages of development of groups is Tuckman's forming, norming, performing and storming to which Brown (1992, p.103) adds the additional stage of ending. It is the forming stage that will be considered here. Manor (2000, p.103) writes that 'the strategies adopted while forming the group influence a great deal of what is to come'. How we start working with a group in a training session is very important as it sets the scene for what follows. It is through careful attention to the forming stage, that the possibility of performing satisfactorily is enhanced. Manor (2000, p.12) also points out that the 'stages in groups are very helpful signposts' as they alert the worker to potential areas of focus.

The beginning stages of a group are crucial to establishing the culture of the group (Brown, 1992, p.104). This is particularly important in training where participants might have very different expectations of the event. For example, in Russia, 'training' often means sitting passively and listening to lectures.

This makes it even more crucial to pay very careful attention to the beginning stages of a training group, so the participants understand what will follow. As Hope and Timmel (1999, vol 1, p.11) point out, 'Dividing people into groups of three to share their ideas and then arranging a climate of genuine listening, when each has a chance to share with the whole group, affirms the wisdom of ordinary people in quite a different way .....' to lectures, but if we are to achieve this outcome we need to pay particular attention to the beginnings.

However, for a training group it is not just enough to be clear as trainers about the processes that are being given attention, it is also important to find a way of communicating them to the participants. Doel and Sawdon (1999) suggest that,

> learning from an experience is not automatic. If the learning is to have an impact on subsequent practice, it needs to be 'named' – made explicit and available for reflection and retrieval. (p.45).

This is as important for trainers as it is for participants. As social action trainers we have to reflect on what is happening and so understand for ourselves the processes involved before we can name them.

As with other aspects of social action work, the practice/action/theory praxis has played a crucial part in the development of the theory of social action groupwork in training. For some time we had ensured that the forming stage of a training session has covered introductions, discussions of why people have come together and what people would like to have learned by the end of the event. But it is only relatively recently, through reflection on our practice, that a colleague helpfully named these stages 'identity', 'purpose' and 'method'. Lizzio and Wilson (2002) suggest that the,

> overall task in facilitating the beginning of any process is to help people achieve a state where they are willing and able to invest in the job in hand. We achieve this by giving attention in our beginnings to design a range of formative activities. (p.11)

It is through the attention to identity, purpose and method that we do this.

The social action approach to group beginnings has evolved into the following framework:

- introductions and warm ups: a short section where purposeful warm up games and exercises are used
- identity: consideration of who is in the group and the nature of their similarities and differences
- purpose: exploration of what it is people want to learn and achieve in the group
- method: agreement on how this group of people are going to work together to achieve their agreed aims

Introductions and warm ups

From the practice we have developed we would agree with Lizzio and Wilson (2002, p.27) when they say 'we should consider our opening comments to a group as more than just a perfunctory social ritual'. In our experience it is not just the opening comments that need choosing with care, but the whole beginning stage. Most of our training sessions begin with 'warm-up' games. Warm up exercises need to be as purposeful as any other training activity, so we carefully consider what we are trying to achieve before deciding what exercise to suggest to the group.

We have many tried and tested games that we use with all groups and in all situations. For example, asking people to tell each other their name and the story behind their name, or a more interactive and dynamic exercise is asking people to group themselves together with others. For example, firstly, to find those whose birthday is in the same month as yours (a fact); second, to find people who share your musical taste (opinion) and, finally, to find people who share your views about something, for example, the capacity of people to create change by themselves (belief). At the same time participants are all talking with each other and establishing what they have in common.

Identity

Following the initial exercises or warm ups, and almost as part of the same stage, we move on to finding out more about who is in the group, how they got to be interested in the training and what they have in common with each other. An exercise we use at this stage is one developed with young homeless people in Moscow, hence the name, the Metro Map.

This exercise is about encouraging people to share with each other their motivations and route into the training event. Each person has a different coloured pen and in turns they talk to the others about the three most significant events or critical incidents in their lives that led them to being at this training event. They draw these as the stations on the map to the event.

In Russia, social workers talked about such things as 'the passion in my heart', 'when I found out about the situation of children in care', 'a realisation of the vulnerability of families', 'a desire to find ways out of this situation', 'having experienced hardship myself as a child', 'empathy with children' or 'a sense of injustice' as being the key events that brought them to the training room. In contrast, items put on the metro maps in America included: 'being told I was stupid', 'becoming involved in community campaigning', 'realising I was a radical at college', 'being frustrated by other teachers' practice', 'dismay at what was happening in my community'.

Another exercise we often use is The Group Name. Once again, we group people. Usually we do this by the well-known method of going around the room counting '1, 2, 3' for as many groups as we need, all the 1's going together and so on. It has the advantage of mixing up people who have probably come into the room and sat with people they know. Someone once wrote on an evaluation form of a Russian training event, that the most useful thing they had learnt on the training was this 'scientific' method of dividing people into groups! Once in their groups they are asked to talk about 'one thing it is important for people to know about you, one thing you believe'. Then they are asked to consider what they have in common, and from this decide on a suitable name for their group. This group is then known by that name for the rest of the training (for example a group might become the Daily Reflection group and so they meet together each day to prepare a reflection on the event so far). Names that the teachers in America have chosen for their groups have included The Negotiators, Passion, Free Radicals, Mavericks and the Lively Learners. In Russia they have also chosen Passion, Concern, Love and Compassion.

Even if participants are reluctant to talk about themselves it is still possible for them to agree a name. Once when working with a group of young people who were not attending school, one group called me over and said that they did not want anyone to know anything about themselves and they did not want to talk about what they believed in. However they were prepared to acknowledge that this was what they had in common and call themselves 'The Unknowns' and, whilst they remained on the edge, they did continue to participate in the event.

We are always on the look out for new exercises we can use or adapt for our training; recently we have taken ideas from Participation: Spice it up (2002) and the Group Games (Fuchs, 2002) series. We have also learnt many superb games and exercises from our training participants. There is great pleasure in taking a 'pen dancing exercise' (an active exercise that builds cooperation and group cohesion) from Russian child care workers to introduce to American teachers, knowing they in turn will use it with their students.

Purpose

Once identity has been considered and people know more about each other and have had the opportunity to talk about things that are important to them in coming to the training, the next step is for the whole group to agree a common purpose for the time they are together. Mullender and Ward (1991, p.59) say that the need to create goals holds true for any group. This fits with Doel and Sawdon's (1999) concept of 'contracting in'. 'The notion of contracting in is designed to help the present collection of individuals begin to reach agreement about what their group might be.

There are three components to contracting in:

• The first is the groupworkers' responsibility to set out their own stall and to set the scene via an opening statement of purpose.

- The second is to introduce group members to each other and to enable them to share their own vision for the group and to agree the processes that will help the group work effectively.
- The third concerns agreement about goals and outcomes, whether these are held individually or commonly. (p.117).

It is this third stage of agreement about goals and outcomes that we call purpose.

Whilst all training events have previously agreed broad aims and objectives that have been negotiated with funders, managers or others (which have attracted people to come forward for the training), it is important that each group agrees their own specific vision and goals. Once two social action trainers ran four consecutive two-day training events for teachers, all with the same overall aims and objectives. However each group identified their own unique purpose within these.

The usual way that social action trainers approach enabling a group to agree purpose is by devising or creating a vision for the event. Initially people think alone, and then share in small groups of about four people the three things they most want to have achieved by the end of the training event. They discuss this in the small groups and then each small group shares with the whole group. There then follows a negotiation process in which the whole group attempts to decide three things which everyone can agree that they want to have as part of their vision. We are usually quite strict about keeping to just three things and about the shared negotiation process. We point out that much work in groups is about negotiation, about getting as many people as possible to agree a common purpose and focus, and that some people may need to leave their own ideas behind. In the negotiation it is important that the trainer explains that all views should be equal, and works to ensure this is the case. The exercise should create involvement and ownership of the process and content of the training event.

Sometimes the negotiation results in some lengthy sentences!

For example: 'to be able to experience, understand, articulate, apply, use and share social action' was once the first thing that people wanted to achieve. Visions often include words such as explore, uncover, gain, experience, understand, articulate, apply or share. When creating visions for training events it is important that group members realise that these set out the things people want to achieve in the training room and so should not include actions beyond the training course; although obviously they often include a desire to be able to apply what they have learnt in the training event when they get back to work.

A vision created by some social workers in Russia on a Training the Trainers course looked like this:

'Our vision is to learn:
- facilitation and social action methods of training
- how to use them in workshops and in other circumstances and with different groups
- how to work together and be as effective as possible (intersectorial working)'

A vision created by one of the teachers' groups in America went like this:

'By the end of the five days we aim
- to experience, understand, own, articulate, apply and use and share social action
- leave here equipped with tools (strategies, stuff) and techniques to open dialogue to establish and build and sustain relationships amongst and within our students, and wider community to advance change through literacy
- establish the means to continue beyond the Institute, using social action within the project, and with each other.'

These 'visions' also form the basis of evaluation at the end of a training event, when the group 'revisit the vision' and consider how far they have achieved what they identified in the exercise.

Douglas (2000, p.38) says that group development is a collection of individuals forming into a coherent group with a common understanding and with collective aims. It is this stage of identifying purpose that social action trainers are trying to create within the groups they are working with.

Method

How things are done is very important in social action work. How one presents something is often as strong a value statement as the content. Social action is about self-direction, so it is important for a group to create their own guidance for their working together in a training session. Preston Shoot (1987, p.25) makes this point also when he writes: 'Group members have the ability to be self-directing and have responsibility for the direction of their learning and change efforts.' Lizzio and Wilson (2002) point out that group maintenance is not just the responsibility of the facilitators, but is shared with group members. They write of making group members partners in creating the group.

> Sharing a model of group or community building with group members may enable them to more systematically and consciously self manage the process of 'growing themselves' as an adaptive group. (p.54)

As always with social action groupwork it is important to start as we mean to go on, by actively involving participants in agreeing how they wish to work together, this begins to create responsibility for group maintenance. We often introduce this stage by pointing out that we all now have information about who is in the group and what they want to do. Now they need to decide how they are to work together as a group to reach the vision they have created.

Once again we have a number of different ways of approaching the task of deciding how we want to work together. Sometimes we ask people in small groups to consider what their hopes and fears are for the training event. Once they have done this and told the rest of the group what they are, each group's hopes and fears are passed on to another group and they come up with actions that group members can take to ensure the fears are not realised but the hopes are. These actions are then discussed in the full group and written up on flipchart paper and left on the wall for the life of the group.

Another way of helping a group think about how they would like to work together is an exercise called Community Vocabulary. This is when we ask participants to suggest all the words they do not want to hear used and those they do want to hear in the training session. This is not about censorship but to liberate people to speak their mind in the group. It is not a game, but becomes integral to how the group is going to work and be together over the period. We find there is often a lot of negotiation and review whilst the words are discussed and agreed. The community vocabulary should become part of the life of the group. Obviously, as trainers, we find that the words tell us a lot about the group. The words they want to hear tend to tell us about aspirations, where they are at the moment. The words people do not want to hear, give us information about their history and past experiences.

From this community vocabulary we sometimes ask people to create a list of Top Tips for participants, and often for facilitators too.

All the exercises are intended for participants to take and use in their own work. We have examples from the teachers in America using this exercise to good effect in the classroom. One teacher tells of how a child referred to the community vocabulary many weeks after it was created to challenge a homophobic comment, and that started discussion about the issue. Participants in Russia have used the exercises in many situations with young people, politicians and professionals.

Facilitation

It is not possible to write about social action work, without, albeit briefly, considering the role of the trainer. Hope and Timmel (1999, p.19) write in Training for Transformation that the 'animator provides a framework for thinking, creative, active participants to consider a common problem and find solutions. People are actively involved in the social construction of knowledge.' Social action has been much influenced by these manuals in its development and continues to look for ways to increase the involvement of people in their own learning and to develop this concept of the 'social construction of knowledge' further.

It is usual, though not always the case, that social action workers carry out training sessions in pairs. The advantages of co-working in groups are well documented. Preston-Shoot (1987, p 64) and Brown (1992, p.79) highlight a number of potential gains through co-working, for example, support and feedback, widening experience in the worker team, security and protection, increasing the range of options, techniques and styles available to the group, thereby ensuring that the group's needs will be understood and met.

Social action workers do not present the same experiences, style, or even personalities. Social action encourages reflection and discussion and so social action trainers are likely to possess a willingness to disagree with or, at least, question each other in the training group, which Brown (1992, p 86) says, 'can be an asset provided it is done in a facilitative and not undermining style.'

Butler and Wintram (1991) mention a further benefit of co-working pointing out that it encourages creativity and innovation:

> The co-worker increases workers' courage in trying out new and more risky exercises because she knows she has someone to help her deal with the reactions to such an approach. (p.40)

These points, combined together, summarise the benefits of co-working for social action. Co-working in a training group can promote review and deeper reflection on the groupwork and learning processes. There are alternative perspectives from which events can be seen. It ensures there is someone else who knows as much about the group as you do, with whom you can discuss what has been happening. Reflection is a vital stage of the social action process and there is no doubt that co-working has enhanced reflection on our training practice and so contributed to its development.

Evaluation by participants

What the participants think of the training is very important for our learning and the development of our work. All our training courses are evaluated, both in terms of content and the process undertaken. We have never evaluated just the first stages of a training event, so the comments below were given at the end of the whole training course.

In the main, people in both Russia and America have come to appreciate the approach, though for many it is a new experience and takes some getting used to. They feel they have developed their skills in communication and also learnt effective methods and techniques and shared knowledge and experience. Most people comment on the relaxed style. The following quotations from evaluation forms will be left to speak for themselves:

> They used a very good approach: encouraged the participants to think and to speak. [Russian Participant]

> Terrific! I want first to thank you for meeting the challenge of working with our large group and for taking us through the process in a way that allowed us to discover and uncover the meaning and purposes of this work. I appreciated the organisation, the progression of the Institute, how it built and led from one concept or strategy into another. I know from my own experience with social change work the balancing act between the conceptual and the concrete, and there were many opportunities to explore both. [American Participant]

> The greatest strength was the way in which we experienced the process of social action through particular strategies. We came to an understanding of SA in an authentic, process-based way. [American Participant]

The facilitators were very patient when the group became impatient about the process and they walked us through everything. [Russian Participant]

Facilitators did a superb job building community to participants. It provided a safe environment for participants to express their sincerest ideas and opinions. [Russian Participant]

Conclusions

It is only after we have worked with a group on these elements of forming, identity, purpose and method, that social action trainers plan the rest of the training in detail, because until this point we do not have enough information to be able to do so. Now that we have some knowledge about and from the people we are working with, we are able to tailor the training to their experiences and needs. Of course, we will have a broad outline plan but we will not complete it until this stage. It is not until these early stages have been completed that we know what the group feels passionate about, what they disagree about, what their aspirations for the event are. Once we have begun to gain this knowledge we can try to ensure the training will be appropriate to them. As Doel and Sawdon comment (1999)

In first and early sessions, as the group is forming, the tension between process and outcome is immediately evident. On the one hand it is important to negotiate agreement around the processes of becoming a group and how the group will conduct itself; on the other is the need to negotiate what the group wants to achieve. (pp.125/6).

This is particularly true with a social action training event, as people sometimes feel it is very slow to get to the 'real work'. It is important to point out that the 'real work' starts the minute people come into the room, but it is sometimes not until the end of the training event that people fully understand this.

How a group is set up has considerable influence on how

they will approach and deal with any issues and problems that may arise later on. However, Lizzio and Wilson (2002, p 53) point out 'The aim is not to facilitate the complete resolution of each area of concern, but rather sufficient resolution to enable subsequent work'. It is not possible to avoid all difficulties in the future; indeed disagreement and mild conflict can be a real stimulation to learning. However, by giving careful attention to the beginning stages it is possible to enable the group to equip itself with solid foundations to be able to deal in the most constructive manner, with whatever arises.

Mullender and Ward (1991) write

> it is not uncommon for workers to expect to swing into action clad in nothing more than anti-authoritarian zeal and a loose commitment to tackling oppression. (p.23).

In social action training we feel we are more adequately dressed than this! We enter a training room with a set of principles and a process that underpins all that we do. We recognise the centrality of values to inform our practice. Social action trainers facilitate and do not lead, because we recognise that people are experts in their own lives, and that by acting collectively they can be powerful. Social action trainers work to create a learning environment where people are listened to, asked to contribute their ideas and encouraged to act on their suggestions, in the hope of enabling reflective groups and developing reflective practice. The early stages of working with a group are the first steps to achieving this and are fundamental in creating the environment in which learning can take place. Combined with this clear and overt value position, social action trainers also have a wide range of tried and tested exercises and techniques which can be used or adapted to most situations. However, we constantly learn from our experiences in training and seek to improve our practice. Dialogue with participants is key to this. We learn much from the groups with whom we work.

Acknowledgements

I could not have written this article without the work of many other people. Ian Boulton was absolutely key, not only in co-delivering and developing the training discussed, but also because of the long and stimulating conversations we have had about it and for many of the original ideas. I also want to acknowledge Lou Wilcox and every teacher and social worker that has taken such an active part in the Institutes and workshops.

References

Badham, B., Blatchford, B., Mcartney, S. and Nicholas, M.(1989) Doing something with our lives when we're inside: Self-directed groupwork in a Youth Custody Centre. *Groupwork*, 2, 1, 27-35

Brown, A. (1992) *Groupwork*. (3rd ed) Aldershot: Ashgate

Butler, S. and Wintram, C. (1991) *Feminist Groupwork*. London: Sage

Doel, M. and Sawdon, C. (1999) *The Essential Groupworker: Teaching and learning creative groupwork*. London: Jessica Kingsley

Douglas, T. (2000) Basic Groupwork. London: Tavistock

Dynamix Ltd. (2002) *Participation: Spice it up!* Cardiff: Save the Children Fund

Fleming, J. (2003) Am I an educator? A collaboration leads to new understandings about education. *The Quarterly*, 25, 3, 2-17

Fleming, J. and Luczynski, Z. (1999) MEN UNITED: Fathers' voices. *Groupwork*, 11, 2, 21-38

Fleming, J. (1999) Working with young homeless people: Lessons from the voluntary sector for social work. *Practice*, 11, 4, 45-57

Fuchs, B. (2002) *Group Games: Social skills*. Bicester: Speechmark Publishing

Harrison, M. and Ward, D. (1999) Values as context: Groupwork and social action. *Groupwork*, 11, 3, 88-103

Hope, A. and Timmel, S. (1999) *Training for Transformation* Vol 1. London: Intermediate Technology Publications

Lizzio, A. and Wilson, K. (2001) Facilitating group beginnings. *Groupwork*, 13, 1, 6-57

Manor, O. (2000) *Choosing a Groupwork Approach*. London: Jessica Kingsley

Mullender, A. and Ward, D. (1991) *Self-Directed Groupwork: Users take action for empowerment*. London: Whiting and Birch

Mullender, M. and Ward, D. (1989) Challenging familiar assumptions: Preparing for and initiating a self-directed group. *Groupwork*, 2,1, 5-26

Peterson, A., Solomon, A. and Young, B. (2000) Centre for Social Action offers teachers powerful tools. *The Voice*, 5,5 , Nov/December, 1, 16-17. http://www.writingproject.org

Preston-Shoot, M. (1987) *Effective Groupwork*. London: Macmillan

Silverlock, M. (2000) Learning beyond the classroom: A role for groupwork. *Groupwork*, 12, 1, 58 -71

This chapter was first published in 2004 in *Groupwork* Vol. 14(2), pp.24-41

At the time of writing Jennie Fleming was Principal Lecturer, Research, Centre for Social Action, De Montfort University

Social action
and self-directed
groupwork:

Section 4
Principles into practice:
Practice

'Nowt to do and always getting into trouble'

The Bulwell Neighbourhood Project:
A social action response

Bill Badham, Michael Bente and Pauline Hall

This paper describes an inter-disciplinary response to young people at risk of offending, and having difficulties, whether at school, home or with the law. The work undertaken involved Social Services, the Youth Service, Probation and two voluntary sector protects'.[1] The young people concerned belonged to two neighbourhoods in the Bulwell area of the City of Nottingham. The work started in the summer of 1984 and ended in the spring of 1988. The article discusses: (1) the background to the neighbourhood work: its origins, the proposal, and social action principles; (2) the neighbourhood work undertaken: working with young people, their issues and concerns, and action taken;and (3). implications for agency practice: inter-agency meetings and consequences.

Background

Origins

There is a firm tradition of neighbourhood work in the Bulwell area, making it a suitable breeding ground for the Neighbourhood Project for three reasons:

1. In the agencies, there was some familiarity with concepts of neighbourhood work and social action (described below), and a broad remit to question current agency practice and to develop appropriate alternatives.
2. Some inter-team initiatives had been tried, and there was a willingness to talk with other agencies.
3. In late 1984 a number of workers from the Youth, Social and

Probation Services were able to pool their experience and ideas, with the advantage of some having worked together before and been on local inter-disciplinary social action training events together.

When representatives of the statutory agencies met to discuss concerns over offending and young people, and the possible need to work across agency boundaries, two actions resulted. First the area intermediate treatment worker recorded the patterns of young people's offending, using the police referral forms which are sent to Probation and Social Services. This pointed to groupings of young offenders in two areas, Bulwell Hall and Highbury Vale. Second, a street survey of local young people was done by Social Services over several weeks. It highlighted groups who did not use local facilities, but who wanted places to meet. The young people talked to also spoke of conflict with the local police and other adults, and of racial tension in Bulwell.

Proposal

Arising from the monitoring of police referrals and the street survey, the area intermediate treatment worker, a social worker, two youth workers and a probation officer (referred to hereafter as 'the worker team') met to discuss the findings and explore the relevance of neighbourhood work in Bulwell Hall and Highbury Vale. As potential co-workers, we began by clarifying our own values and principles, described below. We then put a written proposal to the local statutory agencies, and attended team meetings to discuss the reasons for wanting to work with these young people.

The written proposal highlighted the natural groups of young people at risk in Bulwell, where there were high levels of individual and joint offending and the statutory involvement of more than one agency. Two aims were put forward: first, to work with young people, at risk and in trouble in their own neighbourhoods, in natural groupings, on issues and concerns they would identify: second, to work within an inter-agency context to discuss issues of agency practice and policy, arising from the groupwork process, as well as to check on the progress of the neighbourhood work itself.

The proposed groupwork was to be based neither on activities nor the social skills model. Rather, the term 'social action' was used to suggest that the workers would be examining with the young people, the concerns and difficulties they experienced, the issues they faced and the ways in which they felt that they could both understand their situations better and take action for themselves. The proposal said:

> The workers seek to maximise young people's control over their own lives by increasing their confidence to act on their own ideas, to use resources available to them and to make their needs known to those who have power over resources.
>
> It was proposed that the work should be reviewed regularly on a joint basis by local agencies, and that each worker team should have the help of weekly planning sessions with a consultant.

Principles of the neighbourhood project

By the summer of 1985, the worker team had permission to begin the project. Having worked hard to get to this point, we were eager to 'get started' and meet the young people directly. We agreed, however, that we must first do our own groundwork. Why work with the young people? What are the failings of current, traditional agency responses which seem of limited value to the young people? How can we develop a more relevant response?

The worker team explored these issues, starting with our own dissatisfaction with both current provision and views expressed by colleagues. For example, the youth club leader said that young people need a structure set by adults, need to be provided for, and don't have the ability to take responsibility and action for themselves. Within the probation team, there was resistance to questioning the efficacy of one to one casework, even when the young people themselves expressed dissatisfaction with the service given, and when recent statistics seen by the team pointed to the nature and extent of group offending on Highbury Vale.

Our criticisms were informed by radical social work writers such as Bailey and Brake (1980), Corrigan (1979), and Walker and Beaumont (1981). Agency responses to young people were individualised, and treatment or activity oriented. In consequence the worker's role was generally controlling, setting the agenda and being seen as the expert. Collective issues and concerns were hidden by this divide and rule approach. We acknowledged some new developments but thought these were largely 'old wine in new bottles' (Wilson, 1977). For example, in social skills, the values and methods of the groupwork still focus on an individual's problems, and can be used by course leaders to reinforce feelings of personal inadequacy in group members. 'The wine has been fortified' (Walker and Beaumont, 1981, p. 84).

In contrast, the worker team agreed on some basic principles and values that have continually informed our practice. These are based in part on Freire (1970; 1972), as applied and developed in Nottingham under the term 'social action' (Ward, 1982).

The main principles of 'social action' are as follows:
1. A positive view of young people; young people do have skills, understanding and ability
2. Young people should be heard. They have a right to define their own issues and take action on them.
3. Young people acting collectively can be powerful.
4. Young people's difficulties are not generally a result of 'personal inadequacies'. Social policy, environmental and economic factors, racism and sexism are major forces contributing to young people's problems. Practice should reflect this understanding.
5. The problems that young people face are complex and responses to them need to cross disciplinary and organisational boundaries,
6 Methods of work should reflect principles: practice what you preach.

These principles have been the foundation of our work. Overall, they held firm and informed our practice throughout the life of the project.

The neighbourhood work with the young people

Aims and approach

The aims of the work on the Neighbourhood Project, based on the above principles, were as follows:

1. To work with natural groups in their own areas.
2. To work with the young people at their own pace on concerns that they identify as important to them.
3. To work in partnership with the young people, rather than being seen as 'expert' or 'provider' and doing things for/to them.
4. Through our understanding of the nature of oppression, to develop anti-racist and anti-sexist practice and to challenge racism and sexism among the worker team, the young people and the agencies involved.
5. Believing our agencies' policies and practices to be part of the problem facing the young people, to raise issues and concerns arising from the groupwork, as a means of improving current policy and practice,
6. For ourselves to reflect critically on the work being undertaken, through regular support, sharing and planning with a consultant (see Ward and Burley, 1982).

By Autumn 1985 we were ready to begin contacting the young people. Our social action approach can be seen as a five stage process:

1. *What* are the concerns and difficulties faced?
3. *How* can change be brought about? What information, skills and resources are needed?
4. Forming a plan, and *action* for implementation
5. *Reflection* on what has happened: review action, evaluate, raise new questions and make further plans.

Work undertaken

This section offers an overview of the work with the young people from October 1985 until early 1988. It highlights the issues and concerns they raised, and action taken.

While some of them were known to some of the workers, we wanted our initial contact to be as much on their terms as possible. So, instead of using our contacts to pre-arrange a meeting, both worker teams (the team of five was divided to cover the two estates in the project) began getting to know young people on the streets, where we found they spent much of their time.

Bulwell Hall (MOB)[2]

In the first worker team there were the two sessional youth workers and one local authority social worker. The consultant was also from the Social Services Department. In autumn 1985, links were developed with a group of young people on the streets in Bulwell Hall. There was discussion about what concerned them, especially the lack of facilities and resources on the estate. They wanted somewhere permanent to meet. Workers tried to be clear that they could not 'provide', but would be willing to help the young people look at their concerns in more detail and help them think through what might be done and what action they could take.

The only possible venue was a small hall, attached to a warden-aided old people's complex. Many of them were banned from this hall, but, they looked at the issue, planned, and negotiated with the caretaker themselves. The result was permission to use the hall every Friday evening. It still provides the only indoor meeting place for the young people of Bulwell Hall. In the spring, having achieved their main objective of gaining a place to go on the estate, they sought to develop the facility by trying to get funds and equipment. They arranged and planned a visit by an influential member of the Leisure Services Department. This person met them one evening and promises were made, but not kept.

Although these failed .promises, and school holidays coinciding with a spate of offending, saw a decline in involvement over the summer, numbers again increased in Autumn 1986. The young people showed great commitment to the Friday night group they had established. They dealt themselves with occasional conflict with the caretaker that arose from them using the hall. They invited other young people to come, swelling numbers to 20 or more. They put on a jumble sale that raised over £30. There was much concern also at this time over pending court appearances, and so a probation worker was invited to talk with them about some of their worries arising from the court process. When reports were requested, there were contributions from the project workers, putting the offending in context. They also designed, produced and distributed a leaflet, entitled M.O.B.[2] raising their needs and concerns in the neighbourhood.

During the first part of 1987, this general direction continued and grant applications were made successfully to Probation and Social Services. Some of the young people ably represented their views and concerns at two open meetings between the City Council and the Bulwell Community. Renewed efforts were made to get a grant and a permanent worker from Leisure Services. However, by the autumn, after the expected Summer lull, the nature of the group began changing. First, some moved away and others, being that bit older, found other interests. There were also four on remand in custody, and others facing court appearances. Helped by the consultant, the workers and young people thought about these developments over a number of meetings. They agreed that the social action focus had shifted. It was, therefore, agreed to stop the weekly meetings, but to continue offering support to those in custody, and that the young people would approach the probation worker, were any new initiatives to arise.

Highbury Vale (TOLO)[2]

The other team was the area intermediate treatment worker and the probation officer. The senior probation officer helped in the planning of the work. When first looking around the area one evening, the workers were seen by some young men known to the probation officer. They were in a house belonging to an adult woman friend and we, the workers, were immediately asked in. The welcome was overwhelming and there was much enthusiasm at our wish to be involved on the estate. These young people had access to the attic of the friend's house, which became our meeting place for a short time. They were very clear about their disillusionment with adults, both workers and residents. Previous initiatives had left them high and dry, they said. The workers encouraged the group to look at what troubled them, and they wrote up on a flip chart the following:

Nowt to do
Complaints when we do do
Nowhere to do it
No-one backs you up
When people do back you up they give up after a bit
Always getting into trouble
Whatever we do we get into trouble for it.

The concerns included the agencies, such as Probation and Social Services, solicitors and the courts. The Youth Training Scheme was seen as not being a proper job, boring, and the college as providing nothing. When asked "what do you want?" they talked mainly about wanting to be listened to and taken seriously. Youth facilities in the area were also mentioned.

These young people had a clear understanding of *what* concerns and difficulties they faced. As to *why* these existed, they had experience of adults not delivering the goods and making decisions on their behalf that came to nothing. This realism also caused disillusionment about *how* to bring about change. This may also reflect the feet that they were slightly older than the Bulwell Hall group and increasingly had other things to do, found work or were on schemes, and were more interested in their partners. During the first part of 1986 there was a lull which caused the workers to review progress and go back to the group to look at what had happened, and not happened, and whether they wished to continue meeting. Consistency was crucial if we too were not to confirm 'when people do back you they give up after a bit.

Staying in touch has borne fruit. Some specific matters were taken forward, such as raising concerns that the young people had about a club held once a week at a school in the neighbourhood. They felt this facility was limited and run inappropriately to their needs. Also two or three young men started looking to an 'off the road' facility for driving. Consistent contact has been maintained with these young people ever since. We agreed with them to stop our weekly meetings, because they repeatedly said there was no action they wished to follow up. Yet, the workers have continued to offer support in times of difficulty, including being involved in the preparation of reports, keeping in touch when in prison, and helping friends to visit.

Other issues

The above two accounts have indicated some of the 'products' of the work. Yet, the young people and the workers feel that some of the most important fruits of our involvement together have arisen from the way of working. This is best illustrated by some examples.

Firstly, at Bulwell Hall, the young people gained access to the hall on Friday nights. That was the product. But the process, or the way this happened, was equally crucial. The workers did not hire the hall. It was the young people who had to look at what their needs were and what they could do about it. They had to overcome the barrier of having been banned at the hall before. They had to plan what they would say, who they would say it to, what they wanted and how it would be paid for. Later on, when the group's high spirits have threatened the continuing use of the hall, or when numbers have been depleted and the group disillusioned, this belief in it being their hall and their place to meet has been crucial for their sense of achievement, responsibility and purpose.

Secondly, the leaflet used to publicise the needs of the young people of Bulwell Hall is eye catching and well produced. What is impressive is the manner of its production. If the workers had 'done it for them', then would it not have been adults again speaking on young people's behalf? - one of the very problems they talk about. Helped by the workers, they stated their concern at not being listened to, their need for money and publicity. They decided on using the leaflet and worked out the wording. They wrote to a cartoonist, asking for use of one of his cartoons. They produced the draft leaflet. Then, later, some went to a local advice and resource centre where they were shown how to use the machinery for the leaflet's production. It is not surprising that this episode remains important to the group.

Thirdly, both groups often talked about issues of race and sex, either in general discussion, or through derogatory remarks. Both estates are predominantly white, reflected in the membership of the groups; in Bulwell Hall, particularly, there have at times been a large number of young women involved. When the young people made what was seen by the workers as racist or sexist remarks, the workers' response was to challenge this in the context of how it affected the young people and was relevant to them. While this can cause friction - 'people like you think you're perfect' - it not only avoids collusion, but is consistent with the principles behind the way of working.

In Bulwell Hall, there had always been at least one black worker, initially causing comments like 'you're okay Michael, but Paki's are different'. The group themselves began to question and challenge such views and there is evidence of a lot of learning and a reduction in prejudice and racism. They think through more carefully what they are saying. For example, 'we never used to go to the youth club because of black people; no that's wrong it was because of the drugs around and white people have drugs too'.

A similar process happened with sexism. Comments about what women are only good for often got direct reaction from the group: 'would you say that about your mother or sister? you're talking about people not objects'. In Bulwell Hall, when the young men have tended to dominate, the workers have encouraged the whole group to look at this behaviour. In turn, the young people sought to counter it by, for example, ensuring that one of the signatories to the bank account was a young woman. They have also instituted a 'no violence' rule.

Fourthly, whether there have been specific 'products' or not, both groups have repeatedly said they have found our involvement important because 'you see us as we are'. But, 'In the office you sit in the big chair and we sit in the small chair'. Trust has developed, and the workers have some understanding of the neighbourhood and the nature of the young people's concerns, including their offending. They say they like being listened to and taken seriously by adults, getting the confidence to take decisions and responsibilities.

Implications and evaluation

An important aim of the Neighbourhood Project has been to evaluate the work through meetings of relevant agencies, raising practice issues arising from the neighbourhood work. For the project workers, this has been a key, but very demanding element. It has involved three write-ups of the work, and planning and chairing four inter-agency meetings. One worker, on behalf of the project, has linked with a voluntary housing project to discuss establishing a group for ex-residents, based on similar principles to our work. These links are crucial, if the groupwork is to avoid becoming an end in itself, and for evaluation and accountability.

Implications within the project
If the Neighbourhood Project has been of continuing relevance

for more than two years to the young people concerned and to the agencies involved, we feel three factors have played their part:

1. Careful preparation, clear planning, the establishing of accepted principles of practice among the worker team, and gaining agreement among the agencies to the proposals.
2. The commitment to regular weekly planning by the worker teams, using the help of a consultant.
3. The need for good feedback to teams and the inter-agency forum; write-ups of the work and making sure accurate notes of meetings and decisions are taken and circulated.

Two other points should be considered.

• *Reoffending*
One of the starting points for our work was that groups of young people were offending and at risk of custody. Some have continued getting into trouble, others have stopped. Some have said our involvement directly reduced the amount of their offending (for example, on Friday nights in Bulwell Hall).

Whatever the effect of the groupwork on offending, it was never a specific aim or expectation to reduce offending. However, the young people's concerns frequently included getting into trouble and its consequences. They often talked with the workers about their group or individual difficulties. On their own territory and on their own terms, they have been open about the nature and cause of offending: boredom, lack of money, no jobs ... ... Unlike the labelling and scapegoating comments that characterise the individualised pleading of some social enquiry reports, they did not tend to blame someone else or say they were 'easily led'. Rather, personal responsibility was accepted, but, for example, in the context of limited opportunities, heavy police presence on the estates etc.

It is hard to see how continued offending could undermine the value of the project (unless there was a colossal increase!). There is a risk of testing community action approaches more rigorously in this regard than casework, intermediate treatment or social skills. Unlike these orthodoxies, by working in partnership with people and encouraging collective action on issues they identify to effect change in their communities, social action does acknowledge, and seek to help challenge, the structural causes of much offending. Our work has also helped develop trust and make the 'caring agencies' more accessible, encouraging young people to make demands and get a better deal from their probation or social worker.

- *Evaluation*
  While evaluation of the neighbourhood work may not be easily quantified by, for example, looking at offending figures, critical reflection on practice is an essential part of the social action approach. It is not open-ended in time, or lacking boundaries. Within the project, evaluation occurred at three levels:
  1. By the workers and young people discussing, learning, planning, taking action, reflecting on outcomes, making new plans. Some sessions would specifically brainstorm 'what's good, what's bad and what could be better about the group.' When the focus was slipping, the workers reappraised with the young people the nature of their involvement.
  2. By workers meeting regularly (often weekly) with the consultant. This is essential to air conflicts and successes in the work, set objectives, plan, offer on-going evaluation, assessment and support.
  3. By holding reviews within the relevant teams and having occasional inter-agency forums, involving both main grade staff and management.

Implications for agencies

Whatever the implications for mainstream agency practice, the main reason behind the neighbourhood project, arising out of concern about traditional agency responses to young people, has been to offer a more consistent and coherent response through working with them on their own concerns and issues, in their own neighbourhoods. The interagency meetings were seen as a crucial forum in which to evaluate the work and to learn lessons from the groupwork process. Attendance was not only from the three statutory agencies, but also from relevant voluntary sector workers. It was agreed that the emphasis of such meetings was to look critically at agency policy and practice and not to see how X or Y was doing in a group, or to represent particular issues on behalf of the young people. Good side effects included greater mutual understanding, effective working together, and raising the profile of the needs of the estates.

A more principled practice

Discussions at inter-agency meetings have pointed to the need for clear principles of practice with all people, including young people. We feel strongly that the values behind the groupwork approach are equally valid in traditional youth club settings and the one to one casework model. They have implications, for example, for how workers share information, make decisions, prepare reports, write and give access to records. Do we work with people, or do we tell people what to do, trying to resolve individual problems out of their social and economic context? And what messages do we give by sitting in the big 'flashy' chair and hiding behind the security of a solid desk, rather than meeting people in their own environments and on their own terms?

Court reports

A sub-group of the inter-agency meetings looked at the purpose and contents of reports, with special regard to a community perspective and a better understanding of the context of offending. The neighbourhood work with the young people informed our thinking about the importance of the way reports are written: how easy are they to understand; do we share the report with the defendant; do we go to court to support that person, and do we show some understanding of the neighbourhood? Some reports have begun to include a section on the neighbourhood, such as:

> Through this project, we have come to see the occasional periods of offending by the young people in the context of an isolated and under-resourced estate, with no youth facilities, few employment prospects and a history of limited interest being shown in them.

Further, addenda have been written by the project workers themselves, in consultation with the young people, highlighting the nature of their group and many positive aspects of what they have done.

Youth facilities

The young people have repeatedly raised concerns about the inadequacies for them of centralised youth facilities, based on a youth club that focuses on structured leisure pursuits. Also, when they tried to get funding from the Youth and Community Division of the County Council, they were required to have management structures fitted to adult control and decision making. The inter-agency forum has taken this issue forward with relevant senior management. The local youth club leader has tried, so far unsuccessfully, to gain acceptance for proposals for using an auxiliary worker to resource one of the groups, without taking control of it.

Conclusion

The neighbourhood work took nine months careful planning and development, and it lasted two and a half years. It began by a number of workers questioning the neat agency compartments that were felt to manage and contain, rather than listen and respond to young people and their concerns and difficulties. As one senior social worker said, *"we expect young people to adapt to our structures; yet we must adapt to theirs."*

It is hoped the work described above will give encouragement to do just that:

1. to challenge current practice and agency constraints;
2. to reflect critically on present provision for youth, be it treatment and cure, or structured leisure pursuits;
3. to explore in partnership alternative responses, based on principles that do not label the individual or group, or hide behind the power of the professional;

4. to develop practice, whether individual or groupwork, with people whose difficulties are more likely to be structurally rooted than due to personal inadequacy; who have understanding and ability and a right to be heard; and who can be encouraged to work together to good effect on the issues and concerns they identify.

Notes

1. The two voluntary sector projects are: Family First, Young People's Project, 30 Waterloo Road, Nottingham and Nottingham Young Volunteers, 33 Mansfield Road, Nottingham.

2. MOB (Members of Bulwell Hall) and TOLO (short for Tollerton Green in Highbury Vale) came to be the names the two groups gave themselves.

References

Bailey, R. and Brake, M. (eds.) (1980) *Radical Social Work Practice*. Edward Arnold.

Corrigan, P- (1979) *Schooling the Smash Street Kids*. Macmillan.

Freire, P. (1970) *Cultural Action for Freedom*. Penguin.

Freire, P. (1972) *Pedagogy of the Oppressed*. Penguin

Walker, H and Beaumont, B. (1981): *Probation Work; Critical Theory and Socialist Practice*. Basil Blackwell.

Ward, D. and Burley, D. (1982) *Starting Bloch*. National Youth Bureau.

Wilson, E (1977) *Women and the Welfare State*, quoted in Walker and Beaumont (1981), p. 82.

This chapter was first published in 1988 in *Groupwork* Vol. 1(3), pp.239-251

At the time of writing Bill Badham had been a Probation Officer for five years. Michael Bente had been a sessional youth worker and residential worker in a young people's hostel and was then with a Nottinghamshire Housing Association. Pauline Hall was a social worker and intermediate treatment worker before moving to be a teacher in adult education.

Doing something with our lives when we're inside: Self-directed groupwork in a youth custody centre

Bill Badham, Bob Blatchford,
Steph Mcartney and Malcolm Nicholas

This paper describes the development of groupwork practice at an open youth custody centre in Nottingham from February 1987 to February 1989. It was started by Nottingham Probation Officers linking with a voluntary sector project, and later developed to include Team Resources for Youth, a project working with young black people. The article gives background to how the work arose, both through previous local initiatives, and through careful planning between February and October 1987. It describes the underlying social action principles and values behind the work, and how these affected practice. It concludes with an evaluation of the work by young men and the agencies involved, and suggests implications for future policy and practice.

Background

A number of factors lay behind the initiative to start groupwork with young men at Lowdham Grange Youth Custody Centre (as from October 1988 called Young Offender Institution). First, a voluntary sector youth project (Nottingham Youth Action) and two probation teams in Nottinghamshire had successfully undertaken groupwork in institutions for young men during the previous three to four years. Second, there was interest among a number of Probation teams in the city in developing the style of working, adopted in these projects, to include all young men at Lowdham Grange who were from Nottingham.

Third, the senior probation officer (SPO) at Lowdham Grange

was keen to improve probation worker contact. He told us that there were 22 probation officers involved with 27 young men from Nottingham, and that the service offered was variable and inconsistent, and that probation was often perceived as irrelevant or unhelpful by many of them.

Finally, statistics, published in June 1986, indicated that ten per cent of the probation service workload involved people in youth custody.

Prompted by these factors, an open meeting was called in February 1987. It was agreed there was a need for a better service to young prisoners, and one which they would see as useful and relevant. Groupwork could complement existing contact if it challenged the personal pathology emphasis of traditional casework by addressing the individual within the wider context of social and economic difficulties.

Aims of the proposed groupwork

Arising from the planning meeting, and informed by the previous groupwork experiences the worker team agreed a framework. A positive view of young people which recognised their understanding, ability and skill was seen as essential. In this context, they should be encouraged to define their own issues and take action on them. The workers' standpoint was that difficulties the young prisoners faced were not necessarily the result of 'personal inadequacies'. Social and economic factors, racism and sexism are major forces contributing to young people's problems. Practice should reflect this understanding.

Aims identified included:

1. to work with young people at Lowdham Grange on their concerns and issues in a group setting;
2. to be relevant, accessible, and consistent;
3. to develop critical awareness, challenge attitudes and help effect change, including developing anti-sexist and anti-racist practice;
4. to question the quality of current probation provision, and to propose improvement;

5. to raise relevant issues within the institution, arising from practice;
6. to include other agencies in the project, given that young people's concerns are not the monopoly of the probation service.

The groupwork approach

The way of working with the young men, arising from the above, was to be as follows:

1. to work with them in a group setting at their own pace, on the issues they identified as important to them;
2. to work in partnership with them, rather than being seen as 'experts' or 'provider', and doing things for/to them;
3. to draw on their experience and knowledge;
4. to encourage responsibility among them for actions and decisions taken, and to ensure that attendance was voluntary;
5. to develop anti-racist and anti-sexist practice, and to challenge racism and sexism among the worker team, the group members and the agencies involved;
6. to reflect critically on the work being done, through regular planning sessions and occasional review meetings.

Work undertaken (October 1987-January 1989)

Starting the groupwork

The SPO arranged access to Lowdham Grange for the worker team, and probation management approved the work. The frequency of meetings and the style of groupwork were negotiated with the young men, and explained to prison staff. The first open meeting took place in October 1987, after eight months of planning.

All those from Nottingham at Lowdham Grange were invited by prior letter and a visit to the four separate 'houses' in the institution. This open access to the group allowed for renewing the links and contacts, in contrast to the usual strict segregation. Between 30 and 40 people came. There were six groupworkers, all white and from probation – two women and four men.

The worker team was explicit about certain constraints. For example, fortnightly meetings were agreed, though initially the young men wanted them to be weekly. Further, the worker group could not, except in emergencies, offer to follow up individual requests for help which would overlap with the field probation officer's role. However, individuals were encouraged to channel criticisms through the SPO. Given the principle of the participants working on their own concerns, the worker team established that it would not become the arbiter in disputes, or controller of resources. Thus, any complaints were fed back to the group as their issues, with which the worker team would offer support, but not take over.

It was established that racism and sexism were contrary to the way of working, and could not be allowed, even if the worker team sometimes felt it awkward or difficult to challenge such attitudes. The worker group resisted expectations of 'leadership', aware that their approach contrasted with the hierarchical structures of the institution. Emphasis was on the young men establishing their own agenda, with the team resourcing the work on the issues that resulted. This involved working together in small groups to arrive at some consensus, implying co-operation rather than competition. They adapted quickly, but were not always able to shed the habit of calling the workers 'Sir' and 'Miss'! Although sharing a common experience, the young men were not a natural group. Aged between 15 and 21, they were doing different terms of imprisonment and had different levels of confidence and expectations. This variation, combined with the turnover in the group, meant that momentum was sometimes slow. Yet it was recognised that the pace must always be dictated by the participants themselves.

How the process worked

at the first meeting the young men identified important issues that they wanted to cover, and these were recorded on flip charts. Then a timetable for future meetings and topics was agreed. Being over 30 in number, they decided small groups would allow for greater confidence and sharing. They also decided outside speakers would be of use on occasions, but in order to share information rather than to deliver a lecture.

Through planning between sessions, the workers developed a framework for each meeting to help look at the area of concern identified. This was first checked with the participants and changed as necessary.

At the beginning, views about the reactions of prison staff and others within the institution were aired, so that ways of dealing with possible difficulties could be worked out. (Occasionally, this led to meetings of the worker group and prison staff to overcome what were termed 'organisational difficulties'.) At the end of each session space was always given to allow individuals to seek support and advice from each other and the workers.

Some of the issues discussed

At the young people's suggestion, the third meeting included an outside speaker on welfare rights. The structure of this session set a precedent for the future. Questions to be put to the speaker were worked out in small groups before her arrival. In this way, group members kept a high investment in listening to what she had to say. Time was allowed after she left to check out how the session had gone and to plan for the next one.

Other issues looked at over the following months included housing, parole, legal rights and temporary release from Lowdham Grange. The sessions were dealt with similarly, using outside speakers. At a later stage, the group returned to focus again on the areas of parole, housing and the benefit changes of April 1988. They worked out both what information they needed and how they thought this information could best be presented. Taking this forward, it was agreed to publish three booklets. Over the summer of 1988, the probation department's information officer and a Nottingham cartoonist (BRICK) helped some of the group to identify and undertake various tasks relating to the production of the booklets. These included editing the information, preparing illustrations and designing front covers. Through the young people's involvement, it was hoped to increase the likelihood that the finished booklets would be in a style that would appeal and be read.

Though the young men tended to focus on worries that they had relating to their release, they also looked at concerns within the institution. While wanting to avoid workers in the group acting as an alternative complaints procedure, an assistant governor saw the value of this forum raising points to do with the functioning of the regime. The principal governor attended one meeting to talk with them directly and answer their questions. This they valued, though they questioned whether any concrete action would follow.

Issues of sexism and racism were often raised in group meetings as relevant to specific areas of discussion. For example, had the young men considered the effects on their female partners of their being in prison, and how did their attitude towards them affect their conduct when in the community? In what ways did the parole process discriminate against black people?

With the involvement of black workers from Spring 1988, the worker team was strengthened in its ability to offer support to black people in the group and ensure the maintaining of a black perspective. The group decided it wanted to look more closely at racism over three or four sessions. There was frank exchange and much honesty, with white people thinking through the effects of language and white education structures upon their own attitudes and outlook towards black people. Black members were prepared to share their own experience within this supportive context. All the group were concerned as to how to take this issue forward within an institution where a governor spoke of a few officers having an 'attitude problem', rather than acknowledging the existence of racism.

Evaluation and implications

Reviewing the work with the young people

Each session was reviewed at the end to ensure the group was running in a way that the members found most useful. At intervals of three months, a whole meeting was used to assess together the relevance of what was covered and how it had been covered. This was done in a variety of ways. For example, questionnaires were used. Twenty six young men were present, and all except one took completion of the questionnaire seriously. Comments were generally very positive. What almost all of them wanted from the group was information, advice and 'help'. They enjoyed the relaxed atmosphere where they were 'being listened to', and responded to. The small groups were seen as a good way of sharing and gaining information. Comments about the role of the workers was favourable. They enjoyed 'being together as a group'. Continuing contact with their home probation officer was wanted, though some replies showed that they did not know who he or she was.

Review sessions also allowed workers to assess and feedback their impressions. These were generally very favourable, the manner of work was found stimulating, the motivation of the group members encouraging and the team work supportive. However, the work was acknowledged to be demanding, requiring a considerable degree of commitment to thorough preparation, and consistent practice, and some stubbornness in the face of occasional prison and probation intransigence.

At one review, the sexism experienced by women workers was confronted. The summing up of bad points about the group allowed the workers to be frank about the embarrassment and anger caused by certain looks and remarks, some most unpleasant. Quite a number of the young men approached the women workers later to apologise. They quickly entered into the discussion about sexism and showed sympathy and understanding for the difficult position of women working in an all-male institution. This highlighted their willingness to listen and to enter whole-heartedly into what was being discussed.

A criticism voiced by some of the group members was that not all were prepared to get involved and contribute fully: small groups could be dominated by individuals, though this was seen as rare. There was criticism of the organisation of refreshments, which at one time became rather chaotic. The group wanted the workers to lay down laws and take control. Instead, they were asked to look at the issue themselves and work out their own agreed system. This was done by first brainstorming the question 'what is the current problem with refreshments?'

In small groups they examined why the problems existed and how they could be resolved. Their findings were written on flip charts and the results drawn together in the large group to form the basis of a new system. There were no problems subsequently, and everyone stuck to the rules that they had made themselves.

Reviewing the work within the agencies

There were four open review meetings, involving the groupworkers and other interested practitioners and management from Lowdham Grange, Nottingham Probation and more recently the Youth Service. It was through external publicity that Team Resources for Youth (a black youth work project within the Youth Service) became involved. These meetings, the circulation of the minutes, writing up the work, and going to probation field teams, were the means to encourage wider discussion of the issues raised by the groupwork practice, to ensure the group would continue through recruitment of new workers, and to avoid its isolation from mainstream probation and youth work.

These measures have had some success. For example, the interagency and anti-racist practices were developed through the partnership with Team Resources for Youth. Extending the worker team in this way helped to bring important different perspectives on issues raised and tackled.

It also allowed access to a local prison for a youth organisation that already had contact with some of the young men there. To enable the planning and preparation, an ex-groupworker agreed to act as consultant. Another undertook a development role, with the aim of promoting the work within the departments. However, these successful developments were somewhat undermined by the reluctance of some probation teams in Nottingham to look at the issues raised by the groupwork practice. Further, probation management seemed remote to the groupworkers, and more content to criticise from the sidelines than lend positive support. For example, when information was requested, and therefore sent, it was not acknowledged, or acted upon. This ambivalence raised questions about probation management's commitment to the inter-agency aspect and the development of anti-racist practice within the project. Team Resources for Youth and its management within the Youth Service were increasingly concerned that it was being 'used' by probation as a black resource to compensate for the lack of black probation workers, and the lack of a positive recruitment drive to appoint them.

For the probation field teams fully involved (about half of those in the city), the groupwork was seen to complement individual probation contact with individual young offenders at Lowdham Grange. Statutory responsibilities for throughcare were seen as needing both components. Yet, probation management spoke of duplication and questioned the use of resources (six workers for 30 young men). In turn, this undermined the position with prison staff. When there were significantly fewer young men at Lowdham Grange, there was pressure to fulfil workshop production quotas. Prison management then told probation what its job was: 'Your group still represents work in essence *extra* to the statutory probation links'. Probation management, without consulting Team Resources for Youth, commended and supported this view. The group was closed, though a stay of execution was granted for a fortnight on realising members of the Parole Board from London were due to attend the next session. After 18 months of fortnightly contact, the groupwork .ended in January 1989, with little opposition from probation management, but much anxiety and regret from the young men.

Conclusion and way forward

After 18 months of groupwork, it seemed that the initial aims, as set out in the beginning of this article, were being achieved. The response of the young men was encouraging. They showed great commitment in identifying their concerns, looking at why these existed, and how action could be taken. The worker team gained experience and developed a coherent practice, incorporating an inter-agency and anti-racist perspective. The groupwork revealed wide discrepancies amongst probation officers in the standard of their practice. It suggested self-directed groupwork should form a greater part of throughcare policy. It seemed to offer a model for Nottinghamshire and other probation departments to increase the quality and quantity of contact with young offenders making effective use of resources. It highlighted the need of all probation workers not to let prisoners out of sight be also out of mind. It underlined the need to be conscious of, and involved in, the broader concerns that go beyond individualised problems.

It is hoped the closure of the groupwork initiative is only temporary. There is significant support from the Youth Service and Team Resources for Youth, as well as from many field probation workers and their seniors, for establishing self-directed groupwork as a central component of contact with prisoners. Many issues remain undecided. How would such a model transfer to prisoners on release? Should it not apply to other institutions? If so, how should this be resourced? What encouragement will be given to the active seeking of partnership between probation and local youth workers? Can such creative practice exist under the shadow of further punitive criminal justice legislation, threatening electronic surveillance, tagging and tracking of offenders?

Whatever the unresolved issues, it is hoped that this inter-agency model of self-directed groupwork with prisoners will influence future policy and practice. The groupwork at Lowdham has demonstrated the group members' commitment and enthusiasm to this way of working. They showed the ability to take responsibility and control of their own group, to set their own limits and rules, to identify their concerns and work constructively at resolving them.

One young man said on leaving the group that it had helped 'us to be able to talk about ourselves as individuals; it made you feel as though you *can* do something with your life while you are inside'.

Acknowledgement

This article was informed by all the worker team, in consultation with the young men from Nottingham involved in the groupwork at Lowdham Grange Youth Custody Centre.

> This chapter was first published in 1999 in *Groupwork* Vol. 2(1), pp.27-35
>
> At the time of writing Bill Badham, Bob Blatchford, Steph Mcartney and Malcolm Nicholas were with the Nottinghamshire Probation Service

The Top End Action Group

Neil Ballantyne

The following case study is an example of social action practice written at the end of 1988. It described work carried out in Scotland during the mid 1980s. The study highlights sexism as a key issue. It details dilemmas faced by one team of workers and their response in a situation which will ring familiar to many practitioners.

Background

The setting was Ferguslie Park, a local authority housing scheme on the periphery of Paisley in the west of Scotland with a population in 1981 of 7,615. The housing was a mixture of pre-war and post-war housing and had declined in both number and condition. Over a number of years there had been heavy expenditure on empty housing damaged by fire and effected by vandalism.

Unemployment and associated poverty was another major problem with overall unemployment standing at 60%. Young people under 20 years composed 44% of the population and were hardest hit by unemployment, only 10% of school leavers being in work or at college six months after leaving school.

One result of the extra attention focussed on Ferguslie Park was the use of the urban programme in 1985 to open a youth drop-in centre employing one community worker and three community work assistants. The project operated out of small youth café premises located at the corner of a block of shops in the central area of the scheme.

The youth drop-in centre was created not just in response to deprivation statistics, but also represented the implementation of new developments in the policy framework of Strathclyde Regional Council. In 1984 a member/officer group report entitled *Working with Young People* outlined key directions for the future of work with young people including recommendations on the need for work which aimed at empowering young people:

New ways of involving young people must be found that adopt a direct political approach which ensures young people 'educate, agitate and organise' themselves as a force for change.

Similarly in 1985 the Director of Social Work reported in *A Care Strategy for Young People in Trouble* that:

The major thrust of (diversionary and preventive)... work is to discriminate in favour of those thought to be most at risk by actively encouraging their participation in decision making regarding how to resolve issues affecting them within the locality'.

A social action approach

Accordingly, the team of workers based in the youth drop-in centre adopted an approach to work with young people which viewed them as active participants in joint action rather than passive consumers of a service. They took a positive view of young people 'in trouble' and 'at risk' engaging their strengths as young adults and enabling them to take action. They recognised a link between the private troubles of young people and the public issues arising from their social, economic and political environment.

This approach turned on its head the all too commonly held view of young people as the problem and replaced it with a view of young people as problem solvers capable of taking responsibility, acting collectively, and influencing the world. It is an approach which takes young people through a process within which they can develop new skills, knowledge and attitudes. It is an approach which *empowers*.

The team also recognised that they must operate in partnership not only with young people but also with other agencies and local adults. They had a strong commitment to breaking down inter-agency barriers to change and working jointly with others.

Finally, they determined not to allow the project to be bound by the walls of a building, complementing work within the drop-in centre with outreach work in other buildings and streetwork around the scheme, aiming to overcome the natural territorialism of young people by taking themselves to where they were.

Social action in practice

The young people from the Top End gathered outside the local shops much to the annoyance of local adults and shopkeepers. There was a high incidence of solvent, drug and alcohol abuse and inevitably incidents occurred between youth and adults which led to the police being called in and young people being frequently charged or moved on. In July 1986 the problems associated with the youth from the Top End reached a peak when one elderly resident had his windows stoned by some youths.

The local tenants' organisation convened a meeting between tenants' groups from the Top End and youth workers. The tenants understood that the young people from the Top End were frustrated, bored and angry. The youth workers agreed to make contact with the young people with the aim of engaging them in dialogue about their concerns and helping them to take action.

The four workers involved were clear that they should not react to the problem by running youth provision in the area but to engage the young people in a dialogue about their perceptions of the problems and how they wanted to affect change. Streetwork brought them into contact with scores of young people and several different peer groups with a wide variety of age ranges.

They also recognised that it was not enough to target in on young people – the young people also had to decide whether or not they wanted to work with the workers. For some, particularly those used to the Intermediate Treatment milieu, the fact that the workers were not offering a ready made programme of activities made it difficult for them to understand what was in fact on offer. They expressed a deep cynicism about their ability to do anything for themselves.

Making contact with youth during the early stages was not a problem. Most were eager to talk. One group of young people were initially concerned that the workers might be from the Drug Squad but soon overcame their fears. The workers were very careful to make the young people clear where they stood on a whole range of issues from drug abuse to petty crime to racism and sexism but always listened to the views of the young people with respect.

Through a process of mutual negotiation they began to work

regularly with a group of boys and young men aged 15 to 22. The group had a central core of five and a wider membership of fifteen others who dropped in and out. All of them were or had been in trouble at some stage in their life. They had all heard about the drop-in centre but clearly said that neither they nor any young person from the Top End would use the drop-in centre.

After several weeks of meeting on street corners, in minibuses, and in group members' homes, the group negotiated access to a local community building and started to meet there.

The workers had to work hard at generating enthusiasm in the early days and at giving the group a vision of what was possible. They encouraged the group to brainstorm possibilities, helped them to arrive at consensus and enabled them to turn what seemed like impossible problems into practical tasks.

The main issue for the group, and the one whose resolution would make so much more possible, was the lack of a meeting place for youth use only. They wanted to run their own youth action centre in their own territory. This, they felt, would be the answer to the boredom and depression that led to police harassment and delinquency. Nevertheless, the more pessimistic simply didn't believe that any adult would trust them to 'take a dog for a walk never mind run their own centre'.

At this stage it was agreed that the activists and enthusiasts should form a small steering group of five to meet once a month to progress the long term aims of the youth action centre and that the whole group would meet once a week to work on shorter term goals.

In September 1986 the group submitted an urban aid application to the regional council for empty shop premises to become a youth action centre to provide:

a meeting place for the young people of the area, a base for the development of other youth initiatives, and a café run by the young people of the area.

The workers agreed to support, advise, chivvy, cajole, stimulate, question and enthuse, but not to act in place of the young people themselves.

The initial apathy and defeatism of the group was slowly being replaced by an incredulous self-assurance as they found themselves being taken seriously by adult power holders and decision-makers. They had a meeting with the local regional councillor at which they spoke with such enthusiasm and commitment that they utterly convinced him of the need for their project, so that the councillor became one of their most powerful allies. They impressed the local adult activists so much with their presentation that they were actively sought out by tenants' organisations looking for new activists.

Boys and girls, and sexism

Around March 1987 an issue was coming to the boil concerning the involvement on girls in the group. For some time the workers had been pointing out that there were no girls or young women in the group and that if the group intended to represent the interests of all young people when the youth action centre opened, then they were failing to represent half of the young people.

Ostensibly, the group agreed and undertook to contact young women informally and to make posters to attract them to the group. Their actual lack of support for this proposal was not revealed until a group of girls and young women burst into the middle of a meeting demanding to know why they were not represented on the Top End Youth Action Group. The welcoming smiles and open invitation to participate of the workers was contradicted by the scowls and sullen silence of the young men. This was their group and they were not letting go of it so easily. This confrontation was to herald the beginning of a long and bitter power struggle.

In March 1987 the group heard officially from the Scottish Office that their application had been successful. They were now in control of a project with £58,000 per annum and set about the task of drawing up a formal constitution. They had to make the transition from being an informal friendship group to becoming a voluntary organisation. However, conflict arose over the controlling role of an elected management committee. The boys wanted to specify that there should be two places on a management committee of eight reserved for girls and six places reserved for boys! The girls argued for four places each or else no places allocated for either sex. The workers made it clear that the boys were being sexist and supported the option of four places each.

At the first attempt to have a general meeting the boys flooded the meeting with completely unknown young men, many of whom were 30 years and over. The meeting had to be abandoned and it was agreed to discuss the issue further with the steering group of five boys. At this steering group meeting the workers took a strong line advocating on behalf of the girls and questioning the boys' attempted coup. It was clear they would 'get their own way' all the time. The group of girls were very assertive and mutually supportive with the group. They had already demonstrated considerable organisational skills and it seemed that the boys feared being shown up by the ability of the girls.

Eventually, the boys conceded the absurdity of their position and in fear at the girls dominating the management committee if it were left open, agreed on the option of four places each.

The workers had been caught between their principle of allowing the group to decide and of supporting the rights and interests of the girls. Whilst understanding the boys' fears and their reactions in terms of losing the little power and influence they had as young working class men, the workers decided to act decisively in support of the girls.

Nevertheless the atmosphere in the group worsened. A conflict over the end of a relationship spilled over into the group. Sides were being taken with threatened violence and incidents of harassment of the young women on the streets.

The workers recognised that the group could not get on with its task unless it resolved this conflict and so proposed to enlist the help of two consultants and take the group on a residential weekend to explore the issues, attempt a resolution, and get on with the work of the group. They felt that a new environment and outside help could enable the group to deal with the feelings without becoming lost in mutual recriminations or self indulgence. They also felt that this was a critical moment and learning opportunity for the group to explore the issue of sexism and power relations in community politics.

When the residential weekend was first proposed both boys and girls agreed to participate and seemed keen to get this sorted out once and for all. However, another incident of harassment occurred and when the group were confronted by the workers all but one young man felt that the only way to resolve the issue was for them to drop out of the group. They did not feel that they could work through the issue with the girls and so decided to drop out. They were no longer hostile, simply disinterested.

Although the workers had always been mindful of issues around sexism they had not anticipated the sheer strength of feeling that the issue could generate. In retrospect they are critical of themselves for not pushing the issue of involvement of girls and young women at an earlier stage though they had genuinely believed that the boys were actively trying to recruit girls as they had told them.

The residential weekend went ahead as planned but with a different agenda. The workers now had to enable the girls to seize the initiative and carry the work of the group forward. This meant going over the history of the group and making decisions about future direction. The group emerged from the weekend with a clear agenda for the future including keeping the door open to boys and young men. After a long period of conflict and depression the group was now becoming increasingly enthusiastic and set about the tasks of making plans for the physical design of the youth action centre, managing their new financial responsibility, and employing their community worker.

One new feature of the group was the attitude of male resource holders and decision-makers to a group of young women negotiating with them. The male representative of the regional council architects department was happy for the group to make suggestions about design and colour scheme but baulked when they wanted to choose which companies should be asked to tender for the work. The group wanted to ensure that a local community business was allowed to tender and only won this battle after long negotiations and enlisting the support of the regional councillor.

Assisted by the workers questioning, discussing, brainstorming, and role playing, the group arrived at a relevant and imaginative job description for the community worker. They wrote a bright and witty advert, and handled shortlisting and interviewing with great sensitivity and professionalism.

The Top End Action Group's community worker took up post in February 1988 and their youth action centre opened in October 1988.

Evaluation

The achievements of the Top End Action Group are evident from the process described above. Quite apart from the concrete physical resource of a new youth action centre and workers for the Top End of the scheme, there is now a local youth organisation with roots deep in the community.

The growth in knowledge and skills, and attitudes of the individual young people involved in the project from beginning to end has been noted by themselves and others. The development of local youth leadership and the ripple effect this has both within and outwith the scheme cannot be underestimated. The empowerment of these young people was demonstrated not only in their new found confidence in speaking in public but also in their ability to challenge adults and create change. They became familiar with local and national power structures and how to influence decision making. They understood and could use the problem-solving process.

In retrospect the workers felt they might have better managed the relationship between the local youth and adults by directly engaging the local adults within the group at an early stage. They also felt that the issue between the boys and girls may have been resolved more easily had they taken a more active role in recruiting girls into the group or by supporting the boys and girls separately once the issue arose. These are matters of fine judgement and lessons have been learned for the future.

One piece of graffiti on the door of the shop prior to its conversion into the youth action centre read:

This will be our Centre.

This chapter was first published in 1993 in *Soial Action Journal*, Vol. 21(2), pp.9-12

Neil Ballantyne was a Lecturer in Social Work at Jordanhill College (part of the University of Strathclyde), on secondment from Strathclyde Regional Council Social Work Dept

'All I've got in my purse is mothballs!': The social action women's group

Sandra Butler

This research-based paper gives an overview of the social action women's group of the Radford Shared Care Project, Nottingham, a resource offering a radical approach to keeping children out of local authority accommodation who are at risk of significant harm from their parents. As a vehicle for women's self-development, the practice relevance and effectiveness of the group's value base is unpacked. The groupworkers' style of facilitation is explored in terms of the necessary conditions for the creation of an atmosphere of equality, namely, attending to women's physical needs; encouraging women to establish their own agenda for the group; making connections between individual and collective experience; utilising listening skills and positive reinforcement; and finally, recognising women's power. By examining key recurring themes within and across group sessions, the article validates the structural dilemmas with which group members were faced. Women's sexuality and relationships with male partners became entangled with the processes of racism and the difficulties of bringing up mixed parentage children. Faced with relentless hardships, women easily identified the politics of poverty and central government's punishment of the poor. This process of naming structural and individual experiences is critical to women's empowerment, building a bridge towards the creation of their own solutions and the necessary action to achieve them.

This chapter has arisen out of the first year's work of a five year qualitative research study of the NCH Action For Children/Nottinghamshire Social Services Radford Shared Care Project (Butler, 1994). The project offers intensive, culturally appropriate assistance to families where children and young people are at risk of being removed from home into local authority accommodation. Project workers work with parents in their own homes, addressing issues such as child abuse and neglect, behavioural difficulties and control, and play stimulation. The groupwork programmes complement the family work, focusing on parenting skills and the promotion of women's self-confidence, self-esteem and autonomy.

The social action women's group draws its membership from current project families and women who have recently finished work with their project worker. Women who use the group have extensive and often debilitating experiences of welfare agencies in that their parenting standards have been scrutinised and labelled as 'inadequate'. My analysis will concentrate on the women's group over an eight month period. The group met on a weekly basis for two hours, 9.30 a.m.-11.30 a.m., with creche facilities provided. Group facilitators were an African-Caribbean woman worker from Nottingham Young Volunteers and a white woman paid on a sessional basis. In a group where one quarter of members were Black and half the white women had mixed parentage children, a 'mixed'-race co-working team was essential.

The major principle of social action research and practice is about users taking action for empowerment (Mullender et al., 1993-94; Mullender and Ward, 1991a, 1991b). The research aims to monitor and evaluate the project's work by exploring the formal and informal dimensions of the shared care process, so that learning, development and change in the project can take place. Starting with the issues, ideas and understandings of all project participants, the research moves into an evaluation of the impact of the project's activities and developmental plans. Emerging data is shared with participants, who are enabled to generate their own solutions and the necessary action to achieve them.

Material for this article originates from written evaluations provided by the two groupworkers, taped interviews with the white woman groupworker, the project leader and women's group members. Interviews were transcribed, with the texts only lightly edited. To be consistent with the user-led strategy, I have let the users' and workers' own voices be heard as much as possible. I will begin by reviewing the value base of the group, moving on to explore the groupworkers' style of facilitation and the content and process of group sessions, where structural forces shaped interpersonal discussion.

Value base of the social action women's group

One of the aims of the project is 'to enable parents, individually or co-operatively, to sustain action likely to lead to the greater development of their abilities and self-awareness.' The Joint Service Level Agreement between Nottinghamshire Social Services and NCH Action For Children (1993) states that 'Parents and carers will be invited to join an ongoing group programme aimed at equipping them to take up issues on their own behalf' (4.12, Pg. 6). Whereas British child protection systems tend to pathologise parents and children (Parton, 1991; Frost and Stein, 1989), the Shared Care Project sets itself the objective of confronting the personal and institutional mechanisms through which oppression operates, building upon and emphasising families' strengths. The project recognises key facets of inequality and social injustice which operate in this multi-racial area of Nottingham caused by poor housing, high unemployment, low income, limited educational opportunities and the endurance of racism and sexism. These shape the social construction of differing life choices and opportunities, yielding differential access to services and experiences of discrimination for project families. Women who use the project live in dangerous inner-city areas and housing estates, and suffer considerable racial and sexual harassment.

Within the context of a project whose primary function is to enhance the safety and wellbeing of children, the project leader 'worries' that the project is condoning some aspects of sexism by concentrating on women, their role as mothers and their parenting skills. Groupwork therefore plays a pivotal role in creating space for women's self-development, where members can define the issues that are important to them, other than those tied up with being a parent. Previous research (Fleming and Ward, 1992) revealed that women's empowerment had a positive effect on their children's wellbeing, demonstrating the inter-relationship of women's needs and rights with those of their families.

The groupworkers are committed to socialist values of collective responsibility, meeting community needs and preventative work. They described the aims and values of social action groupwork as enabling women:

1. to set their own agenda of issues, by exploring what are the women's preoccupations;
2. to gain a different perspective on why they are in their current positions, thereby removing the blame and guilt;
3. to recognise that they are caught up in structural events that are historical for them because they have come from families which are disadvantaged;
4. to discover ways of breaking out of these patterns, to find a measure of independence;
5. to discover how they are going to achieve change themselves - what steps they are going to take, what support they might need and what the process is for them to move out of their current positions;
6. to be challenging of themselves, of each other and the groupworkers;
7. to develop a sense of self-worth, recognising the contributions they make to society;
8. to develop a partnership with each other and the groupworkers.

There are many elements of the above which demonstrate the project's aim of sustaining action to enhance women's abilities and self-awareness. The action referred to in items 1-8 is about not only personal change, but also social and structural change. The potential contribution of groupwork to this wider vision is clearly identified in the following extract:

> *The groupwork helps women to question the causes of some of their difficulties and the recognition of the oppression that they're under, that can help their awareness of the world and hopefully even lead to wanting to take some action collectively. This would probably be the biggest thing that the project could achieve* (project leader).

As has been recognised in feminist groups (Butler and Wintram, 1991), the project leader sees the role of groupwork as a vehicle for breaking down the barriers of isolation, as a source of validation and friendship, and as a means of developing and recognising aspects of women's selves that have hitherto been hidden, distorted or suppressed:

> *I think that women are different in groups than in a one-to-one, where they*

can help one another and develop their self-image in two ways. Firstly, that it's not all their fault, they're not inadequate because there are enormous pressures on them and they're not alone. Secondly, that they can say something useful to or befriend somebody else and be valued by them. This can lead to the development of the spiritual and ethical aspects of their lives. So much can be done through a group, to find that they have strengths they didn't know they had (project leader).

The expressed commitment to the principles of the social action group needs to be examined in relation to the effectiveness and the relevance of these values in practice. In the following section, I shall analyse the practical implications of social action values by considering key aspects of the group's content and process, and by revealing the structural dilemmas with which group members were faced.

Content and process of the social action women's group

Groups are dynamic and fluctuating, sometimes conflictual and at other times they assume an organic wholeness, with content and process heavily intertwined. In this section, I will unravel strands of this content and process by analysing the groupworkers' style of facilitation. I will then explore the group's personal/political agenda, and how group process was used to confront racism and sexism.

Groupworkers' style of facilitation: creating an atmosphere of equality

The group has been working at establishing itself and developing an understanding of things through the process of sharing, that is non-stigmatising, that they're not victims (groupworker).

The groupworkers were able to achieve social action aims 1 and 8 because they utilised a style of facilitation which encouraged women to develop the group norms and goals by defining and analysing the problems they faced. Most important, this collaborative style affected the group process:

> *I draw out women's contributions, enabling them to put words around things and stay with what is important for them. I encourage women to talk because some of the women find this so difficult. There's always the woman who wants to talk a lot and the hard work for me is getting the quiet ones involved in talking about their concerns* (groupworker).

Analysis of the interview transcripts and group members' feedback revealed that there were five necessary conditions to the creation of an atmosphere of equality during the group's life. First, careful attention was paid to women's physical needs (food, drink, venue). Given the depths of women's low self-esteem, members felt hesitant about doing even small tasks such as making the tea/coffee or filling the kettle. The groupworkers were empathic in dealing with women's fears in these areas, so much so that after four months, the women were sharing food. Secondly, in carrying out the first aim of social action, the group did not start with a pre-planned programme but instead women were encouraged to establish their own agenda:

> *The group unfolds from where the women start talking. They initiate what it is they want to talk about. The process is about picking up from a very ordinary statement, and turning it into a discussion. What we get into during most weeks is where one member needs a lot of attention, so part of the time is often taken up with the group focusing on whatever crisis has happened. A lot of counselling goes on* (groupworker).

Thirdly, connections were made between individual and collective experience through the process of 'conscientisation' (Freire, 1972), which intimately links knowledge and power:

> *We try to bring out the issues generally for the women from small, personal examples. We share a willingness to discuss issues such as sexuality and we're not shocked. We have to be careful to pull things together a quarter of an hour before the end; this isn't easy when you're in a good discussion. So it's picking out a topic in what women are saying, keeping your ears flapping. For instance, if someone's talking about 'that f—ing Housing Manager', I'll start off by saying, 'It sounds like you had a really bad time'. I acknowledge the feelings and from there we'd develop it in terms of, 'What do you want to do? How might you do it?'* (my emphasis) (groupworker).

Fourthly, listening skills and positive reinforcement were used to undermine the process of stigmatisation and build on women's strengths:

> We listen really hard to their views about what's going on and tell them that they are doing pretty well. I'm very sincere about this because I don't know sometimes how they get through from one day to the next. I don't think they know that because their expectations are quite low. It's our whole manner of being with them, it's so important and affects whether they feel equal or not. Not being patronising, I don't think I am (my emphasis) (groupworker).

Finally, a recognition of women's power was central in encouraging group members to connect personal preoccupations with social conditions and collective solutions:

> The women do tend to be dependent and expect you to do things and always want permission. That makes it all the more important that they can actually feel they've got some power, that they can learn from each other (my emphasis) (groupworker).

The impact of these five conditions is reflected in the perceptions of one group member who talked about the importance of sharing experiences in the group, with trust and safety developing alongside this. She had been enabled to disclose instances of sexual violence in her life:

> We talked about rape and sexual assault in the group. I know I'm not the only person who's gone through it. Everyone is honest and open with everyone else. I don't feel as though I have to keep my mouth shut. I feel safe. Everyone's been through a rough time. It's funny, I've felt as if I've known the women all along. The support has just been there (white woman).

In keeping with social action Aim 8, the style of facilitation enabled the groupworkers to develop a partnership with women because of their belief in women's capabilities and understandings.

Personal/political agenda

The content of the women's group can be untangled through the recurring themes and patterns which emerged within and across sessions. Women's conversation is a broad landscape within which topics meander and flow. However, the explanations and arguments contained within this circularity are the tools with which women construct their social reality. An evaluation of group content against the social action values reveals that aims 1-3 were met in terms of women identifying what the issues were for them. This process of recognition, of naming experiences is critical to women's empowerment. It is an affirmative act of self-definition. I cannot review the complexity of all these themes, but I have selected several which demonstrate the emotional and social reasoning which women go through to make sense of their worlds. There is evidence that the group provided a valuable forum for tackling some fundamental political issues, enabling connections to be made between personal experience and structural forces:

> *Group members do see themselves as victims but we can stress the fact that they are caught up in structural decisions made by men in a wider sense and men in their personal lives who are constantly letting them down* (groupworker).

Within this context, I shall explore the debates women had about their sexuality; their relationships with male partners; racism and bringing up mixed parentage children; and finally, money management, poverty and politics.

Sexuality

In the group, sexuality was treated in terms of whether women had a sexual life and whether this meant having more children. As one woman was pregnant there was much ambivalence in the group about this issue. Women's group members, in keeping with dominant societal beliefs, equated sexuality with penetrative sex, reproduction, sexual behaviour and sexual orientation. They made assumptions about this being exclusively heterosexual:

> *One woman talks very openly about her sexual experiences and about men on building sites and what she'd like to do in graphic detail. If you ask her what she wants, she'll say, 'Ah, I wanna really good bloke', and she gets all raunchy. She says things like, 'The woman next door for instance, she can tell straight away if I've had a good night, if I've had it'. They say things like 'They'd better get some fun out of sex, they'd better get on with it, before*

they're too old', and I remember saying, 'You don't have to worry about that, it might get better'.

Those who haven't got a sexual life at the moment, and are still young, are asking 'Is this all there is to it for me? I'm in my early twenties and there's nothing going on. What can I do about it?' Then there's all this talk about 'Well, I've got a man but he's a rotten lover anyway, so what are you making a fuss about?' It's treated more light-hearted than other issues, but there's an element of huge disappointment for women in terms of their sexuality (groupworker).

This disappointment indicates that women had an impoverished view of their sexual potential. At the same time, being 'sexually attractive' was important to them, with some group members taking harmful slimming tablets purchased from a sex shop as a way of regulating and controlling their weight. Black women in the group were excluded from the standard of the unspoken whiteness of the beauty myth promulgated by the fashion industry and the media. All the women involved in heterosexual relationships were engaged in forms of self-surveillance, complying with the normative narrative scripts which demanded their consent and participation, irrespective of their own sexual or erotic feelings. Whilst women found men disgusting, they also desired them. All of this was compounded by homophobia. For instance, the group discussed one woman's fears about an imminent short prison sentence. She had been told many stories about prison violence, especially incidents perpetrated by lesbians. The group examined the heterosexist assumptions underpinning the 'advice' about lesbian behaviour and how she would survive the experience of prison.

In contrast to the ways in which other topics were handled, women explored their sexuality through humour mingled with sadness.

Relationships with male partners

A great deal of group time was spent in talking and laughing about men. Discussions revolved around women's sense of responsibility towards their male partners, both live-in and non-live-in, and how the pernicious influences of heteropatriarchy shaped male assumptions about their non-participation in child care. Heterosexual women are at greater risk of having inequitable personal relationships due to asymmetrical power distribution (Jacklin, 1993). The contradictions involved in male supremacy were pulled apart in the course of group discussion:

There's a lot of men-hating and laughing at men goes on. They've got little boys as well and I'd like to see them discover the positives in men because of their sons' lives. But they do have a bad time with men. One of them has a live-in partner, who has let her go to prison for a few days rather than he himself pay the TV licence. Another woman has two children by a non-live-in partner who's quite possessive and watches over what she does with the children, but he's never there to let her have a night out, ever. She's not had a night out for six years. Another one has a grown-up son and she gets involved with men who let her down - she gets into abusive relationships. Another two women don't have physically abusive relationships, but their men don't take any responsibility for the children, or for them. They're certainly not nurtured as women in these relationships at all, definitely not (groupworker).

He never helps, never. Bringing up kids is such a tremendous responsibility, but men, they don't see it that way. He might turn up one day. But I wouldn't like that really because he'd upset the kids all over again and I'd have to pick up the pieces. I'd prefer him to keep away all together (white woman).

The group looked at the effect of poverty and 'race' on the quality and consistency of their relationships with male partners. Pressures of lack of money undermined any notion of 'free choice' in relationships. As a result, many group members were exposed to complex feelings of love, lack of respect, anger and sensuality which spilled over, affecting their parenting skills and their determination to carry on in these damaging relationships, despite their utter exhaustion. At the same time, white group members needed to grapple with simultaneous positions of disadvantage and privilege, in that the limited rewards of associating with white men penalised Black women.

One Black woman recognised the effects of this internalised sexism/heterosexism on women's topics of conversation. Her criticism of the group's preoccupation with men's oppressive treatment of women was that she wanted to talk about being a woman and the effects of poverty, poor housing and social welfare services on her psychological wellbeing:

The women only want to talk about what men should do, what men don't do, what's wrong with men, it gets boring. They talk about the same things all the time. Maybe it's because they're all the same kind of women. They've mostly had experiences of violence, so maybe they want to get their own back, I don't know. I just sit there and listen. I'd like us to talk about different things, what you can expect from Social Services, social workers, benefits, everything. But we don't talk about things like that. I'd like to say, 'How would you like to be stuck in a flat with no furniture for four months?' That's how I've had to live. But I don't feel able to say these things. Every week it gets back to the same topic, men, why men can't be left with the kids, let's see if they'd like to do the housework all the while. I know they've got pressures, but I have too. I'd like us to talk about us, women and our ordinary problems (my emphasis) (African-Caribbean woman).

Within the web of women's complex and varied social realities, she saw herself as positioned differently from other Black and white women in the group by virtue of her life-style and status as a lone mother with no current male partner. Her 'difference' was part of a thread of racist discourse and exclusion within the group which was highlighted and confronted through group process and the style of facilitation.

The interplay of racism with heterosexism was addressed through the issue of dual heritage relationships. An instance of racist conflict and discord in the group enabled the dynamics of oppression to be confronted. Group interactions became intense when one white woman walked out of a session because other group members said they did not like white women having Black partners. Other women knew that she had children of mixed parentage, but they had used their own prejudices based on partial, situated knowledge to be 'insensitive, very judgemental and very coarse' (white groupworker). Stereotypes about African-Caribbean men's sexual prowess abounded. When the woman returned to the group, the workers recognised her pain and distress, enabling members to see how offensive their behaviour had been. Both groupworkers stressed the importance of understanding rather than ridiculing these relationships, given the diversity of ethnic identities in Britain.

The group decided to devote one session to increasing awareness about dual heritage relationships. A thirty minute video was shown, charting the history of reactions to these partnerships, followed by a discussion. The group examined its collective heritage in terms of African, European, Asian, Welsh, Irish, American/Italian, Scottish, Irish/Welsh descent. By acknowledging the extent of ethnic diversity in the group, women's different positions could be aired without fear of reprisals. The group realised that opinion about dual heritage relationships was affected by distrust, hatred and even repulsion, with these prejudices determined by not only racism, but also working class dynamics. Whilst poor white women in the group had limited choice and advantages in their intimate relationships with poor white men, they had rendered Black/white heterosexual relationships invisible.

This session was a springboard for the identification of other resources and support systems which could increase group members' knowledge and awareness about the complexity of dual heritage relationships.

Black identity, racism and bringing up mixed parentage children

The most persistent issue for Black and white mothers during the group's life was the problems involved in bringing up mixed parentage children, with women using the group to work through their intense confusions. Lone white mothers needed support to promote Black awareness in their dual parentage children, but the group discovered little current service provision directly aimed at assisting white parents to meet their Black children's diverse needs (Thompson and Fleming, 1993). The group realised that whilst information was available to teach their Black children about self-pride and the nature of white oppression, this did not equip them with the necessary coping strategies when returning to a white household every night where the only significant parent was a white mother. Given the increasing complexity of racial, religious and cultural dimensions in family life, the group played a significant role in assisting Black and white women to gain knowledge of the multiplicity of challenges in identity development for dual parentage children. One woman had two younger mixed parentage children and an older white child, aged six years, who was struggling to understand why his siblings were a different colour to himself. He had a good relationship with their Black father whilst his own white father had rejected him.

The Black groupworker dealt with an African-Caribbean/white woman and her African-Caribbean/white son's denial of being Black by talking about negative images of Black women as bad mothers. Having witnessed the extent to which Black people experienced racism, both mother and son survived their poverty and hardship by identifying themselves as white. The group had to recognise the hostility of the dominant culture towards Black people and confront their own ethnocentricity to offer this woman a glimmer of an alternative perception of herself. Both mother and son gained a great deal from talking about his identity with the Black groupworker, who presented as assertive, was non-threatening, and had an ability to express herself well:

> She said to me, 'Let's stand up, we've got something to say'. She talked to me about not seeing myself and my son as Black, but she did this in a very easy way. It was alright, because it felt as if she was one of us, right there at my side. She didn't point the finger at me (African-Caribbean/white woman).

Such is the intensity of this issue that racist views were expressed in the group which had to be carefully tackled, with groupworkers using skills in challenging and re-education. The dynamics of oppressive behaviour and being oppressed were enacted during an incident where women were talking about confinement in hospital. One group member described 'This Black bastard' (sic) who was a nurse on the ward, adding, 'Well, I'm not racist, I've got Black friends'. She tended to throw out comments and then pull them back. Only one woman challenged her, asking how she would feel if she had a Black partner. The white groupworker took responsibility for confronting white women with their own part in the perpetuation of racism:

> I've got a big responsibility to listen for racism. I have to at least pick it up and see where the discussion goes. I challenged this incident by saying 'Are there any white bastards?' and then I commented on what it meant to others in the group to hear Black people described in this way (groupworker).

In terms of social action Aim 6, the groupworkers recognised that, at this stage in the group's development, they were holding responsibility for challenging instances of oppression whilst offering protection to vulnerable group members:

We're the ones who challenge and we sometimes have to protect some women in the group, certainly from racism. Racism is a big issue. Sexism is there all the time and we have to highlight it. As yet, the women aren't challenging these things themselves; the women who are being hurt, say by racism, don't challenge, they keep silent. Unless you give them some space to talk about their feelings, the women are silenced. It'll be good when women members are able to challenge because they're very hurt by some of the things that are said (my emphasis) (groupworker).

The processes of domination in the group caused pain and distress, with antagonism and struggle replicating power relationships outside the group context. The ideology of 'putting women down' was played out by group members. The facilitators attempted to shift patterns of racism by enabling women to exchange points of view whilst empathising and respecting each other. In terms of interaction, the workers felt that this sharing was encouraging members to have more open discussions about racism and sexism:

The group offers an opportunity to talk about all of this to each other and not just to us. There is now much more thoughtfulness in the group, especially around racism. There's much more of a willingness to pursue things at a deeper level (groupworker).

Money management, poverty and politics

A major priority for women's group members was the effect of poverty on the lives of their children, and their feelings of heavy responsibility for the economic survival of their families. Women were afraid of debt and its consequences and spent a great deal of time examining how they managed their money. Women's health and survival were constantly threatened as they juggled their limited income to secure the basic necessities of food, warmth and shelter. They experienced poverty in its most acute form through their management of the food budget. The weekly cycle of spending was shaped less by families' nutritional needs and more by other financial obligations such as rent, fuel bills, hire purchase and debt repayments. Food is often the main item on which women cut back to make ends meet (Graham, 1993). Running out of money was an ubiquitous experience for women.

During one session, women discussed how expensive food, household items and clothes were and the range of meals they made when there was no money and only a few tins of food left. At these times, women would either miss meals or eat smaller amounts and less nutritional items in order to protect the living standards of their children and male partners, especially when their menfolk expected 'a full meal on the table'. As a result, women compromised their own health to maintain the household. When material and practical resources were few and women's responsibilities many, smoking cigarettes provided group members with temporary relief from the grind of poverty. This small luxury both helped and threatened women's and children's health, but was a means of getting by on an income many would not think twice about spending on a restaurant meal.

The groupworkers commented on how resourceful and strategic they were. During the ensuing discussion it was decided to produce a leaflet for other women in the Shared Care Project, examining how to manage shopping economically, and produce meals which were tasty but cheap (Table 1 is a sample of this work). Women were concerned about their children's futures and their ability to confront these structural forces. As a reflection of social action Aim 4, discussions about money management led to a consideration of ways of breaking out of the poverty cycle in terms of training opportunities, employment and child care resources. Women wanted to return to work, to do something other than care for their children. The need for training was discussed as a means of earning a realistic salary. The group calculated that it would be impossible to afford child-care costs if they were in employment. Women were trapped in the paradoxical situation of being offered free nursery places when there were child care difficulties, but when they had reached the point of being considered 'good mothers' these places were no longer available.

Women were well aware of the increasing scale and intensity of their poverty and that this trend was shaped by wider social divisions, inextricably linked to political and structural forces. The provision of a forum for sharing ideas and experiences enabled women to express their anger and frustration about the political imperatives affecting their lives:

> We were talking about the difficulties of getting their benefits and that how much they get is determined by government. They swear about this and I asked how they can change things, but one said 'I don't bloody well vote for anybody'. Another woman said, 'Oh I vote, but I don't vote for this lot'. They're not daft, they know what's going on. We discussed how women are penalised by all of these policy decisions. We talked about where the government spends its money - they do talk at that level very easily (groupworker).

Conclusion

At the end of this eight month period, the group had not reached the point where women could define how they were going to achieve personal, social and structural changes (Aims 4-5). However, the group's small-scale achievements in terms of understanding the causes of personal concerns were highly valued by the women, facilitating their movement through the project towards a recognition of their skills, strengths and belief in themselves beyond their parenting role. Within the timescale involved, the group made an impact on women in terms of their relationships; their self-care and desire to keep healthy; and their belief that going back to work was something that could now be contemplated rather than being seen as an impossibility. Men still remained shadowy but influential figures in a landscape marked out in terms of what women did for their families. The difference was that the group gave women permission to explore the humour, sadness and strains of family life, and no longer remain silent about these issues.

Group dynamics surrounding heterosexism and racism demonstrated the importance of not assuming an unproblematic, mutually exclusive boundary between the oppressed and the oppressors. Similarities between women were cross-cut by differences which were strongest when discussing dual heritage relationships and bringing up mixed parentage children. These major points of conflict made it possible for women to talk more

SOCIAL ACTION WOMEN'S GROUP LEAFLET
'All I've Got In My Purse Is Mothballs!'

'We don't like being dependent on the State. The children suffer through lack of wide experience, no holidays, and limited activities. It shouldn't really be like this, we should have more choice. We would like to work and earn our own money, getting more than we receive on Income Support.

All the government are bothered about are the rich. They don't care about the poor. Our benefit should go up, not down. The children deserve better than this'.

'All I've Got In My Purse Is Mothballs!'

So..... How to Live on Mothballs (with the kind permission of H.M. Government):

What I've discovered about shopping

'I used to do one big shopping, once a week, but found it used to go quickly - the more food you have in the house, the quicker it goes. Now I get about two bags on the Monday, and about Thursday or Friday I top it up, and whatever I don't have in the house, I just get. I find we are eating just as much, and can buy clothes for the kids. Whereas before, I was like buying one lot of clothes at a time and leaving two children out. Now I can buy three pairs of shoes, and whatever else I see for them.

Women like us still don't get enough money to give our children what they really need. I'd like them to go places instead of doing the same thing. You still feel bad because you can't give them what they ask for.'

Jobs and paying for child care.

They don't give you enough money to live on. When you get a part-time job, you have to pay for all these things:

Nursery places	Food
School dinners	Bus fares
Child minders	Clothes
Rent	Nappies
Bills	Fags

deeply and in greater detail, such that feelings of powerlessness began to crumble:

> I don't think we've seen any big changes so far, but little things have happened. There is no doubt that it's a hard life for women, but they are much more prepared to talk in a more detailed way, rather than use throw-away comments, such as 'We can't change things' and shrugging their shoulders (groupworker).

Acknowledgment

The research on which this article is based was made possible through the financial support of NCH Action For Children. I am grateful to the Shared Care Project's management, staff and women's group members for their commitment to the research process and for their honest expression of feelings and perceptions.

References

Butler, S. (1994) 'Improving Our Lives': The Radford Shared Care Project. Nottingham: Centre For Social Action, University of Nottingham.

Butler, S. and Wintram, C. (1991) Feminist Groupwork. London: Sage.

Fleming, J. and Ward, D. (1992) 'For the Children To Be Alright, Their Mothers Need To Be Alright'. An Alternative To Removing The Child - The Radford Shared Care Project. An Evaluation From the Participants' Viewpoints. Nottingham: Centre For Social Action, University of Nottingham.

Freire, P. (1972) The Pedagogy of The Oppressed. Harmondsworth: Penguin.

Frost, N. and Stein, M. (1989) The Politics of Child Welfare: Inequality, Power and Change. Hemel Hempstead: Harvester Wheatsheaf.

Graham, H. (1993) Hardship and Health in Women's Lives. Hemel Hempstead: Harvester Wheatsheaf.

Jacklin, C. N. (1993) 'How my heterosexuality affects my feminist politics,' in Wilkinson, S. and Kitzinger, C. (eds.) Heterosexuality: A Feminism and Psychology Reader. London: Sage Publications, pp.34-35.

Mullender, A., Everitt, A., Hardiker, P., and Littlewood, J. (1993/94) 'Value issues in research', *Social Action*, 1(4), pp.11-18.

Mullender, A. and Ward, D. (1991a) *The Practice Principles of Self-Directed Groupwork: Establishing a Value-Base For Empowerment*. Nottingham: Centre For Social Action, University of Nottingham.

Mullender, A. and Ward, D. (1991b) *Self-Directed Groupwork: Users Take Action For Empowerment*. London: Whiting and Birch.

NCH Action For Children/Nottinghamshire Social Services Department (1993) *Joint Service Level Agreement for the Radford Shared Care Project*. Unpublished Report.

Parton, N. (1991) *Governing The Family: Child Care, Child Protection and The State*. Houndmills, Hampshire: MacMillan.

Thompson, F. and Fleming, J. (1993) *Nottingham Black Families Project: Background Study*. Nottingham: Centre For Social Action, University of Nottingham.

This chapter was first published in 1994 in *Groupwork* Vol. 7(2), pp.163-179

At the time of writing, Sandra Butler was Lecturer in Social Work at the University of Nottingham

MEN UNITED:
Fathers' voices

Jennie Fleming and Zbyszek Luczynski

This chapter is about a men's group, based in a social services family centre. It sets out how the article was written with the men's cooperation. The account is based on interviews with them and uses their own words to illustrate and emphasise the points raised. The paper does not address the issues of recruitment of members or workers, nor concentrate on roles or methods. Rather, the focus is on ways that self directed groups for men can play a significant part in supporting them in their role as fathers and in challenging the stereotypes of fathers being absent in the care of their children.

Introduction

HA! HA! HA! What a bunch of tossers. . . . That is how I first thought of the men's club - MEN UNITED. I first heard about Men United from a friend who was a regular member who kept asking me to come down. I always said 'No way! Me at a men's club Ha! Ha! Ha!' So that's how it was for a long time, then one day I was bored silly, as the house work was all done, there was nothing to do, nowhere to go except the four walled prison called home. So my friend said to me again, 'Lets go down the men's club?' I just laughed - 'I may be bored but I'm not that bored!' but I was bored and the next 5 minutes seemed like 5 hours - so that is how and why I got involved in the men's club, Men United. I never thought I would benefit out of Men United BUT how could I have been so wrong? I got more benefit out of the Men's Club than I ever thought possible. (from an account by a group member).

This article is about the impact on the lives of members of a group for men who have been meeting together in Radford, Nottingham since June 1995. The group is based on the assumption that men gain from the opportunity to meet with others in similar positions and from talking together about their lives. This paper is an opportunity for the men's views and opinions, about their roles as fathers as well as the role of the group, to be heard.

In an early leaflet about the group the members describe it as a group for

all men who have children and men without children with or without partners, to share their experience of being a man and being a father, talking about everyday things.

The group was originally attached to the Shared Care Project in Radford, Nottingham. This is a joint NCH-Action for Children and Nottingham Social Services project (see Fleming and Ward, 1992, for an outline of the project and participants' evaluation). From the very beginning the Shared Care Project had run a weekly group for women involved in the project (see Butler, 1994). The project manager and the workers at the Family Centre, based in the same building, had for some time been aware of the need to offer more support to men who used the two projects. When a male social work student came on placement, the opportunity to develop a group for men was taken.

The writing of this article

The men in the group have been involved in the process of writing this article. First, they were asked whether they would like the article to be written and how they wanted to take part. The men and the group worker discussed the implications of being involved and also discussed what topics and issues they would like the paper to cover. One author was the group worker, and the members invited the other author to one of their meetings, where we had a tape-recorded conversation on previously agreed topics. This material has been used to form the bulk of the article. The men were shown the first draft of the article and many of their comments and suggestions were incorporated into the second draft. They have agreed to the submission of this article to *Groupwork*.

Men's groups

The quote at the beginning of this paper perhaps reflects views of men's groups which are held by people not only in the community, but also by some professionals as well. Men's groups have not been at the top of the agenda of those working with families - though this is beginning to change. There has been a tradition of work with women, and literature about this (for example, Butler, 1994; Norman, 1994; and Butler and Wintram, 1991). Brown points out that women's groups have been well established and the

> ... need recognised for them particularly in male dominated contexts such as the criminal justice system ... [but] ... Men's groups on the other hand have tended to exist for 'negative' reasons, by which I mean because there is no other choice: as in all-male contexts such as a male prison. (1992, p49)

The men from Men United argue that the support they get from the group is important for them in the female dominated world of parenting. This argument would be supported by others too. Accounts of work with fathers' groups begin to appear in the professional press (for example, McFall, 1998; Young People' Health Network; 1998; Burgess, 1997; and Speak et al, 1997). All these voices confirm the men's commitment to their children and their parenting role and their ability to contribute to and gain from group work. Hart, writing of work with fathers' groups in both Norway and America, says that

> fathering groups are a beginning of a process to having stronger fathers. . . . It may be that the fathering groups can improve the child rearing and the relationship of father and child. (Hart, 1997, p8)

The workers in the group

The social work student mentioned above, himself a father and an experienced worker, was very committed to men coming together, talking and sharing their experiences. When his placement finished he got a job as a Team Leader in the Detached Family Resource Team and continued to come to the group as and when he could. In his place, a local community worker, Zbyszek Luczynski, (then employed by Nottinghamshire Social Services and now, following local government reorganisation, in the Community Division of the Nottingham City Council Leisure and Community Services Department) became one of the workers in the group and has remained throughout, often as a single worker. For a while a social worker from the Specialist Team for Black Families was also a worker, showing awareness of and some commitment to the needs of fathers on the part of Social Services. The workers from the Social Services Family Centre have been very active in encouraging fathers who use the Centre to come to the group.

From the start the need was identified for some level of female involvement. It was felt necessary to have some involvement from a woman as a check against any sexism during the discussions and to enable input from a female perspective. One of the authors, who was already acting as consultant to the women's group, was approached to support the student in the development of the group and has remained in the role of consultant.

There is a crêche available to the fathers. Funding for this has come from the County Council and Children in Need. At present the crêche worker himself is a father and on the days when the crêche is not needed he joins the group.

The City Council (and previously the County Council) give one worker session a week, the room is provided free by the Shared Care Project. Other than this the resources available to the group have been less than £500 in four years. This has been raised through three grants of £150 and car boot sales organised by the men.

The philosophy of the group

The men's group started by a meeting together of a father, who felt the need to meet with others, with a student in a project that states 'if individuals are to make real and lasting changes, they must fully participate in the thinking and choosing of what those changes are to be' (Radford Shared Care Project, 1997, p3). From these roots it was logical that the group developed with an emphasis on empowerment and self-direction.

The group workers all came from backgrounds of community development work or social work and shared the principles of community development set out in the SCCD Charter:

> The Community Development process is collective, but the experience of the process enhances the integrity, skills, knowledge and experience, as well as equality of power, for each individual who is involved.
>
> Community Development seeks to enable individuals and communities to grow and change according to their own needs and priorities, and at their own pace, provided this does not oppress other groups and communities, or damage the environment. (SCCD Charter, 1992)

Another definition of community development work includes a commitment to encouraging self determination and the sharing of power, the development of knowledge and changing the balance of power, challenging inequality and promoting social justice (Skinner, 1997, p100).

The group consultant works for the Centre for Social Action: an organisation based on enabling community members and service users to take action for their empowerment (Mullender and Ward, 1991). All the workers shared a common value base and vision of how the workers should work in the group. Indeed, the group members easily recognised and acknowledged this base as a way of working that was appropriate to them and their development.

The group

Over 50 fathers have come to the regular weekly sessions. However, there has usually been a core membership of between five and eight men. More recently the men have also met at each other's houses for occasional business meetings to pursue the development of work with men through, for example, organising fund raising events and preparing funding applications for a worker, or presentations at conferences.

The membership of the group has been drawn from contacts

made at the Family Centre and the Shared Care Project and contacts of members themselves. The men have also publicised the group in schools, community centres and health centres and occasionally men have joined the group following these endeavours.

The group members have developed their own aims for the group:

- to break down barriers and destroy stereotypes of how men should be,
- to encourage fathers and men to help each other,
- to publicise the benefits of men taking responsibility for supporting each other and their families,
- to provide time and space to share feelings with other men,
- to build a network of fathers' support groups and services for families,
- to provide information and training on men's health, legal and welfare rights, parenting skills, jobs and career opportunities, communication, confidence and assertion skills,
- to build a better understanding of men, women and our children and of different cultures.

(From a leaflet prepared by the men to advertise the group).

Though the group has had fathers with partners, most of those who have remained members in the long term have been single fathers. They have come from the black and white communities in Radford, an inner city area. Over the four years, these men have formed a committee, got funding from the County Council, arranged a 10 session course on men's health with a woman health promotion worker, begun sports sessions after the meetings, run car boot sales, cooked together, and had regular meetings with the women's group to discuss common issues about parenting. They have given presentations to local councillors, run workshops at conferences, been part of research projects about fathers, and undertaken their own survey of local men around issues of being a father. However, the most important thing the group offers the men is mutual support and friendship.

Mutual support

The importance of mutual support for women is well documented (Butler and Wintram, 1991; Dominelli and McLeod, 1989; Flynn et al., 1986) and it is increasingly recognised as a benefit to men; in particular fathers. McFall (1998), Barna (1995), Young People's Health Network (1998) and Luczynski (1999) all recount the importance of the support gained from fathers coming together in groups. The fathers who have attended this group speak of their great relief in finding other men who understand them and their situation – who will listen and help. In the group they feel safe and can be honest and open about the difficulties they are facing. The founding group member writes:

I am a single parent, I was looking after a 6 month old boy. I had lost all of my male friends because they did not think or believe that a man should be looking after a child on his own and because I did not go out boozing and clubbing with them. I felt I was all on my own and isolated. Then when my son was 15 months I got him a place in the nursery at my local family centre - after a time I realised not one man visited the family centre! At a Parent's Committee meeting I decided to have a say and what I said was, 'What about a men's group?' I tried to get men involved, but no luck, then by some fluke there came a student social worker who decided to help me with the men's group and in no time we had three other members. At last I was not alone any more - I knew that at least once a week I could meet with them and talk to men about being a father and what's it like being a father. I thought there must be other men in the same situation as me, who think like me. It took a time - but I always thought they would come.

Another man says:

It was something I was always looking for. I mean every bloke in this room was in the same boat as me. They was all single fathers, they have all had the same hassle as I had. I knew what he had been through and he knew what I was going through. It wasn't what I had expected - but at the same time it was what I needed.

The sharing of a common situation, that of being fathers responsible for looking after their children, creates a strong bond between the men:

My partner abused my kids - not sexually but physically and mentally abused them - I was cracking up. The good thing about the group is you can tell these and they ain't going to laugh - if you go to the pub with your mates they'd laugh, but there he has been through the same stuff and so has he and him too - he ain't going to laugh. It don't matter what problem you come with they will take it serious.

The support they gain from each other is not just about being fathers. The group have also had a series of sessions on men's health with a health promotion worker which has increased their knowledge of their own bodies and encouraged them to talk about other personal issues:

I have also learnt a lot about my health, for example testicular cancer, that is just one thing I should know about but didn't. Where can a man go to ask these things? With his doctor? I don't think so, too embarrassed to go. But when you are in a men's club this is one thing we can talk about - openly, plus it is one thing that is not talked about in the pub!

Position of single fathers

Despite the fact that single fathers are an increasing proportion of single parents (Eurostat, quoted in *The Guardian*, 30th September 1998, p3), the men talk of their feeling that professionals do not take them seriously or recognise them as good parents. This is confirmed by the research the men have undertaken themselves:

Everywhere you go - its, 'You're on your own, on your own with children?' Then it is, 'You can't do that', 'Do it like this', You've got the Health Visitor poking her nose in. I think leave me alone.

However, some had found the support they received helpful:

My missus was abusing the children - once I had decided to look after the children myself social services were really helpful. They came to the nursery here and that is how I heard about the group.

As unmarried fathers they have found their lack of rights (for example, not being able to consent to medical treatment) difficult:

Because I wasn't legally married to my children's mother - I'm nobody. My oldest girl needed an injection and I took her to the doctors and he said I hadn't the right to give the doctor permission to give my daughter an injection. If they needed a life saving operation I couldn't do anything about it. That made me think things should change - that is part of what we are hoping to do with this group - help single fathers get their rights.

The lack of rights for unmarried fathers is beginning to be recognised as an issue for families (Speak, et al., 1998; Buxton, 1996). This issue has been discussed in the press recently (Hugill, 1998; Roberts, 1998; Crace, 1998) and also in research publications (McGlone, 1998) and the group plays an important part for the men in helping them understand their current situation and how they can change it. The men have shared their experiences and supported each other in obtaining parental responsibility for their children.

In the sessions the men have also discussed the images of men in the media and how they often confirm the stereotypes of men,

Like that beer advert saying how awful it would be if men really talked to each other and asked how they were and that. It doesn't help.

Relationships with the workers in the group

In keeping with the philosophy set out earlier in this paper the men were very clear that decisions in the group were made by them collectively. The men decide what happens in the group and how it will be done:

We all do things like arranging the speakers - it depends on who it is - who might know them already and that.

They recognised that the role played by the worker was different from that of the group members:

People like Zbyszek know things we don't. He knows the ropes, the contacts, knows who we need to know - which strings to pull. We learn these things from him. We know about looking after the children and being single dads but not about those other things we need if this group is going to get anywhere.

He gives us information and it is up to us what we do with it. It is not his job or his place to go out and do things.

Women and the group

The men were clear that they did not exclude women from the group, but rather welcomed them, if there was a role for women.

We are happy for women to come to the group when there is a purpose to it - like the health visitor, the solicitor. We wouldn't want to be seen as anti-women, it is just there are some things it is easier to talk about as men.

However, the members felt that theirs was a men's group first and foremost:

Oh yeah, it is crucial. Half the men here wouldn't talk like they do if a woman was always here.

Lessons learnt

What the men felt they learnt from coming to the group was, above all else, that there was a place where men could come together and share their problems, talk to each other and offer support. A consequence of this was that they felt more confident in themselves as fathers:

A: It is great finding other men who want to talk, that men can talk about emotions, worries all that sort of thing.
D: Yeah, men can talk - but not if they feel they will be laughed at.'
The place must be right.
A: Well, it is not just the place is it - it is the people you are with.

The men have also gained confidence from doing the presentations for councillors, at conferences and participating in research. For example, they took part in a research project into black families and family centres (Butt and Box, 1998) and are taking part in a Joseph Rowntree Foundation research project on fatherhood:

When we went to talk to those councillors we was all dead nervous, that was scary. But we did it and we were pleased with ourselves, they said they were impressed with what we were doing and that.

Some of the men felt they had gained personally. Some have gone on college courses and some found jobs, including one man who became a mid-day supervisor at a local school (certainly one of the first in Nottingham): 'That took some courage that did'. One man had cut down on his smoking as a result of the health education sessions.

Difficulties

The group acknowledged they have faced one or two problems both within the group and outside. They talked of how they had responded to a man who had come to the group and been racist:

B: *There was one bloke that came and had been for quite a few weeks and then we was half way through a conversation when it come out he was racist. So there was a big disagreement.*
D: *Basically, we stood up to him.*
A: *It was straight forward racism. At the end of the day it is the racist person what is loosing out.*
D: *Well, he realised he wouldn't get any support for racism here.*

They acknowledged that sometimes the regular members did have differences of opinion, but felt they resolved these satisfactorily:

Yeah, one time two of us were having a go at each other, but we are still friends; we still come and still talk to each other.

Other difficulties they identified included external matters. For example, they were told they would have to move their group meetings as the room was needed for something else. They also discussed the lack of financial support for the group and the difficulties they faced in getting any provision for men and compared their position unfavourably to women in a similar situation. As the following conversation illustrates:

A: *Trying to get anything for the men's group is hard. It seems any women's group I know of seems to have everything this men's group wants. But for us to try and get them is difficult.*
B: *It is supposed to be equal rights and that - but it isn't.*
A: *It would be good if we had our own building - a place just for fathers -*

women have loads of places - but we need places for men.
C: *But some people would argue that men have lots of places they go, where it is not easy for women to go.*
B: *Yeah, but not if you are a single dad. Everywhere you go is women. Here at the drop-in, no men; at mums and toddlers (they call them parents and toddlers but it is all mothers) all women; at school all women. If a bloke walks into a family centre you feel like you are green and you have 4 legs.*
D: *When I went to court to get my parental responsibility order, it was all women - my solicitor, the social worker, the court welfare, the judge all women. I was the only man in that court.*

The men also talked about how it was difficult when they felt the group was being used by social workers. For example, one man had been sent by his social worker to the group and told he had to come without any prior discussion of this with the rest of the group. They felt this affected the balance of the group and interfered with its philosophy.

The Future

The group has achieved much in the time it has been running. However, members have plans for the future.

The group has so far survived on minimal funding. They are now undertaking a needs survey of fathers in Nottingham, which will form the basis of funding applications to set up a twelve months pilot project with their own part-time worker. They hope this will establish the need for an expanded network of fathers' support, activities and groups.

That is our goal: to get our own place, and a worker with more time than Zbyszek has. He only has one day a week max - he is a busy man. We could do with someone full time and that costs - it is down to money again.

The men would like more fathers to come to the group, and have made efforts to attract more men:

We have been to social services offices and written to all of them in the city and told them about the group and suggested they could tell people about the group.

The group also hope to organise a parenting course for fathers, as they have found it difficult to go to existing parenting courses that, they feel, are run more with the needs of women in mind.

A: *We have talked about a parenting course for fathers. Like Ron has tried a couple but they were all based around mothers - he felt it was a waste of time him being there, because he is not a mother, he is a father. It is the same job but it has differences.*

B: *They can be very patronising - I know as I have been to one or two things for parents. I've thought I can't stand this much longer, they tend to ignore you.*

A: *All the materials they use and that - they have photos of women - you would think fathers don't exist.*

One long term goal is to promote wider awareness of the needs of single fathers and to encourage the development of appropriate services. Another aspect of this plan is also to encourage men to work in child care organisations:

Only one per cent of nursery nurses are male - in the whole country - one per cent. Since I've started my training I have had nothing but positives and support - but it would be good if more men thought about this sort of work.

A lot of the help we need is through other people - doctors, schools, social services. It is about them getting more aware of single fathers and what we need and how to provide those things.

Conclusions

The men in this group challenge the stereotype of fathers being uninvolved in the care of their children. They also challenge the stereotype that men can't, won't and don't share emotions, feelings, anxieties and hopes with each other. When men get together in a group such as this; one that lets them set the agenda and talk about issues that are important to them, they grasp the opportunity wholeheartedly.

This group has been very successful in giving fathers confidence and strength to cope with single fatherhood, but it has achieved much more than this. The group also challenges the currently received wisdom that fathers are not suitable carers for their children and actively demonstrates that they can in fact be very good at child care. The result is that the opportunity has been created for fathers' voices to be heard in the predominantly female world of parenting. Perhaps the most important influence behind this development is the groupwork philosophy and method. The self-directed groupwork model (Mullender and Ward 1990) creates ways for people to relate to each other, which in themselves challenge the stereotypes of what 'being a man' and 'being a father' entails in most of the wider world. Unfortunately, this challenge and groups that promote it, are still on the margins of family support.

Perhaps the future will look brighter. The Home Office is planning to set up the 'National Family and Parenting Institute' which hopefully will involve fathers (Sone, 1998), and the Voluntary and Community Unit has started a three year funding programme for work with fathers from last May. Perhaps some of the initiatives arising from these developments will recognise the relevance and power of the model of work described here.

The group members see themselves as part of the larger scheme and recognise that they have overcome some of the problems they face. Those that remain become their agenda for future action:

It seems like we have all these hurdles to jump. It seems people don't expect us to last - but we are still here and still jumping those hurdles.

Acknowledgements

It would not have been possible to write this paper without the cooperation, honesty and openness of the members of Men United. We would like to thank Satvinder, Ron, Rob, Nick and Michael.

Derrick McIntosh sadly died in July 1998. All those involved in Men United acknowledge his memory and his contribution to the group.

References

Barna, D. (1995) Working with young men. *The Health Visitor*, 68, No 5, pp185-187

Brown, A. (1992) *Group Work*. 3rd Edition Aldershot: Ashgate

Butler, S. (1994) 'All I've got in my purse is mothballs!' The Social Action Women's Group. *Groupwork*, 7, 2, pp163-179

Butler, S. and Wintram, C. (1991) *Feminist Groupwork*. London: Sage

Burgess, A. (1997) *Fatherhood Reclaimed: The making of the modern father*. London: Vermilion

Butt, J. and Box, L. (1998) *Family Centred: A study of the use of family centres by black families*. London: REU

Crace, J. 1998) Fathers' day. *The Guardian* July 15th, p8

Dominelli, L. and McLeod, E. (1989) *Feminist Social Work*. London: Macmillan

Buxton, S. (1996) *What is He Doing Here?* London: NCH

Fleming, J. and Ward, D. (1992) *'For the children to be alright their mothers need to be alright' An alternative to removing the child: the Radford Shared Care project* Nottingham: Centre for Social Action

Flynn, P. et al (eds) (1986) *You're Learning All the Time: Women Education and Community Development* Spokesperson Books

Hart, J. (1997) Fatherlessness. The Norwegian National Fathering Project : Strong Families through Strong Fathers. Unpublished paper presented at the 19th Annual Symposium on Social work with Groups, Quebec City, Canada

Hugill, B. (1998) Can't I live with you too Daddy? *The Observer*, 5th April, p8

Luczynski, Z. (1999) Listening, Trusting and Caring for Each Other - Men United Fathers' Group, Nottingham. *Achilles Heel*, 24, pp26-28

McFall, L. (1998) Modern masculinity. *Young People Now*, December, pp 22-23

McGlone, F. (1998) Families. *Research Matters*. April-October, pp50-51

Mullender, A. and Ward, D. (1991) *Self-Directed Groupwork: Users take action for empowerment*. London: Whiting and Birch

Radford Shared Care Project (1997) 'For the children to be alright, parents have to be alright.' Project information pack Nottingham: Radford Shared Care Project

Roberts, Y. (1998) Fathers' little helper. *The Guardian*, April 9th, p4

Sone, K. (1998) The Only Happy Families? *Community Care*, 3rd September, pp14-16

Speak, S., Cameron, S. and Gilroy, R. (1998) *Young single fathers: Participation in fatherhood: Bridges and barriers.* London: Family Policy Studies Centre

SCCD (1992) *SCCD Charter A Working statement on Community Development.* Sheffield: SCCD

Skinner, S. (1997) *Building Community Strengths: Capacity Building in community Organisations* London: CDF

Young People's Health Network, Health Education Authority (1998) Norwich Young Fathers Group. *FOCUS,* 7, p4

This chapter was first published in 1999 in *Groupwork* Vol. 11(2), pp.21-37

At the time of writing, Jennie Fleming was Research Fellow in the Centre for Social Action, De Montfort University (the consultant to the groupworkers), and Zbyszek Luczynski was with Broader Initiatives Development Worker, Nottingham City Council, Department of Leisure and Community Services (the worker with the group)

Involving school students in social action in America: The Youth Dreamers Group

Cierra Cary, Chekana Reid, and Kristina Berdan

The following article describes the work and vision of the Youth Dreamers group in Baltimore, which evolved as a result of young people's involvement in the social action process as part of a school community action course run by teacher Kristina Berdan. In the first part, student members of the group, Chekana Reid and Cierra Cary, describe how they identified their key issue, the need for a youth-run youth centre where young people could go after school to take part in a range of constructive activities. Youth Dreamers started to take action to achieve their goals and have been successful in fund-raising and gaining political support and community support for the venture. In the second part, their teacher Kristina Berdan reflects at length on her experience of the social action process, its educational impact on her students, the contrast between the achievements of the Youth Dreamers group and her regular English class and the differences and sometimes contradictions inherent in her two roles of teacher and social action worker.

Youth Dreamers: The view from the students

The Youth Dreamers are a group of students in grades seven through eleven who decided that they wanted their voices to be heard. We are part of the Stadium School, a Baltimore City Public School that serves about 115 students in grades four through eight from the communities surrounding Memorial Stadium. When we started in 2001, we met for one hour each day. Now, we meet every Wednesday as part of a full day project class, in the evenings, and on weekends.

Our mission is to decrease the amount of violence that involves youth after school. We read that after school many kids just hang out and participate in unstructured activities. This leads to bad grades, bad attendance at school, drug abuse and bad behavior. Our goal is to try to create a youth-run youth centre where these kids can go instead. Our centre will hopefully decrease the amount of negative acts that our youth are involved in today.

The beginning

The first things we did to reach our dream were to:

- write a pledge to show our commitment;
- write a business proposal for possible funders;
- write a one year operating costs budget;
- complete a letter writing campaign.

We wrote over 40 letters and only received replies from three people. We did not stop, we kept on writing, and for those who did not hear us, we kept on fighting.

Fundraising and grantwriting

Our first funding was from Youth As Resources. We requested $3000 for furniture for our centre. To our surprise, we were then written into a federal bill by Senator Milkuski earmarking $70,000 for the creation of our youth-run youth centre. She partnered us with St. Ambrose Housing Aid Center to help us buy the house and Habitat for Humanity to help us renovate it. Since then we have written many other grant applications and now have over $180,000 towards our one-year operating costs budget of $276,000. Even though we were rejected from some of these foundations, we still kept writing and never gave up. We have also run many fundraising events.

All about the Centre

Our youth centre will be run by two adult directors, a Board of Directors that includes youth and adults, up to 23 teenagers in grades seven through twelve, at least eight adult volunteers from the community, Ameri-Corps volunteers, and a janitor. The teenagers will tutor members and teach a variety of classes along with adult volunteers. The centre will include a variety of classes, such as sewing, pottery, mosaics, art, cooking and typing, to name just a few.

Each teenager will commit to working at the centre a certain number of hours each week. They will be paid a small stipend for half of these hours and will earn service-learning hours for the other half. Adult volunteers will get paid a small stipend for their hours. The directors and janitor will get paid a set yearly salary. Finally, we are trying to set up a scholarship fund for Youth Dreamers who serve on the Board of Directors.

Not only will the youth centre serve youth in the community, but it will also serve community members. We will host block parties, open houses, neighbourhood clean-ups and other activities that bring youth and adults together in positive ways. We have been involved in many different publicity events.

This year, four of us went to area elementary schools during the day to work with our future members. We wrote letters to the principals to get permission, and then planned activities and lessons to do with the younger children. Working with younger children is hard, but it pays off in the end.

Four of us also worked with the Baltimore Community Foundation to review proposals for after-school programming in Baltimore. This was a long and hard process, but it gave us a chance to see how proposals are viewed from the 'other side.' We also ran workshops for other middle school students from the city. We helped them identify problems in their community that they wanted to solve. We will continue to work with them to give them advice and help with their projects.

We have learnt a lot over the past two years. We never realised it would be so much work and take so much time. Some of our biggest challenges were not getting responses, staying on task, being comfortable presenting and staying committed. Most importantly however we have learnt that if we stay committed, we can accomplish a lot by working together. We have become good problem solvers and we know how to reflect on our work to make it better. We even researched becoming a non-profit organization, voted to do it, engaged the help of the University of Maryland Law School, and are now the Stadium School Youth Dreamers, Inc. with a board of seven youth and seven adults.

Reflections on the Youth Dreamers: The cycle of successes and challenges and how social action plays its part

The beginning

I am part of the Youth Dreamers because I want to be a part of making a future for the youth of today. [Mildred]

When nine Baltimore City middle school students decided to create a free standing youth-run youth centre in order to provide a safe and stimulating place for kids after school, I actually encouraged them to pick a smaller project. Although I had done successful community projects with other students and had attended several training courses with the Centre for Social Action, I did not see how students were going to be able to mobilize to raise the money and garner the support to do what no other youth group had done on their own. Having taught many of these students who were so easily frustrated by having to revise a paper, I doubted that they had the staying power to stick it out for the years that it would take to accomplish this task. It took little time for me to realize that they were going to do exactly that. Through all of their own efforts, the Youth Dreamers are on the road to seeing their dream become a reality.

Back in March of 2001, I could never have predicted how enormous this project would become, nor how much I would struggle with my role as teacher/facilitator. When I announced 'Community Action' as my elective course, I noted a low, collective groan among the students. Only nine courageous souls signed up for the course, choosing to give up the chance to play basketball, football, or African drums. We began by really talking about the issues in their community that bothered them. The students clearly enjoyed being given the opportunity not only to talk in class, but also to talk about 'their' interests, not the interests of the curriculum writers in their district. When asked to focus in on one issue, the students unanimously agreed on the issue of teenagers being on the streets involved in violent activities after school hours. From that point, I guided the students into thinking about why this problem exists. Utilizing the 'But Why' activity (an exercise used as part of the 'why' stage of the social action process) and additional discussion, the students decided to tackle 'teenagers on the street after school is a problem because they have nowhere safe to go and they are bored.' The idea of a youth-run youth centre was born, and although I did my best to encourage them to take on a smaller project, they were now united and determined. They signed a pledge to commit to the project and I felt like I signed my life away.

From elective course to full day project class

This class is different because in Youth Dreamers we are making change in the community. [Chekana]

During the year and four months as an elective course, I couldn't help but notice the tremendous number of skills the students were learning and applying. Students were enthusiastically writing business proposals, letters of Inquiry to foundations, grants, and budgets. They were planning and executing presentations, making site visits to interview directors of other youth centres and organizing meetings of adults and youth. They were planning fundraisers, evaluating them and calculating their profit. It was a thrill to see the real world connections and application of skills from other classes that these students were showing everyday. But there was never enough time at the end of the day and I was tired of always meeting after school. This was real learning that should be given more place in the daily schedule. I had to speak to the staff. This had to be more than an elective class. But would they agree? And how would we do it?

Fortunately, I work in a 'New School Initiative' school in Baltimore City. This is a Baltimore City Public School run by teachers, parents, community members and students. While we are constrained by the city budget and city and state testing mandates, we are able to write our own curriculum, create our own schedules, determine our own class sizes, etc. When I spoke to the staff about what I had observed in my elective course, they were enthusiastic about taking that class to a different level and taking other projects in the school to that level, too.

Project class

I am part of the Youth Dreamers because we are doing big things together and we're helping people. Also because it seemed fun. [Shanta]

So, September 2002 rolled around and we were now a fully-fledged, all day Youth Dreamers Project Class, with 18 students instead of the original nine. Our day was structured, but full of choice. We began with announcements and from these a list would develop of mini-projects to be completed. Perhaps we needed to do another fundraiser, or research needed to be done to find more grants, or a new grant could have come to our attention, or we could have found out that we were invited to present our work at a community meeting. After announcements, students would decide what they would work on, who they would work with and when they would work. We built in snack breaks, enjoyed a longer lunch period with the whole school, and rounded out our day by coming back together to report on what we had accomplished and set goals for the next class period. The last piece would always be self-evaluation (described later). Occasionally, I would present a mini-lesson on a skill or piece of content that I noted they needed help with, such as business letter form, grant writing, how to speak on the telephone, etc. In later years, as the class grows in size, 'older' Youth Dreamers will be able to take over the job of teaching these mini-lessons to newer members.

Grading

This class is different because you don't learn what most middle school students learn. It is different because you don't really get graded. [Sammy]

While this schedule suited our needs, it was still quite a challenge trying to keep everyone on task for most of the day. And going from a one hour elective class to a full day project class created additional challenges. At first I was concerned that being graded on their work would create a negative, pressure- filled situation that would take away from the sense of community and choice we had created. Fortunately, this did not happen. Students grade themselves on Leadership and Cooperation at the end of each day. I also have a chance to grade them on these outcomes. Students are very honest about their performance, and we find that usually my score matches their own self-assessment. At the end of each grading period, these scores are averaged by the students for their report cards.

There are consistent teacher-developed rubrics used for letter writing, grant writing, and presentations. I developed these rubrics after discussions and mini-lessons centred around these skills. There are standard report forms for fundraising and event planning. I developed these based on whole group reflections that happen after every fundraiser and event. Students are utilizing skills from core classes to accomplish numerous goals. They are understanding why business letter form is important and how to use their math skills to balance our cheque book and modify our budget. And as a full curriculum, connected explicitly to state and city outcomes and standards, I feel protected from people who want to question the validity of what I am doing in my classroom.

The transformation

I felt that the Youth Dreamers would be an organization where my voice would be heard and my opinion would be heard. [Chantel]

I noticed a phenomenal transformation in this class in comparison to my seventh grade English class. In my English class, students refused to write a short story, but in the Youth Dreamers, they would write 10 page grants. In my English class, I would come up with creative, interactive ways to teach how to address an envelope and notice that whenever they needed to do so, they were unable to do it correctly. Switch to the Youth Dreamers - when a student pulled me aside to ask how to address an envelope, I showed her once, she filled out the envelope that held the grant that went to the foundation, and I never had to show her again. In my English class, asking a student to revise a paper became an emotional disaster. In the Youth Dreamers, students would come to me to ask if they had left out any important information in their letter of inquiry to a foundation. When rejection letters rolled in and I prepared myself with Winston Churchill quotes—'Success is nothing but failure after failure with undiminished enthusiasm'—the students would look at me and then ask, 'So who should we write to next?' This was an aberration from the classroom when they would fall apart if they did not receive a grade they expected on a paper.

In my English class, students would constantly bicker over trivial matters, fight for attention and rarely respect the contributions of others. In the Youth Dreamers, students would democratically decide who would get to be the one student who was interviewed on the morning news. As a class, they then decided to each write down their top three choices for a representative, and they tallied the votes to come up with one representative and a runner-up. These two students worked together to prepare for questions that might come their way. In addition, the students would recognize the strengths and contributions of others when deciding on mini-project groups.

At one point, I had students begging to be part of the Youth Dreamers, particularly students who did not typically work very hard in regular classes. One of my English Language /Arts students who did very little work in class asked if he could join. I responded with, 'It's a lot of hard work and you don't do very much work in class.' He surprised me when he said, 'But Youth Dreamers is important. They're really doing something.' I didn't know whether to be upset at the notion that he thought we weren't really doing 'something' in English class, or thrilled at the realization that he saw the Youth Dreamers as a group of students taking responsibility for making positive change in their world.

Individual students in the Youth Dreamers were baffling me. Tenika was failing all of her other classes but was the leader in the Youth Dreamers, organizing and running fundraisers, starting a group to plan and run the Talent Show, writing a 5 page grant to have a block party in the community. Students were begging to stay after school in order to plan a presentation. Instead of bemoaning the school-wide Halloween party that only raised $5.00 for the Youth Dreamers, we decided during our reflections that it showed what good planners they were and that they could organize and control a whole student body on a holiday. We moved it from the Fundraising part of our budget and included it in reports for funders to show these strengths. Again, attitude seemed to evaporate and enthusiasm took its place. I stayed up nights wondering: What is happening here? Why is it happening here? Why isn't it happening in my English Language /Arts class? Is it going to go away? Should I not talk about it for fear of it going away? Should I ask them about it? Is it just a case of luck or magic? I was constantly pondering these questions to help me better understand the effects of social action and what I was doing 'wrong' in my regular classroom.

The classroom vs. the social action project embedded in the classroom

How do you get them to do all that work? [Teachers]

I don't. They do. When I first began the elective course, I invited students to join the class to 'make change in their world.' They came to the class by choice. This is very different from how students come to my English class, who attend because they are forced to be there. They are learning what is prescribed by the city, not necessarily what they want to learn. For the most part, I am teaching what I am told to teach, not what I can see they need to learn.

In the Youth Dreamers, I used the social action process in its true sense to guide them. They came up with the issues, they brainstormed why the problem exists, they decided how they were going to address it, they take action and they reflect on almost every step along the way. Unlike my traditional classroom where students have little control of their own learning, the Youth Dreamers have total ownership of what they are doing and why they are doing it.

The climate of the classroom has changed from traditional teaching (even though I consider myself to be an untraditional teacher) to working on a social action project as a team. The only time I am teaching in the traditional sense is when I am presenting a mini-lesson in reaction to their needs. At all other times, students are choosing what to work on, who to work with and how to best accomplish the task at hand. In response, students have begun to perceive Wednesdays in a very different way. They speak about it as a 'fun day,' even though they are doing more work on that day and they are still being graded on it. According to a survey given in March 2002, 80% of the Youth Dreamers surveyed responded that they learned more and completed more work in this class than in other classes. In addition, of thirty skills listed, they identified learning 70% as a Youth Dreamer, 3% in other classes, and 27% in both Youth Dreamers and other classes.

My role

Ms. Kristina don't tell us what to do. We do it with our own free will. [Chris]

As the facilitator of the Youth Dreamers, I wear the hat of a social action worker, using the skills I have as a teacher to help facilitate a student-chosen goal. I am no longer seen as their teacher, but more as their guide and a resource. I enjoy being able to float through the classroom to help with particular questions or general needs. I am able to create mini-lessons based on real needs (such as how to write a business letter or address an envelope), rather than what I think are real needs. This often makes me reactive, rather than proactive, which is not how I am used to teaching.

As a worker, it is often the case of the blind leading the blind. I never know what will happen next, what direction the students will choose to go, or how they will handle the next challenge. This can be a very uncomfortable position to be in because you feel a real lack of control. But the structure of our days, the goals we have in common, and the desire to see a dream become a reality bring self-control to the classroom. The students perceive me as peripheral in the project. When asked what the role of the adult ally is in the group, the students responded, 'Well, we really do everything. She just organizes our thoughts on chart paper around the room.' I was both thrilled and disappointed with this response. After all, I do a bit more than serve as their scribe, BUT I am pleased to see that they are confident knowing that they really are in charge of their project.

I struggled for a long time about the difference between what was happening in my English class and my role there, with what was happening in the Youth Dreamers and my role there. After much reflection and discussion, it has become very apparent to me that being a teacher and being a social action worker are not the same. The principles and process of social action do not align perfectly with teaching because teaching is not about bringing a group with common issues together to make change. Teaching and social action may share philosophies/principles and they may be influenced by one another, but they are not the same.

On Wednesdays, I am a social action worker working in the confines of a classroom. I use my skills as a teacher to provide mini-lessons and guidance and grading is injected. I am working with a group of students with a shared goal. The rest of the week, I am a teacher, guided by the principles of social action and good teaching, incorporating those theories into my practice. I am working with a group of students with very different needs, no common goal, and a required curriculum. So I just keep both hats in the closet and make costume changes every now and then.

My struggles

You spend entirely too much time with your students. [a friend]

As a facilitator and not a teacher, I feel that I sometimes lack credibility among my colleagues. My guidance has come into question because people assume that these students are just making all kinds of decisions on their own. On the contrary, students do a tremendous amount of research, make decisions collectively with adults they bring in to help, and are never just allowed to do something without planning. I have a responsibility as their teacher to maintain a safe and secure environment, which means I monitor, participate, guide, and sometimes obstruct. I struggle with how much guidance to give them, whether to give input about direction, and how to deal with having to tell them that their choice may not be an appropriate option. And because I often don't know what is around the corner, I can't prepare myself for anything. I have made mistakes, but have grown much more comfortable admitting to other adults that I need help from them.

While there are those who are willing to help, there are also those adults who either refuse to believe that this project is youth driven, refuse to believe that it can happen because it is youth-run, don't follow through on their promises, or ask for a one-year operating costs budget the next day. When Senator Mikulski was considering funding the project, her projects director wanted to meet with me, not the students. Against my better judgement, I attended the 10 minute meeting alone, laden with photographs and work that the students had done. She had no interest in my 'evidence,' she just wanted to know about our demographics and test scores. When larger foundations are approached by the students, they are often unwilling to even consider that the project is possible because it is youth-run. At a Housing Meeting with adult allies from the community, students asked for help in finding a building and finding someone to take title to it. The adults set tasks to be completed by the next meeting and then did not even show up at that meeting where the Youth Dreamers presented all the research they had completed in the interim. Writing a one-year operating costs budget took the students weeks, not the day in which it was expected. Adults do not understand that time frames for students are very different from time frames for adults. And given the role that I have chosen, I simply cannot just do it for them in order to have it turned in on time. Fortunately, these struggles end up being more of my burden than a burden on the students. They tend to chalk it up to another adult not believing in them and then they move on to the next task that will take them further to accomplishing their goal.

Although I am more of a social action worker in this role, the teacher in me often wants to jump in and 'fix' things or just 'finish' them on time. But I have learned that the most valuable lessons come from students fixing and finishing themselves. Figuring out that the riot at the entrance to the Benefit Basketball Game could be avoided by having two students, instead of one, standing in front of the door blocked by a table is much more valuable coming from them instead of me. Choosing to finish a grant in the eleventh hour, rather than giving up on it because of the time constraint, really taught Tenika that leaving things to the last minute can be an uncomfortable, unenjoyable situation. But she did it, bragged to everyone else, and then received the money.

Finally, I struggle tremendously with time. Initially, I was thrilled at the prospect of having a full day with the Youth Dreamers. We would finally have enough time to get things done without having to meet in the afternoons and on weekends. My life had become the Youth Dreamers and I was looking forward to returning to a more balanced lifestyle. The reality is that there is still not enough time and my life is still not my own. The students are constantly working to meet deadlines. Teaching three classes on top of managing the Youth Dreamers has become totally overwhelming. Getting students to presentations and meetings outside of school involves getting coverage for my classes or working late into the evenings and/or on weekends. While I have tried to delegate some of my duties to our adult allies, they are often unavailable because of their own busy schedules. There have been times when I just wanted to run away screaming when a student suggested meeting on another Saturday. But having begun this project with them two years ago, I have never felt that I could just walk away. If they are willing to sacrifice a Saturday, shouldn't I be willing to do the same? This is something I still struggle with, something that I know needs to change; I just don't know quite how to change it.

And I struggle with additional questions: Is it always going to be the blind leading the blind? Am I qualified to deal with what is lurking around the corner? Are they focusing too much on this goal by spending all these additional hours working on it? How is this perceived by the school and our community? What in the world is going to happen when they actually get this centre opened? Then what will happen to my life? Will we be able to successfully run this youth centre the way we have successfully worked towards the goal?

Their struggles

A lot of adults think our project is 'cute.' They don't really believe that we are doing all of the hard work to accomplish our goal. [Astarte]

The students face their own set of challenges and struggles. I hear their complaints during class time and I saw their frustrations on paper when they completed the survey in March 2002. They have been discouraged by the attitude of adults who don't take them seriously because they are youth: 'Youth really have talent! You just need to develop it.' They are frustrated by the media's portrayal of youth: 'The newspaper and TV talk about bad stuff too much. They need to see the positive sides of Baltimore.' They often have trouble staying on task and get irritated when students don't do their part: 'The most frustrating thing is people not doing their job as a Youth Dreamer.' Although they respond by writing more letters, students are frustrated 'when we write letters to people and they don't write back.' They, too, feel the effects of how much time this project has taken: 'The thing that frustrated me was that things didn't happen right away. It took some time in school and after school. It seemed like we were going nowhere.' Many have had trouble staying committed to the goal, while others have never strayed: 'I have learned the importance of commitment and that all of us is better than doing it yourself.' The lessons learned seem to overpower the frustrations, as expressed by Chekana, 'If you really want to do it, then do it. Don't give up. You may come across rejections, but keep going, never stop.'

But in the end it works for us because ....

Being so immersed in this project has made it difficult for me to step back and view what is happening in an objective way. Although blurred by all these questions that swirl about in my head and the struggles I see the students grappling with, what I do see is very clear … I see the smile on Cierra's face when she found out that she had secured $20,240 worth of funding from a grant she wrote. I also see her mother bragging to a community member at our festival about how hard her daughter is working towards this dream. I see Tenika walking around the classroom with a huge grin after faxing her four page grant taunting, 'What did you do today? Anything? I wrote an entire grant.' I see Sammy after a presentation/skit for 30 bankers interested in reinvesting in the community being asked, 'So, were you at the meeting with

the developer who might donate a house to your organization?'
To which he replied, 'I wrote him the letter, planned the meeting,
and ran it.' I see Astarte running into the room breathless after
a call to the Senator exclaiming, 'The bill is on the President's
desk. He is going to sign it!' I see Rebecca and Tiye running into
the classroom after convincing an elementary school principal to
allow them to tutor her students who will soon be members of our
centre, 'She's letting us come on Wednesday afternoons, and she
was so impressed with our proposal ... everyone was asking us if
we wrote it!' I see Astarte and Chris waiting on their doorsteps at
3:15 am so they can help open the school and setup for the Angel
Soft Media Blitz. I see Chris arm in arm with Jane Kaczmarek from
Malcolm in the Middle walking through the classroom pointing out
all of the work the Youth Dreamers have done. I see Shani sitting
on a board of adults and youth helping to decide which after
school programs should get funding in the city. I see adults and
youth sitting around a table adjusting by-laws so that they don't
read President and Chairperson, but instead President and Youth
President. I see the shock on Nathan's face when we get to Walmart
only to be presented with an overflowing shopping cart of toys and
craft supplies because of a letter he wrote to five corporate officials.
I see Chris, Mildred, Chantel, and myself on the other side of the
table, now serving as Youth As Resources Board members, not
youth coming to them for money. I see Jade smiling and sighing
with relief after presenting her first workshop to middle school
students. I see the look of shock on Chekana's face when the Youth
Dreamers were presented with a Resolution from the Baltimore City
Council after their own presentation. I see 16 students showing
up for a meeting in the middle of the summer, enthusiastic about
setting goals for the new year. I see youth who have accomplished
more at age 13 than many will accomplish in a lifetime. I see youth
who have a ticket to college having written letters and grants; been
interviewed on TV and the radio; presented at major universities
and in front of numerous groups of adults; researched and started
their own non-profit organization; and organized, planned, and run
their own community block party. I see youth who are stakeholders
in their community, and hopefully, will come back to serve their
community in the future. I see youth who believe in their project

and its lasting effects: 'Because of our project, I would like to see less youth on the corner and more youth going to college and being successful.'

Ultimately, I see a group of students who embody the principles of social action because they believe that they:

- Have the skills, experience, and understanding that they can draw on to tackle problems they face;
- Have the right to be heard, define the issues facing them, and take action on their own behalf;
- Can work collectively and have power; and
- Can make decisions for themselves and take ownership of whatever outcome ensues.

The most exciting part of this project has been seeing the things we want to happen actually happen. [Shanta]

This chapter was first published in 2004 in *Groupwork* Vol. 14(2), pp.64-79

At the time of writing, Cierra Cary was Formerly Stadium School Student, and current Board Member of the Stadium School Youth Dreamers, Inc. Chekana Reidwas Formerly Stadium School Student, and current Youth Secretary of the Stadium School Youth Dreamers, Inc. Kristina Berdan was a Teacher at the The Stadium School

The role of groupwork in social action projects with youth

Joan Arches

This chapter presents a case study, and puts forth an approach to social justice work with young people, that impacts youth development, empathy, and social change by applying two social work models, Self-directed groupwork, and its model for stages of group development, along with concepts of expressive and instrumental social roles in groups.

The personal growth for the youth was demonstrated by their increased confidence, greater academic interest, and more positive perceptions by teachers. Socially they exhibited heightened understanding of others, communication skills, and teamwork. The result for the community was seen in the social change skills they acquired and the project they implemented.

Introduction

The social action project with urban middle schoolers and university service-learning students discussed here resulted in the youth taking on the issue of *adultism* in their school. *Adultism* is the abuse of power by adults. In the course of the project the youth identified the issue, analyzed its causes, designed a survey to see if others had the same experience, analyzed the data, and came up with a pledge to stop *adultism* which the teachers will be asked to sign. By the end of their semester, the youth had presented their work at several venues and were already seeing results.

Practitioners and academics are recognizing the impact of social activism on positive youth development and community transformation. Increasingly we are seeing examples of youth involved in social change using participatory action research, social action, and other participatory methodologies (Barbera, 2008; Ginwright & Cammarota, 2002; Ginwright, Noguera, & Cammarrota, 2006; Rodriquez & Brown, 2009). Individual growth and civic engagement together are coming to the forefront of youth development work.

This article reviews the literature on approaches to youth activism and social justice that incorporate the aforementioned concepts. Based upon the review of methods and projects taking place with groups of youth, only self-directed groupwork (Mullender & Ward, 1991) addresses group development as a significant factor needing attention in the engagement process. Recognizing the importance of groupwork theory and practice skills in working with youth on social change projects adds value to the growing field of activism and engagement with young people. With this as a focus, I present a social groupwork approach toward working with youth that employs self-directed groupwork and another model for stages of group development (Garland, Jones & Kolodny, 1973), along with the concepts of expressive and instrumental social roles. The results yield personal growth for the youth demonstrated by their increased confidence, greater academic interest, and more positive perceptions by teachers. Socially they exhibit enhanced empathy, communication skills, and teamwork. The impact for the community is seen in the social change skills they acquire and the projects they implement.

In the following case example, the stages of group development and Self -directed Groupwork, along with British social action, were applied in a partnership involving university service-learning students and urban middle schoolers, who identified their issue as *adultism,* abuse of power by adults, and then developed and implemented a plan to address it in their school. This case study will demonstrate the importance of applying knowledge of group dynamics and stages in social justice work with youth, to provide the tools to facilitate change on individual, interpersonal, and organizational/societal levels.

Literature review:
Social justice approaches to youth activism

Youth activism refers to programs and projects that encourage youth voice, agency, critical thinking, and reflection in youth led activities for social transformation. These approaches are all carried out collectively by youth, in groups, usually with adults as partners, facilitators, or co-facilitators. Social justice and groupwork are embedded in the pedagogy, process, and products. An understanding of power reflects an empowerment perspective that is woven into all aspects of the groups (Arches & Aponte Pares, 2005; Barbera, 2008; Ginwright & Cammarota, 2002; Kilroy, Dean, Reipe, & Ross, 2007; London, 2007; Pearrow, 2008; Rodriquez & Brown, 2009; Watts & Guessous, 2006).

An example of an activist approach applied with youth, participatory action research (PAR), directly involves young people affected by a problem in the design and action to rectify the youth-identified issue. They participate in every stage as co-researchers and problem-solvers. PAR validates the knowledge of local people, in this case youth, and values their role as co-creators of knowledge (London, 2007). PAR is frequently carried out with university researchers who share their claim to expertise and authority with local young people, who would ordinarily be the subjects of their research agenda. The boundaries between subject and researcher are blurred. The young people experiencing an issue are recognized as possessing a unique and legitimate understanding of the problem and how it should be addressed (Kilroy, Dean, Reipe, & Ross, 2007). The process includes identifying an issue, designing research and collecting data to substantiate it, conducting a structural analysis to get at root causes, and carrying out action to change the conditions. This is a powerful pedagogy for young people who are too often blamed for their troubles and left out of the problem solving process. It allows them to locate their issues in the public, rather than private domain, and motivates changes in power dynamics based on collective action (Arches & Aponte, 2005; Barbera, 2008; Rodriquez & Brown, 2009).

Similar to participatory action research, social justice youth development includes understanding the impact of social, economic, and political factors that impact the lives of young people, manifesting themselves as personal problems (Ginwright & Cammarota, 2002). It highlights the role oppression plays in maintaining the structural components of inequality that underlie issues youth face. (Ginwright & Cammarota, 2002). Social justice youth development is also carried out in groups with a process defined by critical thinking, consciousness-raising, and social action.

Incorporating the concepts discussed in participatory action research and social justice youth development, British social action is values-based and carried out with groups, challenging unequal power relations, while creating opportunities for improving conditions in the environment, and changing systems. Social action is a philosophy and theory for social change based on the work of Paolo Freire, (1970), the tenets of popular education, and influenced in the United Kingdom by the disability movement, black activists, and the women's movement (Castelloe & Watson, 1999; Dominelli & McCleod, 1989; Evans, 1994; Oliver, 1992). Like participatory action research, and social justice youth development, it is carried out with groups who are experiencing an issue and generating the solutions (Breton, 1995; Fleming & Ward, 1999). This approach is guided by the belief that acting collectively through groups is powerful, and that people, of any age and status, can improve their lives by taking action on their own behalf to achieve their collectively identified goals. In social action groups members identify issues, analyze why they exist, design and carry out action, and reflect (Berdan et al, 2006; Matthies, Jarvela, & Ward, 2000; www.dmu.ac.uk/dmucsa).

Self-directed groupwork

Attuned to the importance of the group as the basic unit of social action, only self-directed groupwork identifies group theory and process in the youth activism literature. Created to address the need in social work practice for a groupwork method that was empowering, self directed-groupwork puts forth a non-oppressive practice model in which workers and participants share power. It provides an avenue to work for social transformation in the larger social structure by challenging traditional power relations within the group and the broader environment. It incorporates an explicit values base committed to social justice and anti oppressive practice in which group participants: *define their own problems, set their own*

Fig. 1

Self Directed Groupwork (Mullender and Ward, 1991)	Stages of Group development (Garland, Jones, Kolodny, 1973)
Stage A: **Workers Take Stock** • •Preplanning/Agreeing on empowering principles for the work before meeting with users. • Assembling a co-worker team and establishing a mechanism for external feedback through consultation and reflection	Stage 1: Pre-Affiliation • **Potential group members approach the group with ambivalence** • Workers are mindful of the tentativeness of members' participation • Initial meetings are engaging, fun, and not overly demanding • The group explores their values, goals and process
Stage B: **The Group Takes Off** • Workers engage with users as partners to build a group with 'open planning' lines. • Users set norms, define, and analyze the problems, and set group.	Stage 2: Power and Control • Members commit to the group but are still wary about their roles and participation • Testing behavior and power plays are characteristic • Workers plan agendas in which members have power and control • Planning takes place as the group establishes the guidelines, values, and mission
Stage C: **The Group Prepares to Take Action** • The group explores the questions: • WHAT is the issue? • WHY does it exist? • HOW can we change the conditions that are causing it?	Stage 3: Intimacy • The group functions as a family and work is carried out as a unit • Participants feel aligned with the group • Roles are evolving
Stage D: **The Group Takes Action** • Participants move from recognition to action • Learning takes place, and plans may change, as reflections accompany action	Stage 4: Differentiation • A division of labor emerges • Members take on unique roles based on their interests, talents, and skills • The group is engaged in its work.
Stage E: **The Group Takes Charge** • Users are running the group • They make connections between WHAT, WHY and HOW and focus on broader issues and next campaigns • Workers retreat and may leave the group altogether. • Participants are learning to take control of their lives and how they are perceived by others	Stage 5: **Termination/separation** • Participants are given ample notice of when the group will end • The group reviews achievements, reflects on the learning, and discusses next steps • Celebratory events punctuate the formal end of the group

goals and act on their own behalf (Mullender and Ward, 1991, p.2). Mullender and Ward identify five stages in this model.

In the *Pre-planning Stage* (Stage A), the team is assembled and clarifies its values before meeting with youth. With the values in place for the facilitators, the youth join and the *group takes off* (Stage B) as it establishes guidelines and starts the process of defining its issue. Participants select and analyze the problem, and determine an action plan (Stage C). The facilitators guide the process of deciding which issue the group will address, posing questions, and encouraging creative ways of looking at problems, analyzing root causes, and creating an action plan. As they answer the questions related to why this issue exists, the group takes on a consciousness-raising function. Participants are able to see connections between what they thought were their own personal problems/troubles and the social structures that give rise to these issues and experiences. It is through this process that a change in the social relationships occurs referred to as the *politics of interpersonal relationships*. Empathy deepens as the ways of relating to other oppressed groups become more collaborative and mutual. As the power dynamics change communication, especially listening, is enhanced.

With the issue identified, and the problem analyzed as a public issue, as opposed to a private trouble (Mills, 1970), the *group takes action* (Stage D). Reflections are ongoing. The cycle is complete when the *group takes charge* (Stage E). The power dynamics completely change and the group takes ownership. These stages are not purely linear and with each obstacle it faces, the group could find itself back at an earlier stage.

Minding the gap: Group stages, dynamics and roles

Self-directed groupwork responds to the need for an empowerment process in groups to define their issues, set their goals and determine their course of action. In addition, there is a need to understand the *stages of group development and how expressive and instrumental group roles* contribute to effective groups (Vinik & Levin, 1991; Johnson & Johnson, 1997; van Linden & Fertman, 1998; Cohen & Mullender, 1999). Yet, the significance of groupwork techniques and skills that contribute to successful outcomes with youth activism are not adequately addressed (Galvin, Guttierez, & Galinsky, 2004; Getzel, 2006; Pearrow, 2008).

The field of social work highlights the connections between social groupwork and social activism (Berman-Rossi, 2002; Cohen & Mullender, 1999; Garvin, Guittierez, & Galinsky, 2004; Vinik & Levin, 1991). In assessing effective groups in community-based research, Shultz, Israel & Lantz (2004) refer to the characteristics of groups that engage the skills of all members. Finn, Jacobson, and Campana (2004) identify the importance of the group as central to social transformation in their work with participatory research, popular education and popular theatre. Cohen & Mullender (1999) caution that group practice should not be constrained by approaches that focus on only one system level such as micro, meso or macro, but rather group processes can be applied to foster goals on all three levels. Mondros and Berman-Rossi (1991) two decades ago, spoke of the role that social groupwork practice models play in community organizing. They made the connections between successful groups, knowledge of group development stages and effective organizing campaigns. But despite this, currently most of the literature on groups, and the youth civic engagement and activism literature, remain separate.

Incorporating an understanding of group roles, the stages of group development, and Self-directed groupwork into social change projects with youth enhances the likelihood that outcomes will be successful. (Fig. 1). By focusing on the immediate context in which the youth operate, the facilitators can support individual needs for growth along with group process and action. Starting with an understanding of what to expect as groups develop, the facilitators can be mindful of the types of social interactions and individual concerns with which members may approach the group. Garland, Jones and Kolodny (1973) identified five stages of group development which can aid in the successful planning and implementation of empowerment and social transformation groups with youth.

As a group begins to form, (*Forming or Pre-affiliation* stage), potential members approach it with ambivalence. There is a lack of trust as members try to figure out whether they want to join the group. They need time to develop trust, decide what they think about the group, and make a commitment. Facilitators select activities and icebreakers that are fun, and geared towards getting to know each other, but with limited and non threatening self-disclosure. Icebreakers may include asking: *How did you get your name? What is something I wouldn't know to look at you?*

In this first stage, which is similar to the initial stage of self-directed groupwork, facilitators guide the process of setting group goals, establishing group values, and developing group guidelines. To build on strengths and start to identify possible group roles, facilitators might do an exercise in individual asset mapping. They are encouraging group and ownership cohesion by asking: *What do you bring to the group and what might your role be?* Consistent with the stages of self-directed groupwork, these activities all help establish ownership, identify the values that will guide the work, promote communication, as well as, align with the positive side of the youth's ambivalence. The work, in this stage, is geared towards building relationships, and developing trust. Facilitators recognize that individuals need to feel comfortable and see a role for themselves before they can act as a group (van Linden & Fertman, 1998).

The next stage is characterized by *power and control issues*. Actions reflect the theme: *Whose group is this?* Facilitators avoid power struggles. They introduce icebreakers in which youth may be asked to identify their own strengths and assets, and the things about themselves they are proud of, as they start to share more and identify what they might contribute. The youth determine the group's goals and codes of conduct, and firmly establish that it is their group. To recognize their expertise the youth are asked to identify issues that are of concern to them. They might give the group a name to further promote ownership (Fleming 2004).

Moving to the third stage, the group achieves a level of *intimacy* that allows them to productively work together. In self-directed Groupwork, this is referred to as, *the group takes action*. Rules are applied, trust continues to build, working relations are in place, and the group functions somewhat like a family. As roles and tasks are clarified the group enters the fourth stage, where *differentiation* takes place and members build on their own strengths and leadership skills. The group moves closer to its goals. Each member takes on a role that contributes in some way.

The last stage, is *separation/termination*. This stage can be particularly difficult for the university students, or facilitators, who might want to deny that the group and their relationship with the youth is ending. To provide closure and reinforce the accomplishments, facilitators review what was achieved and highlight strengths. End of group celebrations can support a positive termination. If successful, this last stage will correspond with the self-directed groupwork stage *the group takes charge,* and the youth will take ownership and continue.

Group roles and dynamics:

At each stage group cohesion propels the group forward, on task, with all members in some way participating. Members need to feel the group satisfies their needs (Toseland, Jones & Gellis, 2004). Social cohesion, a core ingredient in maintaining effective groups, is strengthened by paying attention to expressive and instrumental roles for each participant of the group (Toseland, Jones, & Gellis, 2004). Expressive roles meet the members' socio-emotional needs. They may connect to socialization, affiliation, or recognition, and include roles that allow for humor, caring, connectedness, integration, conflict resolution, empathy, participation, and ownership. They reflect the needs, as well, as the strengths of the members. Instrumental roles are those necessary to complete the tasks, and reach the group goals. They include focusing, keeping track of time, planning, summarizing, explaining, teaching, researching, and in some cases writing, editing, presenting and fundraising. Skilful facilitators identify strengths and reinforce the roles that are emerging. Members who perform positive group roles feel greater ownership of the group.

The case study and service-learning

In this example, the work took place in a public middle school located in a low income, high crime section of a large Northeastern city, with a sizable African American and immigrant population mostly from the Dominican Republic, Haiti, Cape Verde, and Somalia. Plagued by political, social, and economic obstacles, the school is remarkable for its positive spirit. Only eight years old, it is beautifully constructed and well maintained. Because it has a large enrolment, the school is divided into four identical academies, each led by its own staff and head master. Since it is located in between rival gang territories, the youth are required to wear uniforms to ensure their safety walking to and from school. Precautions are in place to make sure the youth do not wear colors identified with a specific gang. It is not unusual to hear gunshots while waiting for the bus at the end of the day, or for the school to go into lockdown after a shooting where the perpetrator is still at large. Yet the school is much better described by its welcoming atmosphere, community involvement, and commitment to positive youth and community development. Named after a local female activist who organized the community to effectively transform land that housed a dump into a much needed middle school, the school still reflects the commitment to the community. At any given time there are community groups meeting on school grounds and visitors are always welcome.

The youth who volunteered for the project ranged in age from 11-14 and were in grades six and seven. Those who volunteered were all participants in an afterschool enrichment program for students who had been identified as needing additional social, emotional and/or cognitive support. As participants in the program they were able to select one of five groups for their after school activity in addition to mandatory homework groups. Members of the University service-learning class recruited the youth first by handing out flyers and talking to the middle schoolers during their lunch hour, and then by presenting information on the group at an after school meeting where the youth made their final choice for afterschool program activities. The youth who took part reflected the diversity of the school's ethnic composition however the majority were males. Each semester only one female student was engaged. Consistent with the tenets of Self-directed Groupwork (Mullender & Ward, 1991) the membership was voluntary and open. Participation varied from week to week, and across the semesters, but five core members were consistent in their attendance and participation. Because the group had open membership the group dynamics required attention to ensure group cohesion and continuity. Over the course of a year, we met once a week for an hour in the library of the school. Each week anywhere from four to ten youth participated, with the core group of five regulars.

Building on the theoretical foundations of social action and Self-directed Groupwork along with social groupwork concepts, five ethnically diverse university students, ages 19-55, enrolled in a service-learning class and facilitated the group. While they all attended each group session, along with the professor, each week one student was the primary facilitator, with others leading the ice breaker, group reflections, and assisting in the process. Understanding the issues regarding affiliation in the beginning stages of a group, the student facilitators established a tradition of beginning each meeting with an icebreaker that was short, encouraged movement as the youth had been in class all day, allowed for transitioning from class to group, and always made everyone laugh. They selected this taking into account ambivalence as new members approached a group. They wanted the group to be fun, engaging, and to appeal to the positive side of any ambivalence the youth might have had.

The university facilitators knew they needed to meet the expressive needs of the group for fun. One such activity is called, *pass the power*, everyone stood in a circle, one person began by passing a *Clap* to the person next to them who had to catch it as they passed it on to the person next to them, catching it and clapping at the same time as the person who passed it. The activity had variants such as speeding up, and changing directions, but it was fun and became part of the group culture.

The first few meetings were spent identifying instrumental and expressive roles and tasks, establishing values, goals, and working relationships expected in the *group takes off* stage, along with sharing interests, culture, and concerns about the community. The university students had already established their values in class activities before meeting with the youth in the *pre-planning stage*.

During the third session, in a discussion about community and school assets, the youth mentioned how hurt they were when during the previous year someone who shadowed their principal for a day, as part of a city initiative, wrote what they felt was a disparaging article about their school and, by implication, about them – the middle school students. The university students located the article and brought it to the next meeting where we all read it out loud, giving each member a chance to participate, and the youth elaborated upon their concerns. They were pleased and surprised when the university students suggested that they might write a response to the letter and try to get it published. Now in the power and control stage the university students wanted to ensure that the youth knew they had the power to direct the action of the group. The youth needed to know that they were in control of the agenda. The letter that emerged built on their skills, accentuated their strengths, and brought out their unique contributions. This activity contributed to the group cohesion and as a consequence they felt empowered and expressed it. A copy of the letter was given to their principal, and sent to the newspaper which published it.

In the next few meetings the youth discussed problems in their community, made posters of the movie that would document it, and analyzed some of the issues. They focused on violence and impressed us all with their skill in analyzing the causes. They created webs uncovering root causes and connections between political, social and economic factors that contribute to violence. Indeed they were demonstrating higher order skills in critical thinking and analysis. They worked well as a group in the intimacy stage learning about each other and sharing the work. The group made decisions by a majority vote, following group discussions.

As the first semester ended they selected the topic of violence as their action project for the next semester, and started to think about what research they would carry out to help them decide on an action. But as the second semester began the youth were clearly stuck. They felt overwhelmed by the task, and the issue, and always diverted the discussion to issues about their day, their feelings about teachers who disrespected them, and the powerlessness they felt as students, even in a caring school. They had identified the *what* and the *why,* and were feeling comfortable with each other in the intimacy stage, but the group did not feel able to able to *take action.* It was at this point that the university students were reading about *adultism*, the abuse of power by adults (Bell, 1995). They mentioned to the youth that their experiences with their teachers might just be a manifestation of that public issue. The youth were elated as they embraced the concept and asked to read the article.

From there we moved to *the group takes action*, and were firmly enmeshed in the *differentiation stage* as well. It had become clear to the group members that this was not their individual problem, but an issue of abuse of power by adults. They applied the personal to the political as they clarified what they experienced by creating collages from magazine pictures. Individual talents and skills emerged as the youth embraced their roles in the group. Artistic and humorist roles came to the forefront in beautifully crafted and quite humorous collages that showed exactly how they experienced *adultism* in school. As they started to see how oppression is internalized and manifested in their daily lives, the way they related to each other changed. We observed examples of how empathy deepened as they became more collaborative.

For the next two months the group worked at a rapid pace designing a survey to enable them to find out if this was an issue for other students, as well as to get others on board in the action. They learned about creating surveys as they clarified the purpose, and designed criteria for questions to ensure they collected needed information. One youth who had been quiet in discussions until that point, emerged as a powerful force in thinking about and expressing the issues, once he sat down at the computer and started a draft of the survey. Sitting in the group he was quiet, but once he put his hands on the keyboard a leader appeared. All were quick to notice this and commented on it. From then on his strengths and skills were supported as he led the group forward.   Another youth who was on the verge of failing, and who was regularly kicked out of class for being disruptive, showed himself to be a master editor helping the group to clarify the questions, avoid redundancy, and arrange the statements in a meaningful order in the survey. The afterschool program director who showed up at one meeting said his teachers would never believe that he had the skills and knowledge that he was exhibiting. A member who wanted to be a psychologist was supported when he showed his understanding of others. Each participant was encouraged to develop the roles that matched their personality and skills. These youth who, in the classroom, were not generally recognized as contributing anything but trouble, thrived as their contributions were recognized and supported.

Once the survey was completed the group continued to take action as they approached the principal and presented the survey, along with the request that they be allowed to distribute it in every homeroom in the school. It was a tense few moments as they made their presentation about *adultism* to this no nonsense principal to whom none of them had ever spoken before this time. Their presentation was flawless, and the impressed principal not only agreed to let them disseminate the survey, but requested that they present their findings, along with recommendations, at a teacher development meeting.

Survey administration met some resistance from academy heads who had reasons not to allow it to be distributed on time. With the help of the afterschool program director, the youth did manage to distribute nearly a hundred surveys, which they analyzed, and presented in a PowerPoint at a city-wide afterschool program event attended by members of the City Council, the School Committee, and the Superintendent's Office. As part of their display they explained what they did, why they did it, and what they found to elected officials and others who had authority over the schools.

The youth, some of whom, had never been in this part of the city before, showed efficacy and confidence as they explained their work which included in the recommendations a pledge from teachers committing to address their own *adultism*. As we approached the semester's end we all felt that the *group had taken off*. This was not a negative experience for anyone involved because the university students consciously worked to integrate what they were learning about termination. The youth reflected on all the learning that had taken place, the knowledge they had created, and commented how it was so different from being in a class. The university students were moved and impressed by the accomplishments of the youth and the power of the social action and self-directed groupwork process. They embraced the concepts of group development and roles. Their reflections underscored how difficult it was initially to let go, allow the youth to take charge, and set the agenda. This experience had changed the way they viewed youth and youth work practice.

Discussion

Social action, and other activist approaches to social change, combined with mindful groupwork facilitation, can impact both individual and community development. Youth who are not necessarily strong in traditional classroom settings can shine when given the opportunity to participate in experiential learning projects such as those building on social action, PAR, and self-directed groupwork. For many this can provide a new way to approach learning. Experiential learning occurs when actions are reflected upon and the lessons learned can be applied to other situations. It makes the learner an active participant in his/her own learning (van Linden & Fertman, 1998). The experiential learning cycle reflects the similar components presented in self-directed groupwork referred to as the *Information-Action-Reflection cycle*.

In these settings youth can build much needed twenty-first century skills working in teams, honing critical thinking, building communication skills, learning to access information, and developing technological prowess. Encouraged by knowledgeable facilitators, they learn how to research, and become co-creators of knowledge as they develop social interactions and civic engagement competencies. This provides a strong alternative, or complement, to the classroom which does not always accommodate a range of learning styles.

Within the traditional classroom, teachers schooled in these methods and techniques can find they are having success with students they had previously thought were hard to engage. By acknowledging the techniques embedded in activist youth work and groupwork methods, teachers and other adults working with youth can find more opportunities and approaches that develop individual growth and civic engagement. Social interactions change. Viewing the class as a group, and applying knowledge of developmental stages, and roles may enhance its functioning. Youth who are turned off learning and alienated from the community can find a place to reengage. Young people who are active in civic engagement projects can learn about themselves and groups while making a difference in their communities. For all participants, knowledge of working with groups will enhance individual competence and later civic engagement work as well.

Conclusion

Acknowledging the significance of groupwork theory and practice skills in working with youth on social change projects adds a missing component in the growing body of literature on activism and engagement with youth. For over twenty years the Centre for Social Action has acknowledged the role groupwork plays in social justice work with youth. The model of self-directed groupwork, which accompanies social action, is unique in responding to the need for a model of group stages that applies to the social change process. Because young people spend so much time in groups it behoves those working with them to understand the dynamic nature of these contexts.

In addition to Self-directed groupwork, applying an understanding of social groupwork's developmental stages and group roles can add value to the impact and effectiveness of the group. When the university service-learning classroom is also seen as a group, these same theories can be applied to promote connected-learning. The social change process which depends on the group cannot help but improve. While the theories underlying this work were carried out in the community with youth, the university students were simultaneously learning about themselves, power, and social change.

Acknowledgement

The author wishes to thank the youth and the staff of the middle school, as well as, those at and the University of Massachusetts students without whose commitment, talent and skill this project never would have succeeded.

References

Arches, J. and Aponte-Pares, P. (2005) Challenges and dilemmas in university-community partnerships. *Humanity & Society,* 29, 3/4, 205-227

Arches, J. and Fleming, J. (2007) Building our own monument. *Practice,* 19, 1, 33-45

Barbera, R. (2008) Relationship and the research process: Participatory action research and social work. *Journal of Progressive Human Services,* 19, 2, 140-159

Bell, J. (1995) *Adultism.* Retrieved February 1, 2011, www.freechild.org

Berdan, K., Boulton, I., Eidman-Aadahl, E., Fleming, J., Gardner, L., Rogers, I., and Solomon, A. (Eds) (2006) *Writing for a Change: Boosting literacy and learning through social action* California: Jossey Bass

Berman-Rossi, T. (2002) My love affair with stages of groupwork. *Social Work with Groups,* 25, 1/2, 151-158

Breton, M. (1995) The potential for social action in groups. *Social Work with Groups,* 18, 2/3, 5-18

Castelloe, P. and Watson, T. (1999) Participatory education as a community practice method: A case example from a comprehensive head start program. *Journal* of *Community* P*ractice,* 6, 1, 71-89

Cohen, M. and Mullender, A. (1999) The personal is political, *Social Work with Groups,* 22, 1, 13-21

Dominelli, L. and McCleod, E. (1989) *Feminist Social Work.* London: Macmillan

Evans, M. (Ed.) (1994) *The Woman Question.* London: Sage

Finn, J., Jacobson, M. and Campana, J.D. (2004). Participatory research, popular education, popular theatre. in C. Garvin, L. Guttierez, and M. Galinsky (Eds.) *Handbook of Social Work with Groups.* New York: Guilford (pp.326-343).

Fleming J (2004) The beginnings of a social action group. *Groupwork,* 14, 2, 24-42

Fleming, J. and Ward, D. (1999) Research as empowerment: The social action approach. in W. Shera and L. Wells (Eds) *Empowerment Practice in Social Work.* Toronto: Canadian Scholars' Press (pp. 371-389)

Freire, P. (1970) *Pedagogy of the Oppressed.* New York: Seabury

Garland, J. Jones, H. and Kolodny, R. (1973) A model for stages of development in social group work. in S. Bernstein (Ed) *Explorations in Group Work*. Boston: Milford House (pp. 1-71)

Garvin, C., Guttierez, L. and Galinsky, M. (Eds.) (2004) *Handbook of Social Work with Groups*. New York: Guilford

Getzel, G. (2003) Groupwork and social justice: rhetoric or action. *Social Work with Groups,* 53, 12, 53-64

Ginwright, S. and Cammarota, J. (2002) New terrain in youth development: The promise of a social justice approach. *Social Justice,* 29, 4, 82-97

Ginwright, S., Noguera, P., and Cammarrota, J. (2006) *Beyond Resistance*. New York: Routledge

Harrison, M. and Ward, D. (1999) Values as context: Groupwork and social action. *Groupwork,* 11, 3, 88-103

Kilroy, S., Dean, R., Riepe, A., and Ross, L. (2007) Youth voice in urban high school transformation: 'We're talking is anyone listening?' *Children, Youth, and Environments,* 17, 2, 389-408

Lewis-Charp, H., Cao Yu, H. and Soukamneuth, S. (2006) Civic activist approaches for youth in social justice. in S. Ginwright, P. Noguera, and J. Cammarota, (Eds.) *Beyond Resistance*. New York: Routledge (pp. 21-36)

London, J. (2007) Power and pitfalls of youth participation in community action research. *Children, Youth, and Environments.* 17, 2, 406-432

Matthies, A., Jarvela, M., and Ward, D. (Eds.) (2000) *From Social Exclusion to Participation*. Jyvaskyla, Finland: Jyvaskyla University Printing House

Mills, C.W. (1970) *The Sociological Imagination*. Harmondworth: Penquin

Modell, E. (2006) Youth-initiated research as a tool for advocacy and change in urban school. in Ginwright, S., Noguera, P., and Cammarrota, J. (Eds.) *Beyond Resistance*. New York: Routledge (pp. 111-128)

Montrodros, J. and Berman-Rossi, T. (1991) The relevance of stages of group development theory to community organization practice. in A. Vinik, and M. Levin, (Eds.) *Social Action in Group Work*. Binghampton, New York: Haworth (pp.203-222)

Mullender, A. and Ward, D. (1991) *Self-Directed Groupwork*. London: Whiting & Birch

O'Donoghue, J. (2006) Taking their own power: Urban youth,

community based youth organizations. in S. Ginwright, P. Noguera, and J. Cammarota, (Eds.) *Beyond Resistance*. New York: Routledge (pp.229-246)

Oliver, M. (1992) Changing the social relations of research production. *Disability, Handicap and Society*, 7, 2, 101-114

Pearrow, M. (2008) A critical examination of an urban-based youth empowerment strategy: The teen empowerment program. *Journal of Community Practice*, 16, 14, 509-527

Rodriquez, L. and Brown, T. (2009) From voice to agency: guiding principles for participatory action research with youth. *New Directions for Youth Development*, Fall, 123, 19-35

Shultz, I. and Lantz, P. (2004) Assessing and strengthening characteristics of effective groups in community-based participatory research partnerships. in C. Garvin, L. Guttierez, and M. Galinsky, (Eds.) *Handbook of Social Work with Groups*. New York: Guilford (pp. 332-349)

Strobel, K., Osberg, J. and McLaughlin, M. (2006) Participation in social change: Shifting adolescents' developmental pathways. in S. Ginwright, P. Noguera, and J. Cammarota (Eds) *Beyond Resistance*. New York: Routledge (pp. 197-214)

Toseland, R., Jones, L., and Gellis, Z. (2004) Group dynamics. in C. Garvin, L. Guttierez, and M. Galinsky, (Eds.) *Handbook of Social Work With Groups*. New York: Guilford (pp.13-30)

Van Linden, J. and Fertman, C. (1998) *Youth Leadership*. San Francisco: Jossey-Bass

Williamson, H. (1995) *Social Action for Young People*. Dorset: Russell House

Watts, R. and Guessous, O. (2006) Socio-political development: The missing link in research and policy on adolescence. in S. Ginwright, P. Noguera, and J. Cammarota (Eds.) *Beyond Resistance*. New York: Routledge (pp. 59-80)

This chapter was first published in 2012 in *Groupwork* Vol. 22(1), pp.59-77

At the time of writing, Joan Arches was Professor, College of Public Community Service, University of Massachusetts, Boston

Social action and self-directed groupwork:

Section 5
Principles into practice:
Research

Postscript
Social action research:
A methodology for addressing 'how it is'

Dave Ward

The conference at which this paper was presented was hosted by the Centre for Social Action. Like these researchers, the Centre is committed to an approach, be it in practice, training or research, which starts from the issues, ideas and understandings of service users, rather than from a professional's definition of their needs. For the Centre, a key consequence is the responsibility of practitioners and researchers to set in motion a process of participation whereby people come to identify and define their own needs, and work on common issues and concerns that can then become agendas and goals for change. This means that, although special skills and knowledge will be employed, these do not accord privilege and are not solely the province of researchers and practitioners. In effect, methods that are used should reflect non-elitist principles (Mullender and Ward, 1991, Chapter 2) and should empower users to come to make decisions for themselves, and to control outcomes.

These assertions will be readily recognised both by researchers with a qualitative orientation, particularly where contextualised within 'passionate scholarship' (Du Bois, 1983) values, and by workers in a range of settings (community, social and youth work, health, housing, planning and adult education, for example) who have a 'development' orientation. However, in Social Action Research we have developed an approach in which such user participation is the core dynamic in a convergence of research and development work.

Good community development and social work practice involves assessment; qualitative research, if given a participatory and anti-oppressive framework, gives great attention to the implications for social and personal change. Social Action Research combines these traditions. Social Action Research recognises the importance of a high level of inter-personal/groupwork/development skill for the researcher, but additionally it sets a thorough and defensible research methodology as an essential feature for the practice of development work.

The Social Action research method

Methodology

The theory and methods of the approach are grounded in a combination of practice and research approaches, which are explicitly concerned with empowerment through partnership with communities and service users. We draw from the practice of social education and community development work (Mullender and Ward, 1991) interpreted and complemented by feminist (Roberts, 1981), disability (Oliver, 1992; Zarb, 1992) and black (Ahmed, 1989) research insights and perspectives. Within this framework we have adopted and utilised the techniques of grounded theory (Strauss and Corbin, 1990), 'new paradigm' research (Reason, 1990) and qualitative data analysis (Miles and Huberman, 1994), to develop an ethnographic research approach (Everitt et.al., 1992) which emphasises collaboration, participation and mutual respect. Our focus is on analysing what is happening on the basis of people's felt experience and, from this, to contribute to developing measures which can explicitly empower those involved at a local level to shape their environment and bring about improvements in their material conditions.

As far as is feasible, we work together with all the parties involved at all levels, at all stages of a research project. They participate in the refinement of the objectives, in the formulation of the questions to be addressed and the methods of information collection, and, in due course, in the interpretation of the findings. This forms the basis of a collaborative research approach which draws out qualitative and quantitative data, using a range of data collection methods. Where appropriate, local people are involved, and are provided with training, as 'peer researchers'. They are able to elicit data and, in their own right, contribute perspectives out of reach of external information gatherers (Dyson, 1995; Dyson and Harrison, forthcoming).

The value of the whole method lies particularly in the depth and richness of the qualitative data gathered, providing vivid descriptions and clear insights into problems and opportunities. By using such a collaborative format and a combination of methods, a range of perspectives are brought to bear on data and meanings attributed to them, to achieve both sensitivity to participants and, through triangulation, research validity (Patton, 1990). Working in this way has made us well aware of the ethical dimensions of research. We take very seriously concepts of confidentiality, informed consent and open and honest communication with all participants and consider that the Social Action research approach is particularly valuable in that it provides a means of directly addressing ethical issues with participants (Fleming and Ward, 1996).

Social Action research builds on the expectations, understanding and experience of all participants to offer concepts which they can engage with and apply to their own circumstances. Findings are disseminated and shared with people in terms they can understand and use. Benefits lie in securing widespread ownership of findings and in achieving support for implementation of conclusions. We have found that the process also engenders knowledge, skills and structures which can be sustained after research involvement is over. What takes place is a seamless interaction and progression of research and development work.

Process

Social Action research usually falls into nine main phases. These are not separate and discrete; there will be some overlap between stages:

1.   Orientation (including Literature Review)
2.   Setting up of a research steering group
3.   Defining the parameters of the research
4.   Gathering and analysing the data
5.   Presentation and discussion of interim findings

6. Further information collection
7. Analysing the information collected
8. Preparation and presentation of final report
9. Wide dissemination of the findings

Orientation

This is a period for the researchers to meet and establish working links and systems of communication with the key relevant people in the subject area and to familiarise themselves with:

- the range and structure of the subject area;
- geography, demography and scope of the area/locality;
- all relevant written materials;
- other relevant research literature so that the study can draw on existing knowledge and experience.

Setting up a research steering group

A research project will usually be guided by a group of people with knowledge and expertise in the subject area with relevant experience in the field of Social Action research and with local knowledge. Its function is to be a forum to discuss issues arising from the research, in particular process and practice as well as method and findings. This ensures the quality and relevance of the research.

Defining the parameters of the research

Conventional research seems to be obsessed with defining 'research questions'. Social Action research works on the basis that research should not be detached from practical activities. Projects should learn from the information produced by the research as it emerges, and should incorporate it into the process. This means that people at all levels must have close links with the research and a commitment to take on the process and its results into their own activities. Thus, all parties are involved in discussions about what information should be collected, why and from whom, how it should be collected, and how it should be presented and used. What is important at this stage is not to specify a number of predetermined questions based on researchers' or funders' perspectives, but to ensure that the research methods deployed are sufficiently flexible and open for issues to be introduced by participants and to be added from emerging data.

The researchers spend time with participants to identify what the parameters of the research will be. They look at the multiplicity of interests and concerns and the consequent plurality of legitimate matters for attention (Powell and Goddard, 1996) and work with participants to establish which are the key areas, processes, practice and outcomes upon which the research will focus initially.

Gathering and analysing the data

Data collection methods are finally decided with participants and the steering group. We believe that users have much to contribute in deciding the most successful ways of collecting information.

A variety of information collection methods are available to achieve this. These include:

- **review of secondary sources** minutes of meetings, policy documents, correspondence, newspaper articles;
- **direct observation;**
- **guided conversations** with key individuals and groups;
- **maps and diagrams** e.g. resource and facility maps;
- **critical incident analysis** to look at how certain problems arise and are dealt with;
- **drama workshops;**
- **case studies** of organisations or individuals;
- **work diaries** of paid and unpaid workers and community members;
- **focus groups;**
- **SWOT analyses** (looking at the strengths, weaknesses, opportunities and threats in particular situations);
- **questionnaires** (ranking and scoring);
- **statistical data;**
(see also Mikkelsen, 1995, Chapter 3).

Where appropriate, information collection is undertaken by 'peer researchers' or by using translators. All instruments are pre-tested to ensure their clarity and relevance. Interviews and focus groups are taped with the permission of the participants.

A purposeful sampling strategy is used with contrast sampling to ensure diversity (Patton, 1990). This allows for the identification of common patterns or variations between groups. Efforts are made to reach the opinions of the 'unorganised', those who are not necessarily active in groups. We have found that the 'snowballing' sampling technique is an effective way of achieving this (Browne and Minichiello, 1994).

Data are analysed throughout the research period by a variety of means. Thematic coding of the qualitative information can be undertaken. Coding schemes are devised as the research develops with the collaboration of those involved in the projects. Codes can be derived from research questions or evolve in the early stages of the research, using the 'interoder comparison procedure' suggested by Miles and Huberman (1994) to ensure adequate reliability and validity. Emergent themes are discussed with the participants and in the steering group. By having a range of people and methods of looking at the same situation, it is possible to allow for some triangulation. Computer packages can assist in the analysis of quantitative and qualitative data (for example, QSR NUD-IST and SPSS).

Presentation of and interpretation of interim findings

The consultative nature of Social Action research may mean that it can take longer than other research approaches. However, because of the significance to participants of the research, there is an interim presentation of progress and findings part-way through by means of a short interim report of findings and interpretation seminar(s) for participants.

Further information collection

The research process continues after the interim report and seminars. It is adapted and adjusted to take into account the discussion of the interim report. Avenues identified in the interim interpretation are further investigated.

Analysing and interpreting all the information collected

The analysis of all the data collected is undertaken by the researchers within a framework agreed with the participants. It is intended that the interpretation of the information, after analysis, should involve as much participation as possible. This will take place through workshops, discussion groups and draft reports circulated for comment. These enable people to be involved in giving meanings to the information and discussing its implications for policy and practice.

Preparation and presentation of the final report of the research

In practice the findings of the research are fed back to the participants on an on-going basis. This allows it to have the greatest possible influence on the development of practice and policy. In addition, the research is likely to have several written outputs.

Dissemination of the results

We are absolutely committed to the research having as wide as possible an impact. We have a track record of sharing information and promoting learning through our publications, training courses and seminars.

By its collaborative nature, such a research process itself has an impact on individuals, groups and communities involved. Local residents, community organisations, partners in the voluntary, private and public sectors all have been involved in setting the issues for attention and in the evaluation of these. Our experience shows us that this is a learning, empowering and change process for all concerned.

This 'action-research' approach has been used in a wide range of research projects and evaluations in the UK, all of which have been focused towards identifying directions and processes for achieving change, on the basis of an analysis of existing circumstances.

They range through health needs and assessments sponsored by statutory organisations, to project and service evaluations and feasibility studies on behalf of user and community groups, national and local voluntary organisations and statutory bodies. They have invariably left in place action and development plans and frequently structures and access to resources for carrying these forward. Often, the Centre has been asked to continue involvement by providing consultancy and training for these next steps.

Projects have taken place in a diverse range of ethnic and cultural environments, for example, the Asian community of the City of Derby, the African Caribbean community of Nottingham, the Somali community in London. Outside the UK, the methodology has been successfully utilised in a Malaysian 'planned village' context, to evaluate structures and processes of community participation within national development programmes (Abu-Samah, forthcoming). The methodology has also been central to a training approach used extensively by the Centre for Social Action in Russia and Ukraine.

References

Abu-Samah, A. (forthcoming) 'A qualitative-ethnographic approach as an empowering research process', *Groupwork*

Ahmed, S. (1989) 'Research and the black experience' in Stein, M. (ed.), *Research in Practice: Proceedings of the Fourth Annual JUC/BASW Research Conference, Leeds University, September 1988.* Birmingham: British Association of Social Workers

Browne, J., & Minichiello, A. (1994) 'The condom: why more young people don't put it on', *Sociology of Health and Illness,* 16(2), pp.229-25

Du Bois, B. (1983) 'Passionate scholarship: notes on values, knowing and method in feminist social science' in Bowles, G., and Duelli Klein, R. (eds.) *Theories of Women's Studies.* London: Routledge and Kegan Paul

Dyson, S. (1995) 'Clients as researchers: issues in haemogrobinopathy awareness' *Social Action,* 2(4), pp.4-10

Dyson, S., and Harrison, M. (forthcoming) 'Black community members as researchers: working with community groups in the research process' *Groupwork*

Everitt, A., Hardiker, P., Littlewood, J., & Mullender, A. (1992) *Applied Research for Better Practice*. Basingstoke: Macmillan

Feurstein, M. (1986) *Partnership in Evaluation - Evaluating Development and Community Programmes with Participants*. London: Macmillan

Fleming, J., and Ward, D. (1996) 'The ethics of community health needs assessments: searching for a participant centred approach' in Parker, M. (ed.) *Ethics and Community*. Preston: Centre for Professional Ethics, University of Central Lancashire

Mikkelsen, B. (1995) *Methods for Development Work and Research: A Guide for Practitioners*. London: Sage

Miles, M., and Huberman, M. (1994) *Qualitative Data Analysis*. Second edition. London: Sage

Mullender, A., and Ward, D. (1991) *Self-Directed Groupwork: Users Take Action for Empowerment*. London: Whiting and Brich

Oliver, M. (1992) 'Changing the social relations of research production', *Disability, Handicap and Society,* 7(2), pp.101-114

Patton, M. (1990) *Qualitative Research Methods*. London: Sage

Powell, J., and Goddard, A. (1996) 'Cost and stakeholder views: a combined approach to evaluation services', *British Journal of Social Work,* 26, pp.93-108

Reason, P. (ed.) (1990) *Human Inquiry in Action: Developments in New Paradigm Research*. London: Sage

Roberts, H. (ed.) (1981) *Doing Feminist Research*. London: Routledge and Kegan Paul

Strauss, A., and Corbin, J. (1990) *The Basics of Qualitative Research*. London: Sage

Zarb, G. (1992) 'On the road to Damascus: first steps towards changing the relations of disability research production', *Disability, Handicap and Society,* 7(2), pp.125-138.

This chapter was first published in 1997 in *Social Action Journal* Vol. 3(2), pp.29-32

At the time of writing, Dave Ward was Professor of Social and Community Studies, De Montfort University, and Director of the Centre for Social Action

Black community members-as-researchers: Working with community groups in the research process

Simon Dyson and Mark Harrison

This paper will compare the experience of two sets of research projects involving members of black and minority ethnic communities in the role of researchers. The projects involved working with groups, firstly, in providing support and advice to groups as a whole; secondly, in approaching respondents as a group; thirdly, in the project's concern with communities of interest (communities potentially affected by sickle cell and thalassaemia in Leicester) as well as geographically defined communities (the refugee Somali community in Tower Hamlets). Learning points to emerge include the importance of research diaries and debriefing workshops in community research and the importance of including this reflexive data in reports; the importance of devolving organisational aspects of research to community members; the benefits of interested partisan community researchers contrasted to disinterested 'objective' professionals; the pros and cons of monetary reward for community researchers; the attention required to health and safety and quality of research materials in planning research; the importance of revealing the contextual production of all research reports to commissioners; the features mitigating in favour of successful collaboration between academics and community researchers; the nature of the required commitments to feedback; and the limits to further pressurising clients who live in challenging social circumstances.

Introduction

This chapter will consider the relevance of working with groups to the research process by comparing the experiences of two sets of research projects involving members of black and minority ethnic communities in the role of researchers. The projects involved working with groups in three senses. Firstly, the projects involved providing support and advice to groups as a whole. Secondly, the projects entailed an approach to respondents as a group. Thirdly, the projects were concerned with communities of interest (as well as geographically defined communities).

Following Mullender and Ward (1991), the authors take the view that working with groups in this way presupposes a certain value basis to research formulated around a set of six key principles, principles which inform the activities and research of the Centre for Social Action. These principles include:

1. Rejection of the notion that work by community members, because they are not professional researchers, is fatally flawed by lack of skills or lack of objectivity. On the contrary, it will be argued that there are weaknesses in professional data collectors which community researchers do not share, and conversely strengths the community researchers possess which are generally missing from professional data collectors.

2. As we shall see in relation to the organisational arrangements of the research, the right to define the nature of research intervention and to define what community educational issues should operate in tandem with data gathering are vital aspects of the research process.

3. The complexities of problems facing communities cannot be reduced to the identification of deficiencies located within individuals. The false complaint of professionals about non-response levels must be understood in relation to challenging economic, social and environmental conditions one of which is the research process itself to the extent that, as Hillier and Kelleher (1996) have recently acknowledged, communities are over-researched without concomitant benefits flowing from that research to those communities.

4. People may derive power from working in groups. Thus we will indicate that in this respect community researchers gained confidence by interviewing in pairs; provided mutual support through group meetings; and were able as groups to question and challenge the authors where they felt issues were being overlooked.

5. The use of research support workshops or debriefing interviews reflect the principles that any research skills of the authors should not confer a priori a privilege to determine validity of research findings. Community researchers can determine research outcomes.

6. Working with community researchers can help to challenge oppressions based on social differentiations. So, for example, we will look at the role of the community researchers in challenging age-based hierarchies and the stigma of disability in their communities.

We begin then with a brief description of the two projects concerned; identify the three levels of working with groups inherent in these projects; and look at the similarities and differences between the contexts of the projects. We then move to a more detailed consideration of the specific methodological, practical and political benefits we feel may derive from working with groups of community researchers. In conclusion we try to outline recommendations for research practice with groups based on the commonalities of issues we found across the different contexts of the projects concerned.

The projects

The first project involved two parallel surveys of community awareness of sickle cell anaemia and beta-thalassaemia in Leicester (Dyson and Goyder, 1994a, 1994b). These two inherited haemoglobin disorders particularly affect peoples of African-Caribbean and South Asian descent respectively, although both conditions are found to some extent in many other ethnic groups. The research interviews were conducted by members of the local self-help groups (The Organisation for Sickle Cell Anaemia Research and the Thalassaemia Society) and generated several potential learning points for future research involving community members in the research process.

These points were taken up in the second set of projects which related to work alongside the refugee Somali community in Tower Hamlets in East London. This community is thought to number around 30,000 people, principally displaced by the civil wars in Somalia, and mostly without asylum status. Building on contacts made in the course of a research project identifying housing needs of refugees (Harrison, 1993), the Centre for Social Action was commissioned by the Tower Hamlets Race Equality Council (THREC) to look at the take up of welfare services by the Somali community in the Bethnal Green City Challenge Area (Harrison et al., 1995), and is currently moving to work alongside SOYAAL a Somali self-help group. This THREC project tried to take up learning points from the haemoglobinopathy surveys in using members of the Somali community in the research. The collection of data was preceded by a workshop based around ten issues that had arisen in the Leicester surveys (Dyson, 1995).

Working with groups

These projects demonstrate the importance of working with groups at three distinct levels.

Firstly, the projects entailed an approach to respondents as groups by interviewers who themselves constituted groups both by self-definition and self-organisation and also by the working conceptualisations of the authors. Whether the groups are of African-Caribbean, South Asian or Somali descent, interviewers and respondents share in common experiences of racism, albeit that the extent and nature of both the experiences of racism and resistances to it may vary within and between different groups (Modood et al., 1994). Involving communities with interviews recognises both that people have skills and understanding which they can bring to bear on their own circumstances and permits at least the possibility that white workers may share their skills and not keep what Bourdieu characterises as cultural capital to themselves (Bourdieu and Passeron, 1977).

Secondly, the authors attempted to provide advice and support to the community interviewers as a group. This reflects the importance of not proceeding to the other extreme in turning projects over to black community members wholesale, leaving people unsupported in circumstances made challenging by economy, policy and environment. As such this research approach tries to avoid the problem of setting up black projects to fail. Following Sivanandan (1991), funding of disparate 'ethnic' projects may divert responsiveness away from black communities and towards the system of funding itself. Or, to develop Bourne (1980), funding black community projects may be a strategy of socially controlling previously autonomous initiatives. That control may be effected through monitoring requirements (e.g. in research terms, does data pass tests of validity and reliability?) which are to be questioned not because they are inappropriate (as Reed and Proctor, 1995, seem to imply) but because they are set against over-idealised versions of how they are applied elsewhere, for example in statutory contexts.

Thirdly, the projects were concerned with communities of interest (as well as geographically defined communities) or what has in credit union terms been defined as a 'common bond'. Specifically in connection with the processes of research, there are the issues of what may be termed research scepticism and research fatigue in the black communities. The former refers to the feeling that researchers take statistical and other information from communities or produce ethnic monitoring but those communities do not see the benefits of changes (see Booth, 1988; Ohri, 1988; Ahmad, 1993; Johnson, 1993; Hillier and Kelleher, 1996). The latter alludes to the degree of monitoring that can take place where marginal groups become the continued targets of researchers. Only by black and white workers successfully working together, it may be argued, can a situation be avoided whereby research participants are not themselves estranged from the research process (Oliver, 1992). Only by conducting research which effects change and provides community feedback can the conditions for changing the social relations of research production (Oliver, 1992) begin to be established.

Continuities and contrasts

Before turning to a critical examination of the application of these issues in the two settings, it seems appropriate to outline some immediate differences between the populations and contexts of the two series of projects. One overriding factor the African-Caribbean and Asian communities in Leicester and the Somali communities in Tower Hamlets share in common is the experience of racism. However, there are several factors which suggest that the Somali communities are even more disadvantaged.

On the one hand, the Somali community comprises primarily those with refugee status, notwithstanding the very long history of Somali seamen in Britain. This provides for even greater insecurities of residency than might otherwise be the case for Britain's black population. Secondly, whilst patterns of postwar migration have led to African-Caribbean and Asian populations having a younger age structure than the white population (Smaje, 1995) and whilst women and children were indeed separated in some cases for years from menfolk before being able to join them in Britain, the degree of distortion of these structures in the Somali community reflect much more recent migration and the violence of the civil war as the impetus behind the migration. It is for these reasons that it is particularly young men, ex-warriors in the civil war, who are over-represented as a proportion of the population. Thirdly, their high levels of unemployment, low levels of access to housing, welfare, health, educational and interpreting services are further compounded by the failure of statutory authorities to recognise them as a group with distinctive needs. In this respect basing service provision on the 1991 Census figures misrepresents them in several ways. Firstly, and most obviously, in many cases the migration simply post-dates 1991. Secondly, many would not have been eligible to complete the Census return, others may not have been accorded the appropriate opportunity to do so by interpreting services. Finally, they may have been subsumed in the generic Black (African) ethnic category.

On the other hand, notwithstanding the divergencies of structure and experience between Leicester and Tower Hamlets, one continuity is the importance of being sensitive to diversities within black and ethnic minority communities. The Leicester South Asian community mainly comprises Gujarati Hindus and Moslems, but Punjabi Sikhs, Moslems and Hindus are also represented as are smaller proportions of Pakistani, Bangladeshi and Chinese communities. The Leicester African-Caribbean communities represent many different Caribbean islands, especially a number of smaller islands such as Montserrat. The Somali refugee community is predominantly Moslem, but is based around one particularly important divide. The West London Somali community is mainly drawn from refugees from Somalia, a former colony of Italy. The Somali community in East London comprises refugees from Somaliland, that is Northern Somalia, with Britain in the role of former colonial power. This divide is one major basis for determining the opposing factions in the civil war and not surprisingly proved an important source of tension in the data collection.

Providing advice and support to people as a group

Critical commentary on validity and threats to validity

A vital aspect of the research process proved to be the ability of the community members to comment on their perceptions of the validity of data they are engaged in creating. They may be privy on the one hand to sensitivities of a shared experience of racism and of local community strategies for dealing with racism which may affect what people are prepared to say and to whom. Equally they may be attuned to internal divisions within a community which may appear to professional outsiders as an homogeneous grouping, divisions which may well influence what people say or claim at interview. For instance, in Leicester, especially in the thalassaemia research, interviewers provided insights to the effect that couples appeared to be hiding their knowledge of thalassaemia in front of the mother-in-law or the wife from the husband because of the perceived stigma an inherited condition might bring on the family.

In the Somalian study checks on validity also came from the workshop format for supervision where through open discussion the researchers debated responses and findings and consensus was achieved. The important distinction from the work of Roth (1966) is that the negotiated meaning of responses took place with community researchers. This meant they held the dual roles of data collector and data interpreter (not separate as in Roth's experiences) and the collector-coders were also people who could themselves have been respondents and not outsiders to the situation studied, again in contrast to Roth. Where there were still unresolved questions, these were checked out with other Somali community professionals who formed an informal support group to the study.

Personal rewards of research

Whilst it must surely be the aim of any collaboration with community members to secure professional rates of pay for comparable work where the worker so desires, there do seem to be important extra-monetary rewards which may motivate community researchers. From the Leicester experience these appear to include escape from social isolation; acquisition of new skills such as interviewing; self-clarification of views; increased confidence; and an opportunity to challenge community stigma. Payment may, in some instances, rob the activity of its symbolic meaning to the community, and this certainly echoes the concerns of Illich (1978) that professional work strips the community of its folk skills and lay strategies. Seeing the value of work only in monetary terms may indeed be the first step in crystallising a community activity into professional work.

In the Somali community older, higher status women respondents tended at first to undervalue the contribution of the young interviewers who were in their mid-twenties. However, the process of research eventually appeared to entail an enhancement of community status for these young interviewers. Because status in the Somali community is related to age as well as to tribe, the work of the young interviewers helped to break down these age-related status divisions within the community. As there was a general lack of understanding about the basics of the British welfare system, questions about the accessibility of that system were not meaningful to respondents. For instance where the elder concerned did not know about Britain's welfare services they sought to defer to the researchers to complete the questionnaire on their behalf. In situations such as these the questionnaire format was to some extent abandoned as the researchers took on an educational role in explaining to their community the meanings of service provision such as social services and education. On the other hand the Somali interviewers were paid at professional rates of pay (University Research Scales). In retrospect the research supervisor felt that it would have been more appropriate to set the level of payment at a lower level (as the researchers were neither qualified nor experienced in research) but to pay longer hours (which would more closely reflect the real amounts of time spent on the study). Lower levels of researcher pay would also leave more monies for research supervision to support the community interviewers.

Valuing community researchers

The Leicester projects underlined what should have been apparent, namely the importance of demonstrating to the community how their contributions are valued, not only by words but by the actions of the professional members of the research team. This means such things as having in place strategies for ensuring the personal safety of community researchers in terms of freedom from physical or sexual violence, or health and safety regulations covering unfamiliar buildings community members are asked to frequent. It also means that any tangibles of community researcher status (clipboards, pens, folders, notebooks, identity badges, typed guidelines) are of good quality, and do not convey the hidden message that cheap, second-hand, used or hand-written materials are 'good enough'. If training workshops are to be part of the process, then the basic minimum would seem to be to provide appropriate refreshments, and to dovetail the timing with the cycle of community religious or cultural commitments (e.g. collecting children from the mosque).

These lessons from the Leicester study were raised with the Somali interviewers. Issues of personal safety were raised in the preparatory workshop. The interviewers felt that the work did not expose them to dangers over and above the very real threats to well-being attendant upon being black in an area of London infamous for the level of racial attacks. Meanwhile the researchers were supplied with University business cards and official documentation to ensure their status as bona fide interviewers was not questioned. All supervisory meetings were scheduled around pre-existing commitments of the community members. A full range of equipment needed for the research was supplied including clipboards, tape recorders, maps, pads of paper etc...

Approaching respondents as a group

Delegation of organisation of work

Within the broad parameters of the research design and funding there exists the potential for delegating many organisational features to the community members. This may include factors such as relative workload and the particular division of labour to be employed. Thus in the Leicester studies it was found to be beneficial encourage this self-organisation as it permitted decisions such as whether male-male match-ups for interviews were more or less appropriate than female-male; to enable a married couple to interview jointly as a team when interviewing other married couples; and to decide whether, in cases where a community interviewer was well known to a potential respondent, it was more appropriate for the interview to be conducted by someone well-known, someone not immediately known, or to leave the decision to the respondent.

In the Somalian study the decisions about who should interview whom in the community were once more left to the community researchers. The assumption was made that they were the experts in knowing their own community, and the role of research supervisor was restricted to areas of research methods. Questions of gender, age and tribe were discussed with the supervisor acting as a sounding board. A great deal was learned about the community by this process and community cynicism (about whether the interviewers represented a particular local political faction) and suspicion (related to the civil war) seemed to be more significant than gender in gaining successful interviews. In fact the young female interviewer experienced some difficulties in obtaining interviews from older women (who enjoy higher status in the community) and eventually concentrated on interviewing men. The male interviewers interviewed women. Decisions about who would interview whom were again made on the basis of who knew whom.

Contrasting the 'hired hand' mentality

The use of community members as part of a research team lends itself to potential criticism by researchers (and indeed research funders) for 'when community groups generate their own research their methods are seen as idiosyncratic and often cause concern to the more experimentally inclined practitioner' (Daly and McDonald, 1992, p.4). In fact, as Roth (1966) has argued, using professional but disinterested interviewers as 'hired hand' researchers can bring with it quite systematic data collection avoidance and fabrication. This poor quality data can be seen to be the product of a hierarchical division of labour in which those responsible for collecting data have no vested interest in the procedures and research outcomes. As has been pointed out in the realm of official statistics, ostensibly neutral 'hired hands' do not have the motivation to identify implausible data to the research team, nor the initiative to get the issue resolved (Government Statisticians Collective, 1979). The Leicester experience suggested that community volunteer researchers have precisely that motivation. They returned to an address several times rather than give up; they traced people to new addresses where the original one listed was out of date; and they persevered in the face of full-time jobs, child-care commitments or both.

For the Somalian study to be successful it had to be carried out by an institution and Somali researchers who had credibility in the community. If this had not been achieved access and information would have been denied and we believe where access was gained the information gained would not have been accurate. The combination was critical in this instance. Without the outside institution, there is the strong possibility that the Somali community would have been concerned that a Somali only initiative represented a particular sectional interest group. Some local projects had, in the absence of proper statutory authority support, collapsed and monies been misappropriated. But an outside agency alone would have been viewed with the suspicion that information gathering was being employed as the substitute for services and for the provision of infrastructure and support to local projects. This is an important reminder that we need to move beyond sterile dichotomies of insider v. outsider or community v. institution.

Different truths

The expectation that respondents will speak freely and truthfully to members of their own ethnic group, but hide at least parts of those truths away from white researchers is at best a simplistic assumption (Rhodes, 1994). Relative success in securing agreement to be interviewed must be conceptually distinguished from the degree of commentary elicited concerning people's views of the research taking place, and from eliciting their views on a sensitive subject which is the substance of the interview. In Leicester, African-Caribbean interviewers appeared to enjoy good co-option rates, eliciting expressions of anger from the community about research which gave nothing back to the community, but equally to meet some resistance to an open discussion of the sensitive issue in question, namely sickle cell anaemia, a discussion the one African-Caribbean interviewer felt would have been more open with someone outside the community.

The Somali interviewers experienced difficulties in eliciting responses from some community members in a number of respects. These were a cynicism of the value of research born of the perception that there existed corruption within the community. This can be traced to the 'failed' initiatives where monies had gone missing following the collapse of a community project where neither the buildings nor skills development of workers had been adequately resourced. Having the University as an outside research institution provided the researchers with an identity distinct from any local vested interest group. This allowed them to proceed more openly than might have been possible than if a local agency or community organisation had been the employing body.

Working with communities of interest

Building trust over time

In Leicester two community conferences (Leicester OSCAR, 1988; Williams, 1990) are just part of the legacy of a ten-year collaboration between the community groups and the author. It is uncertain how successful any collaboration with community researchers can be as an initiative starting cold. Questions such as 'Can people trust you as a professional worker?' will only really be answered by actions over a considerable period of time. It may be judged on factors such as 'Will you attend community meetings in your own time? Will you become involved in self-help activities? Will you make professional resources such as photocopying available to communities?' It may also be judged by the success of smaller joint ventures and by your willingness to share professional expertise (e.g. to make and disseminate notes in plain language where professional information is only available in jargon). This does suggest that a major joint research venture would be difficult, if not impossible, as a first initiative.

A proven track record and credibility within the community were essential for the Tower Hamlets research. The Centre for Social Action had been working in the Somali community for three years and were originally invited in by a professional/voluntary body that enjoyed the respect of the local community. The results of this first piece of work had a high degree of community involvement and produced tangible results for the community. The housing feasibility study developed a range of housing for the Somali community and led to the appointment of a 0.5 Somali Housing Development Worker. These successes meant that the researchers identified with the research as did the wider community such that the interviewers were able to gain access to all sections of the Somali community.

Feedback

A major complaint raised with interviewers in the Leicester projects was of no feedback received or action taken on the basis of previous research which communities had responded to. Once more the basic minimum would seem to require a willingness to make results known in accessible formats (community newspapers, self-help newsletters, community centre conferences etc.), to discuss the meanings of results found with the communities themselves (which is in any case a well-established feature of qualitative social research - Miles and Huberman, 1994) and to conceive of research as concerned with engaging with change, a conception which, in contradiction to Reed and Proctor (1995), can and is the legitimate concern of those who work in academic institutions.

In Tower Hamlets consultation with key community members was carried out before, during and after the completion of the research. A follow-up workshop was held with community professionals and leaders to check out the findings and make additions and amendments as appropriate. A conference is being planned to feedback the results of the study to which the community and local agencies will be invited. Whilst the research process is seen by the community as being very successful the research will ultimately be judged on whether anything changes and whether additional resources and services are secured. Failure to deliver the recommendations will increase the community's disillusionment and make future research more difficult to carry out.

Reflexivity in research

Reflexivity draws on the notion that people's reactions to being researched and the experiences of the research process may tell us as much about the situation studied as the 'official' data. So, for example, the high level of inaccuracies and omissions in the officially recorded addresses for the black and ethnic minority populations are arguably a reflection of the level of priority accorded to those communities by statutory agencies. In order that this evidence not be lost, one recommendation is that the community interviewers be asked to keep research diaries of their experiences during the course of the project, and that these diaries be the subject of focused de-briefing interviews towards the conclusion of the research. This may have to be completed using cassette tapes where there is lack of self confidence in writing skills. However, the importance of writing out one's thoughts should not be underestimated as a mechanism for stimulating critical reflection on one's own point of view (Plummer, 1983) and thus reinforcing the insights offered by the process.

In the Tower Hamlets research the supervision was carried out through regular meetings which were run as workshops where the participants were encouraged to talk about their experiences and observations from the research. With the Somali refugee community there is little or no official data. This placed a heavy responsibility on the young community members who were recruited as researchers. The observations of the researchers provided as much information into the community as the 'official' answers.

Without community members as researchers subtle changes in circumstances would not have been picked up or understood. For example, at one point in the study the researchers reported that they were experiencing difficulties in obtaining interviews. The reason for this was a flare up in the civil war in Somalia. Without community members as researchers this subtlety would, we believe, not have been detected.

Clients under pressure

If the research enterprise is conceived of as making a contribution to the community whose members participate in the research process, then policing of timescales, completion rates and the like begin to seem Draconian if they are at the expense of personal illness, family and community commitments and work schedules of the community researchers. It seems that the supreme effort involved in fighting back needs protecting from a willingness to take on over ambitious demands, and this requires mutual clarification of anticipated commitments from the outset.

All the anticipated timetables and targets overran in the Tower Hamlets study. However, they were renegotiated by the Centre for Social Action with the commissioning organisation. The reasons for the delays were in the main outside of the control of the researchers. We saw it as our main job to take as much of the management pressure in order to free the workers to undertake their roles. All the commitments were met but in double the original timescale. This has provided valuable lessons for future projects of this nature to allow more time to complete the research tasks.

Conclusion

Notwithstanding the important differences in context that we have outlined many lessons about working with community members collectively in research seem to have been transferable between situations, and lead us to make the following conclusions:

1. The critical reflections of the community interviewers on the validity of the findings they themselves generate should be an integral part of the data presentation. At the same time it is incumbent on the research supervisors to ensure that, for example, these validity checks are not misinterpreted by commissioning bodies as evidence of poor quality data, but to draw attention to the equivalent missing (or even suppressed?) checks in other data that a commissioning body may be relying upon.

2. The pros and cons of monetary payments for community research work should be discussed with the community members at an early stage of planning. Where those members themselves feel that the team should be paid, and that payment is not compromising an important voluntary service ethos, then we feel that the following points be addressed. The rates of pay should be on professional scales, but at a point of such scales reflecting the level of research experience of the community members, and reflecting the real level of hours work involved, and with proper allowance made to adequately fund research support and supervision.

3. Particular attention be paid to health and personal safety issues at the planning stage, and that community members are given at least the protection of identification and official documentation to carry with them in their work. Even within restricted budgets we feel that an important informal message of valuing people is conveyed by the allocation of good quality research materials to community members.

4. Decisions about the division and organisation of labour and about who interviews whom should be devolved to the community themselves. This recognises that they are the experts in their own community dynamics. It avoids a rather programmatic imposition by the researchers about the

meanings of social differentiations such as age and gender to respondents and interviewers. And it allows judgements about the importance of personal networks in securing interviews and obtaining appropriate match-ups to be made on the ground.

5. It is important to assert that employing interviewers who might be regarded as partisan appears to strengthen rather than weaken the quality and completeness of the data collected. On the other hand it is equally vital that the attempt to flatten the hierarchy of research relationships does not leave the community members unsupported. In this respect we recommend that ongoing supportive workshops are arranged throughout the period of data collection and beyond, and that community leaders other than those directly engaged in the research should have an acknowledged role in providing a complementary sounding board to the one also offered by the research supervisors.

6. An awareness is required of the manner in which research evidence is an account produced in a particular context rather than regarding different contexts as more or less likely to provide a privileged access to an external truth. Again this places a responsibility on research supervisors to expose to commissioners of research the processes in the production of other research information upon which they may base planning judgements.

7. The possibility of developing collaborative work with community members depends on establishing a long-term relationship with community groups. Factors thought likely to help establish trust include demonstrating a commitment to work beyond professional boundaries; to work outside 9-5 hours; to contribute unpaid work of your own; to be accessible to researchers (e.g. giving home telephone numbers as contacts as in Oakley, 1992); to make offers to contribute your expertise (e.g. in Leicester this involved 'translating' a form rich in medical jargon into plain English for the self-help group); not to wait to be asked; and to maintain contact over a long time-scale.

8. There are additional concerns regarding the importance of

providing feedback to the community at large. This involves not only disseminating results widely in accessible formats (community conferences; newsletters etc.). It also means having regard to the possible consequences of revealing information about less powerful groups to powerful decision makers where this is not in the interest of the community themselves; providing opportunities to check the interpretation of results with community members before dissemination; and demonstrating a commitment to see action taken on the basis of the results.

9. The possibility of learning lessons through thinking reflexively about the research process was confirmed in both cases. Difficulties in accessing the respective populations highlighted, in Leicester, the lack of care in health service record keeping for black clients, as well as an unwillingness to trust information provided by the communities themselves, and in Tower Hamlets the invisibility of the Somali communities to welfare services in the absence of a commitment to seek more up-to-date information than the 1991 Census. We have therefore come to the conclusion that research diaries and debriefing workshops should be an integral part of any community research.

10. It is important not to replicate the failures of statutory funders of services in using small, inadequately-funded and supported projects as a means of buying off community discontents. In other words it is vital to have and to show an appreciation of the place of research in the lives of community researchers, to tailor the pacing of the research to their work, and to their family and community responsibilities. Ultimately this may mean, as in the Leicester project, putting desired developments on hold so as not to unduly pressurise those who already live in challenging circumstances.

Acknowledgements

The authors would like to thank the following community members whose hard work we hope we have properly documented here: Carol King, Winston Nurse, Erskine Cave, Theo Badu, Pauline Samuel, Monique Pinks, Nila Kataria, Viresh Kataria, Hanif Ebrahim, Soraya Ebrahim, Hina Patel, Jyoti Thakkar, Daxa Parmar, Mohammed Ismail, Rhodda Saeed, and Abdirashid Gulaid. We should also like to thank and acknowledge the participation of the community respondents in the various projects.

References

Ahmad, W.I.U. (1993) 'Making black people sick: 'race', ideology and health research' in Ahmad, W.I.U. (ed.) *'Race' and Health in Contemporary Britain*. Buckingham: Open University Press, pp.11-33.

Bhat, A., Carr-Hill, R. and Ohri, S. (eds.) (1988) *Britain's Black Population*. Second Edition. Aldershot: Gower.

Booth, H. (1988) 'Identifying ethnic origin: the past, present and future of official data production' in Bhat, A., Carr-Hill, R. and Ohri, S. (eds.) *Britain's Black Population*. Second Edition. Aldershot: Gower, pp.237-266.

Bourdieu, P. and Passeron, J.C. (1977) *Reproduction in Education, Society and Culture*. London: Sage.

Bourne, J. (1980) 'Cheerleaders and ombudsmen: a sociology of race relations in Britain', *Race and Class*, 21(4), pp.331-352.

Culley, L. (1996) 'A critique of multiculturalism in health care: the challenge for nurse education', *Journal of Advanced Nursing*, 23(3), pp.564-570.

Daly, J. and McDonald, I. (1992) 'Introduction: the problem as we saw it' in Daly, J., McDonald, I. and Willis, E. (eds.) *Researching Health Care: Designs, Dilemmas, Disciplines*. London: Routledge, pp.1-11.

Dyson, S. and Goyder, E. (1994a) *Sickle Cell Anaemia: Current Carrier and Community Awareness in Leicester*. DMU Haemoglobinopathy Series, No. 1. Leicester: De Montfort University.

Dyson, S. and Goyder, E. (1994b) *Beta-thalassaemia: Current Carrier and Community Awareness in Leicester*. DMU Haemoglobinopathy Series, No. 3. Leicester: De Montfort University.

Dyson, S. (1995) 'Clients-as-researchers: issues in haemoglobinopathy awareness', *Social Action*, 2(4), pp.4-10.

Government Statisticians Collective (1979) 'How official statistics are produced' in Irvine, J., Miles, I. and Evans, J. (eds.) *Demystifying Social Statistics.* London: Pluto Press, pp.130-151.

Harrison, M. (1993) *Housing Feasibility Study on Behalf of Praxis Housing Committee.* Leicester: Centre for Social Action.

Harrison, M., Boulton, I., Abdirashid Gulaid; Mohammed Ismail, and Rhodda Saeed (1995) *Research into the Needs of the Somali Community in the City Challenge Area of Tower Hamlets.* Leicester: Centre for Social Action.

Hillier, S. and Kelleher, D. (1996) 'Considering culture, ethnicity and the politics of health' in Kelleher, D. and Hillier, S. (eds.) *Researching Cultural Differences in Health.* London: Routledge.

Illich, I. (1978) Disabling Professions. London: Marion Boyars.

Irvine, J., Miles, I. and Evans, J. (eds.) (1979) *Demystifying Social Statistics.* London: Pluto Press.

Johnson, M. (1993) 'Equal opportunities in service delivery: responses to a changing population?' in Ahmad, W. (ed.) *'Race' and Health in Contemporary Britain.* Buckingham: Open University Press.

Leicester OSCAR and Leicester Thalassaemia Society and Leicestershire Health Promotion Department (1988) *The First Community Conference on Sickle Cell and Thalassaemia.* Leicester: Leicestershire Health Promotion Department.

Miles, M. and Huberman, A. (1994) *Qualitative Data Analysis.* Second Edition. London: Sage.

Mullender, A. and Ward, D. (1991) *Self-Directed Groupwork: Users Take Action for Empowerment.* London: Whiting and Birch.

Modood, T., Beishon, S. and Virdee, S. (1994) *Changing Ethnic Identities.* London: Policy Studies Institute.

Oakley, A. (1992) *Social Support and Motherhood.* Oxford: Blackwell.

Ohri, S. (1988) 'The politics of racism, statistics and equal opportunity: towards a black perspective' in Bhat, A., Carr-Hill, R. and Ohri, S. (eds.) *Britain's Black Population.* Second Edition. Aldershot: Gower, pp.9-28.

Oliver, M. (1992) 'Changing the social relations of research production', *Disability, Handicap and Society,* 7(2), pp.101-114.

Plummer, K. (1983) *Documents of Life.* London: Unwin Hyman.

Reed, J. and Proctor, S. (eds.) (1995) *Practitioner Research in Health Care.* London: Chapman and Hall.

Rhodes, P.J. (1994) 'Race-of-interviewer effects: a brief comment', *Sociology*, 28(2), pp.547-558.

Roth, J. (1966) 'Hired hand research', *American Sociologist*, 1, pp.190-196.

Sivanandan, A. (1991) 'Black struggles against racism' in Central Council for Education and Training in Social Work (ed.) *Anti-Racist Social Work Education: Setting the Context for Change*. London: CCETSW.

Smaje, C. (1995) Health, *'Race' and Ethnicity: Making Sense of the Evidence*. London: King's Fund.

Williams, J. (1990) *'The Second Leicestershire Conference on sickle cell and thalassaemia'*, MIDIRS Midwifery Database Information, Pack 15, December.

This chapter was first published in 1996 in *Groupwork* Vol. 9(2), pp.203-220

At the time of writing, Simon Dyson was Principal Lecturer, Department of Health and Continuing Professional Studies, and Mark Harrison, Director, Centre for Social Action, De Montfort University, Leicester.

Empowering research process: Using groups in research to empower the people

Asnarulkhadi Abu-Samah

This article discusses how a qualitative research approach is appropriate for research in a context where groups are a central focus. The approach, which is ideologically and philosophically based on the 'second tradition' that values people's interpretation of their social world uses an interactive technique of data collection involving in-depth interviews, follow-up interviews and group discussions. These techniques, administered in a dialogue fashion, generated information which showed that people are becoming empowered through experiencing the participation process within groups in their community. In addition, while sharing and feeding back information within the techniques used, people are learning and becoming empowered. As they became accustomed to this, they began to realise the significance of the research approach used.

Introduction:
Philosophy and ideology in social research

Obtaining and gaining data or information from the people studied is the basic aim of social research. To achieve this, social scientists/ researchers such as sociologists, anthropologists, community workers/developers or social workers use different methods of data collection to approach and to understand the subject matter studied. These can be classified broadly into two approaches, quantitative and qualitative. There are philosophical debates and competing views between these two approaches (Bryman, 1988) as to how the researcher should 'treat' social reality: the people to be studied who live in their own world. Social scientists who uphold the positivist viewpoint use approaches such as surveys or questionnaires as their data collection tools to capture and understand the subject matter under scrutiny. This 'positive' tradition believes that social realities and phenomena can be explained 'scientifically', based on the regularities from the data obtained. Most researchers who take this standpoint aim 'not to disturb the world they are studying: their aim, instead, is to trawl their data collecting net quietly through the social world' (Graham and Jones, 1992, p.239).

In contrast to the 'positive' tradition is the interpretive tradition in which an understanding of the social world and the subject matter studied is generated from the people. This second tradition is more concerned with understanding social reality and phenomena, and interprets them from the viewpoint of the people themselves (Denzin, 1970a, 1970b). These are basic principles held by phenomenologists and interactionists. The argument is that human beings are active participants who live in a changing environment. As they interact with the social world in their everyday lives they adapt and adjust to the situation. Thus, the people's active response to social reality possesses some meaning which cannot be interpreted by a snapshot survey. It is through the process of 'going native' with the people that the meaning behind their reactions and actions towards certain situations can be explained.

Working along the same principle, participationists move a step further. Researchers not only aim to understand what meaning and significance the social world has for the people, but also explore the social world, its 'properties' and nature. These are developed, generated and verified by and with the people themselves based on their 'grounded experiences' (Glaser and Strauss, 1967). Concurrently involving the respondents in the whole research process enables them to become active participants in defining and interpreting their actions, collectively and actively with the researcher, which can enhance their understanding about their own living environment. Thus, the notion of empowerment is embedded in this research approach. Further, by taking and shifting the paradigm of researching social realities from 'researcher-centred', where the research problems are predefined or 'controlled' by the researcher, to 'researched-centred', where research issues are being defined and scrutinised together with the people through dialogue, this enhances the values of consciousness raising and empowerment.

Based on this second tradition, this article shows how a research process, by involving the respondents from the initial stage, facilitates them in reflecting on and understanding their actions in community life. This writing is based on a case study of a Malay rural planned village settlement in Malaysia. The aim of the study was to understand the people's participation in community development and community work activities - establishing groups and organising community group-based activities. Each group had its own particular interests, ranging from taking care of community welfare, offering communal services, providing community and adult education, safeguarding vulnerable youths from drug problems, and securing and controlling rights of land possession.

Groups as a central part in the research process

First and foremost, in carrying out social research one has to remember that we, the researchers, are dealing with human beings, individually or collectively in their own living environment. One common feature of people's behaviour is that they live and interact within a group. Groups can take various forms and size; the simplest and smallest may be self-help groups or neighbourhood groups, while the biggest and more complex ones may take the form of associations or one community. Regardless of the size and type of groups, individual life within the group is dynamic. The researcher needs to be sensitive to the context and life of the researched within the respective groups in the community. Therefore, in order to grasp a true picture of people's behaviour, action and endeavour, or in the case of this study people's participation in which individual's experience is the fundamental source of information, it is necessary to study them within the dynamic context of the group. This requires a sensitive and interactive methodological approach, which takes into consideration the group element as a central focus.

The qualitative-ethnographic approach

From this researcher's experience the ethnographic participative approach has particular value for research with and about groups. The interactive techniques of data collection, such as personal in-depth interviews and group discussions, provide a sensitive way of collecting data. The unrestricted and open-ended nature of data collection techniques which are based on guidelines consisting of loosely-formed questions, provide freedom for the respondents to express their views and experiences. The researcher who may follow-up with more probing questions, must listen and record carefully. The techniques have an empowering element, in that respondents have the opportunity to reflect on their past experiences of working as a group and of seeking to achieve group goals.

Qualitative-ethnographic research, which is often denoted as 'thick description' (Greetz, 1975) among anthropologists is holistic in nature and the time spent researching the subject matter is relatively long compared to the survey method. It provides opportunities for the researcher to examine other pertinent and emerging issues related to the subject studied throughout the study period, thus enriching the information collected.

Research as empowerment

The basic principle underlying my research is that the respondents were encouraged to be involved actively in the research process. It was through their direct involvement that the subject matter studied could be scrutinised in depth, based on people's first hand experiences. From the point view of basic research, people's experiences are significant in order to understand and explain in what ways and why they react to the environment. Empowering research moves a step further. Facilitated by the qualitative-ethnographic approach, the research method offers an interactive relationship between the researcher and the respondents, not only in terms of acquiring information but also in terms of its use, during and after enquiry sessions.

The interactive and responsive data collection techniques of in-depth interviews and group discussions were carried out in a dialogue style. The unrestricted, open-ended framework of loosely guidelined questions, encouraged the respondents to explore the subject matter collaboratively with the researcher in a 'non-monopolistic' manner (see Fals-Borda, 1991). These interactive techniques enabled the respondents to be directly involved in this research activity. In this interactive and participative process the relationship between researcher and respondents was not just a researcher-object or researcher-researched relationship, but more a researcher-subjects relationship. Treating people as subjects meant that they had the right to speak and to be heard and minimised manipulation.

In contrast to conventional research, where research questions are predetermined or derived from existing bodies of knowledge, in interactive research questions can be developed and refined throughout the research process. Through an induction and deduction process of acquiring the information from respondents individually and collectively, the subject matter can be understood clearly in the context of peoples' own experiences. By enabling them to explore their own world through dialogue, their involvement as active partners throughout the research is enhanced. This framework of investigation also creates a mutual consciousness between researcher and subjects, and, in this way, a more comprehensive understanding of the subject matter. This can subsequently act as a basis for further 'empowering' action by the subjects, having realised that they have the capability to define needs and problems, and to take action on them.

How these underlying principles have been employed to motivate and mobilise research subjects to engage themselves, and subsequently to benefit from their direct involvement in the research process is explored and discussed below.

'The welcoming tone'

Like any other ethnographic study, meeting the people, the study subjects, was crucial. The importance of their involvement in the research was not only in terms of their position as the source of information, but also in their willingness to participate in the research, and their expectations that the research would be productive for them. This positive attitude towards the research activity was observed clearly during the first meeting, before embarking on the actual data collection activity. In this meeting the issue of data collection techniques excited them. Realising that the method to be used in this study would be quite different from previous studies carried out and experienced by them, one of the respondents requested that the findings be shared with him later:

> It's good to have research like this. I think it is quite different from the previous one...and I would like to see the results from your research later...At least if you can spare me a synopsis or summary of the findings. So, I can know about my village, my people, what they want..., on what they disagree with me. Then I can react on it later, if possible. (Mr Wan)

On another occasion before engaging into a group discussion, one of the respondents from the youth club said:

> That day, you, brother (referring to the researcher), wanted to meet all my friends from Embun Hidayah (name of the youth club). Hah! Today I bring them all. At least they can share in our discussion today. Possible isn't it? You can hear and confirm from them what I narrated to you a few months ago... (Mr Sofi)

Using an interactive data collection technique created a situation which encouraged people's involvement in the research activity. Mobilising the people towards this activity was made possible because the stand taken by the researcher was that the people themselves are more knowledgable about the environment in which they live. This stand was reiterated by the researcher during the first meeting with respondents (group members from each of the community groups) in the village, as illustrated in the examples below:

> ...to learn from you all how you get engaged with the activity...and share some information that I don't have.

> I am eager to know about your experiences of how you became involved with and organised the activity, if you can share these with me...

These answers were given as a response to questions asked such as: 'Why do you want to know about our activities?' and 'What is so special about us here?'. Within this stimulating interaction with the people, facilitated by open-ended and unstructured interviews used in a dialogic fashion, much information about group activities and the members' involvement was gathered in this preliminary discourse. Respecting their position as subjects who possessed the real experience and knowledge about their community life, and demonstrating the researcher's readiness to learn from them, encouraged them to reveal information. It was also noted during this preliminary dialogue that the subjects, regardless of their gender (members from the men's groups or women's groups) were motivated to show and share how they became involved in organising group activities by inviting the researcher to attend their group meetings. This encouraging and stimulating atmosphere shown by the subjects gradually diminished the researcher's own worries and doubts about carrying out research in women's areas and groups, an issue that has been raised and debated by feminist researchers (Oakley, 1981; Ramazanoglu, 1992; Finch, 1993). The positive attitude and willingness to share experiences is evident from the illustration below:

Is it okay if I bring along my friends to our meeting today? Both are my neighbours. Yesterday I went to their house and simply invited them... Today they're willing to follow me, to hear about our meeting. They are our group members. Sometimes they join me in the activity. You can ask them questions too! (Mrs Fira)

In a similar vein, on another occasion before the group discussion started, one uninvited participant came and asked permission to participate:

Can I join the meeting, is it okay or not...? I want to know exactly what's going on. Three days ago you invited my friend but not me to the meeting today. I asked her what's going on. I'm not busy body...She said, if I would like to know, just follow her today, it is a discussion about our group activities. Can I join in? (Mrs Aminah)

In other words, it can be argued that it is the empowering framework of research adopted, allowing people to participate in the information gathering, which mobilised them to engage in the research process.

Choosing the sample

As more information was disclosed by the subjects about their group activities and members involvement, more preliminary data were captured, and this enabled me to develop a sampling strategy, in this case a snowball technique. In relation to studying people's participation in community work and community development activities, the issue of sampling is worth considering. Randomly choosing the community members to be included into the sampling frame or sampling list as advocated by the quantitative method may not reveal a true picture of people's participation. This is because by using such technique, the chances of including individuals who may not be involved in community group activities is great, and this certainly could distort understanding of the subject matter.

The close and interactive relationship with group members in the preliminary dialogue sessions helped to minimise and monitor these issues. Through group members' recommendations, names were gathered. These names were then accumulated and validated along the research process when each respondent was asked about other members' involvement and contribution in their group activity through probing questions incorporated into the interviews, together with the researcher's own observations from attending group meetings, some secondary documents obtained, and a recorded video tape lent by a group. Names that were mentioned at least twice by respondents were interviewed. There are two reasons or rationale for employing this interactive strategy. The first reason was, in relation to the phenomenological aspect of this ethnographic approach, that the understanding of the subject matter (in this case people's participation) should be grasped from the point view of the subjects. Therefore, to misjudge the sample could mislead the understanding of how respondents organised themselves to participate in community work activities. This further has some connection with a second reason, in that only individuals who had experienced the participation process could reflect on those experiences. In reflecting, they empowered themselves by realising that they had the capability to act and decide for themselves. More on this issue is discussed below.

In short, methodologically, the approach used created a situation that encouraged the subjects to participate directly in the research process, and simultaneously acted as a useful device to verify the information gathered through a process of deduction and induction incorporated within the interviewing process.

Induction and deduction process

The qualitative-ethnographic approach enables both induction and deduction to take place simultaneously in the research process. It is a cyclic process of verifying data gathered by checking and cross checking both with and between respondents. Starting from the first day of observation and interview, data were gathered and some ideas were conceptualised, deduced and adopted. As the interviews continued more ideas were developed and concepts generated. These, and other interrelated concepts, were clarified and verified by converting them into more questions, a process of analytical induction. All ideas and concepts deduced from the last interview were checked against another respondent in next session. Therefore, it was within and between the interview(s) that deduction and induction took place which verified ideas and concepts as data accumulated. These interrelated ideas and concepts then emerged as themes, which guided and focused the researcher's probing and prompting questions until they reached saturation and refinement.

The checking and cross-checking process in this study not only took place between respondents within a single method but also between methods. Through paying careful attention during the interviews, some important keywords, phases or clues were jotted down as theoretical memos, and personal observations and impressions were also recorded in field notes as part of the deductive procedure. The researcher also engaged in the deductive process by making notes while listening to what the respondents said in the interview tapes. Again, these data were checked against the deductive ideas from memos and personal impressions recorded from earlier notes. In these ways grounded concepts or categories and their relationships were generated. These interrelated concepts were again refined, compared and checked against the themes generated from transcribed interviews. Through deduction and induction (interchangeably at this stage), more concise concepts and themes grounded in the data were constructed. Both the concepts and themes were then brought back to share and debate with the respondents through the follow-up interviews and group discussions.

This process was possible because the qualitative-ethnographic approach allows the researcher to step backwards and forwards during the research process, internalising and testing data against other respondents or sources of evidence, either by questioning or observing, to set the meaning in context. In other words, the concepts developed during data collection are validated throughout the research process by triangulating (Denzin, 1970) within and between the methods, with the same respondent and between respondents, during the in-depth interviews and group discussions. By triangulating within and between different sources of evidence, data collected were enriched and thus able to overcome the limitations of using a single method. The multi-method approach also allowed for convergent lines of interrogation of different sources of evidence, thus, eliminating bias and promoting the validity of the data collected.

Reflecting and sharing information

The in-depth interview and group discussion were the techniques used to gather information from the respondents. Intensive focusing on research subjects in a dialogic style was the primary source of information in this study. A paramount issue in the process of obtaining information was the flexibility of the technique used. As a method of 'conversation with a purpose' (Kahn and Cannell, 1957:149), the techniques were based on the 'unstructured interview' (Burgess, 1982, pp.107-110; Burgess, 1984, pp.101-122; Patton, 1990, chap.7). Open-ended and unstructured in-depth interviews based on loosely guideline questions were easily adapted to particular settings and were applicable to respondents' experiences, which in turn helped to ease interaction during the interview sessions. This made the dialogue or conversation process more dynamic and lively, and enriched and encouraged respondents to talk and share more information about themselves, while at the same time their active involvement promoted the integrity of the understanding reached the people's participation through the respondents' active involvement. Thus, the technique used which centrally focuses on groups - so as to obtain members' grounded experiences - was also, in large part, a groupwork-based research approach.

A paraphrasing or recapitulating technique was used in the process of questioning. Probing questions rather than directing, encouraged respondents to share information. When answering questions, respondents made some reflections on their experiences and reasoned out actions taken. For example, in explaining the reason why he participated in a group activity (religious study circle), Mr. Azha said:

...I think my main reason for joining this study group is to gain new information, new knowledge...and also to help the study group members. I suppose my involvement is my social obligation to support them...and at the same time I gain some knowledge working together with them. (Mr Azha)

Mrs. Fira voiced the same concern, along similar themes in explaining the reason for her involvement as she said:

What would happen if you don't have knowledge on Islam...what would happen to us? This knowledge is very useful for our daily lives...I mean I can use it myself, I know what is wrong and what is right...how to deal with people, to respect people. That's why I always attend this class. (Mrs Fira)

On another occasion during the interview session, Mrs. Eton, who is one of the leaders of the Crockery Association, reflecting upon the problem that the women faced before the establishment of the group, explained:

Hah! at that time it was difficult to hold a 'kenduri' (feast). I still remember, Ali (not his real name) wanted to marry off his son. His wife just passed away a few months before the ceremony. He, like all the families here, are poor...

*owned only a few bits of crockery, pots and pans, not many...We decided that
each household should lend him five plates, bowls, cups and spoons for the
marriage feast...From this incident, we, Mrs. Yati, two other friends and I
then discussed and decided to set up this Crockery Association.* (Mrs Eton)

These are just few examples to illustrate that by giving people
a chance to share their experience in initiating and participating
in their group activity and by being ready to hear their ideas
the researcher was enabled to understand their reasons for their
involvement in those activities. Although it is beyond the scope of
this article to delineate each of the reasons given on each type of
community group or community activity initiated by the people,
the study showed that the people had much understanding about
their problems and the needs of their community, and as a result
of thinking about the problems they began to seek solutions. Thus,
the interaction between researcher and respondents in this dialogue
style of in-depth interview produced a 'joint construction of reality'
(Agar, 1980 c.f. Crabtree and Miller, 1992, p.76). The researcher's
and respondents' interactions fused the ideas into one perspective.
In responding to the questions, the respondents described the
process they had undergone, based on their experiences, and at the
same time the researcher tried to understand the meaning within
a context that would reflect what had been described.

Consciousness raising

Dialogue involves a two way process of interaction between the
person who intends to hear and encourages the other person
(people) to talk about their experiences, ideas, feelings, problems,
hopes, etc. in a non-authoritarian relationship. The process involves
understanding, clarifying, describing and explaining activities. As
such, it gives the freedom for people to express their reasoning,
expectations and perceptions as to how they perceive the world
they live in. It is about giving people the right 'to name the world'
(Freire, 1972), that is 'the right to name one's reality' (Breton, 1993)
and to define one's own issues (Mullender and Ward, 1991). All
these processes developed in the interviewing sessions within
which self-reflection and self-realisation took place simultaneously.

Both have a consciousness raising element in that by reflecting on the experiences that they had undergone, they are actually making sense of their past experience of involvement in group activity. Consequently, through sharing their experience, respondents became more informed about their actions. This can be seen in the descriptions below.

In describing his involvement in establishing Embun Hidayah (a youth club), for example, Mr. Amsul began to realise that his previous effort was worthwhile, as he said:

> *I think my involvement to set up the group last year was not wasted. Now, the parents in this village can see with their own eyes that we, the EH members, can help together in developing their children in this camp (religious camp activity).* (Mr Amsul)

This self-realising process, taking place during sessions, generates a form of self-judgement about one's actions, efforts and ability to bring some improvement. With regard to this, it can be argued that the method of inquiry is empowering in itself. It enables subjects to evaluate their capability and to realise that they possess the potential to act for themselves and for other people.

In another session, Mr. Azli who led the Parents and Teachers Association in campaigning for better school facilities, voiced his reasons for changing the initial strategy from cooperative action and close working relationships with the school authority, to firmer action - by demanding and bargaining for appropriate changes to be made at the school. He realised that the new strategy or action was put forward when the former strategy failed to achieve the parents' expectations:

> *When I saw that soft action didn't work, I called for another meeting. In the meeting, I suggested to my friends that we take signatures of all parents who send their children to the school (Religious Primary School), to be sent to higher school authority...So in the covering letter we expressed our dissatisfaction towards them (the School Division of Selangor Islamic Department) about their slow action...no action taken. We also demanded a male teacher (ustaz), and again we forced them to improve the congested classroom condition.* (Mr Azli)

In another instance through reflecting on the same action - i.e. demanding a change for a new head teacher for the Primary School - a group discussion showed that the parents were aware and responsible for the action to achieve their common interes, better achievement by their children at school:

...this was my first experience in such a thing. I had never experienced it before but after discussion with the youth leader, I agreed to join his action in sending a petition to the District Education Officer, to show that we, the parents, take this matter seriously. (Mr Sidi)

...it is better to do like this...if we are not satisfied we should act promptly, if not, the problems drag on ... (Mr Wan)

It was also noted during the discussion that after having realised their action was successful, this motivated them to take further action if the responsible authority should fail to keep their promise:

I think this issue struck them (the District Education personnel), when we demanded to change the new head teacher...That's why they quickly responded to our request, and promised to monitor the school administration...Let's see, if nothing happens we will fire them again. (Mr Fizol)

Dialogue interaction not only enabled the raising of respondents' awareness about what had happened, what sort of action they had been involved in, or what significant experience had been gained, but it also created and raised respondent's consciousness about the importance of their participation in the group. As more probing questions were asked, respondents became more aware and understood their role in facilitating other community or group members' participation in community development activities, and appreciated their talents and contributions. This can be observed clearly from the illustrations below:

I admit that most of our members (in the Crockery Association) consist of senior mothers, no young people. They couldn't even read or write. From my experience with them, they have difficulty in writing down the borrowers names or how many plates rented out. They can write a little in Jawi (Malay-Arabic writing). Pity them! I realised their problems...that's why I take the trouble to teach them how to note down the transaction made (who has borrowed what) in a book. If there's no one like me to teach them who else will direct them? We, the ones with the brain, the energy should guide them, that's what I think... (Mrs Anum)

We, people like me who are quite knowledgeable and know more or less how to organise, to develop oneself, should teach or hand down this knowledge to the village people. If not, what's the use of me being the youth leader here? While working with them, we can also discuss together and show ways to organise an activity, learn together while being involved in the activity. I like this kind of involvement. (Mr Fizol)

The two examples above show that respondents realised that they have the capability to help and facilitate the group or community members in pursuing their group activities. In another perspective, this could also eventually help in stimulating them to sustain their contribution in the group, and thus maintain the group and its activities.

Social learning process

The information obtained from such conversations is not only useful for the researcher, but also for the people themselves. This is because sharing in the dialogue interaction, either in in-depth interviews or group discussions, based on reflecting on the respondents' past experiences, is a shared social learning process. Respondents giving responses to the questions asked, and researcher feeding back the ideas by incorporating them into more probing questions, enables them to speak more about themselves. Since the dialogue takes place in a non-authoritarian context where the position of researcher and the people is a subject-to-subject relationship, therefore with such mutual trust, respect and reciprocity, the information, as knowledge, is shared together. Giving and sharing this knowledge is an empowering learning process. The process involved is not to 'fill the empty vessel' - the 'banking process' or 'depositing' an idea to be 'consumed' by the people (Freire, 1972), which has the 'domestication' effect, but rather facilitates people to be learners in their own world.

This empowering effect was clearly observed in this piece of research. As the study progressed, more questions pertaining to the subject matter were explored, and during the process of feeding back information about themselves through paraphrasing and probing, respondents began to discover and learn that they have gained something from their past action. This was particularly true among respondents who selected and joined the Group Replanting Scheme, in the rubber replanting programme, after rejecting the mini-estate scheme proposed by the authorities. Below are some of the comments gathered during the in-depth interviews and group discussions, which exemplified that they have learned from their action in taking control over the contractors who maintain the plantation, and this was reinforced during sharing information sessions:

> Yes, when I think back about the Group Replanting Scheme I think we, here, made the correct choice. If we had not formed a group like this how could we control the contractors, because we were not strong enough. In a group like this we are more confident to take action on the contractors...that's how I feel participating in this Group Replanting Scheme. (Mr Baba).

> No more worries. Now we, all the committee members (referring to the group replanting committee), are well-versed in our action. Nobody taught us. I think it was our patience to learn from our previous mistake...What did I say to you six months ago? 'Bad experience is a good lesson!'. I want to share this with you. Remember next time, no matter what problem you face, learn from it. The more you can take it, the more experience you gain. Don't give up. (Mr Mumtaz)

From the examples above, it can be concluded that people learned from their involvement and experience, and this was notified and verified in the sharing of information during the dialogue. In this dialogue process they have grasped the idea that through understanding the bad experience, in this case being exploited by the contractors, taking collective action to form the group replanting committee enabled them to regain some power to control the contractor.

While elaborating on and responding to questions asked, describing their experience of involvement, respondents also began to value and appreciate their own actions and the 'power' that they possess. Gaining the understanding that they had acquired such an ability in the course of their actions was a stimulating self-learning process, shared during follow-up interviews and group discussions:

Yes, actually, as I told you, I never gave up fighting for my people. If this doesn't work, we'll try another way. Now, I'm very familiar with their character (the school authority). We must be firm. There's no point waiting and trying to persuade them to visit us here. It doesn't work that way. That's why we changed our strategy, sending a petition like this is much better. It gets a faster reaction from them. (Mr Azli)

Now I know, the next time if we want to deal with any government agency, not only with the school authority, we have to deal straight-forwardly with them...[because] if we do it gently, sending letters telling them we have a problem here, they never entertain us, but if we threaten them, they will do something. (Mr Baba)

From the examples given above it can be concluded that enquiring about and exploring the subject matter in its own setting, through a qualitative-ethnographic approach and techniques, encouraged social learning, and this was an educative element in the approach used. The empowering aspects of the approach do not end when phenomenon studied is understood, but the effect of the method used also helps to strengthen people's own belief that they have the ability to act, either individually or collectively. Sharing information during conversation interaction is a process of gaining self knowledge based on their actions. At this point knowledge is a source of power, and this is particularly true when people became more aware of their capabilities.

Empowering research process: the 'products'

As discussed in the earlier part of this article, an empowering research process facilitated by the interactive techniques of data collection is able to raise people's consciousness. Through dialogue interaction the respondents critically reflected on their involvement, and action taken, during participating in various community group-based activities. Their experiences of learning through participating in various group activities were shared with the researcher in the conversation discourse. This further enhanced their understanding about their capability to overcome common problems and to achieve their needs. Resulting from this interaction with the people, towards the end of the research process, as part of the shared learning activity promoted by the approach used, they also experienced some changes in themselves. These changes related to people's growing capacity and ability, and include changes in their confidence, skills and knowledge. These three significant elements represent an enhancement of their individual empowerment. In due course, by being closely engaged in the research process, people were able to evaluate their group activities, diagnose organisational problems, and identify remedies.

Developing confidence

The development of self-confidence was one of the most prominent aspects gained by the members from participation. Obviously, self-confidence is the driving force behind the initiation of, and participation in the groups, as a response to the problems they encountered.

The development and accumulation of self-confidence among community members can be seen from the descriptions below, which emerged after reflecting upon their experiences. The expression and nature of the confidence gained differed between members. Among those who had experience in developing, enabling and guiding group members (the leaders), the confidence they gained related primarily to the process of organising people, and secondly, to the activity itself:

...I gained a lot of experience from organising this activity (referring to the My Home My Heaven project). At first, I was a bit doubtful about doing this because it was a big project. But after the first, second and followed by the third ad-hoc meetings with members from different groups, I gained more confidence. Once I was confident, I was encouraged to help my friends to carry out the project. (Mr Kamar)

...I have learnt so many lessons from organising these activities. Now I'm confident that we, the women, can work as a group. That's why I never gave up encouraging my friends, young and old, to participate in the study circle. In fact, with the success of these joint-ventured activities with the mosque

committee (referring to the religious talks and feasts), I believe in future I would be able to mobilise more women to participate in such activities, or organise other activities that will benefit us. As I said just now, many younger people are already showing their interest recently... (Mrs Anum)

In the individual and group sessions, as the respondents reflected on their past actions, they were consciously evaluating and assessing their involvement and their capabilities. Their self-confidence developed as they realised and defined themselves as capable and worthy people. Discovering their capability to perform certain actions increased their confidence. Believing in themselves and being able to act effectively, based on the confidence developed and accumulated, is the essence of empowerment. This phenomenon can be seen clearly from the comments made by Mr. Azli and Mrs. Fizi respectively, reflecting upon their experiences:

Of course I have to believe that I can do this - organising a meeting, calling parents and friends, for example - before starting any action. Believing in yourself that you can do it is very important, if not, you can't go anywhere. You have to start from zero, from scratch, don't you?...My confidence increased as the group began to shape up. It assured me that I could easily guide them as a team in deciding the activity. (Mr Azli)

I gained new and invaluable experience working together with the local women, organising the Women Smallholders' Association. As I mentioned before, I am new here, just got married to a local guy. Moreover I was worried because the community is divided, but I forced myself to take up this challenge. From participating with them, I slowly built up my confidence. Now I am sure that I can work with both groups, women of my age and the older people, because they accept me. (Mrs Fizi)

Self-confidence, as empowerment, strengthens the on-going capability of an individual to take further action. The connection can be seen from Mr. Azha's effort, who is a member of the UMNO Youth Club, but later led and organised the formation another community project, the bill paying service. This is evident where he says:

In helping Mr. Kamar and Mr. Fizol to carry out the group activities, I actually did two things at once. Of course, firstly I helped them conduct the projects but at the same time I also learned how they organised the activities. To me, it didn't seem difficult once I knew how to organise people, furthermore, most of my friends share my interests and ideas. Once you are confident you can do it. (Mr Azha)

A similar experience was also portrayed by Mr. Kamar in reflecting upon his involvement in organising two community projects, the Islamic Family course and 'My Home My Heaven' project, as he said:

...anyway, I think the first project I had with the community - the Islamic Family Course in 1991 - was a turning point for me. I learned a lot from it and I used the knowledge gained to organise my second community project, the 'My Home My Heaven' project. The first project provided me with confidence, and encouraged me to do the second one. (Mr Kamar)

This increasing level of individual capability ultimately helped to build the groups' collective capacity to achieve commonly shared interests. The confidence gained by group members in supporting and helping to organise and participate in activities, varied according to different groups. These variations resulted from, and reflected differences in, the working practices of carrying out the activity:

Well, I enjoyed helping Mr. Kamar organising the 'My Home My Heaven' project and campaigning for the TAHFIS school. I learned a lot from them...Carrying out the task that I chose gave me more confidence. When I performed it, something seemed to push me to do more. That's how I felt...That's why I enjoyed it, compared with participating in WI (Women's Institution) activities. With the WI, I feel that I'm not 'free'...I think that's the correct word to use here. (Mrs Wani)

...yes, with the Embun Hidayah group, I gained lots of experience handling the Religious Camp for the school children. Although I am also involved in WI, between the two, I am more comfortable with the Religious camp. In the Religious Camp we share the work together as a team. Dealing with our own people here gives me confidence that I am able to contribute to my people...but not with the WI, because although I participated in the essay writing competition, I felt like I was just one of the contestants. I wasn't directly involved. (Mrs Mona)

I'm really satisfied to be involved from the beginning - thinking about and discussing the activity, then directly participating in carrying it out and seeing with my own eyes what actually took place. I feel it like this. When

I'm satisfied, I'll be more confident to carry it out in the future...Not only in the community sports activity, but also other youth projects that I'm involved in...I'm not saying that I'm not confident to carry out activities proposed by the leader, but I would prefer activities that are initiated by us. (Mr Radi)

It is important to note here that the interactive process in interviewing allowed the respondents to reflect on their participation experiences. In these reflections, as portrayed in the above descriptions, they were able to identify and realise that as a product of their involvement, there was a change in themselves. They were consciously aware that they had acquired and developed self-confidence. It was also observed that through this reflection they were able to judge the extent of benefit obtained from the different situations. They understood the limitations and advantages of different approaches that they had experienced, one which was directed by an external body or induced by a leader, and the other which was self-directed. Furthermore, for some members, especially in the WI (Women's Institution) organisation, this process of reflection during the interview encouraged their critical analysis of the activity and the group itself. This critical analysis, sparked off in individual interviews blossomed during a group discussion, when group members and leader shared and began to tackle the problems and limitations. (More on this is discussed later).

Developing skills and gaining knowledge

Accompanying the development of self-confidence were skills developed and knowledge gained. As individuals participated together in the process of identifying, planning and implementing activities to solve their problems and achieve their common goals, skills were also developed. 'Skill' here refers to the ability to do something. Skills are not in-bred, but were attained through a learning process. Acquiring skills is part of personal development.

Identification of these skills was based on people's experiences and reflections, also supplemented by data obtained by the researcher through direct observation of some of the groups' processes in organising and carrying out their activities throughout the study period. This information was also verified and elaborated during the 'information sharing' session with the respondents in the follow-up interviews and group discussions. The 'classification' of the skills, however, is not mutually exclusive. In practice, skills are integrated together; while performing one skill to show a particular ability, others follow simultaneously in a complex interlocking process. Therefore, this 'classification' is for purposes of analysis only. Three types of skills developed among the respondents are identified and examined in this study, namely, organising skill, problem solving skill, and technical skill.

Organising skill

Although the group or activity initiated was inspired by a few members, the process in which they raised and focused on specific issues or unresolved problems together with their friends reinforced their ability to organise themselves, and to form collective action. Experiencing the action process in turn provided them with more knowledge about organising skills. This aspect was clearly described by the respondents in reflecting on the benefits of this action process, as illustrated in the statements below:

> Actually, organising people is something like testing your own talents. I feel that way. I'm happy because the more I'm involved in organising an activity, the more new things I gain...more chances for me to test my talents, my skills...I think if you are in that position, you also can get the pleasure, even more if you succeeded. And this keeps me trying again and again in other activities. (Mr Kamar)

> I admit it was quite challenging the first time I tried it, but as I kept on doing it - calling them for meetings, discussing and deciding together with the members - now organising an activity is routine to me. It's like cooking, you know! The first time you cook the dish it won't be very delicious but as you keep on practising you develop the skill, how much sugar to put in, salt, and so on...Yes, participating in organising the activity is something like creating and developing your own recipe. (Mrs Anum)

Experiences of participation in this respect have an empowering effect. In participating, the individuals were not simply contributing on a 'trial and error' basis. They also reflected on their action.

Appropriate actions were perceived as new things, new knowledge that developed and enhanced their skill in terms of organising people and organising an activity. These skills were then used in further undertakings, where they are adjusted to suit situations or the nature of the group to be organised, which eventually upgrades their skills. Here, there is a continuous and cyclical relationship between experiencing participation, and reflection. It is in this chain action and reflection process that new insights and skills are obtained, which are later consolidated when this body of knowledge is 'tested' in further actions, in more challenging situations.

Experiencing the process of establishing a group or carrying out an activity helps to widen understanding about organising an action, as elaborated in the examples below:

...Last time I didn't realise it but now I know that organising ourselves in a group like this is good...[because] we can achieve what we want. If we hadn't organised in a group I don't think RISDA would have approved the setting up of this Women Smallholder's Association. (Mrs Maria)

...There is a Malay proverb - 'Bersatu kita teguh, bercerai kita roboh' [which literally means, 'We are strong if united but weaken if we dispute'] and I believe in this. This applies to our group here. When we are in one group we can organise many things, for example in the case of threatening the contractor, and also the school authority. (Mr Baba)

Through the continuous engagement with a group or group activities, participants were able to understand the benefit of using collective action to pursue objectives. As they experience the process, they learn and subsequently appreciate the strategic skills of organising. As group members sharpened their insights about the importance of organising themselves to pursue any action, they also strengthened their belief in collective endeavours. Although the degree of competence between individuals who had gained and used their skills in organising people (as in the case of the leaders) was relatively high compared with those who just understood and valued the skill and principle of organising, the fact that the latter group appreciated the leaders' skills shows that they had cultivated an elementary knowledge of it. This enabled the leaders to develop collective action with members to achieve their group goal. In other words, by involvement, the members learned, developed and enhanced their organisational skills, which advanced their collective action towards solving their problems or taking action against, or to influence, others.

Problem solving skills

Virtually the whole process of community action examined in my study concerned community members' own efforts to solve commonly shared problems. While struggling to achieve needs and goals, they also strengthened and enhanced some aspects of problem-solving skills. Some of the skills developed are related to solving a group's internal problems, and have significant consequences for maintaining the group and its activity By sharing information with the respondents in the follow-up interviews and in some of the group discussions, they became more aware of the skills they had developed, and this understanding brings with it self-realisation:

> *Yes, after being involved in many community activities I can see my potential. Before this I never realised that people like me, a factory worker, could do something for the community...Yes, all this started when I got involved in running the TAHFIS school, and helping to solve some financial problems faced by the school and students in their education, besides assisting in conducting the religious talks...* (Mr Izam)

> *Yes, I admit I discovered something here. Now I realise that working together in a group is beneficial...we can help to solve not only the problems faced by us here but also in carrying out group activities. I think I'm not too late in discovering this, though I'm nearly 70 years old, aren't I?* (Mr Hasif)

> *Let me tell you something...I prefer doing work rather than just talking a lot and not taking action. Because the more I do it, the more experienced I'll be. I think that's how I've developed my ability...helping my group when a problem arises, that's only one example. Ah! it's a very pleasant experience once you are committed to doing it. It gave me inspiration to do more once I saw the outcome. That's why I've always persuaded my friends to join the study groups, let them experience what I'm experiencing now.* (Mrs Rosi)

As reflected in the statements above, it was through the process of mobilising members, initiating the group or activity, and solving some of the internal problems in the group activity that some members were able to exploit the opportunities to advance their skills. As a process, such participation provides experience for individuals, and such experience generates more insight and understanding of working together and the benefits this brings. The more they worked together the more they internalised and understood this, and more skills were developed. Hence, the experiences gained are the essence of empowering learning for community members.

Technical skill

Another equally important skill which was generated was technical skill. In sharing information with the respondents and in the process of 'feeding back' the information to them during group discussion and in the follow-up interviews, two types of technical skills, namely communication skill and managing skill, were reaffirmed by them.

Communication skills

One of the interesting phenomena discovered in this study was the ability of the community group to organise a strategic way of channelling and disseminating news or information. It was observed that every group had its own informal representative in each neighbourhood. These representatives acted as the contact or liaison persons for the respective groups and were responsible for informing and encouraging their friends on matters concerning their group affairs. The emergence of these skills was reflected in their action in mobilising their friends, drafting invitation letters and encouraging them to get involved in community group activities. The development of these skills once again was confirmed when they stressed the usefulness of experiencing the task they had performed. For example, both Mr. Azha and Mrs. Lina admitted they had improved their writing and communicating abilities, as illustrated from the statements below:

> ...as I told you before, I learnt a lot from this, the more I did it the easier it became. I think, yes, it gradually improved my writing skill. I believe they get my message clearly...[because] most of them who receive my invitation

letters are prepared to discuss the matter directly, compared with the last time when the letter did not spell it out clearly. (Mrs Lina)

My argument is this. We, human beings, are not perfect. But for me, if I do it several times I can master it. I'm able to communicate with my friends just by sending them an invitation letter. Of course, there are some other means - phoning them, for example. (Mr Azha)

I never got credit from anybody before. You are the first one to recognise our ability here. It is true. That's how we organise ourselves here. Like myself, I'm the representative for this hill area, about 13 houses around here. So, informing friends about the group activities, encouraging them to attend any group functions is my responsibility...As long as the group needs my service I would like to keep it on. (Mrs Fira)

It was also perceived from the detailed analysis that this skill played an important role in maintaining the community groups' activities, and assisted and allowed members to continue and take other actions. Sharing and feeding back information increased their personal knowledge, competence and self-efficacy, and practising the skill also encouraged the cooperative, mutual-help and self-help spirit among individuals in pursuing groups' intended goals.

Managing skills

Managing skills were another kind of competency developed by members in administering their group activity. These involve taking and keeping minutes, managing and keeping accounts and assets. These competencies were acquired and practised as they worked together. The principles of 'learning by doing' and 'practice makes perfect' were shared by them in reflecting on those experiences when they said:

Now, since I became the group rapporteur I know why keeping minutes is just as important as in the government meeting. It's easy for me or my committee to check what decisions we agreed earlier. If we didn't, it would be difficult for us to proceed with our next follow-up action. (Mr Kamar)

To tell you the truth, before this I had never heard what a ledger is. But now, after five years managing the group replanting account, not to say I'm an expert, but I know what it is about. Once you get into it, you learn it...If you asked me now how much we had spent over the last 9 months and how much is left, I should be able to tell you. (Mr Ibra)

I'm not embarrassed to show you our group's financial record book, here... Nobody showed me how to do this. I never learnt this during my school-days either. But I tried it myself. I simply followed the examples shown in my youngest son's commerce text book (school text book). I learnt it from here. But, when I went through it, doing it, I knew how it works. Good! It's a real good experience...I apply the same principle, more or less, in recording how much crockery is borrowed and returned from my friends. (Mrs Anum)

Although it can be argued that only a few individuals, especially those who were responsible for carrying out certain tasks in managing the group, could benefit significantly from these experiences, the benefit from one or two people's ability in maintaining the group is shared among members.

People's reflections, as has been depicted, show that through working together people were able to acquire skills and knowledge. This then became new knowledge when they assessed the differences before and after. Together with confidence, knowledge and skills were accumulated, sharpened and widened, as they applied and practised them during their action. As more confidence was developed, people were encouraged to accept and undertake more responsibility, which helped to broaden their skills and knowledge, and, as such, constituted an arena for informal learning and empowerment.

People's evaluation

The continuity and overlapping of respondent's involvement in various group activities enabled them to assess the activities and the groups in which they were involved. This evaluation took place during the sharing sessions in which they identified, defined, and verified their personal development, and it was during these sessions that their self-evaluation intensified.

People's evaluation of the activities emerged gradually during the follow-up individual and group sessions. From a close examination of the information gathered and noted, most comments and suggestions related to working practice in conducting an activity. This was especially true for women who had experienced participating in both externally-directed activities (i.e. WI activities), and community-initiated activities, where they could compare the two. In the group discussion this issue was again raised. Some of them disclosed their regret that too much attention was given by the WI leader to carrying out external activities, rather than focusing on internal activities for the benefit of all members. The comments made were based on their perception and sensitivity to what had been going on since the establishment of the WI, as pointed out by respondents in the statements below:

...it's like I said before, if our WI activities focus mainly on helping the district WI, there's nothing much our women here can benefit from them... (Mr Wani)

Yes, I agree with my friends. Living in one community in a village like this, we need to keep up our spirit of mutual help. That's for sure. But, what I'm trying to say here, if we could have a specific project just for our women, it would be much better. (Mrs Nor)

As the discussion proceeded they eventually came to a point where they identified that inadequate group meetings and poor planning contributed to the low priority given to local needs. From the information given by the respondents during the discussion, it was found that the leader only called meetings to inform and direct/ instruct the members to be involved in the District WI activities. Although the group has a 'general' meeting, this is only conducted every two years. The issue of group meetings was raised:

The problem with our WI group is that we never have regular meetings... Meetings are only held when something needs to be done for the main WI organisation. So, we can't plan, how to discuss suitable activities for the group members...yes! to me planning is important, especially if we could have a yearly plan... (Mrs Lina)

Actually, I've never had the chance to voice my opinion like this...[because] there is no open discussion like this (referring to the group discussion). Meetings are specifically meant to organise our members for the District WI activities. I think we should try this kind of discussion in our group, at least we could share our ideas - what we need for our own good. (Mrs Mona)

Yes, I do agree with that. We don't have proper planning, that's the main thing. Regular meetings may not be necessary, we could have one or two, but we must discuss and plan the activity properly. (Mrs Wani)

After sharing and hearing the problems and the needs of the members in the group discussion, the leader took a positive stand and was prepared to take action in relation to planning their group activity, as she said:

Well, it's easier said than done. Anyway, next year in January we are going to have our general meeting. So I suppose you all can come together...Off hand just to tell you all, in the meeting next year we are going to have a leadership election. Maybe new faces, like Mrs. Fizi or Mrs. Lina can take the lead...In the meantime we can think about any good projects for our group, maybe in sport or other activities...But the main thing, we, together must come and plan, not like the last two years, where only few turned up, how can we plan...? (Mrs Wan)

Among the men's groups, they were more concerned about the 'inter-group problems' and a reduction in inter-group cooperation in the village. Involvement had come to be based on the political division of the community into two camps. By and large, this political division limited cooperative work among groups, and threatened the traditional mutual-help and self-help spirit. The 'in-group' nature of participation and the implication of this phenomenon was translated into some members' worries, as can be seen quite clearly in the statements below made during follow-up interviews and group discussions:

What I see is that if the activity is organised by the 'mosque people', other group members don't seem to bother much. Of course, they never boycott our activity, but you know, they just attend it, hear the talks (religious)... which is quite fair...But it would be better if they could come and help each other, wouldn't it? (Mr Azli)

...four or five years ago we lived in harmony. But now things have changed. Group activities have been politicised. Everyone blames each other. So, what can you expect? Luckily we can still work together in the Group Replanting Committee. If we couldn't, it would be a disaster. (Mr Ibra)

Can I add some more? For me, nowadays it seems that the mutual help spirit is decreasing...Not like before, where all the village activities were done together...but now only certain groups, certain people join in. The problem is when political matters infiltrate into community life, the whole thing goes haywire...It's only in certain activities, like the religious talks and religious classes I see both groups participate together; the rest I can't see any. (Mr Baba)

These men were aware of the problems. As perceived by them, political divisions or cliques were the central issue, and threatened harmonious community life. Furthermore, this problem had spread across gender, and at least two generations.

Although it was not the intention of this study to solve this 'political issue' which is affecting community activity, having gone through the information sharing sessions with the respondents in small group discussions, opportunities were revealed for them to re-establish and restore the spirit of cooperation. The ideas put forward by potential mediators of the two factions, Mr. Azli and Mr. Kamar in follow-up interviews showed this possibility:

Well, so far I can see one possibility is through the religious activity, for example the religious talks...because the men and women from both sides can contribute their part...but of course, we need to find some means to discuss this matter. I'm confident I can influence all my friends towards this effort if we really want to work this out. (Mr Azli).

...but what I'm trying to do is to establish an educational cooperation assembly. I am going to invite representatives from all groups - the Parent and Teacher Association of TASKI and TAHFIS, the Primary Religious School, primary school, Women Smallholders' Association, Women's Religious Circle, the mosque and surau committee members, and so forth. Any groups that have an educative element in their activity, I will call them. I will contact Mr. Azli directly, that's not a problem for me. I believe he's willing to sort out these problems...I'm sure we can try from here as a starting point to re-unite our members. The basic priority that I will emphasise is education. (Mr Kamar)

Coincidentally, their ideas were quite similar. The opportunity was enhanced by encouraging 'promises' made by members of both factions, although there were some cases where respondents were sceptical about the possibility. These encouraging promises were noted during the group discussion sessions with both sides:

What is most important to me is who wants to make the first move...I suppose the Village Development and Security Committee members can initiate this. I think Mr. Kamar is the right person...don't think about his age but his capability, he is young of course.

Let me put it this way, first and foremost, the intention must be clear, no political interests. Otherwise we will be back to square one, there's no point. If the main aim is to 'save' the community, I can assure you all here that I'll be the first one to support it.

I'm 50-50, maybe yes, maybe no. But there's no harm in trying. For me I have no reservations. It's better for me and for the younger generation.

I will give my full support, don't worry about that. But in my opinion the best place to start is at the mosque because this is our central point. Many activities can be organised here. To me there's no reason why we can't work together.

In general, both factions' members had similar hopes and there was an intersection of ideas. The recognition by the opposition group of Mr. Kamar's capability, and realisation by the second group that the mosque is an appropriate place for organising the activity signifies this intersection. Building on this idea could help to accelerate the integration process. This constructive agenda, which could foster future community development, had been promoted by the interactive method of data collection of this study.

Conclusion: empowerment as a product of the research process

In order to understand the process of participation, people's experiences, as the primary source of information, were scrutinised. To facilitate the data gathering process, a qualitative-ethnographic approach was used. The interactive and responsive techniques of data collection of in-depth and follow-up interviews, and group discussions, advocated by this approach allowed the people to be directly involved in the research process and helped to facilitate an understanding of their participation in the activities of the community. The conversation style, dialogue, and the interaction between researcher and researched also played a key part in the research process. 'Story telling' (Reason and Hawkins, 1990) was the most significant way used by the respondents to express their experiences and views, and, as such, involves reflection during the dialogue. It was during this reflection that respondents became more aware about what was happening, while narrating their experiences, and in this way, a self-realisation, consciousness raising and self-evaluation process took place. The methodology used also empowered the respondents. The information drawn out was purely based on what they said, and sharing and feeding back the information to them during the interviews and discussions enabled them to begin to realise they possessed the abilities and capacities to act and to affect some changes in their living environment, and collectively gain more control over their lives. The affirmation that they have developed in their personal abilities in the course of their involvement in group activities was explored within this sharing process, which in turn empowered them more to seek solutions to some of the pertinent issues in their community, including to restore the spirit of co-operation among group and community members.

Thus, an interactive technique of data collection was not limited simply to understanding the processes which have taken place. It developed and enhanced group members' ability and confidence to comment and make suggestions grounded in their own concrete experiences, and, as such, demonstrated an empowering capacity in the approach. The evaluation of the group and its activities was a 'critical comparison-reflection', based on members experiences of participating in various groups. Suggestions which emerged during the research discourse represented members own ideas for collective solutions, based upon enhanced understanding of the problems and issues to be faced.

Ethnographic participative research methods offered an interactive approach to studying people in a group context. From the beginning of the research process, before actually becoming engaged in the real process of gathering data, the 'welcoming tone' from the people signified the credibility that the technique has to offer. The trust that the people showed in the researcher, facilitated by sensitive and interactive data collection tools, encouraged them to get involved in the research process. At the outset of the research process people were eager and confident to share their experience with the researcher. As they became further engaged along the research process through in-depth interviews and group discussions, respondents realised that the techniques had benefits for them. This can be seen from remarks made during group discussion about the method used:

...Today, I think there are many more issues concerning our group which arise from this kind of discussion (referring to group discussion). I think it is good to follow the style of this discussion, very detailed, deep down to the root...we can give it a try in our next meeting. (Mr Sofi)

I just want to add another point. I don't know whether what I'm going to say here is relevant to our discussion or even to your work (referring to the researcher's intention) today, but this is what I feel. After being interviewed, and today in the discussion, after talking and talking, I realised that we, the older generation, are not weak. Our past action in the Group Replanting Committee proved that we can work it out. As long as we work in a group I think in future we can still manage our own affairs... (Mr Sidi)

...I think we should try this kind of discussion in our group, at least we could share our ideas- what we need for our own good. (Mrs Mona, requote)

Yes, I do also agree with Mrs. Mona. Like I said just now, having group meetings or discussions like this means we can plan our activities more systematically. So far we have not tried it before. No harm in trying! Sooner or later we could benefit from it. (Mrs Lina)

References

Anyanwu, C.N. (1988) 'The technique of participatory research in community development', *Community Development Journal*, 23(1), pp.11-15.

Blumer, H. (1969) *Symbolic Interactionism: Perspective and Method.* New Jersey, Englewood Cliff: Prentice Hall.

Bogdan, R. and Taylor, S.J. (1975) *Introduction to Qualitative Methods: A*

Phenomenological Approach to the Social Science. New York: Wiley.

Brannen, J. (ed.) (1992) *Mixing Methods: Qualitative and Quantitative Research.* Aldershot: Avebury.

Breton, M. (1993) 'Partnership and empowerment', *Social Action,* 1(2), pp.13-19.

Bryman, A. (1988) *Quantity and Quality in Social Research.* London: Unwin.

Burgess, R.G. (1984) *In the Field: An Introduction to Field Research.* London: Allen & Unwin.

Burgess, R.G. (ed.) (1982) *Field Research: A Sourcebook and Field Manual.* London: George Allen & Unwin.

Crabtree, B.F. and Miller, C.L. (1992) *Doing Qualitative Research.* London: Sage.

Denzin, N.K. (1970a) *The Research Act in Sociology.* London: Butterworth.

Denzin, N.K. (1970b) 'Symbolic interactionism and ethnomethodology' in Douglas, J. (ed.) *Understanding Everyday Life.* Chicago: Aldine, pp.261-286.

Fals-Borda, O. (1991) 'Some basic ingredients' in Fals-Borda, O. and Rahman, M.A. (eds.) *Action and Knowledge: Breaking the Monopoly with Participatory Action-Research.* London: Intermediate Technology Pub., pp.3-12.

Fals-Borda, O. (1981) 'Action research', Development: *Seeds of Change, 1,* pp.66-61.

Fear, F.A., Carter, K.A. and Thullen, M. (1985) 'Action research in community development: concepts and principles' in Fear, F.A. and Schwarzweller, H.K. (eds.) *Research in Rural Sociology and Development.* Greenwich, Connecticut: Jai Press, pp.197-216.

Finch, J. (1993) 'It's great to have someone to talk to: ethics and politics interviewing women', in Hammersley, M. (ed.) *Social Research: Philosophy, Politics and Practice.* London: Sage in assoc. with Open University.

Freire, P. (1972) *Pedagogy of Oppressed.* London: Penguin.

Glaser, B.G. and Strauss, A.L. (1967) *Discovery of Grounded Theory: Strategies for Qualitative Research.* Chicago: Aldine.

Graham, H. and Jones, J. (1992) 'Community development and research', *Community Development Journal,* 24(3), pp.235-241.

Greetz, C. (1975) *The Interpretation of Cultures.* London: Hutchinson.

Hall, B.L. (1981) 'Participatory research, popular knowledge and power: a personal reflection', *Convergence,* XIV, (3), pp.6-27.

Hall, B.L. (1975) 'Participatory research: an approach for change',

Convergence, VII(2).

Hammersley, M. and Atkinson, P. (1995) *Ethnography: Principle in Practice.* London: Routledge.

Heron, J. (1981a) 'Experiential research methodology' in Reason, P. and Rowan, J. (eds.) *Human Inquiry: A Sourcebook of New Paradigm Research.* Chichester: John Wiley, pp.153-166.

Heron, J. (1981b) 'Philosophical basis for a new paradigm' in Reason, P. and Rowan, J. (eds.) *Human Inquiry: A Sourcebook of New Paradigm Research.* Chichester: John Wiley, pp.19-35.

Jick, T.D. (1979) 'Mixing qualitative and quantitative method: triangulation in action', *Administrative Science Quarterly,* 24, pp.602-611.

Kahn, R. and Cannel, C. (1957) *The Dynamic of Interviewing.* New York: John Wiley.

Kolb, D.A. (1984) *Experiential Learning: Experience as the Source of Learning and Development.* Englewood, N. Jersey: Prentice-Hall.

Litchty, J.R. and Kimball, W.J. (1985) 'Analysis of an action research project' in Fear, F.A. and Schwarzweller, H.K. (eds.) *Research in Rural Sociology and Development.* Greenwich, Connecticut: Jai Press, pp.217-237.

Mullender, A. and Ward, D. (1991) *Self-Directed Groupwork: Users Take Action for Empowerment.* London: Whiting and Birch.

Oakley, A. (1981) 'Interviewing women: a contradiction in terms' in Roberts, H. (ed.) *Doing Feminist Research.* London: Routledge & Kegan Paul.

Patton, M.Q. (1990) *Qualitative Evaluation and Research Method.* California: Sage.

Rahman, M.A. (1981) 'Participation of the rural poor in rural development', Development: *Seeds of Change,* 1, pp.3-9.

Rahman, M.A. (1981) 'Reflection', Development: *Seeds of Change,* 1, pp.43-51.

Ramazanoglu, C. (1992) 'On feminist methodology: male reason versus female empowerment', *Sociology,* 26(2), pp.207-212.

Randall, R. (1981) 'Doing dialogical research' in Reason, P. and Rowan, J. (eds.) *Human Inquiry: A Source Book of New Paradigm Research.* Chichester: John Wiley, pp.349-361.

Reason, P. (ed.) (1990) *Human Inquiry in Action: Developments in New Paradigm Research.* London: Sage (reprinted).

Reason, P. (1994) 'Three approaches to participatory inquiry' in Denzin, N.K. and Lincoln, Y.S. (eds.) *Handbook of Qualitative Research.* California:

Sage, pp.324-339.

Reason, P. and Hawkins, P. (1990) 'Story telling as inquiry' in Reason, P. (ed.) *Human Inquiry in Action: Developments in New Paradigm Research.* London: Sage, pp.79-101 (reprinted).

Tandon, R. (1981) 'Participatory research in the empowerment of people', *Convergence*, XIV(3), pp.20-27.

Voth, D.E. (1979) 'Social action research' in Blakely, E.J. (ed.) *Community Development Research: Concepts, Issues and Strategies.* New York: Human Science Press, pp.67-81.

This chapter was first published in 1996 in *Groupwork* Vol. 9(2), pp.221-252

At the time of writing, Asnarulkhadi Abu-Samah was a PhD Student at the University of Nottingham.

Postscript
Where do we go from here?

Jennie Fleming and Dave Ward

We hope this collection of papers is of interest to groupworkers committed to empowerment and change, be they paid workers, volunteers or peer members. The articles reproduced show the relevance of the Social Action and Self-directed Groupwork across many settings and have considered the working methods and skills involved and the necessary transformation of conventional working practices to reflect a set of essential practice principles.

We had always believed that the approach had an immensely wide applicability. Indeed, there is no reason, in terms of its ability to encompass the complex causation of contemporary social problems and to provide a methodology for tackling them, why Social Action should not be the norm for people seeking to create change in many contexts, leaving currently more accepted approaches on the periphery.

The group, of course, is an essential feature of this landscape. The practice described and examined in the articles has shown that what the approach has to offer is not merely a new configuration of descriptive features or a new menu of techniques. Rather, it is a clear statement of the principles from which flow methods of working together and interacting with other people. In particular, there is a distinctive collaborative commitment to achieving group aims, goals and purposes on issues recognized, identified and owned by the group members themselves. Both this commitment and the values from which it springs are a world apart from those to be found, explicitly or implicitly, in much current work.

Social Action is an approach that can readily be adopted by all those who share the goals of social justice and emancipation. It is a people-centred model and, at the same time, is rooted in anti-oppressive values and a vision of structural social change. The principles and values that underpin the social movements of black, Asian and minority people, of women, of lesbian, gay, bisexual and transgendered people, and of disabled people, and all related struggles, are embedded in it. Practitioners and activists are challenged to combine their own efforts with those of oppressed groups without colonizing them to achieve change. Group members, assisted by the facilitation of peers and groupworkers, chip away at the forms of inequality that lie at the heart of oppressive social arrangements and which affect them all, across boundaries of diversity and intersectionality.

However, those who talk about empowerment must be clear about their responsibility *and the skills* they need to possess if they are to support effectively those seeking their own empowerment. Nothing is more inexcusable than raising expectations and creating commitments that then flounder because group facilitators do not know how to deliver their contribution. Social Action is, therefore a highly disciplined and skilled approach requiring training, support and consultancy. Just as the model has been tested and modified over the past thirty years, it will continue to be refined in the light of continuing practice and experience.

The importance of values in marking out the distinctive nature of the approach cannot be overemphasised. These values, in binding together in a complementary way the knowledge, skills and experience of group members and groupworkers, form an essential platform for this systematic, structurally grounded challenge to the degrading and stigmatizing conditions that are the practical manifestations of oppression.

Social Action transcends conventionally defined boundaries between disciplines. Practitioners and activists in many settings can work in an empowering way if they fashion their practice in a manner that is congruent with its principles and value-base, formulated within an understanding of wider political perspectives and if they then translate its implications into their practice. They can transpose well-intentioned, committed but, sometimes, undisciplined work into a dynamic and refined approach that can sustain a clear commitment to social change objectives and stand up to critical scrutiny. Asking the questions 'WHAT?', 'WHY?' and 'HOW?' lies at the heart of this process.

This collection demonstrates that Social Action is as relevant today as when the articles were written. It continues to be relevant to peer, volunteer and professionally facilitated groups addressing a diverse range of issues and across different societies. The values and methodology have taken root in a number of disciplines. Social Action continues to sustain the mind-set and practices needed to achieve social justice through Social Action and community empowerment.

However, while acknowledging and celebrating these achievements, there is a continuing responsibility to invigorate, revitalize and galvanize to meet new challenges. This is all the more important in times of austerity, in an increasingly hostile and regressive political, social and economic environment. In such times, it is vital to re-engage with the core vision and mission and to re-energize open and honest collaboration with community members and users of services as partners in change. This is likely to be uncomfortable as it challenges and even threatens established practice and leadership, a business model based on contracts not local need, organizational and professional power rather than common ownership of process and solutions.

Organizations and all people within them need to think about doing things differently for the sustainable benefit of the community. Such reframing of what we do and why we do it in turn impacts upon relationships and behaviours of all involved wherever people meet together, privately and publicly. What this collection shows is the act of trust made by adopting the underpinning principles. The consequent practice of Self-directed Groupwork can make a difference that goes beyond what might previously have been seen as possible. It liberates opportunities never previously seriously considered. It means going beyond a culture represented by targets and outputs to developing a different ethos in the way people interact, work and, indeed, live together. This is not a technical exercise. It calls upon professionals, volunteers, peer activists and in fact anyone who finds themselves in a position where they are facilitating and supporting people to achieve change, to think again about the basics of 'what' they are doing, 'why' they are doing it and 'how' to go about their involvement.

To sustain such innovation requires engaging in an alternative culture with an established history, turning conventional processes on their head. Process comes first, with the confidence and expectation that 'product' will emerge from this. Instead of planning and then involving, it means starting off with engaging with people and moving thence to planning. It involves a double-sided value commitment: on one side, to push towards greater social justice; on the other, albeit pulled back by fear, reluctance and conventional wisdom, to surrender and share power. For many, this is will be a journey into the unknown but, once engaged in Social Action paid workers, activists, researchers and managers can find, as the articles in this collection show, that it is a process that works. We want to enable people who have not yet taken the steps outlined above now to have the confidence to do so, to try it for themselves – and to make a difference!

www.ingramcontent.com/pod-product-compliance
Lightning Source LLC
Chambersburg PA
CBHW060956280326
41935CB00009B/738